Cornerstone of the Confederacy

CORNERSTONE
OF THE
CONFEDERACY

Alexander Stephens and the Speech that Defined the Lost Cause

KEITH S. HÉBERT

The University of Tennessee Press
Knoxville

Library of Congress Cataloging-in-Publication Data

Names: Hébert, Keith S., author.
Title: Cornerstone of the Confederacy : Alexander Stephens and
the speech that defined the Lost Cause / Keith S. Hébert.
Description: First edition. | Knoxville : University of Tennessee Press, [2021] |
Includes bibliographical references and index. | Summary: "This book traces the
curious history of the Cornerstone Speech. As Alexander H. Stephens's formal defense
of the new Confederacy, delivered on March 21, 1861, the Cornerstone Speech
was an uninhibited overture to a new nation founded on white supremacy and slavery,
and an instant sensation. While the speech is widely cited, no full-length treatment of the
work and its legacy exists—and it is poorly understood. Hébert examines how Stephens
initially considered it, then how, with the help of others, he reinterpreted it to shore up
major tenets of Lost Cause ideology after the Confederacy was defeated on the battlefield.
The book also shows how this reactionary interpretation would inform Neo-Confederate
ideas that abide to the present day in American culture"—Provided by publisher.
Identifiers: LCCN 2020048866 (print) | LCCN 2020048867 (ebook) |
ISBN 9781621906346 (hardcover) | ISBN 9781621906520 (PDF)
Subjects: LCSH: Stephens, Alexander H. (Alexander Hamilton), 1812–1883—Influence. |
White supremacy movements—United States—History. | Slavery—Southern States—
Justification—Sources. | African Americans—Southern States—Social conditions—
19th century. | Racism—Southern States—History—19th century. | United States—
History—Civil War, 1861–1865—Anniversaries, etc. | Southern States—Intellectual
life—Sources. | United States—Race relations—History—19th century.
Classification: LCC E645 .H43 2021 (print) | LCC E645 (ebook) |
DDC 305.800973/09034—dc23
LC record available at https://lccn.loc.gov/2020048866
LC ebook record available at https://lccn.loc.gov/2020048867

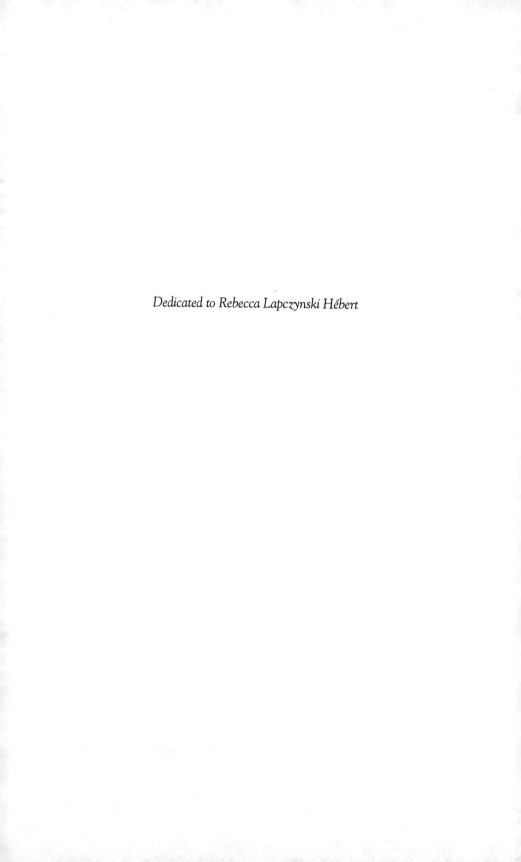

Dedicated to Rebecca Lapczynski Hébert

Contents

Illustrations

Acknowledgments

This book would not have been possible without the assistance and encouragement of a cadre of supporters both personal and professional. Foremost, I wish to thank my students at Auburn University. This project began during a historical methods course as I tried to model research and writing techniques to a new generation of budding historians. I tell students that it is best to write something daily to hone your skills. In response to this advice, a particularly gifted student asked, "What have you written today?" That brought me up short, and I dusted off some languishing research to rediscover the Cornerstone Speech. Although I contemplated abandoning this project on several occasions, conversations with students about my work and its connection to our contemporary society reminded me of its potential value.

Within my department, I would like to thank those faculty and professionals who participated in our southern history seminar. Melissa Blair, Jason Hauser, Kenneth Noe, Jenny Brooks, and Lyn Causey all provided exceptional feedback and suggested revisions that dramatically improved the manuscript. When I had doubts that this topic could be transformed into a monograph-length study, Kenneth Noe encouraged me to continue pushing the subject matter into areas that I had not previously considered. For twenty-five years, Noe has been my teacher, mentor, friend, and colleague. His influence on my historical analysis and writing can be seen throughout this book.

Although my work often criticizes how contemporary Neo-Confederates and Confederate heritage enthusiasts interpret history, my frequent interactions with those groups as an invited speaker or tour guide had a major impact on this work. Despite our obvious disagreements, their frank conversations about their views provided valuable insights as I tried to document their worldview. They reminded me that, although it is far easier to ignore those whose views differ from our own, maintaining a dialogue with those whom we disagree remains America's best hope for building a better world.

Without the exceptional resources developed by the creators of Newspapers .com, Google Books, and the HathiTrust this project would have foundered. The ability to search millions of records in seconds and locate even the slightest mention of Alexander Stephens or the Cornerstone Speech provided an enormous source base. Honestly, there are parts of this story that could not have been discovered without the use of these modern research tools. Locating the proverbial needle in the haystack has never been more possible and has opened new avenues for historical research and analysis that will bear much fruit in the coming years.

University of Tennessee Press director Scot Danforth played an instrumental role in transforming my drafts into readable text. When I doubted whether a publisher would be interested in a book-length examination of the Cornerstone Speech, Danforth graciously reviewed some early draft chapters and offered me a clear path forward that reignited my confidence in the book's merits. His exceptional editing helped me think deeper about this topic and discover new methods of communicating my findings to a broader audience. He has been patient, kind, and professional as we have collaborated. I could not have asked for a better editor to guide this manuscript.

Several scholars reviewed the work and provided excellent suggestions as the book moved toward publication. Alexander Stephens's biographer Thomas E. Schott graciously reviewed my efforts to reinterpret the Confederate vice-president's legacy and offered an honest assessment. Likewise, Christopher C. Moore gave my work a thorough examination and offered numerous strategies for its improvement. Finally, an unidentified University of Tennessee Press board member pointed out several analytical weaknesses that subsequent revisions rectified.

Personally, I would like to thank my family. Living with a historian who is obsessed with his research day and night can be taxing. Thankfully, Rebecca Hébert is a great listener and historian. She probably knows more about Alexander Stephens than she cares to know, but without her this book would not have happened. During the many months that I contemplated whether to devote myself to this or that project, she reminded me that I got more excited whenever I talked about the Cornerstone Speech and that I always do my best when I follow my passions. Her faith in me is my cornerstone. Likewise, Inman Hébert has become an exceptional thinker who asked probing questions about my work and its significance. Inman's love for learning and zeal for life helps me remember that there are many things far more important and fulfilling (and potentially more interesting) than being a historian.

Finally, I would like to thank the educators who helped me pursue larger ambitions than I might have otherwise achieved. Where I come from no one dreams of becoming a writer. Those who seek out lofty goals are often told only of the obstacles that await. Thankfully, I encountered people in my life who were dreamers and encouraged students to be confident that the greatest obstacles in life are self-imposed.

Abbreviations

ANV	Army of Northern Virginia
CCC	Civilian Conservation Corps
CSA	Confederate States of America
DNR	Georgia Department of Natural Resources
GAR	Grand Army of the Republic
KKK	Ku Klux Klan
LOS	League of the South
NAACP	National Association for the Advancement of Colored People
NPS	National Park Service
SCLC	Southern Christian Leadership Conference
SCV	Sons of Confederate Veterans
SPLC	Southern Poverty Law Center
UCV	United Confederate Veterans
UDC	United Daughters of the Confederacy
WPA	Works Progress Administration

Cornerstone of the Confederacy

Introduction

On the evening of March 21, 1861, Confederate States of America Vice-President Alexander H. Stephens delivered the Cornerstone Speech before a celebratory crowd in Savannah, Georgia.[1] A few days earlier, Stephens had played a major role in drafting the Constitution of the Confederate States of America. Two months earlier, Stephens had been Georgia's leading critic of secession. By late March, Stephens had acquiesced to Georgia's decision to secede from the Union and had accepted a role in the new Confederate government. In Savannah, local leaders had asked Stephens to deliver some remarks comparing the United States Constitution with its Confederate counterpart. Stephens, despite his high-pitched voice and small stature, possessed exceptional oratorical abilities. Without prepared remarks, Stephens took the stage celebrating the Confederacy's birth. A few minutes into the speech, Stephens delivered this oft-quoted passage: "Our new government is founded upon exactly the opposite idea; its foundations are laid, its corner-stone rests upon the great truth that the negro is not equal to the white man. That slavery—subordination to the superior race—is his natural and moral condition."[2]

Stephens's white-supremacist declarations were more than spontaneous remarks delivered to a raucous crowd. His opinions on that cool moonlit night in Savannah were his own: measured, reasoned, and dispassionate. He believed that the Confederacy had offered an improved vision for America—one that explicitly acknowledged black inferiority and asserted white supremacy.[3]

The Lost Cause remains one of the most influential falsehoods in American history.[4] Confederate Vice President Alexander H. Stephens's Cornerstone Speech provides historians a useful lens to analyze this dishonest intellectual tradition. The speech espoused deceitful fallacies about white supremacy and black inferiority and was subsequently repudiated by Stephens and Lost Cause promoters as part of a postbellum misinformation campaign to cleanse the Confederate States of America of the indelible stain of slavery. Without the Cornerstone Speech, few Americans would remember Alexander H. Stephens; his place in American memory is tethered to it.[5] How Americans remembered Stephens usually depended upon whether they accepted or rejected the speech's explicit message. For generations, the Cornerstone Speech persevered, despite Lost Cause efforts to distort its lucid meaning, thanks to the actions of emancipationists, who kept the document's hard truths alive in American public discourse. *Cornerstone of the Confederacy* examines the convoluted trail of ways Americans have remembered Stephens's speech over the past 150 years.

Prior to the Civil War, white supremacy had not been a central ideology used by American political parties to rally support among white male voters. To be sure, racist attitudes pervaded all aspects of American society, but a distinction should be drawn between racism and white supremacy. Although both share much in common, the latter did not evolve into a major part of American political identity, especially among Democrats, until emancipation. Historian Mark Neely has warned that historians should avoid blurring distinctions between antebellum racism and white supremacy. Neely criticizes scholars who fail to recognize that white-supremacist identity politics did not fully emerge until the Civil War. My work embraces Neely's criticism of past assumptions about antebellum white supremacy and argues that the Cornerstone Speech is a representative example of how American political identity during the Civil War era was transitioning from expressions and representations of racism to more aggressive articulations and assertions of white supremacy. When Stephens's Cornerstone Speech used the rhetoric of white supremacy to forge a new national identity, his words and actions represented a shift in American politics as he unsuccessfully tried to unify white southern men under the Confederacy's white-supremacist banner. In fact, Stephens believed that the Confederacy's newfound white-supremacist identity would attract northern white men and Europeans to the Confederate cause.[6] After the Confederacy's defeat and emancipation, white-supremacist political rhetoric became more pronounced in national public discourse and subsequently began playing a greater role in shaping how postbellum Americans remembered the Civil War. The Cornerstone Speech provides a useful text to analyze how generations of Americans have articulated explanations of slavery, race, and white supremacy as they remembered the Civil War. Today, many Americans remember Alexander H. Stephens as a white supremacist whose words and actions demeaned African Americans and justified slavery's central role in antebellum history. Others reject those depictions. Those disagreements have produced a vibrant public debate about the Civil War's legacy.

Not only did Alexander Stephens endorse white supremacy, he also believed that such ideas bound white people together by ameliorating divisions created by disparities in wealth, sectional disagreements, and politics. Like Stephens, many historians have argued that expressions of white supremacy forged bonds of unity among white southern men. Historian Ulrich B. Phillips once argued that race had been the central theme in southern history. Likewise, historian Samuel S. Hill argued that southern "racial traditions and practices have served as the cement for the South's cultural cohesion" and that white supremacy was the "primary component" of southern culture.[7] Rooted in nineteenth-century pro-slavery defense rhetoric, white supremacy has evolved since emancipation into a dynamic belief that has touched all aspects of southern life. According to historian George Fredrickson, white supremacy played a central role in the South's nineteenth- and twentieth-century development. Expressions of racism delivered by politicians, clergymen, writers, and others molded the South into a "herrenvolk democracy" that united white men across class lines by eliciting a common commitment to white supremacy. Given the chance to forge a new government in the weeks that followed secession, the Confederate States of America, according to Fredrickson, deliberately chose to emphasize racial subordination rather than states' rights. "Many governments," as Alexander H. Stephens declared in the Cornerstone Speech, "have been founded on the principles of subordination and serfdom of certain classes of the same race; such were and are in violation of nature's laws. Our system commits no such violation of nature's laws. With us, the white race, however high or low, rich or poor, are equal in the eyes of the law. Not so with the Negro. Subordination is his place."[8] Any white unity gained through white supremacy was based on a series of lies intended to include poor whites while maintaining black inferiority.[9]

Some distinction should be drawn between white supremacy and racial prejudice. Many Americans, including Republican Party leaders like Abraham Lincoln, held deep rooted racial prejudices that questioned the place of African Americans in American society. The brand of white supremacy endorsed by Stephens and most Confederate leaders went much further: they argued that enslaved labor was the natural and divine condition of black people due to the latter's inferiority and inability to be fully reformed into prospective citizens. Many Americans held racial prejudices that also limited what roles African Americans might play in the nation's future, but nonetheless opposed slavery for a wide array of reasons. No white supremacist in antebellum America opposed slavery or endorsed the abolition movement. Meanwhile, many opponents of slavery and abolitionists held prejudices against black people that would have a profound impact on slavery and emancipation. White supremacists like Stephens saw slavery as the logical result of black inferiority and in many cases had convinced themselves and others that enslavement offered enslaved laborers protections that would have been stripped from them following emancipation.

White supremacy exists beyond the confines of the American South, but its influence in the South has been substantial and understanding its origins and dissemination is essential to analyzing the region's development.[10] After the Civil War, journalist and Lost Cause promoter Edward A. Pollard argued that building a southern society on a foundation of white supremacy had been one of the Lost Cause's goals.[11] As Gunnar Myrdal argued in *An American Dilemma*, the link between slavery and segregation "in the South . . . is psychologically direct. Even today the average white southerner really uses the race dogma to defend not only the present caste situation but also *ante-bellum* slavery and, consequently, the righteousness of the Southern cause in the Civil War."[12] The Cornerstone Speech stands at the junction between the Old South and the New South. A new road was forged out of the old. New postbellum articulations of white supremacy would mirror Stephens's words and help ensure that the New South, with regard to race, was not particularly new at all. The speech represented the evolving beliefs of a slave society that transformed racist assumptions about African Americans into a white-supremacist identity that challenged every aspect of black post-emancipation life in America. After emancipation, the speech continued to find new expressions among southerners who sought to expand white supremacy. An in-depth analysis of the Cornerstone Speech's place in American memory sheds much light upon evolving notions of race over time.[13]

While the speech appears in Civil War memory scholarship, no historian has examined how the Lost Cause, emancipationist, and reconciliationist visions of Civil War memory used Stephens's words to shape postbellum debates concerning the war's causes and white supremacy's continuity in American society. As defined by historian David Blight, the emancipationist view of Civil War memory portrayed the conflict as a struggle to end slavery. Promoted by many American Army veterans and African Americans, emancipationists cast the war as a moral crusade. Meanwhile, Blight also identified another version of Civil War memory: reconciliationist. This expression of memory grew more pronounced during the late nineteenth and early twentieth century as white Americans, north and South, put aside their sectional animosities to forge a new brand of nationalism dedicated to foreign territorial expansion. Both sides downplayed the role that slavery had played in the war. In the north, proponents ignored the contributions of African American Union soldiers. In the South, black enslaved laborers were remembered as loyal servants who had supported the Confederacy with the same zeal as their white enslavers. Nor has any scholar placed the Cornerstone Speech in a timeline that traces the emergence of white-supremacist ideologies from earlier expressions of racism. The Cornerstone Speech deserves extended analysis because it is an explicit declaration of support for white supremacy and contains other ideas, such as states' rights, that later became central to the creation of Lost Cause memory.[14] The speech is one of many from that era that can help historians understand the transition and distinction between racism and white supremacy. Any scholarly conversation on the evolution of white-supremacist rhetoric and its influence upon Civil War memory must consider the Cornerstone Speech. Stephens's declaration that the newly formed Confederate States of America rested on a cornerstone built upon slavery and white supremacy made explicit what most antebellum politicians and Civil War–era Confederates implied. After the war, the speech became an inconvenient truth for ex-Confederates, especially Stephens himself, who sought to cast their defeat as a noble cause lost in defense of states' rights, not as a failed revolution launched to preserve slavery and white supremacy. As the Lost Cause's misinformation campaign gained strength, the Cornerstone Speech evolved from a declaration of the war's causes into a rhetorical weapon wielded by emancipationists who challenged those lies.[15]

Historians play central roles in shaping, evangelizing, or rebutting historical memory. Forays into American memory can shed light on the development of the historical profession and the relationship between scholars who claim membership in the academy and amateur writers who are often perceived as less rigorous in their methods and documentation. Because public audiences rarely acknowledge those distinctions, historians of various skill levels, especially with the advent of the internet and digital publishing platforms, can influence historical memory. Overt partisans sought historians whose writings either intentionally or unintentionally validate their ideological reconstructions of the past. Memory, much like scholarly historiography, remains dynamic and resistant to monolithic orthodoxy. The Lost Cause's persistence throughout post-bellum American history symbolizes the important influence of professional historians in the memory making process.[16] Journalists, such as Edward Pollard and Horace Greeley, began shaping Civil War memory long before the Army of Northern Virginia surrendered. Despite their biases and sectional partisanship, those works remain an invaluable part of this topic's historiography as later commentators returned to those writers. Numerous studies of Civil War memory have appeared over the past century. Paul H. Buck's Pulitzer Prize–winning *The Road to Reunion: 1865–1900* (1937) offered scholars an analysis that concluded that the central theme of Civil War memory had been national integration rather than sectional divergence.[17] Along a similar vein, Thomas Pressly's *Americans Interpret Their Civil War* (1954) argued that, by the early twentieth century, a nationalist interpretation had allowed both sides to justify the war. Most believed that the war had been inevitable and thus no one could be blamed for its devastation.[18] Most notably, David Blight's *Race and Reunion* (2001) established a persuasive framework for analyzing the evolution of Civil War memory. He identified three competing visions—reconciliationist, emancipationist, and white supremacist—that have defined the war's memory. According to Blight, by the war's fiftieth anniversary, the North and South had achieved a sectional reconciliation that rejected emancipationist hopes for a racial reconciliation. American memory celebrated the bravery and honor of Union and Confederate veterans alike but ignored discussions of the war's causes and African American contributions to the nation's central conflict. Blight admitted that no single volume could examine every facet of American Civil War memory. Thus, his scholarship ignores references to the Cornerstone Speech found among reconciliationists, emancipationists, and white supremacists between 1865 and 1911. By examining the speech's memory, this book offers an interpretation of Civil War memory that contrasts with Blight's sectional reconciliation claims. The debate between white supremacists and emancipationists over the speech's meaning suggests that neither vision achieved reconciliation. Also, neither vision was monolithic. Perhaps at the time of the Civil War's semicentennial, support for sectional reconciliation and Lost Cause unity was less prevalent than Blight suggests.[19]

This book supports the findings of Caroline Janney's *Remembering the Civil War* (2013), Keith Harris's *Across the Bloody Chasm* (2014), and Adam Domby's *The False Cause* (2020). Janney argues that the many visions of Civil War memory never reconciled and continue to compete for attention today. Among those visions, however, the Lost Cause interpretation became the most visible and widespread because it contrasted sharply with its fragmented competitors.[20] Likewise, Harris challenges Blight's argument and asserts that Union and Confederate veterans promoted a sectional memory. Rather than white Union veterans ignoring black veterans, as Blight describes, Harris argues that emancipation became central to white Union veteran memories. Meanwhile, Confederate veterans labored to separate slavery from the war's causes.[21] Those labors required some linguistic maneuvering as explicit statements of white supremacy, such as the Cornerstone Speech, were explained away as benign expressions of states-rights ideology. Unfortunately, like other Civil War memory scholars, Harris's excellent work devotes only a passing mention to either Alexander Stephens or the Cornerstone Speech. Blight, Janney, and Harris, as well as numerous other scholars, interpret white supremacy as one of many elements of Lost Cause memory. Adam Domby's *The False Cause: Fraud, Fabrication, and White Supremacy in Confederate Memory* (2020) places white supremacy at the center of Civil War memory. Domby argues that the Lost Cause was founded on lies used to buttress white supremacy. However, like other Civil War memory scholars, Domby's study of Civil War memory in North Carolina ignores Stephens and the Cornerstone Speech.[22] Like Domby's work, my book places white supremacy at the center of Civil War memory and the Cornerstone Speech at the center of changing expressions of white supremacy in post-bellum America. Expressions of white supremacy, and justifications for preserving such ideas in a post-emancipation society, can be found in Confederate postbellum memorials, cemeteries, histories, speeches, organizations, politics, and more. By memorializing the Confederacy, a nation founded upon evolving expressions of white supremacy, post-bellum Lost Cause advocates used the power of historical memory to exert contemporary political influence through identity politics. Whereas the Cornerstone Speech failed to unify white Americans under the banner of white supremacy, post-bellum efforts to transform white supremacy into a political identity proved to be far more successful nationwide. Consequently, a major strand of white supremacist identity emerged in postbellum America, the Lost Cause.[23]

The study of commemorations provides a lens through which historians can view disagreements within society. Few commemorations lack contestation because the very need to commemorate is often in response to another group's efforts to define history. Commemorations, like memory, are highly selective and subjective displays intended to demonstrate meaning without much concern for historical fact. They are performances designed for both consumption by perpetrators, victims, and bystanders.[24] Private and public funds are used to support commemorations. Powerful private individuals and organizations often lobby elected officials to provide public financing. Such commemorations often advance and then recede as private organizations lose political influence. However, the physical reminders of past commemorations, such as monuments, cemeteries, markers, museums, street names, etc., often persist long after the original promoters' societal influence declines. Without influential backers capable of delivering political capital, commemorations and commemorative sites become vulnerable to new individuals and groups who seek to change the commemorative landscape. Alexander H. Stephens's important role in developing Lost Cause ideologies had a profound impact on commemorations honoring the fallen Confederate States of America. His writings and actions helped build the intellectual veneer that cloaked the Lost Cause's distortions of American history and memory.[25]

Most biographies of Alexander H. Stephens have glossed over or ignored the Cornerstone Speech's significance to both their subject's life and Civil War memory. Historians have analyzed how Americans remember Confederate civil and military leaders, such as Jefferson Davis, Robert E. Lee, James Longstreet, Nathan Bedford Forrest, John Mosby, John Bell Hood, and Stonewall Jackson, but Stephens has escaped their gaze.[26] Thomas E. Schott's biography remains the best scholarly work on the Confederate vice president. Schott's cradle-to-grave biography, however, devotes no attention to Stephens's legacy and posthumous role in shaping Civil War memory. Schott does an exceptional job detailing Stephens postbellum political career but underestimates his important place in the development of the Lost Cause. During his postbellum congressional career, Stephens, the former Confederate vice-president, became a symbolic target for emancipationists who never let him forget what he had said back in March 1861. Also, while Schott included an account of the Cornerstone Speech, he underemphasized the speech's enduring relevance to Stephens's postbellum career and to the Lost Cause.[27] Likewise, William C. Davis's excellent *The Union that Shaped the Confederacy: Robert Toombs and Alexander H. Stephens* (2001) downplays the Cornerstone Speech's impact on Stephens and the Confederacy.[28] Most historians have confined Stephens's Civil War-era influence to his various roles in the creation and administration of the Confederate States of America. Surprisingly, both Stephens and the Cornerstone Speech have received little attention from scholars interested in Civil War memory despite the frequency both appeared in historical sources, especially newspapers and organizational meeting transcripts. Ultimately, Stephens was more responsible for the development and perpetuation of Lost Cause distortions of Civil War history than scholars have acknowledged. *Cornerstone of the Confederacy* examines how the Cornerstone Speech evolved into its modern-day usage. The bitter divisions surrounding the speech's meaning continues to divide Americans between those who have accepted and now defend dishonest ideas inherited from the Lost Cause and those who continue to draw connections between contemporary social injustices in America and the lies told by Confederate leaders.

CHAPTER ONE

Laying the Cornerstone, 1830–1860

The rhetoric employed by Alexander Stephens in the Cornerstone Speech was rooted in evolving antebellum American constructions of race. Stephens's speech provides a lens through which to examine the evolving expressions of those falsehoods. White southern male understandings of race—especially white supremacy and black inferiority—constitute the central theme that connects the Cornerstone Speech to the causes of the American Civil War. Stephens spent a lifetime debating those questions. Subsequent critics of the Cornerstone Speech attempted to diminish the speech's credibility as evidence of the centrality of slavery to the Confederate experience by claiming that Stephens's opinions failed to represent southern society. However, the Cornerstone Speech mirrored emerging late antebellum white-supremacist rhetoric that Stephens and others championed in their defense of slavery, southern society, and ultimately the Confederate States of America.

Politically, Stephens remained committed to the Union until after Georgia seceded in 1861. He believed that the US Constitution was slavery's best protector. Equally beloved and despised among white southern men, Stephens often occupied the lonely middle ground between political extremists on all sides. His opinions on race, however, lacked the same level of moderation as his politics. Stephens believed that the American people should determine slavery's future in America because he thought most white male voters shared his views on black inferiority. Stephens might have originally been a reluctant Confederate, but his support for white supremacy and slavery never wavered. His belief in America was contingent upon the nation's endorsement of white supremacy. He joined the Confederate cause and betrayed his nationalist loyalties because the new southern government made support for white supremacy and slavery explicit at a time when "Black Republicans" questioned slavery's future. Before the Civil War, Stephens spent decades crafting the white supremacist rhetoric found throughout the Cornerstone Speech.[1]

Stephens was an avid reader of non-fiction. He preferred non-fiction to fiction because it revealed more about human nature. Stephens believed that the intense observation and study of humanity was essential to both his legal and political career. He saw himself as an ethnographer who devoted a lifetime to observing others. Liberty Hall, Stephens's Crawfordville, Georgia, plantation house, contained a large private library. Like most educated white southern men, Stephens had an extensive knowledge of classical literature, philosophy, and history. By setting aside scheduled reading times daily, Stephens absorbed large amounts of contemporary works of social science, anthropology, history, and theology. For example, Stephens had read George Fitzhugh, Arthur Gobineau, Henry Hotze, Josiah Nott, and other racial theorists. Friends and supporters routinely sent Stephens pamphlets, news clippings, and books that reflected his broad intellectual interests. Before the Civil War, Stephens often received requests from newspaper editors to lend his name and pen to the development of new literary magazines.[2] As a successful man who rose from humble origins, Stephens prided himself in the high level of education that he had attained.[3]

A man with Stephens's thirst for knowledge never struggled to find antebellum southern politicians espousing their opinions on race in America. The various strands of racist assertions that pervaded antebellum American society did not come together to form a coherent expression of white-supremacist ideology until the late antebellum period. Racism had been part of America's political identity from the start.[4] However, explicit articulations of a white-supremacist ideology first appeared on the eve of the American Civil War. Stephens's speech represents a confluence of racist ideas that, by the start of the Civil War, had merged to form a new ideology, white supremacy.[5]

Stephens's views on slavery had much to do with his personal experiences as an enslaver. Stephens saw no conflict between his white-supremacist beliefs and his reputation as a benevolent enslaver. At the start of the Civil War, Stephens owned thirty-four enslaved laborers. Supposedly, none of his slaves ever ran away. He taught some to read. Field hands worked under a task system that provided rewards for good work. Stephens's enslaved laborers never worked on Sunday. They also received Thursday and Saturday afternoons off. During the week of Christmas, Stephens permitted them to rest and visit family and friends on neighboring plantations. On Christmas Day, he hosted a large feast and supplied his human property with ample amounts of whiskey. Physical punishment, such as whipping, was prohibited, and he was never suspected of fathering children with his female slaves. Upon witnessing a runaway slave being publicly flogged near his home, Stephens fell into a deep depression because such brutality darkened his already dim view of humanity. Stephens opposed breaking up slave families and recognized marriages and extended family groups. Before the war, he reunited one enslaved family who had been broken up during previous sales.[6] All his slaves had permanent passes that allowed them to leave the plantation at night or whenever they had finished their assigned labor tasks. Stephens prohibited slave patrols from his property. When one of his slaves, known as "Uncle Dave," got into a dispute with a white woman, Stephens reportedly gave the slave money and told him to leave the area as fast as possible.[7]

Stephens's legal and political career often required extensive travel. He spent long stretches away from home. During his many absences, Stephens placed his cousin, Lordnorth Stephens, in charge, who according to former slave Georgia Baker, "let us do pretty much as us pleased." Lordnorth relied heavily on an enslaved driver, known as "Uncle Jim," to manage the estate. To be sure, Stephens bought humans to work his lands. He believed that his slaves were both members of his extended family and examples of an inferior race that required his supervision and care. He was also keenly aware of the physical brutalities that most enslaved laborers endured. Yet, decades after emancipation, Stephens's enslaved laborers recalled that white men referred to them as "Stephens' free niggers" because of their enslavers perceived leniency Perhaps his empathy for black enslaved laborers never extended beyond those he owned and whom he considered to be friends and fictive kin.[8]

The various white-supremacist themes found in the Cornerstone Speech came from a wide array of source material that Stephens would have been exposed to throughout the antebellum period. In 1835, South Carolina Governor George McDuffie delivered *The Natural Slavery of the Negro* before a packed state legislature in response to growing criticisms of slavery among northern abolitionists. "No human institution," McDuffie decried, "is more manifestly consistent with the will of God, than domestic slavery, and no one of his ordinances is written in more legible characters than that which consigns the African race to this condition. . . . That the African negro is destined by Providence to occupy this condition of servile dependence, is not less manifest. It is marked on the face, stamped on the skin, and evinced by the intellectual inferiority and natural improvidence of this race. They have all the qualities that fit them for slaves, and not one of those that would fit them to be freedmen." McDuffie argued that South Carolina's black enslaved laborers were in a better "condition" than "that which remains in Africa totally unblessed by the lights of civilization or Christianity." McDuffie bragged that enslaved laborers enjoyed superior working and material conditions than European factory workers. In the care of white southerners, McDuffie claimed, enslaved laborers were "cheerful, contended, and happy, much beyond the general condition of the human race." The sole reason an enslaved laborer dreamt of anything beyond what white enslavers had provided was due to "those foreign intruders and fatal ministers of mischief, the emancipationists." McDuffie's white-supremacist beliefs were commonplace in the antebellum South. Stephens agreed with McDuffie's justifications for slavery and gradually adopted most of his rhetoric.[9]

Stephens believed that all white men shared a stake in the benefits of slavery. Generations of white southern men had drawn a connection between slavery and their rights as members of a master race. During the late antebellum period, many secession zealots tried to convince other white men to join their cause by appealing to their shared notions of white supremacy. They depicted slavery not as an institution that provided some white men with enormous economic benefits, but rather as a shared responsibility among white men of all social classes. The sole defense against abolitionists would be to unify white men to protect slavery. Secession zealots predicted that emancipation would result in the loss of white male privilege in America. Stephens lacked the same zeal for secession as others, but he certainly saw white supremacy as a form of social glue that held together an American democracy reserved solely for white men. He struggled to understand why slavery and racism had failed to unify the nation.[10]

Stephens believed that slavery created a classless society of unified white men who equally enjoyed the fruits of liberty.[11] This white man's democracy had helped the nation avoid the kinds of internal class conflict that had engulfed France at the turn of the nineteenth century.[12] White unity was an essential component of American exceptionalism. The roots of the Cornerstone Speech's expressions of white unity can be found in Abbeville, Virginia, politician George W. Williams's fiery rhetoric. Williams warned that a "war of the races has commenced" that would require those "who advocate white supremacy . . . to unite." Williams saw secession as necessary to "preserve the ascendency of the white race" and accused abolitionists of trying to "bring white and black to the level of a common degradation." He accused abolitionists of manipulating westward expansion to give "public lands to foreign paupers" in order to prevent white southern men from taking their slave property to these new sections of the country. Like Stephens, Williams asserted that "the negro must be governed, must have a master, the good of both races demand it." Any threat that weakened slavery, according to Williams, would destroy the rights and liberties that southern white men enjoyed.[13]

Religion also played a role in the development of white supremacy as, in the minds of racists, certain biblical texts justified slavery. Some observers incorrectly suspected Stephens of being an atheist. He believed in divine providence but questioned the church's agency. He was a member of the Presbyterian Church, but rarely attended services. Nonetheless, Stephens did not prevent his enslaved laborers from forming religious bodies of worship. Nor did Stephens outright oppose the reading of the Bible by slaves or visits from itinerant preachers on his plantation. He welcomed all guests into his home. Traveling ministers were commonplace. Stephens's endorsements of Christianity's virtues grew more pronounced when employed in defense of slavery. As a Christian slaveholder, Stephens had encountered the writings of proslavery theologians who argued for slavery's divine origins. Stephens believed that the spread of Christianity among slaves was the greatest religious movement in world history. He and others who shared such beliefs tended to depict a desire to spread Christianity to Africa as a major part of the rise of the Atlantic slave trade. Stephens portrayed enslavers as Christian missionaries spreading the Gospel among Africans as the Apostle Paul had. When Stephens explained to non-southerners slavery's central role in southern society, he relied heavily on biblical imagery to make his case. Ordinarily, Stephens, who at times was described as either a devout Presbyterian or a lonely atheist, refrained from using biblical references in his political speeches.[14]

Stephens's Cornerstone Speech echoed many ideas found in Rev. Josiah Priest's popular *Slavery, As it Relates to the Negro, Or African Race*, which was later reprinted under the title *Bible Defence of Slavery or, The origin, history, and fortunes of the Negro race*. Published in 1843 and reprinted throughout the 1850s, Priest's work gained an international audience. Priest sought to prove that God had created black people to be slaves. Priest traced the origins of a white race of people to Japheth and a black race of people to Ham, both sons of Noah.[15] Priest proclaimed that Ham, whom he described as "a woolly headed, black eyed man" was "the first negro of the human race." Thus, according to Priest, "the cause of the negro's color" was determined by "the arbitrary will and wisdom of God."[16] Many nineteenth-century theologians had attributed the enslavement of Africans as evidence of a curse that Noah had placed on Ham's descendants. Priest's interpretation differed, however, as he attributed Ham's "whole character and nature" as the reason "that the curse of slavery was entailed on his race."[17] Priest's descriptions of the origins of the white race emphasized how their skin color united them in ways that made it impossible to become an inferior race. "It is utterly impossible to reduce the whites by any process," wrote Priest, "whatever to so low a condition, as is found to be the universal state of the negro race, on account of the possession of superior mental faculties, moral feelings, reason, reflections, sympathies, and all the train of qualifications, constituting the image of God."[18] Meanwhile, the black race, according to Priest, possessed superior recuperative healing powers and physical traits that made them ideal slaves. Ultimately, Priest argued that the black race needed to be supervised by a white race that possessed superior mental and moral faculties. The supposed "burden" that nature had placed on the white race to care for the black race was also central to Stephens's defense of slavery.[19]

On one significant point, Stephens disagreed with many racial theorists on the future potential of the black race. He believed that enslaved laborers were capable of intellectual and moral improvement. Stephens could imagine a distant future when black enslaved laborers might achieve a level of "civilization" comparable to their white enslavers. He would have disagreed with writers like John Campbell, who asserted "that no amount of education or training can ever make the negro equal in intellect with the white . . . under no circumstance has the negro race ever been able to compete with the white."[20] By contrast, Stephens encouraged enslavers to educate their enslaved laborers and worried that the failure to do so had impaired American society. Stephens disliked the word "slavery" because he saw the relationship between enslavers and enslaved laborers as a positive force for all. He often referred to black enslaved laborers as servants.

Stephens believed that slavery made all white men equal. He empathized with poor whites. He lost both of his parents at a young age. That experience as an orphan child from a family with modest means shaped his entire life. As a youth, he benefited from the charitable aid provided by his extended family and community members. He felt grateful for the assistance and seemed to genuinely try to extend such charity to others for the rest of his life. Stephens's correspondence was filled with numerous requests from orphans or impoverished children seeking aid. For decades, Stephens paid for students to attend private schools and colleges. He often used his influence to help poorer students access educational opportunities. Widows also contacted Stephens in search of relief. He tried to help most of the people who asked for help.[21] By the start of the Civil War, Stephens was a renowned philanthropist with a special place in his heart for poor white people who wanted access to education.[22]

During the antebellum period, Stephens most extensive remarks on slavery came during congressional debates over the annexation of Texas. Proposals to acquire and admit Texas into the Union as a slave state placed southern members of the Whig Party in a difficult position. Democrats enthusiastically endorsed immediate plans to annex Texas. Northern Whigs disagreed and worried that annexing Texas would instigate a war between the United States and Mexico. In 1844, Whig senator and presidential candidate Henry Clay of Kentucky proposed to delay annexation. Georgia Whigs supported annexation but also urged the country to delay so that proper terms for a peaceful agreement could be negotiated with Mexico. Stephens himself had been among those Whigs who called for "the annexation of Texas to the United States, at the earliest practicable period, consistent with the honor and good faith of the nation."[23] According to historian Anthony Carey, "Whigs lost the pro-southern high ground by trying to make timing the issue on Texas annexation."[24] In November 1844, Democrat James K. Polk defeated Clay in a presidential contest shaped in part by their differing positions on Texas annexation.

After the election, congressional Democrats, with some assistance from southern Whigs, including Stephens, pushed for the immediate annexation of Texas. Stephens occupied the awkward position of maintaining his allegiance to the Whig Party while defending the westward expansion of slavery. Many of his northern Whig Party friends had accused the South of using the debate over Texas to initiate a war with Mexico for the sake of expanding slavery into new southwestern territories. On January 25, 1845, Stephens broke with his party and threw his support behind immediate annexation. His explanations for why slavery should expand westward mirrored many ideas that he would later expound upon in the Cornerstone Speech. "I am no defender of slavery in the abstract." Stephens declared, "Liberty always had charms for me, and I would rejoice to sell all the sons of Adam's family, in every land and clime, in the enjoyment of those rights that are set forth in our *Declaration of Independence*." However, according to Stephens, slavery was a divinely sanctioned institution that "will prevail wherever the Anglo-Saxon and African races are blended in the same proportions." Slavery was as inevitable as the sun rising in the east and setting in the west. Whether Congress approved of slavery or not, it would continue to be necessary wherever the white and black race coexisted. Later, Stephens joined eight southern Whigs and Democrats as they ratified Texas's annexation.[25]

Northern Whigs and southern Democrats found Stephens's remarks equally shocking. His declaration that God endorsed slavery's perpetual expansion upset northern Whigs, who feared that Texas annexation would lead to the acquisition of additional new slaveholding territories.[26] Meanwhile, Stephens's pronouncement that he was "no defender of slavery in the abstract" drew the ire of southern Democrats who interpreted his defense of slavery as weak. The *Georgia Telegraph* accused Stephens of being "an improper representative for a slaveholding state" whose "constituents regard [slavery as] a vital principle of their welfare, guaranteed by the Constitution and sanctioned by the Bible." Stephens, the newspaper claimed, had weakened the region's defense of slavery by "promulgating to the world his abhorrence of the abstract principle of slavery." In 1846, Stephens did not embrace slavery as a "positive good." Instead, he continued to view slavery as a "necessary evil" thrust upon the white race by God. He also agreed with Thomas Jefferson and others who hoped that slavery might vanish in some abstract future.[27]

Throughout the 1850s, Stephens remained committed to preserving the Union. He believed that compromises that could ameliorate rising sectional tensions were possible. As a southern member of the national Whig Party, Stephens sometimes found himself awkwardly trying to protect southern interests in slavery while advancing his party's agenda that increasingly opposed the territorial expansion of slavery. Stephens neither claimed to be a party partisan nor did his stances always align with the South's sectional interests. As he was throughout his life, Stephens was unafraid to take an unpopular stand in defense of what he judged to be necessary to serve the nation's best interests. Stephens's efforts to explain his positions were often complicated and contradictory, but he remained committed to compromise and nationalist policies until Georgia's secession in 1861.[28]

During the fight over the Compromise of 1850, Stephens supported Illinois senator Stephen A. Douglas's comprehensive effort to settle the nation's sectional disputes. Stephens believed that Congress had the power to regulate slavery in western territories but lacked the authority to abolish it. Realistically, Stephens knew that slavery had little chance of extending into new territories such as New Mexico and Utah, but he opposed the efforts of northern congressmen explicitly to dictate that decision. Like Douglas, Stephens supported a policy of popular sovereignty that allowed state governments to determine slavery's legality. Ideally, new territories would endorse slavery, but Stephens was not an idealist and understood that the best compromise white southern men could attain from their northern counterparts would be to place the decision in the hands of territorial citizens. Stephens preferred having slavery prohibited by locals rather than Congress. His support for the Compromise of 1850 left him as a man without a party as northern Whigs strongly endorsed prohibiting slavery in the west, and many southern Democrats launched threats to secede from the Union. Undeterred, Stephens returned to Georgia, where he joined Robert Toombs and Howell Cobb in an aggressive campaign for the Compromise of 1850. Together the men traveled hundreds of miles across the state delivering numerous speeches and engaging in several debates with southern-rights proponents. Previously, the state legislature had passed a resolution calling for a statewide convention if Congress passed the Compromise of 1850. On November 25, 1850, Stephens's Unionist allies won a decisive victory over their southern-rights foes, attaining more than a 22,000-vote majority. Like Stephens, most Georgia voters remained committed to preserving the Union.[29]

What this majority supported, however, was not the Compromise of 1850. The Georgia Platform, passed by the convention to contest elements of the Compromise, reflected Stephens's nationalist sympathies. Although the platform's fourth resolution warned that Georgia would secede if the federal government acted to restrict slavery, overall the document struck a conciliatory tone. The potential transgressions that could ignite secession were either unlikely to happen in 1850—such as a secession trigger that would occur in the case of the prohibition of slavery in Washington, DC—or carefully worded to provide additional room for compromise, such as congressional prohibition (not regulation) of the interstate slave trade. Stephens continued to believe that many allies across the nation would come to the region's defense if anti-slavery forces threatened the institution.[30]

In 1851, Stephens left the Whig Party and became a leading figure in the Unionist Party—a coalition of former Whigs and southern Democrats who opposed secession. As the Whig Party collapsed as its southern and northern wings could not resolve differences over the issue of slavery, Stephens dreamt of creating a "sound national organization upon broad—national—republican principles."[31] He was concerned that the nation's political parties were becoming too divided along sectional lines.[32]

During the Kansas-Nebraska Act debate, Stephens fretted that the national parties would desintegrate. In 1854, Illinois senator Stephen A. Douglas proposed legislation that would create two new territories, Nebraska and Kansas, located north of the Missouri Compromise 36° 30' line that had set the boundary for where slavery would be permitted during westward expansion. Stephens wholeheartedly endorsed the Kansas-Nebraska Act and argued that the Missouri Compromise was never intended to be a contract between North and South limiting the future expansion of slavery. Since 1820, Stephens argued, the North had failed on several occasions to fully enforce the 36 °30' line and had leaned toward allowing territorial residents to determine for themselves if slavery should exist in their area. Stephens questioned why northern politicians should fear popular sovereignty, given their immense population advantages and foreign immigration. "Are your 'free-born sons,'" Stephens mocked, "who never 'breathed the tainted air of slavery, such nincompoops that they cannot be 'trusted without their mother's leave?'"[33] According to biographer Thomas Schott, Stephens's implied "that slavery was not so bad after all" and that the sole way "to keep 'wise, intelligent, and Christian men, even from New England itself, from adopting' slavery was to have Congress prevent it."[34]

Above all, Stephens's disdain for states'-rights Democrats motivated his enthusiastic support for the Kansas-Nebraska Act. Stephens criticized them for manipulating fears and refusing to compromise. He held a steadfast conviction that he knew what was best for the South. The Kansas-Nebraska Act, a bill proposed by a leading Democrat, offered Stephens the chance to prove to states'-rights Democrats that compromise did not necessarily pose a threat to the South's interests. He urged southern Democrats to accept Douglas's bill as a symbolic victory that admitted that slavery's future should be in the hands of voters rather than of Congress. Stephens remained convinced that most Americans supported slavery and shared his white-supremacist views. When it appeared as if the bill's opponents would successfully delay a vote, Stephens's use of an obscure house procedural rule rescued it. The bill's passage owed much to Stephens's determination. "I took the reins in my own hand and drove with whip & spur until we got the 'wagon' out of the mire," Stephens's exalted to a friend. He considered his role in the passage of the Kansas-Nebraska Act to be "the greatest glory of my life."[35] Not a single northern Whig supported the bill. Stephens's actions helped destroy his party. During the secession crisis, states'-rights Democrats were also dissatisfied: they denounced Stephens's support for the Kansas-Nebraska Act. According to some, his compromising stances had jeopardized southern interests.

During the 1850s, Stephens began to transition away from a position like Jefferson's expressed hope that slavery might fade away to a position that defended slavery as a "positive good." Stephens possessed a genuine concern for the downtrodden in American society. He believed that government policy and Christian charity could help the poor and weak advance in America. Those ideals, combined with his white-supremacist values, shaped his opinions on slavery. "For a man so naturally compassionate toward the unfortunate, weak, and poor," wrote biographer Thomas Schott, "he betrayed little sensitivity to the fate of the millions of southern blacks."[36] However, as historian John Patrick Daly argues, "evangelical morality and proslavery ideology constituted the heart of southern identity."[37] Thus, like most southern evangelicals, Stephens believed that what slaves and white southern men had gained from the religious conversion of the former far outweighed any possible negative consequences caused by chattel slavery. For Stephens, the power and success of white society to lead black people to Christ was both pragmatic and divine. Slavery's future place in American society, according to Stephens, had already been decided due to black inferiority and the immense wealth it created nationally and internationally. In a letter to his brother Linton Stephens, Stephens mused "if the comforts of a people or race are to be comported according to their natural increase and rapid multiplication the race is certainly vastly better off in this country in their present condition than it ever was in their own with all the liberty of nature." Emancipation seemed impractical, inhumane, and improbable for Stephens.[38]

Within the House of Representatives, Stephens emerged as a vocal defender of slavery. In 1856, during a debate over the admission of Kansas, Stephens argued that slavery was the result of "Christian philanthropy." "The negro," Stephens urged, "is inferior to the white man; nature has made him so . . . all attempts to make the inferior equal to the superior is but an effort to reverse the decrees of the Creator." "Do what you will" Stephens continued: "a negro is a negro, and he will remain a negro still. In the social and political system of the South, the negro is assigned to that subordinate position for which he is fitted by the laws of nature." Explicitly echoing the language of the Cornerstone Speech, he argued that God's covenant with humanity "is the corner-stone of the whole Christian system." No law Congress enacted could reverse "the laws of nature." Stephens expressed concerns that abolitionists might sabotage slavery while America was still on the rise socially, culturally, and economically. Furthermore, if abolitionists and Congress abolished slavery, Stephens admonished, relations among white men in America, where "no castes or classes" existed, would be thrown into chaos. Stephens described the South as a distinctive American region bound by white unity.[39]

Virginia lawyer James Holcombe influenced Stephens's pro-slavery rhetoric. In 1858, Holcombe delivered an address titled "Is Slavery Consistent with Natural Law?" at the annual meeting of the Virginia State Agricultural Society. Two decades later, Stephens included a full transcript of the speech in an appendix to his *A Constitutional View of the Late War Between the States*. Holcombe declared that "equality" had never been allowed by God in a "society where the inferior race constituted an element of any magnitude." The survival of the black race, Holcombe contended, "may become a question between the slavery, and the extinction or further deterioration of the inferior race." Freedom would have placed African slaves in competition with white men that for the former "must either terminate in its destruction, or consign it to hopeless degradation." Like Holcombe, Stephens eventually saw slavery as essential to preserve and uplift an inferior race through contact with a superior race. Holcombe's rhetoric inspired Stephens's subsequent speeches:

> Slavery has weaned a race of savages from superstition and idolatry, imparted to them a general knowledge of the precepts of the true religion, implanted in their bosom sentiments of humanity and principles of virtue, developed a taste for the arts and enjoyments of civilized life, given an unknown dignity and elevation to their type of physical, moral and

intellectual man, and for two centuries during which this humanizing process has taken place, made for their subsistence and comfort, a more bountiful provision, than was ever before enjoyed in any age or country of the world by a laboring class.[40]

Black liberty was possible, but "the refining influence of Christian servitude has yet given no signs of living and self-sustaining culture." Holcombe proclaimed that white southern men could be proud of the achievements both white and black races attained because of slavery.

Beyond elevating the black race, Holcombe and Stephens believed that slavery reconciled "the antagonism of classes" among white men. Without slavery, Holcombe declared, white southern men would have fallen into "discord" internally plunging the nation toward revolution. Slavery had become "the great peace maker of our society," Holcombe said, "converting inequalities . . . into pledges of reciprocal service and bonds of mutual and intimate friendship." Abolitionists threatened the peace, security, and liberty that united southern white men. If slavery ended, the loss of the exceptional civilization built upon widely held notions of black inferiority would end the "happiness and advancement of mankind." Holcombe's words reverberated throughout the Cornerstone Speech.[41]

In 1859, after sixteen years in Congress, Stephens retired. During his trip home, Stephens delivered a farewell address in Augusta, Georgia. The town was in a celebratory mood as planned Fourth of July festivities loomed. He previewed many ideas that would become central to the Cornerstone Speech two years later. Simultaneously, Stephens struck both nationalist and sectional chords as he continued to resist pro-secession zealots and promote bipartisan compromise. Specifically, Stephens disputed the wisdom of major western philosophers, scientists, and politicians whose great works failed to recognize that "subordination is the normal condition of the negro." Without acknowledging the supremacy of the white race, none of their theoretical ideas could work in practice. The Declaration of Independence had misled the nation that "all men were created equal." This central misunderstanding of the "laws of nature" had created many of the animosities among the sections that plagued antebellum America. Stephens claimed that the South, however, had discovered a pragmatic truth that God had ordained white supremacy. Acceptance of that divine truth had allowed the region to thrive while enslaved laborers benefitted from Christian virtue.[42]

If left alone, Stephens speculated, the South would reach the zenith of human civilizations. Stephens declared: "If slavery, as it exists with us, is not the best for the African, constituted and made as he is; if it does not best promote his welfare and happiness, socially, morally, and politically, as well as that of his master, it ought to be abolished. But if it does this, then we stand upon a rock as firm and impregnable as truth."

Although he saw abolition and sectional partisanship as threats to southern society, he continued to oppose secession in the hopes that all sides would cling to a "higher law"—the US Constitution. He applauded southern leaders for forcing the country to recommit itself to slavery through their constant agitation. He urged them to continue their protests.[43]

Most of the speech contained ideas that Stephens had repeated numerous times with one major exception. In his zeal to convince others of slavery's virtues, Stephens argued that the country needed more slaves to continue its "Christian philanthropy." Africans achieved so much thanks to slavery, Stephens announced, that America should reopen the African slave trade. Without a new supply of enslaved laborers, Stephens said, it would be useless for the nation to expand slavery into the western territories. Few southern politicians, except for a handful of pro-secession zealots, ever spoke of reopening the African slave trade.[44]

Why had Stephens broached such a taboo subject? By 1859, sectional tensions had reached a boiling point. Southern radicals interpreted the adoption of an anti-slavery constitution in Kansas as a symbol of the national Democratic Party's impending collapse. Some blamed Stephens for what happened in Kansas because of his support for Stephen Douglas and "squatter sovereignty"—the derogatory term most white southern men used to describe the idea that territorial populations should decide whether their territories should allow slavery, which was Stephens's own position. According to the *Charleston Mercury*, Stephens "has been prominent in influencing the great events which have brought the South into a position of weakness and peril." Pro-secession Democrats often accused Stephens, a former Whig, of either being "sympathetic to abolitionists" or a "submissionist." Stephens had always doubted whether slavery could expand into Kansas and other western territories because the South lacked the surplus population that would have enabled a mass migration of enslavers and enslaved laborers. By 1859, Stephens dreamed that the African slave trade would be reopened because of the enormous annual expense enforcing the ban had imposed on both the British and American governments. He also felt that events in the Caribbean and other places that had experienced emancipation would convince Americans of the folly of black liberty. Rather than focus its protests on extending slavery into the west, Stephens advised white southern men to revive the African slave trade. If the South had a large surplus of enslaved laborers, the nation would be less able to halt slavery's spread. Plus, by allowing the African slave trade to remain dormant, the South had surrendered the moral high ground that justified the enslavement of the black race as an act of Christian philanthropy. Stephens, whose rhetorical style had been described as a blend between a preacher and teacher, was instructing his impatient pro-secession zealots on why they needed to adopt a long-term pro-slavery strategy.[45]

The Augusta crowd responded to Stephens's white-supremacist rhetoric with thundering applause. The *Daily Constitutionalist*, an Augusta newspaper, praised Stephens as "a faithful soldier" who "if there be a retired statesman upon earth with purer hands, we would make a pilgrimage to kiss them."[46] Stephens's Augusta farewell speech attracted national attention. The *New York Day Book*, a Democratic Party–affiliated publication, applauded Stephens's frank commentary on slavery. "No speech made by any southern statesman," the newspaper declared, "has excited such profound interest in the North as this one" because it was "so bold, so striking, so full of moral force and true humanity, that the Abolitionists of the North are confounded." Had other southern politicians been willing to provide "a proper explanation of the great truths upon which the institution of negro subordination or 'slavery' rests . . . southern institutions [would be] as safe in Massachusetts as in South Carolina." Most Americans, the newspaper predicted, agreed with Stephens's white–supremacist rhetoric.[47]

Some newspapers challenged Stephens's use of the US Constitution to defend slavery. The *National Era* in Washington, DC, blasted Stephens's contradictory rhetoric. Editors accused Stephens of falsely presenting himself as a constitutional expert when his interpretations shifted with "the every-varying currents of popular feeling." If Stephens and his allies succeeded, the newspaper declared, they would use the federal government to force local governments to accept slavery. The paper reminded readers of Stephens's endorsement of popular sovereignty. Now, "he has no fixed principles or policy to carry out, but has only exhibited the qualities of an adroit and successful demagogue." According to the newspaper, no one could trust Stephens.[48]

Pro-secession newspapers, such as the *Charleston Mercury*, despised Stephens. They labeled Stephens as a "traitor" to southern interests who falsely equated "prosperity" with "liberty." Stephens, they claimed, had collaborated with Stephen A. Douglas and "black Republicans" to admit Oregon to the Union as a free state without forcing Congress to admit Kansas as a slave state. The pro-secession newspaper urged southern white men to "save themselves from their southern politicians no less than from their northern enemies."[49]

The election of 1860 further exacerbated Stephens's relationship with pro-secession Democrats. Many Democrats believed that Stephens had retired from Congress to run for president in 1860. Had Stephens sought a presidential bid, the Georgia Democratic Party was prepared to nominate him, but he discouraged those plans. Instead, he endorsed Stephen A. Douglas—a candidate whom many Georgia Democrats disliked because of his strong endorsement of "squatter sovereignty" and the Freeport Doctrine. At the 1860 Democratic National Convention in Charleston, South Carolina, Georgia Democrats stormed out of the convention when Stephen Douglas refused to support congressional protection for territorial slavery. Even Stephens's best friend and former Whig Party nationalist ally Robert Toombs had swung to the pro-secession faction, arguing that Douglas's platform had forced southerners to endorse positions contrary to their regional interests. Toombs was prepared to split the Democratic Party and warned delegates that if a "Black Republican" were elected in November he would lead the South out of the Union. Stephens, on the other hand, remained committed to the national Democratic Party. Dividing the national party, he believed, would hand the Republican Party an easy victory in November. When Georgia Democrats again refused to support Douglas's nomination at the Baltimore Convention, Stephens and a group of Georgia Democratic nationalists, including Herschel V. Johnson, remained committed to Douglas. In Georgia, support for Douglas was strongest in Stephens's old congressional district, centered on Augusta. Elsewhere, pro-secession Democrats provided strong support for southern-rights candidate John Breckinridge of Kentucky.[50]

Nationally, Stephens emerged as a moderate voice in a radicalizing southern faction of the Democratic Party. A Philadelphia newspaper commented that despite his "unnaturally small" features Stephens was a "Hercules in statesmanship . . . [and a] Titan in mind, and a Knight in chivalry and in courage." To some northern Democrats, Stephens appeared to be a martyr who sacrificed his political prospects by refusing to bend to the will of pro-secession zealots. Newspapers emphasized that anyone who could befriend Abraham Lincoln, Stephen A. Douglas, and Robert Toombs could help reunite the nation through sensible compromise. They encouraged Stephens to "take the stump in Georgia, and sweep the disunionists into lasting obscurity." Although those compliments appealed to Stephens's vanity, he knew that Douglas's campaign would fail.[51]

Stephens remained confined to his residence, Liberty Hall, throughout most of the 1860 presidential election due to a terrible fall that disabled him for months. Meanwhile, perhaps due to his growing concern about secession, the severe headaches he had endured throughout his life returned. Finally, in July, Stephens delivered his first public speech endorsing Douglas's presidential campaign. He returned to Augusta to partake in another Independence Day celebration. An energized Stephens took the stage for three hours, convinced that fanatics and demagogues had led the nation along a path toward "disruption" and "anarchy." He proclaimed that despite its problems the United States of America was "the best government on earth, and ought to be sustained, if it can be, on the principles upon which it was founded." The sole national candidate in the race was Stephen A. Douglas. Any hope of maintaining the Union rested upon his successful campaign. The southern-rights faction of the party had broken away without a clear platform and ultimately adopted most of the same stances that Douglas supported. Douglas's views on slavery, Stephens claimed, would never pose a threat to southern interests. Douglas supported the Dred Scott decision, fugitive slave laws, and shared Stephens's beliefs in the black race's inferiority. According to Stephens, Douglas "holds that the negro is of an inferior race—that he is not and cannot be a citizen of the United States—that he was not intended to be embraced in the Declaration of Independence—that subordination to the white race is his natural and normal condition." Whereas Douglas's critics had accused him of supporting "squatter sovereignty," Stephens declared that he was "perfectly willing for the pioneers of civilization who quit the old States for new homes in the west to form and regulate their own domestic institutions in their own way, and make all other laws according to their liking." Stephens questioned whether southerners could demand states' rights while denying western settlers the privilege of determining slavery's fate locally. He reminded the crowd that most of them had descended from squatters whose sole desire had been to govern themselves. Only Douglas could preserve the Union.[52]

One month prior to the November election, a *New York Herald* reporter traveled to Crawfordville, Georgia, to interview Stephens. Though the correspondent arrived unexpectedly, Stephens warmly greeted him. Stephens warned the reporter that "northern people" had underestimated the popularity that pro-secession forces had acquired across the South. The North, Stephens claimed, did "not know what slavery is, and are ignorant of its first principles." Nonetheless, "the popularity of slavery" had grown nationwide, including within the Republican Party. If the nation was forced into an "irrepressible conflict" that pitted the free labor North against the slave labor South, Stephens confidently declared that "it would end in the triumph of slavery." Stephens told the reporter that support for slavery had grown worldwide because "no government has successfully proposed a substitute for African slave labor." When asked why he supported Douglas, Stephens replied "the course I am taking in the present canvass is dictated by a desire to do all I can to prevent a catastrophe which I believe to be not only imminent, but certain, in case of Lincoln's election." Stephens accused southern extremists of ignoring their earlier support for congressional nonintervention in the territorial expansion of slavery. By forcing Douglas to promise congressional action to thrust slavery upon territorial governments, Stephens claimed, pro-secession Democrats had placed themselves in an impossible position: they had destroyed the candidacy of the one politician, Douglas, who could defeat Lincoln. To make matters worse, pro-secession Democrats had selected as their southern-rights candidate John Breckinridge, who was both a Unionist and an opponent of congressional intervention. Brandishing his underappreciated humor, Stephens quipped that Breckinridge would have to be the first to hang if disunionists managed to win the election. Stephens criticized "fanatics on all sides" for endorsing "demagogues" who have silenced "statesmen and patriots" and sacrificed "principle and honor" in pursuit of selfish ambitions. Unless something unexpected happened, Stephens predicted that Lincoln's election would unleash an uncontrollable "whirlwind" leading toward secession and civil war. Stephens painted a bleak picture.[53]

Despite Stephens's efforts, only 10 percent of Georgia voters cast a ballot in support of Stephen A. Douglas. Nationally, only Missouri provided the Illinois senator with any electoral votes. Republican Abraham Lincoln's election sent shockwaves across the South as secession advocates increased their calls for slave states to remove themselves from the Union. Stephens supported secession in the abstract but initially felt that the South had little to fear from the new Republican-controlled federal government.

After Lincoln's election, the Georgia legislature voted to hold elections on January 2 to select delegates for a January 16 state convention to debate secession. Georgia's leaders quickly formed into two primary camps. Immediatists, such as Howell Cobb and Robert Toombs, sought to remove Georgia from the Union as soon as possible without any further efforts to negotiate with the federal government. They argued that Georgia needed to secede before the Lincoln administration took office on March 4, 1861. Cooperationists wanted to offer the federal government an opportunity to strike a compromise that would preserve the union but most also endorsed Georgia's right to secede. Few Cooperationists referred to themselves as Unionists. They doubted whether the federal government would support the kinds of guarantees to preserve slavery that they demanded. Primarily, Cooperationists were concerned with how and when Georgia would secede. Unlike Immediatists, Cooperationists recommended that Georgia only secede if joined by other slaveholding states. Secession, in their opinion, had to present a unified front to be recognized by the rest of the world. Among Cooperationists, Stephens held a minority view that Georgia should only secede if the Lincoln administration violated the Constitution or northern states infringed on individuals' right to carry their human property anywhere. Few shared Stephens's position. Most agreed that secession was inevitable. Neither side, however, questioned the region's commitment to slavery. Both groups believed that abolitionists and Republicans posed serious threats to slavery's long-term survival. Each faction explicitly recognized that the current sectional controversy was rooted in debates over national protections for slavery and that southern society was distinctive and needed additional protections from perceived northern aggressions. Compromising slavery to heal the nation's festering sectional divide was nonnegotiable.[54]

For weeks after the election, Stephens's emotions paralyzed him at a crucial moment. The combined election returns for John Bell and Stephen A. Douglas bested Breckinridge by more than a thousand votes. The sole chance for Georgia to avoid immediate secession was the formation of a coalition of Bell and Douglas supporters. The only politician in Georgia capable of building such an alliance was Stephens, yet he shrank from public view when opponents of secession needed him most. Three days after the election, Stephens confided to his brother Linton that "no power [could] prevent" secession. "Our destiny seems to be fixed."[55]

As Stephens sulked, Immediatist leaders organized an effective campaign to secure convention delegates as Cooperationists struggled to articulate their position. Immediatists possessed a rhetorical advantage. They only had to convince voters to endorse secession now. Cooperationists, however, had a far more complicated set of conditional proposals. As fears of "Black Republican" rule spread across Georgia, the Immediatists seized the momentum. Meanwhile, Stephens did nothing to help organize the Cooperationist campaign. Instead, he moped at home. Douglas's poor showing in Georgia had embarrassed Stephens. His best friend, Robert Toombs, had opposed Douglas and now led Immediatists toward secession. Across the state, several of his former nationalist allies had switched sides. Georgia had fallen to the very demagogues Stephens detested. The desperate situation plunged Stephens into depression as he failed to campaign against secession.[56]

As Stephens had done so many times in his political career, the opportunity to resist against overwhelming odds and in the face of steep opposition cured his depression. The Georgia legislature invited Stephens to deliver some remarks on the crisis. For more than a week, Georgia's political leaders had traveled to Milledgeville to present a case for why or why not the state should secede from the Union. The night before Stephens's address, his old friend turned political rival Robert Toombs had delivered a thundering emotional appeal for immediate secession. "Strike, strike," Toombs pleaded, "while it is yet time . . . make another war of independence."[57] Stephens denounced Toombs for allowing his emotions to best his logic. Unlike many of his impromptu stump speeches, Stephens spent several days crafting his address. This would be his last chance to persuade his opponents that secession, rather than the Republican Party, presented the biggest threat to slavery's future. On the night of November 14,

Stephens delivered a powerful speech, later referred to as the "Union Speech," before the Georgia legislature in Milledgeville. This was the speech that he wanted to be remembered by.[58]

"In my judgement," cautioned Stephens, "the election of no man, constitutionally chosen to that high office, is sufficient cause for any State to separate from the Union. [The South] ought to stand by still and aid in maintaining the Constitution of the country." By seceding from the Union, Stephens claimed, the South would violate the will of the people by trying to overthrow a fair election. Lincoln lacked neither absolute power nor unanimous support among Republicans, according to Stephens. If the South seceded, it would surrender any power it held in the national government to the Republicans. Secession might be the one issue that could unify the Republican Party against the slave states. Stephens reminded his white southern male audience that disrupting slavery would require an enormous level of political power that no one in Washington, DC, was capable of wielding. If the South left Congress, no one would be left to check the power of the Republican Party. Stephens closed his remarks by drawing a comparison between secession zealots and the snake that had tempted Eve in the garden of Eden. Secession might reveal the South's "own nakedness" as it lost the protections afforded by the Union.[59]

Stephens implored white southern men to cling to the US Constitution for protection from northern tyranny. He predicted that secession would lead to a devastating war that would threaten the South's principal wealth, slaves. Rather than casting northern politicians as a danger to southern interests, Stephens argued that time and time again the South's supposed enemies had compromised on the issue of slavery. Stephens listed the continuation of the African slave trade following the Constitutional Convention, the three-fifths clause of the Constitution, the Fugitive Slave Act, and the annexation of Texas as evidence of the North's willingness to bend on the issue of slavery and its expansion. He predicted that a new Republican-led government would never endorse universal emancipation. Beyond the impracticality of emancipation, Stephens argued, northern capitalists would be reluctant to free the slaves because of the damage such an act would have on the American economy. If the slaveholding states left the Union, Stephens warned, the South would be at a major disadvantage in a war due to their small white male population and lack of industry and manufacturing. A war would bankrupt the South and cost "tens of thousands of your sons and brothers slain in battle." Stephens accused unscrupulous men of spreading fears of northern oppression to further their own political ambitions. Secession, in his opinion, had less to do with constitutional liberties and the future of slavery than satisfying the foolish ambitions of zealots seeking attention and power. Once the slaveholding states left the Union, Stephens argued, the region would never again enjoy the benefits it had achieved under the protections of the US government. "For you to attempt to overthrow such a government as this . . . in which we have gained our wealth, our standing as a nation, our domestic safety while the elements of peril are around us," Stephens exhorted, "is the height of madness folly, and wickedness, to which I can neither lend my sanction nor my vote."[60]

Northern newspapers celebrated Stephens's speech. He became a national hero, celebrated by the northern press to remind the nation that moderates who supported the Union still existed in the radicalizing South. The *Bradford Reporter* praised Stephens for taking "strong conservative ground" by calming the secession movement.[61] The *Philadelphia Inquirer* reprinted large sections of Stephens's speech and encouraged its readers to review them carefully because they represented Georgia's founding principles—"Wisdom, Moderation, and Justice."[62] The *Detroit Free Press* called Stephens "an influential voice for the Union." "It is most fortunate for the cause of the Union," the newspaper pronounced, "that Mr. Stephens is enlisted under its banner, for no other statesman of the extreme South has so great power as he to hold the tide of disunion."[63] The *Buffalo Daily Republic* lamented that Stephens had not run for president during the recent election. The *London Times* reprinted most of Stephens's speech.[64] In December 1860, President-elect Abraham Lincoln contacted Stephens after reading the Milledgeville speech. "You think slavery is right and ought to be extended," wrote Lincoln, "while we think it is wrong and ought to be restricted. That I suppose is the rub. It certainly is the only substantial difference between us."[65] Stephens replied by urging Lincoln to denounce "fanaticism" within his own party and to condemn John Brown's raid. "A word fitly spoken by you now would be like 'apples of gold in pictures of silver,'" responded Stephens.[66] Stephens basked in the attention. He left Milledgeville convinced that he had used all his oratorical powers to preserve the Union. According to fellow Cooperationist Herschel V. Johnson, without Stephens's opposition Georgia might have left the Union without a public referendum.[67]

Unfortunately, during the six weeks between Stephens's Milledgeville speech and the January 2, 1861, convention election, Stephens and other Cooperationist leaders failed to maintain any momentum that his remarks might have generated. During this critical period, Stephens delivered only one speech. He did not canvas the state raising the alarm against his immediate secession enemies. Perhaps, despite his initial optimism, Stephens had accepted defeat.

In December, the governor of Mississippi sent Judge William Harris to Milledgeville to urge the Georgia legislature to join Mississippi and South Carolina and immediately secede without additional debate or public referendums. Harris's speech failed to change Stephens's views on immediate secession, but in the months that followed, he adopted many of the judge's principal ideas. Harris accused Republicans of plotting to destroy white supremacy in the South. "Our fathers made this a government for the white man, rejecting the negro, as an ignorant, inferior, barbarian race, incapable of self-government, and not, therefore, entitled to be associated with the white man upon terms of civil, political, or social equality." If Republicans succeeded, Harris warned, they would force upon the South "their new theory of the universal equality of the black and white races." Harris told the legislature that white southern men must be prepared to fight to avoid "submission to negro equality." As his hyperbolic address drew to a close, Harris proclaimed the he would rather see all white southerners sacrificed "in one common funeral pile [pyre]" than submit to negro equality and Black Republican rule. The secession crisis had led many white southern men to explicitly declare white supremacy's central place in the Cotton Kingdom.[68]

When South Carolina seceded from the Union on December 20, 1860, even the most steadfast Cooperationists believed that the die had been cast. On January 2, 1861, Immediatists in Georgia won a slim 2,510 vote majority—or 51.5 percent of the votes. Despite their poor organization and unenthusiastic campaign, Cooperationists nearly halted the rising tide of secession. Seventeen days later, the Georgia Secession Convention voted to leave the Union by a 208 to 89 vote margin. Stephens opposed secession during that final vote. Despite his opposition, convention members chose Stephens to help draft the secession ordinance and selected him as one of ten delegates to represent Georgia at the Southern Convention in Montgomery, Alabama.[69]

Georgia tasked Stephens's longtime friend Senator Robert Toombs with writing a justification for secession. Toombs made it clear that slavery had been the central cause of secession. "For twenty years past, Abolitionists and their allies in the Northern states, have been engaged in constant efforts to subvert our institutions, and to excite insurrection and servile war among us." Toombs blamed Republicans whose "avowed purpose is to subject our society, and subject us, not only to the loss of property but the destruction of ourselves, our wives and our children, and the desolation of our homes, our altars, and our firesides." Despite Stephens's opposition to immediate secession, he endorsed Georgia's declaration of causes and often repeated its message.[70]

Anxieties over the future of slavery in America occupied the minds of many state secession convention delegates. South Carolina's secession convention declared that the Republican Party had launched a war "against slavery until it shall cease throughout the United States." Mississippi claimed that the abolitionist-dominated Republican Party "advocates negro equality, socially and politically, and promotes insurrection and incendiarism in our midst."[71] In Alabama, delegates accused Republicans of being "avowedly hostile to the domestic institutions and to the peace and security of the people of the State of Alabama." Likewise, Texas delegates suspected that president-elect Abraham Lincoln would enact the Republican Party agenda to procure "the abolition of negro slavery" and "the recognition of political equality between the white and negro races." Lincoln, according to the Texas delegation, had proclaimed "the debasing doctrine of the equality of all men, irrespective of race and color—a doctrine at war with nature, in opposition to the experience of mankind, and in violation of the plainest revelations of Divine Law." Those who attended the various state secession conventions clearly viewed slavery as the central issue that had necessitated their radical actions.[72]

Stephens had hoped Georgia would delay secession until most slaveholding states decided to leave together as a sign of strength and unity. That did not happen. Instead, Georgia sent commissioners to Alabama, Louisiana, Texas, Arkansas, North Carolina, and Virginia to urge those states to secede as soon as possible. As historian Charles Dew has documented, the pro-secession argument delivered by those commissioners reveals much about the Civil War's causes. When the Virginia secession convention opened on February 13, 1861, Georgia commissioner Henry L. Benning was present. Five days later, Benning, a former Georgia Supreme Court justice, and Fulton Anderson, a commissioner sent from Mississippi, addressed the convention. Anderson opened the day's proceedings with a scathing critique of the Republican Party, which intended to "abolish the internal slave trade" and give "public land to immigrant settlers, so as, within a brief time, to bring into the Union free States enough to enable it to abolish slavery within the States themselves."[73]

Benning followed Anderson's speech with an impassioned plea for Virginia to secede in order to preserve the rights of southern enslavers. Why did Georgia secede? Asked Benning. "It was a conviction, a deep conviction on the part of Georgia, that a separation from the North was the only thing that could prevent the abolition of slavery." Benning laid out a series of standard southern fears of Republican Party rule, which included the predominance of abolitionists in their organization and the party's implicit support for radicals such as John Brown. The former Georgia jurist laid out a frightening scenario in which slavery would be first abolished everywhere except for the Deep South. Isolated and politically impotent to halt the abolitionist agenda, even the Deep South would be forced to abolish slavery. "By the time the North shall have attained the power, the black race will be in a large majority, and then we will have black governors, black legislatures, black juries, black everything." When the audience laughed at Benning's prognostication, the jurist implored the "white race" to take a stand before it was too late. If abolitionists succeeded in abolishing slavery, Benning decried, "we will be completely exterminated and the land will be left in the possession of the blacks, and then it will go back to a wilderness and become another Africa or St. Domingo."[74] Commissioner speeches delivered before secession conventions received little press or commentary from observers. Nonetheless, Stephens had likely heard Benning and others express those same dire predictions throughout the Georgia secession convention. Previously, Stephens had used some of this rhetoric in his public addresses. As he moved beyond secession, Stephens and his rhetoric began to resemble Benning's dire prediction of a devastating race war.

As a divided Georgia left the Union, Stephens had several options. He could retire peacefully to his Crawfordville home and abstain from whatever calamity followed. He could continue to oppose secession by building a coalition of Unionists. Or he could accept secession as the will of the Georgia people and do his part in helping the state move forward. Ultimately, Stephens chose loyalty to his state over maintaining his own political positions. As much as he believed secession to be a major mistake, Stephens could not sit idly by and not help Georgia navigate its self-made crisis. Stephens's unwavering commitment to slavery and white supremacy enabled him to abandon his pre-secession unionism and to embrace post-secession Confederate nationalism. He continued to believe that secession threatened slavery, but he dedicated himself to ensuring that he played some role in trying to curtail that looming disaster. If, as Stephens believed, slavery had played a central role in building a superior southern civilization, then he was willing to surrender his nationalist ideals in defense of the South's cornerstone. Stephens grew convinced that white racial unity was required to defend the South from external forces that threatened to unravel its slave society. By throwing his support behind secession and the new Confederate government, Stephens thought he was doing his part in preserving the southern way of life. To expand support for the Confederacy among white southern men, Stephens began to employ more overt expressions of white-supremacist rhetoric to draw a clear distinction between "us" and "them."[75]

In his later years, Stephens considered the time that he spent in Montgomery, Alabama, as part of the Confederate Provisional Congress tasked with forming a new nation, as his finest hour. Stephens's usual pessimism had been replaced by atypical displays of optimism. Over those few days, Stephens had received the attention and respect that he had always craved. Playing the combined role of senior statesman, parliamentarian, and constitutional scholar, Stephens's fingerprints were all over the new Confederate government; even its name, the Confederate States of America, had been his suggestion. In Montgomery, people who had journeyed to central Alabama to witness the birth of a nation treated Stephens like a celebrity. Stephens's distinctive personal appearance attracted gawkers, who rapped upon his door at all hours to see him for themselves. Others lobbied Stephens for positions in the new government. Among his fellow congressmen, Stephens had enemies, such as Howell Cobb and Tom Cobb, but even his adversaries recognized his superior parliamentary skills. The congress leaned heavily on Stephens and he basked in the spotlight.[76]

Throughout the convention in Montgomery, the Georgia delegation had hoped that one of their own would be selected to lead this new nation. Bitter internal divisions among Georgia's delegates, however, undermined those chances. By the morning of February 9, convention delegates had chosen Mississippi Senator and former US Secretary of War Jefferson Davis to be the Confederacy's first president. Shut out from the nation's highest office, Georgia's delegates quickly put aside their quarrels and rallied behind Alexander H. Stephens for the vice-president post. Delegates had debated whether Stephens should be president. Ultimately, his name was removed from consideration by a faction who believed that the president should be someone who had enthusiastically endorsed secession. Stephens's nomination surprised many who recalled that he had only recently been a leading critic of secession. His central role in shaping the new government in Montgomery, combined with his extensive legislative experience and reputation for brokering compromises among divided factions, helped secure his election. Stephens's election surprised many nationwide. A Pennsylvania newspaper speculated that Stephens's election had been "a forced one; that he did not desire . . . and [accepted] it only for the purpose of exerting his influence for reconstruction and reunion." The paper hypothesized that his election had been necessary because secession proponents lacked the support of most southerners who shared Stephens's more "conservative" views.[77] His rise to the office of vice-president placed a bright spotlight on Stephens—one that he enjoyed. At least for the moment, people around the country wanted to hear what Stephens had to say about the Confederate States of America. He had gained the audience that he had always wanted.[78]

On the evening of February 10, a crowd of supporters in Montgomery urged the new vice-president to address the state of the new government. "Our republic," said Stephens, ". . . must be supported by the virtue, intelligence, integrity and patriotism of the people. These are our corner-stones, upon which the temple of liberty must be constructed." The provisional congress had inspired Stephens to describe the new government as a virtuous republic helmed by intelligent and patriotic leaders with integrity. He was proud of the work the congress had performed in service of the rebellion. As he identified the new government's strengths, Stephens's proclaimed that "King Cotton" "control(s) the commerce of the world." His remarks alluded to slavery as one of many "assailed" institutions that exist "in strict conformity to nature and the laws of the Creator." Creeping closer to the rhetoric he would employ one month later in the Cornerstone Speech, Stephens declared that "it is our mission to vindicate the great truth on which [our institutions] rest, and with them exhibit the highest type of civilization which it is possible for human society to reach." The following day, on February 11, Alexander Stephens took the oath of office to become the first vice-president of the Confederate States of America.[79]

Not everyone appreciated Stephens's newfound support for secession. Following Lincoln's election, northern newspapers had praised his resistance to secession. Now, months later, those same editors called him a traitor who had been seduced by his former pro-secession enemies to "identify him with their nefarious cause." They accused Stephens of being a political opportunist who traded his integrity for the office of vice-president. The former "chivalrous champion of the Union," the newspaper decried, had transformed into a "conspirator" whose "brave words were swallowed before they were cold."[80]

Stephens kept his public remarks restrained ahead of Jefferson Davis's inaugural address. He believed that Davis should set the new nation's agenda and offer the public an explanation for its creation. Jefferson Davis arrived in Montgomery at 10:00 p.m. on February 16 after a grueling five-day journey by train and steamboat. That night Davis offered some coded but unmistakable remarks that defined why secession had been necessary. From his hotel balcony, Davis told a large crowd "Fellow Citizens and Brethren of the Confederate States of America . . . we have henceforth, I trust, a prospect of living together in peace, with our institutions a subject of protection and not defamation." He clearly saw slavery as the Confederacy's central "institution" in need of "protection."[81]

On Monday, February 18, 1861, Davis delivered his inaugural address from a wooden platform constructed on the steps of the Alabama state capitol in Montgomery. Over five thousand people attended the event. The former Mississippi senator gave a reserved speech that avoided any direct mention of slavery. Davis alluded to slavery when he claimed that the Confederate Constitution had "freed" the nation "from the sectional conflicts which have interfered with the pursuit of general welfare." According to Davis, the South had a right to secede because the Declaration of Independence had proclaimed states to be sovereign entities joined by a mutual compact. For reasons that Davis only vaguely defined, the North had violated that compact and had forced the South to secede. Unlike Stephens's later comments, Davis de-emphasized the revolutionary nature of the Confederate government. Davis interpreted what had transpired as a conservative movement built largely out of an existing example of just government. The president avoided laying out specific changes the new government had made to the old constitution as it sought to strengthen slavery by restricting the Confederacy's powers to regulate the "peculiar institution." Davis declared that the Confederacy consisted of an "agricultural people" determined to preserve "peace" and "the freest trade which our necessities will permit." If Davis had hoped to avoid controversy by limiting his remarks, he succeeded. In the days that followed his speech, newspapers across the nation and in Europe paid little attention to his inaugural. While a transcription of the speech appeared in numerous publications, editors provided little additional commentary or reaction to Davis's measured statements.[82]

Nearly a month after Jefferson Davis's inaugural address, Alexander Stephens delivered a rousing speech that made explicit statements that the president's earlier remarks had only implied. On March 12, 1861, a massive crowd gathered in Atlanta to honor Stephens as he passed through the city for the first time since the creation of the Confederate States of America. Atlantans showered Stephens with their affections. A large band performed. Local women delivered gifts to the bachelor statesman. State and local dignitaries and business leaders gave Stephens the type of welcome that a president might expect. Public support for him was at an all-time high. The scene must have been quite satisfying for Stephens who, despite his introverted personality, craved recognition for his intellect and leadership. Rarely did Stephens allow his emotions to overtake his usual cautious rhetoric. He had never been one to cater his speeches to excite the crowd. Yet, Stephens was keenly aware that he had just spent the last few weeks creating a new government. One of the reasons he mentioned the Founding Fathers so often in his addresses during this period was because he saw Thomas Jefferson and James Madison in himself as he helped lead a new southern nation. Stephens knew that he was making history.

As Stephens's West Point and Atlanta Railroad train arrived in Atlanta, the swelling crowds that spilled across several acres along the train terminal elicited emotions within him that impacted his rhetoric. That night, as Stephens spoke, he played to the crowd, eager to receive their adulation. He craved their applause. An experienced orator, Stephens knew how to inspire a crowd. Filled with adrenaline, Stephens took the stage and declared that the "cotton states" had launched an unprecedented bloodless revolution. Although he had loved the US Constitution, "he did not hesitate to declare that the new [Confederate Constitution] was an improvement upon the old." For the first time, Stephens criticized Jefferson, Madison, and Washington for accepting "the fallacy of the equality of races as underlaying the foundations of republican liberty." During the 1787 Constitutional Convention, those leaders, according to Stephens, "all looked forward to the time when the institution of slavery should be removed from our midst as a trouble and a stumbling block." By failing to insert explicit protections of slavery in the constitution, the Founding Fathers had fallen under the "delusion" and "heresy . . . that all men, of all races, were equal, and we had made African inequality and subordination, and the equality of white men, the chief corner-stone of the Southern Republic." Stephens pronounced that the new Confederate States of America was a model government that would soon have "the admiring gaze of the world." During the speech, the crowd erupted in applause several times, halting Stephens impassioned remarks. As he concluded his impromptu address, the crowd shouted "three cheers" for Stephens the "tiger" of the Confederacy. This important address was an important warmup in style, rhetoric, and crowd pleasing to the Cornerstone Speech, which would be delivered in nine days.[83]

A few days later, on Thursday, March 14, another exuberant crowd of supporters welcomed Stephens to Augusta, Georgia. Located about 60 miles from his Crawfordville home, the people of Augusta had been among his most steadfast political supporters during his previous congressional career. As he stepped off the train, the Washington Artillery and Clinch Rifles fired salutes in his honor. Outside the Planters' Hotel, a large crowd gathered anticipating that Stephens would oblige their calls to address them. Appearing on a second-floor balcony, Stephens compared secession to removing a bad tooth that "no longer served the purposes for which it was formed." After a brief discussion of Confederate taxation and fiscal policies, Stephens turned his attention to "the great question which was the prime cause of our separation from the United States—I mean the question of African slavery." He again repeated his claim that the US Constitution "was founded upon the idea that African slavery is wrong, and it looked forward to the ultimate extinction of that institution." In contrast, the Confederate government was founded "upon the principle of the inequality of races." He assured the crowd that other slave states would join the rebellion once they accepted slavery's central role in the movement. Gradually, Stephens predicted, once slavery's reputation improved Mexico, Central America, and the Caribbean Islands would join the Confederacy as well as the northwest territories. Pointing to a Confederate flag fluttering in the nighttime breeze, Stephens prophesized that their new nation's flag "may wave in land a thousand miles away—and where people do not now even dream of it." Stephens remained convinced that the Union would allow the Confederacy to leave without a fight.[84]

Others shared Stephens's opinions about slavery's central place in southern society. The *Southern Literary Messenger* of Richmond, Virginia, defined an abolitionist as anyone "who does not worship [slavery] as the corner-stone of civil liberty . . . [and] does not adore it as the only possible social condition on which a permanent republican government can be erected." Like Stephens, the newspaper depicted slavery as a "divine institution" worthy of being "extended and perpetuated over the whole earth, as a means of human reformation second in dignity, importance and sacredness alone to the Christian religion."[85]

Stephens newfound zeal for secession created some odd bedfellows. During the secession crisis, *Charleston Mercury* editor Leonidas W. Spratt had been one of Stephens's most vocal critics. His opinion of Stephens began to change as the latter's public proclamations of the Confederacy's support for white supremacy grew. Like Stephens, Spratt also believed "the South is now in the formation of a *Slave* republic." Spratt urged Confederate leaders to explicitly recognize the natural inferiority of the black race. The South, according to Spratt, had developed a superior society because its democracy was governed by a small group of well-educated elites. In the North, Spratt claimed, "the reins of government come from the heels, in the [South] from the head of society; in the one it is guided by the worst, in the other by the best, intelligence." Spratt declared that slavery had played a central role in providing social, economic, and political stability in the South because it lacked a large class of free laborers whose demands for equality in the North and across Europe had pushed nation's toward revolution. Spratt's criticism of the excesses of democracies paralleled Stephens's politics. Both men ascribed to forms of democracy that limited mass participation and placed affluent white men at the head of government. Stephens's embrace of white southern male solidarity viewed equality as a natural law that produced white supremacy. Governing a white supremacist society, however, required extreme deference toward elite white men who could both expect and demand to lead. Although all white men were created equal, according to Stephens and Spratt, building a political system that recognized universal white male equality was both impractical and dangerous. Non-elite white men remained important to the South because their existence provided ample numbers to either help enforce slavery or dissuade enslaved laborers from rebelling.[86]

In the weeks prior to the Cornerstone Speech, northern writers responded to the formation of the Confederate States of America by proclaiming that secession had abandoned the cornerstone values of American society. As Jefferson Davis only hinted at slavery's role in secession, abolitionist William Lloyd Garrison pronounced that "the only question of to-day is SLAVERY." Slavery's continued presence in America, according to Garrison, had violated "the very corner-stone of the new Republic" that had been founded to preserve "the inalienable rights of all men." From its inception, the nation had compromised on the issue of slavery despite its contradictory relationship with the teachings of Jesus Christ. Garrison argued that Jesus demanded that men treat one another as they would want to be treated. Now that many slave-holding states had left the Union, Garrison predicted that those who remain would come to their senses and move toward banishing it. "Now is the turning point," Stephens declared. "Slavery will go out, if we refuse to purchase its stay." Garrison believed that secession provided the nation with an opportunity to rebuild its cornerstone that rested upon the ideals of liberty and justice for all.[87]

The *Chicago Tribune* blasted northern members of the Democratic Party for being "trembling doughfaces" who had "already sunk in the filth of slavery." If slavery was the "corner-stone" of secession, the newspaper declared, then the Confederacy had been built to protect "a legalized crime." Secession had brought the American people "nearer to the true issue which must be met and decided. The Confederacy's actions had "brought into the clear light" an issue that many previously had been ignored. With the South's removal from the Union, "all the lovers of their country and lovers of the human race" could unite to end the "monstrous blasphemy" that had defied both "heaven and Earth." The *Chicago Tribune* did not need Stephens to tell them what had caused secession.[88]

By early 1861, Stephens had abandoned all hopes of preserving the Union and had become an enthusiastic advocate for the Confederate States of America. Although Stephens's politics changed throughout the antebellum period, his rhetoric on questions concerning race in America remained consistent. Like many southern enslavers, Stephens was a Christian planter who believed that slavery was both divinely sanctioned and necessary for the protection and advancement of an inferior black race. Stephens spoke of slavery as a glue that bound together the South's white men under a common banner of white supremacy and Christian virtue. He struggled to understand why the federal government would do anything to restrict the expansion of slavery due to its economic benefits, potential to reform a downtrodden race, and role in advancing an exceptional American civilization. Stephens held a common belief shared among most southern white men that slavery and southern civilization were inseparable. By early 1861, the need to defend slavery from "Black Republicans" had inspired Georgia and other southern states to secede from the Union to form a new government founded on the advancement of slavery and white supremacy.

CHAPTER TWO

The "Corner Stone Speech," 1861–1865

O n March 21, 1861, Confederate States of America Vice-President
Alexander H. Stephens delivered what became known as the
"Cornerstone Speech" at the Athenaeum Theater in Savannah,
Georgia. Of the numerous speeches that Stephens made, history would most
remember the Cornerstone Speech. Although the speech was presented without
prepared notes, Stephens gave a thoughtful, impassioned oration intended
to rally the crowd, the nation, and the world around the new Confederate
government. As he promoted the Confederacy, Stephens determined that the
Cotton Kingdom's greatest virtue was its explicit acknowledgment of racial
inequality. While his public admission of slavery's central role in secession drew
the ire of many Confederate officials and northern newspapers (for different
reasons), his words reflected the beliefs of most Confederate leaders. The
Cornerstone Speech was not a one-time confession. The speech represented
the confluence of decades of proslavery and secession rhetoric that had become
accepted truths among southern white men. When Stephens delivered his
Cornerstone Speech, he was not speaking solely of his own opinions but shared
what he knew to be the pulse of Confederate public opinion. In short, the new
nation had been founded to protect a civilization whose cornerstone was slavery
bolstered by new expressions of white supremacy.[1]

Stephens delivered the Cornerstone Speech extemporaneously. He did not
create or leave behind any notes or commentary that he may have prepared in
advance of this speech. The sole transcription of the speech was published in
the *Savannah Republican* on March 23, 1861. On March 25, 1861, the *Southern
Confederacy* of Atlanta became the first newspaper to reprint the *Savannah
Republican* transcription. Within a few weeks, the speech was reprinted in more
than two hundred newspapers worldwide. During the war, the speech appeared
in several published collections. After the war, Stephens claimed that he had

been misquoted and misunderstood, but his later revisions never altered the original transcription's substance. Stephens never contested whether he said that slavery was the cornerstone of the Confederate States of America. He only argued that his message had been misunderstood. The first book to include a transcription of the speech was Garrett Davis, Hon. *Garrett Davis, of Kentucky. African slavery the cornerstone of the Southern confederacy. Speech by Hon. Alex. H. Stephens, of Georgia* (1862). The following year, historian John Abbott's history of the Civil War, published in multiple volumes during the war, was the first work of history to include any analysis of the speech.[2] Throughout this book, my research uses the 1861 *Savannah Republican* transcript as the official version of the Cornerstone Speech.[3]

As the newly elected Vice-President of the Confederate States of America, Stephens was partly intent on telling the new nation more about himself and his leadership abilities, even though he had already been a national political figure, having served in Congress for more than two decades. In the weeks that followed his election, numerous papers published extended physical descriptions. A Vicksburg newspaper reported that Stephens was "without doubt, the most unprepossessing man in appearance in America." Many worried that his poor health might prevent him from fulfilling his duties as vice-president. "He looks like a man in the last stage of sickness," a Confederate paper reported, whose "head is shaped something like a mashed pumpkin." By March 1861, Stephens was an experienced orator who had delivered hundreds of public addresses. Accounts describing the sound of his voice vary. Some reported that "he has at first a shrill sharp voice, but as he warms up with his subject the clear tones and vigorous sentence roll out with a sonorousness that finds its way to every corner of the immense hall."[4] Others compared his voice to a flute—akin to a pre-pubescent male. Few ever complained that Stephens could not be heard. Stephens also loved to prove that despite his relatively small stature and chronically poor health, he possessed the physical stamina to deliver speeches lasting up to three hours with ease. Most left his speeches impressed that a man so slight could speak with such force.[5]

He often began speeches with a display of false humility, declaring his opinions to be either unimportant or in need of further study. Stephens's self-perception, however, was more assured in his intellectual abilities and moral righteousness than this rhetorical feint would imply. He spent a lot of time reading nonfiction, especially history and philosophy. Well versed in classical literature and William Shakespeare, he often incorporated select quotations from a broad range of writers in his speeches and writings. Stephens often incorporated "a dash of keen satire" and humor into his remarks, often at the expense of his adversaries. He especially enjoyed pointing out an opponent's contradictory statements or supposed misreading of the Constitution.[6]

For several days, news had spread that the new vice-president would visit Savannah on Thursday, March 21. Upon his arrival by train, a local committee, which included the mayor, urged Stephens to regale the public with his intimate knowledge of the creation of the Confederate government. As usual, Stephens appeared to reject the invitation, but quickly consented to deliver some remarks that evening after dinner. Expecting a large crowd, the committee chose to host Stephens at the Athenaeum Theater—the largest public building in Savannah. Built in 1818, the Athenaeum, located on Bull Street, adjoining Chippewa Square, previously had been known by several names, including the Savannah Theater. The building hosted events ranging from concerts and plays to political conventions and debates. By 5:00 p.m., an excited audience had filled the theater. Soon the crowd spilled out across Chippewa Square. Locals wanted to see the new vice-president. By the time Stephens arrived, over two thousand people had gathered.

Around 7:30 p.m., after receiving a flattering introduction from Savannah Mayor C. C. Jones, Alexander H. Stephens basked in the "deafening sounds of applause." Stephens took the stage and declared that "we are in the midst of one of the greatest epochs in our history. The last ninety days will mark one of the most memorable eras in the history of modern civilization." Outside, the surging crowd complained that they could not hear Stephens. They asked Stephens to deliver his remarks from the square rather than the theater. People grew restless after Stephens resisted their request. Several members of the Savannah committee interceded, offering to deliver summaries of Stephens's remarks periodically throughout the address. No precise account survives of what those committee members said. The jovial throng remained in the square during the speech as they celebrated the birth of the Confederate States of America.[7]

As Stephens resumed his speech, he described the new Confederate government as a "revolution" that had "been accomplished without the loss of a single drop of blood." In previous speeches, Stephens had drawn comparisons between the Confederacy and the American Revolution. Usually, he did so to make a case that despite the South's smaller population and manufacturing capacity, it could achieve independence against a larger foe just as the American colonists had cast off the British Empire. The revolution had cost thousands of lives. Stephens continued to hold out hope that the US federal government might allow the Confederacy to secede without deploying its military. A few months earlier, as Stephens unsuccessfully tried to persuade Georgians to remain in the Union, he had presented a far more pessimistic view. At that time, he seriously doubted whether secession could be achieved without a costly war. Earlier, Stephens had worried that a war would disrupt slavery and threaten southern society. In Savannah, the customarily gloomy Stephens presented a rosier picture.[8]

Like a good lecturer, Stephens organized his speech around a handful of major arguments supported by specific examples and source references. The primary purpose of the Cornerstone Speech was to demonstrate how the Confederate Constitution had surpassed the achievements of the US Constitution. Stephens had spent the last three decades of his political career labeling himself a staunch defender of the American Constitution. He fancied himself a constitutional scholar who often lectured his fellow congressmen on its proper interpretation. In January, at Milledgeville, he begged his fellow Georgians to use the US Constitution to protect themselves and slavery without having to resort to secession. After Georgia seceded, Stephens joined a provisional congress in Montgomery that drafted a new constitution in four days. He felt a great sense of pride in the new constitution. While he continued to question secession, Georgia's removal from the Union gave him the opportunity to fulfill a lifelong dream—to emulate America's Founding Fathers. He received the unprecedented chance to revise the US Constitution to better suit the needs of his beloved southern civilization. Stephens admitted that he disliked some sections of the new constitution, but he told the crowd that he would avoid those discussions tonight. "I have no hesitancy," Stephens declared, "in giving [the Confederate Constitution] as my judgement that it is decidedly better than the old." The crowd erupted.[9]

As the applause faded, Stephens turned his attention to tariffs, which he claimed had been a national problem since the 1832–33 nullification crisis. Ironically, the man who began his congressional career with an impassioned defense of federal tariff policy, now labeled that same policy as one of the principal causes of secession.[10] He accused the federal government of "fostering one branch of industry [northern manufacturers] to the prejudice of another [southern cotton planters]." The Confederacy prohibited trade duties to ensure the "principles of perfect equality." Several months earlier, Stephens had told the Milledgeville convention that the dispute over tariffs had been resolved to the South's benefit. Georgia's secession, however, had motivated Stephens to alter several of his previous political stances. By the time he arrived at Savannah for his infamous speech, Stephens had embraced Confederate nationalism and wanted to endorse policies that he believed would foster unity among white southern men.[11]

Following another raucous ovation, Stephens broached a long-held source of southern animosity toward the US government—federally financed internal improvements. As a former Whig Party member who had traditionally supported using federal tax revenues to finance public works projects, he accused Congress, which southern representatives dominated throughout the antebellum period, of unfairly spending taxes raised from southern agriculture to build railroads, roads, canals, ports, and other internal improvements in northern states. Prior to 1861, Stephens tended to see federal expenditures from a nationalist perspective, i.e., what was good for one region of the country was good for the entire nation. Most federal internal improvement projects were created to advance westward expansion across the Midwest. Generally, Stephens had endorsed those expenditures. Georgia's secession, however, seemed to have erased Stephens's memories of his nationalist stances. Citing Georgia's Western & Atlantic Railroad (W&A) as an example, Stephens applauded the South's willingness to raise local funds to support internal improvement. The W&A had cost Georgia taxpayers approximately twenty-five million dollars. Unfortunately, as Stephens described, American protective tariffs placed on foreign iron importers forced Georgia to "pay into the common Treasury several millions of dollars for the privilege of importing the iron after the price was paid for it abroad." Stephens questioned the "justice . . . in taking this money, which our people paid into the common Treasury on the importation of our iron, and applying it to the improvement of river and harbors elsewhere." In the Confederate government, if Savannah wanted to improve its railroad and port the local government would have to finance those improvements. Steadily, Stephens built support for this claim that the Confederacy had been founded on "the broad principle of perfect equality and justice" in response to an inequitable and unjust federal government. The crowd appeared to agree with that description as they applauded each time it was mentioned.[12]

He also addressed the improvements he perceived in the new Constitution. The Confederate Constitution also changed the relationship between the executive and legislative branches of government and imposed new term lengths and limits for elected officials. Unlike the US government, the Confederate legislative branch would allow executive cabinet members and advisors to participate in congressional debates. Stephens believed that this new process would enhance communications between department administrators and legislators. Also, Confederate presidents would serve a six-year term rather than a four-year term. No president would be allowed to serve more than a single term in office. Stephens claimed that these changes were necessary to ensure "that under our system we shall never have what is known as a government organ."

Any Confederate president, Stephens proclaimed, would be solely motivated to serve "the good of the people, the advancement, prosperity, happiness, safety, honor, and true glory of the Confederacy."[13]

With the audience worked up to a frenzied state, Stephens turned his attention toward slavery. The Confederacy "has put at rest, forever, all agitating questions relating to our peculiar institution." Those "agitating questions," according to Stephens, had been "the immediate cause of the late rupture and present revolutions." Which questions had the Confederate government resolved? The Founding Fathers believed that the "enslavement of the African was in violation of the laws of nature" because "they rested upon the assumption of the equality of races." Stephens argued that the Founders had built a nation on a "sandy foundation" that had toppled in the storm.[14] What Stephens said next would dog him for the rest of his life and beyond. "Our government is founded upon exactly the opposite idea; its foundations are laid, its corner-stone rests upon the great truth that the negro is not equal to the white man. That slavery—subordination to the superior race—is his natural and moral condition." According to the Savannah newspaper reporter, an emotional Stephens glared from the stage as members of the audience leaped to their feet and let loose a loud roar of approval. The jubilation spread across the moon-lit square. Stephens had pronounced that white supremacy was the Confederacy's cornerstone, and the crowd agreed. He had declared in public ideals found throughout the Confederate Constitution that few Confederate leaders had made explicit in their public remarks. According to Stephens, the Confederate government would be "the first in the history of the world" to recognize white supremacy as a "physical, philosophical, and moral truth."[15]

Stephens described the Confederacy's endorsement of white supremacy as a revolutionary idea. Until recently, Stephens claimed, even white southerners had not fully accepted the relationship between white supremacy and slavery. Stephens labeled anyone who disagreed with white supremacy as either insane or a fanatic. Citizens of the North, Stephens said, "assume that the negro is equal and hence conclude that he is entitled to equal privileges and rights with the white man." Although England, France, and many American states had abolished slavery, Stephens could not "permit" himself "to doubt the ultimate success of a full recognition of this principle throughout the civilized and enlightened world" because the Confederacy was "the first government ever instituted upon principles in strict conformity to nature, and the ordination of Providence." Slavery had often fallen in world history because those societies had violated the laws of nature by enslaving classes of the same race. Africans, however, "by nature" and "by the curse against Canaan" were destined to be the white man's slave. God had made one race different from another. The

Confederacy was "founded upon principles in strict conformity with those laws." By rejecting the idea that all men were created equal, the Confederacy had accepted the "truth" of black inferiority as fundamental to recognizing nature's role in human affairs and God's divine sanction of black slavery.[16]

Despite Stephens's glowing depictions of slavery as a civilizing Christian force for good, he refrained from calling for the reopening of the African slave trade in the Cornerstone Speech. Stephens had supported reopening the slave trade in the late 1850s as part of his plan to create large surpluses in enslaved laborers to encourage more enslavers to settle in western territories. In Montgomery, the issue of reopening the trade had been a hotly debated question among members of the Confederate provisional government. For reasons that remain unclear, Stephens did not endorse reopening the slave trade as part of the new Confederate Constitution. Article 9.1 of that document prohibits the "importation of negroes of the African race from any foreign country" and required Congress to pass laws banning the foreign slave trade.[17] The Confederate government's foreign slave trade prohibition attracted criticism from many pro-secession zealots because to build a new nation on slavery and then use the powers of that new nation to prohibit the purchase of additional African slaves seemed contradictory. Charleston Mercury editor and fire-eater Leonidas W. Spratt chastised the Confederate government for recognizing "the toleration of slavery as an existing evil by admitting assumptions to its prejudices and restrictions to its power and progress." By not universally endorsing the righteousness of slavery, Spratt declared, the Confederate government "re-inaugurate[d] the blunder of 1789."[18] Banning the African slave trade was one of many sections of the US Constitution that reappeared in its Confederate imitation.[19]

In the Cornerstone Speech, Stephens speculated on how the world would respond to the Confederacy's endorsement of what it considered one of nature's laws. He openly acknowledged that most nations had rejected the natural law that the Confederacy endorsed. Most abolitionists, Stephens predicted, would embrace slavery once they accepted the black race's natural inferiority.[20] He again defended slavery as a positive good that had benefited Africans. Stephens alleged that prior to slavery, Africans lacked the ability to clothe and feed themselves because of their poor work ethic. Africans, Stephens claimed, had to be taught how to work. After nearly four hundred years of African slavery, Stephens argued that enslaved laborers still needed to be taught lessons that Adam learned in the Garden of Eden: "in the sweat of thy brow shalt thou eat bread."[21] Again, the crowd applauded Stephens's account of black inferiority.

Stephens asked what the Confederacy's future might be like if no other states or nations joined the Confederate States of America. Could the Confederacy achieve independence and defend itself from a numerically superior foe? Stephens's response to those questions confounded both his Confederate contemporaries and outside observers. As Stephens spoke, the Confederate government had dispatched diplomats to other slave states to convince them to join its cause. Prior to secession, Stephens had warned fire-eaters that their dreams of independence were unattainable because the slave states lacked the human and capital resources necessary to defend its territory. In Savannah, Stephens presented a far rosier picture of the Confederacy's future. Although he was confident that many Border States would soon join the new government, Stephens told the audience that Confederate independence did not depend upon adding new states to their rebellion. The confident crowd cheered wildly after being assured that the current Confederate States of America had the resources needed to procure independence.[22]

Stephens gave the crowd a series of glowing and optimistic descriptions of current affairs. Uncharacteristically, Stephens praised his fellow members of the Confederate provisional government as an "abler, wiser, a more conservative, deliberate, determined, resolute and patriotic body of man I never met in my life." The Confederate Constitution, pronounced Stephens, "will be a lasting monument of their worthy, merit and statesmanship."[23]

As Stephens extended his remarks, he again returned to the subject of slavery. He questioned why the North, which opposed the expansion of slavery, would "be equally determined not to part with an inch 'of the accursed soil.'" "Notwithstanding their clamor against the institution," Stephens continued, "they seem to be equally opposed to getting more, or letting go what they have got." He lambasted the North for being "disinclined" to surrender the economic rewards they gained from slavery's profits. If there were to be a war, slavery, Stephens proclaimed, would be at its center. "The spoils is what they are after," Stephens mocked, "though they come from the labor of the slave." Stephens believed that the same cornerstone that was foundational to the Confederate States of America would force the Union into a war to restore what it had lost.[24]

At this point in the speech, the *Savannah Republican* reporter stopped transcribing and began to summarize Stephens's thoughts on the Confederate Constitution. Stephens discussed the treasury, legislative branch, and tariffs—none of which excited the crowd. After nearly two hours, Stephens ended his address by declaring the Confederacy to be "the highest type of civilization ever exhibited by man." According to the reporter, "Mr. Stephens took his seat amid a burst of enthusiasm and applause such as the Atheneum has never displayed within its walls."[25]

The next morning, the *Savannah Republican* published an account of the address that applauded Little Aleck's performance but offered no analysis. The newspaper referred to the event as "Mr. Stephens's Speech." No mention was made of Stephens's cornerstone remarks. Although the paper described the large crowds that had attended the speech, the event was not front-page news and was confined to a brief description found on the second page. That day's leading stories related to the recent passage of the new Georgia State Constitution, reports of the failed secession vote in Arkansas, and news of the federal Navy resupplying Fort Pickens in Pensacola, Florida.[26] The first speech transcript appeared in the March 23, 1861, edition of the *Savannah Republican*. Savannah's other newspaper, the *Daily Morning News* failed to mention the speech in its March 23 edition.[27]

As the Cornerstone Speech began to appear in newspapers across the country, editors examined what Stephens had said on March 12, nine days before the Cornerstone Speech, in Atlanta. The *Chicago Tribune* labeled Stephens a traitor, guilty of slandering the Founding Fathers. The newspaper condemned Stephens for calling Washington, Jefferson, and Madison "fancy politicians" who had been infected by the "delusion" of "the fallacy of the equality of races as underlying the foundations of republican liberty."[28] According to the editor, the Confederacy intended to destroy the Union to build a "negro oligarchy extending all the way to Central America."[29]

Most southern newspapers, such as the *Southern Confederacy*, applauded Stephens's Atlanta speech. Under the heading "A White Man's Government," the newspaper quoted the vice-president's words: "In that instrument we solemnly discarded the pestilent heresy of fancy politicians, that all men, of all races, were equal, and we have made African inequality and subordination, and the equality of white men, the chief corner stone of the Southern Republic."[30] The editor applauded Stephens's efforts to define the Confederacy as the defender of white supremacy. The editor predicted that northern white men would respond to the example set by the Confederate government and seek to remove from power the "Abolition lecturers" and "negro equalityites" responsible for "corrupting" the federal government. Other newspapers referred to the speech as "the emanation of a great mind, of a pure man, and a patriot of enlarged experience and comprehensive statesmanship." Stephens appeared to be the ideal politician to lead the revolution.[31]

Likewise, the *Southern Banner* urged every paper in Georgia to print the Atlanta speech. The Athens, Georgia, newspaper, however, worried that some editors might ignore the speech because it "characterizes faction and fault-finding in just terms, and rebukes those who are seeking to poison the minds of the people against the Government." Promising to print the entire speech later, the March 27 issue of *Southern Banner* offered only a few lines of commentary. Rather than focus on the Stephens's white-supremacist declarations, the paper instead applauded his predictions that the Confederacy would supplant the federal government as the supreme continental power. The paper avoided any discussion of slavery.[32]

Some observers commended Stephens's white-supremacist declarations and sought after the vice-president to issue additional comments in support of his pronouncements. Dr. Harvey Leonidas Byrd, a professor at the Oglethorpe Medical College, had been among the large crowd that had gathered in Chippewa Square to hear the Cornerstone Speech. Unable to speak to Stephens in person, Byrd penned a letter to him two days later. Byrd shared Stephens's opinions on "the subject of the 'origins of the races of men.'" Beyond its "deep and absorbing" scientific interest, wrote Byrd, the matter was "connected and associated with the white and black races of our new and glorious Confederacy." Byrd urged Stephens to collaborate to produce an article for the Oglethorpe Medical and Surgical Journal—a publication whose entries were reprinted in medical journals across the nation and internationally. The professor believed that Stephens's endorsement would add support to the scientific arguments for African inferiority. Byrd seemed ecstatic that the secession crisis had fused science and politics in defense of white supremacy.[33]

Stephens received several letters of support from people who attended the Cornerstone Speech. Cornelia V. Grant of Savannah told Stephens that his remarks made her "proud for Georgia my own native state and for our Southern land." She urged Stephens to seek God's guidance in the days to come to ensure that the Confederacy remained in His hands. Like most people who wrote Stephens, Grant followed her praise for him with an appeal for assistance from the newly minted vice-president. Imploring Stephens to honor her request in "the memory of his [deceased] mother," Grant sought Little Aleck's help in securing a position in the Confederate government for her son. Most of the letters that Stephens received in the weeks that followed the Cornerstone Speech were requests for government and military appointments.[34]

Although the Cornerstone Speech's white-supremacist passages drew the most attention, some Confederates contacted Stephens to protest the new government's import tariffs. In the Cornerstone Speech Stephens had told the crowd that the Confederacy would continue to collect an import tariff to fund the government. The Confederate tariff disappointed many Confederate supporters, who thought secession would end those taxes. A group of merchants from Macon, Georgia, told Stephens that they were "sorely troubled about paying duties on goods" when it was believed that the new government would support free trade. Merchants warned Stephens that the duties raised to support the Confederacy would threaten merchant businesses and lead to consumer price inflation. They urged him to return to Montgomery and advocate for the removal of all import tariffs during the upcoming legislative session.[35]

The Cornerstone Speech represented the eroding middle ground between secessionists and Unionists that Stephens had once occupied. The inclusion of moderate men, such as Stephens, in the Confederate government ameliorated some of the ill feelings lingering from the secession crisis. Moderates could look to Stephens as an example to follow in their transition from Americans to Confederates. "More than to any other of our public men," claimed the *Augusta Chronicle and Sentinel*, "they look to [Stephens] for counsel and guidance." Many felt assured that Stephens would "raise the banner of the people's rights" in the new government. The Cornerstone Speech had inspired Stephens's followers to think beyond the immediate political issues that had led to secession. Stephens's speech proclaimed that Confederate independence was essential to the preservation of a southern civilization founded upon racial inequality. If Stephens appeared willing to fight to defend the South, then large numbers of white men would likely follow his lead. By exposing the "true cause of secession" Stephens had drawn more southern white men to the Confederacy's cause.[36]

Many newspapers chose to reprint the Cornerstone Speech in its entirety. Others, however, elected to provide readers small sections of the speech. Some newspapers refrained from either publishing or commenting on Stephens's remarks on slavery. The *Alabama Beacon* and *The Independent*, for example, never mentioned his commentary on black inferiority, but chose to print the vice-president's descriptions of the South's human and natural resources and its desire to see other slave states join their nation. Beyond a few paragraphs that contained some of the speech's most benign assertions, those newspapers never referenced the speech again.[37]

When Stephens delivered the Cornerstone Speech, eight slave states— Maryland, Delaware, Kentucky, Missouri, Tennessee, North Carolina, Arkansas, and Virginia—remained in the Union. The Confederate government had dispatched diplomats to each state to urge its immediate secession. The Cornerstone Speech appeared in Upper South newspapers as those states debated secession. Stephens's remarks appeared to have little effect on those debates, but his words resonated across a broad section of white southern men who feared the "Black Republican" government that controlled Washington, DC.

By late March 1861, North Carolina voters had narrowly rejected secession during a statewide referendum. The *Wilmington Daily Herald*, a newspaper that had opposed secession, was among the first North Carolina publications to comment on the Cornerstone Speech. The paper's editor, Alfred Moore Waddell, shared much in common with Alexander H. Stephens. Prior to the secession crisis both men had belonged to the Whig and Constitutional Union parties. Neither man had initially supported secession. However, Stephens and Waddell were devoted white supremacists who used their intellectual talents and public platforms to slander the black race. Stephens's acceptance of Georgia's secession and embrace of his leading role in the Confederate government had given Waddell a prelude for what his life might become if North Carolina seceded. Summarizing Stephens's remarks, the paper reiterated Stephens's assertions that the inferior black race had benefited enormously under the "great lessons" taught through their contact with white men. The old government had been "built on a false foundation." The Confederacy "had for its foundation a great truth, and like truth would stand the test of time." Waddell agreed with Stephens's assessment that slavery united southern society and "that the institution was never so strong as now." Like Stephens, the editor compared the Confederacy to the thirteen colonies on the eve of the American Revolution. Whereas the colonies faced enormous disadvantages compared to the mighty British, Waddell assessed that the South had enough of an advantage in wealth, trade, and labor to secure its independence from the North. If North Carolina remained in the Union, wrote Waddell, it would miss its chance to join a "perfect system of government" filled with "brave, virtuous, and intelligent people." Waddell placed the story on the front page next to a series of reports that condemned "Black Republican" activities in Washington, DC, and questioned North Carolina politicians who opposed secession. Waddell hoped that the Cornerstone Speech would lead "wise" moderates such as himself to embrace the Confederacy if North Carolina seceded. Perhaps the only thing Waddell feared more than Black Republicans and secession was a North Carolina government dominated by rabid secessionists.[38]

Elsewhere, North Carolinians responded to the strong reactions that the Cornerstone Speech had elicited among some northern audiences. According to the *New Bern Daily Progress*, Stephens's speech had forced Republicans to reveal their intention "to fight for the freedom of the negro." According to the newspaper, Republicans had ignorantly clung to the Founding Fathers' pronouncement that all men were created equal. "This is the policy openly avowed or covertly concealed under devotion to the Union, by these Abolition traitors and villains now in possession of the government at Washington," wrote the *New Bern Daily Progress*. "Great God!" the paper continued, "what is our country coming to, when the sacred name of freedom is polluted by such heaven-defying traitors to their country and their race!"[39]

In Tennessee, the Cornerstone Speech left some secession opponents questioning if compromise could ever restore the broken Union. Politician Henry S. Foote penned an open letter to Kentucky Senator John J. Crittenden urging him to encourage the Bluegrass States to recognize the Confederate States of America. Foote, Crittenden, and Stephens had been among the most vocal opponents of secession before the Confederacy was formed. In the US Senate, Crittenden had proposed a series of Constitutional amendments that would have strengthened national protections for slavery and, he believed, restored the Union. The measures failed due to Republican opposition. Crittenden remained convinced that a bargain could be struck even as the Deep South seceded. After reading Stephens's "able and manly" speech, Foote, a former Whig who had opposed secession, decided that the Confederacy might offer slaveholding states a better government that "retain[ed] . . . all the better features of the one under which we have so long lived, and avoiding those defects which the experience of seventy years has disclosed." The liberties that Stephens described as fundamental to the Confederacy made it impossible for those states to "ever again voluntarily place themselves amidst the innumerable dangers and perplexities from which they are now so happily relieved." Foote echoed Stephens's proclamation that "a more contented, united, and happy people have never been delineated upon the page of history" than the Confederate States of America. Stephens's assertions that slavery and white supremacy represented the cornerstone of the Confederate government attracted Foote's attention. He warned that slave states who remained in the Union would be at the mercy of "Black Republicans." "They are only postponing the day of their destruction," Foote predicted, "until their long-cherished scheme of injustice can be executed." Faced with the prospect that those states that seceded would never willingly rejoin the Union, Foote urged Tennessee and Kentucky to recognize the Confederacy formally before it was too late. Only recognition could prevent the "most sanguinary and destructive conflict that the world has yet known."[40]

The *Civilian and Telegraph* of Cumberland, Maryland, accused Stephens of misrepresenting the Founding Fathers' views on equality. Whereas Stephens had declared that Thomas Jefferson and others had incorrectly proclaimed that "all men were created equal," William Christian, editor of the *Civilian and Telegraph*, asserted that "what they did affirm was the equality of human right, despite all diversities of color, capacity, statue, culture, and ability." Christian stated that America had been founded upon the ideal that "equal rights as human beings are not affected by [our] differences." Stephens's government, Christian proclaimed, was "founded on directly antagonistic principles to those of Jefferson and the Fathers." Unfortunately, secession supporters had failed to realize the contradictory statements on liberty that their new constitution provided. Some predicted that the Confederacy would fail when its citizens realized their new government's undemocratic foundation.[41]

Northern conservative newspapers sympathized with Stephens. An editorial that appeared in the Democratic Party–aligned *New York Express* warned readers that Stephens's descriptions of the South's human and natural resources should be taken seriously. They cautioned that any war to restore the Union would be catastrophic.[42]

Some northern newspapers used the Cornerstone Speech to examine the relationship between the US Constitution and slavery. The *Lowell Patriot* argued that Stephens and abolitionist William Lloyd Garrison shared a common interpretation of the US Constitution. Both sides had asserted that the Constitution was a pro-slavery document. Neither Stephens nor Garrison, according to the newspaper, could prove that the Constitution protected slavery. The paper documented that the word slavery and its protections, such as fugitive slave laws, were absent from the Constitution. Therefore, the question of slavery was not a federal issue but rather one "to be regulated and controlled by the States." The *Lowell Patriot* condemned both secessionists and abolitionists for advocating "erroneous" and "inconsistent . . . teachings of our early fathers."[43]

The Cornerstone Speech sparked a debate over white supremacy's intellectual underpinnings. If the white race was superior, as Stephens supposed, how could a man of such inferior physical qualities as Stephens represent the master race? Furthermore, if obvious distinctions of physical, intellectual, and moral qualities exist among white men what, if anything, would prevent enslavers, who have judged themselves to be the best examples of a master race, from using the "lash" to abuse free laborers? The newspaper cited numerous examples in world history when white men had enslaved other white men. If the Confederacy gained independence, enslavers would extend their control over other white men. Stephens had claimed that slavery and white supremacy were divinely sanctioned institutions. The *Chicago Tribune* declared that Stephens's theological assertions were false and urged southern churches to excommunicate him. Although slavery existed in the Bible, the newspaper argued that little evidence existed that it was either divinely sanctioned or determined by race. Science also contradicted Stephens's argument. The *Chicago Tribune* referenced results from the latest German scientific research that disproved perceived inequalities among the races. Citing the recent scholarship of anthropologist Theodor Waitz, the newspaper concluded "that nothing in fact yet ascertained proves any want of vitality, or power of propagation in mulattoes, or in crossed of any human race." Waitz's research directly contradicted Josiah C. Nott and George Giddon's *Indigenous Races of the Earth* (1857)—a book that most southern intellectuals, like Stephens, used as scientific evidence of black inferiority.[44]

Stephens received several letters from northern supporters who shared his views on race and states' rights. Henry Phillips of Deerfield, Massachusetts, requested a handwritten copy of the speech and the vice-president's autograph. Phillips believed that the speech ranked among the greatest in American history.[45] Bayaro Thomas of Independence, Iowa, hoped that Stephens would "live to see the Southern Confederacy expand, bud & blossom to a mighty Republic, and may it be a terror to Northern abolitionists & Black Republicans." Thomas, a native southerner who had moved to Iowa as a child, agreed with Stephens that some free states as well as nations around the globe would join the Confederacy to escape the tyrannical Lincoln administration. The Iowan mourned that the North lacked a "Statesman of the highest order," like Jefferson Davis. He accused Republicans of colluding with John Brown and urged southerners to surrender their lives to protect the new more perfect government. Thomas reminded Stephens that many white northern men shared his views on black inferiority and opposed abolitionism.[46]

Likewise, William C. Wallace, a native southerner living in Newark, New Jersey, wrote a letter of support to Stephens after reading the Cornerstone Speech. After expressing regret that the South had failed to abide by Stephens's efforts to prevent secession, Wallace advised Confederate leaders to "as far as possible on every point, place herself in the sight before the world." The North, Wallace decried, had "no right to interfere about slavery, and that in the general the treatment was right in the sight of God." Wallace accused abolitionists of espousing a "fanatic sentiment" that far surpassed the "dreadful sins" that might be associated with slavery. The South had always compromised on the issue of slavery, Wallace wrote, until abolitionist agitation made further negotiation pointless. Wallace expressed his agreement with the Cornerstone Speech: "I believe slavery to be the greatest blessing to the Negro, but our consciences are not clear if we do not adopt the blessings of the Gospel to their conditions."[47]

Most northern newspapers condemned the Cornerstone Speech. The *Guardian* of Buchanan County, Iowa, accused Stephens of flip-flopping on Stephen Douglas's popular sovereignty platform. During the speech, Stephens had thrown "off the Douglas mask, and comes out flat-footed in favor of the Divine origins of slavery." The editor accused Stephens and the Confederacy of reversing the will of the American people as expressed in the presidential election returns. When the final vote favored the Republican Party, the Confederacy decided that slavery could not be protected within a democratic nation. The paper mourned that many northern Democrats shared Stephens's divine justifications for slavery. "If they had the honesty of Mr. Stephens," the newspaper declared, "they would openly avow it." The paper warned that the looming war would be unable to ignore the question of slavery because the Confederacy had made it central to their rebellion. White supremacy, divinely appropriated, "must hereafter be the corner-stone of the Democratic temple," wrote the newspaper editor, "and all who will not bow down and worship it, will be stigmatised [sic.] as enemies of 'Southern rights!' Stephens had made clear that the issue of states' rights could not be removed from the debate over slavery's future in America.[48]

The *New York Evening Post* referred to the Cornerstone Speech as the Confederate "manifesto." Its editor declared that Stephens had admitted that "slavery [was] the basis of the new Confederacy."[49] Likewise, the *Massachusetts Spy* pronounced that the Cornerstone Speech was "one of the most significant and decisive pronouncements in favor of slaveholding as a fundamental principle of good government which has been yet put forth." The editor expressed shock that Stephens had defended the right to own slaves as sanctioned by God and nature. The paper labeled the Confederate government as regressive compared to democratic political movements that had spread across Europe. While Italy, Russia, and Austria moved toward "liberal and progressive policy," the Confederacy has "set up a government upon the basis of the worst form of absolutism and tyranny which the world knows." Regardless of Stephens's assertions that the Confederacy would succeed, many northern newspapers believed that "nature, history, and all right principles are against them."[50]

Stephens received letters from northern abolitionists who questioned slavery's divine sanction. Edward Bunker, an abolitionist from Brooklyn, New York, agreed with some of the assertions found in the Cornerstone Speech, but he remained unconvinced that the Confederate government, or any government, had the authority to continue slavery indefinitely. "I am an abolitionist," Bunker proclaimed, "that is to say, I am opposed to African slavery, and prepared to use all honorable means for its extinction." Bunker rejected Stephens's declaration that God had cursed Africans and questioned how a new nation so dedicated to individual liberty could be founded on such a contradictory institution as slavery. If the black race was inferior, wrote Bunker, how could Stephens explain a great mind such as Frederick Douglass? Bunker broached the taboo subject of interracial sexual relations between white masters and black slaves. If enslaved women were naturally inferior, why were there so many mulattos and quadroons throughout the South. "Will the race springing from your lust," questioned Bunker, "remain the social inferiors of southern white men?"[51]

Other abolitionists accused Stephens of betraying his conscience and country. Edward Williams of Boston criticized Stephens of hypocrisy after joining the Confederate government following months of trying to prevent secession. "I warn you of the fate of traitor," wrote Williams. "Beware of implicating yourself against your better judgment, in the plots of those conspirators who have already dragged down the Cotton States from their proud position as members of a great and powerful republic, to that of a petty, feeble, confederacy.

. . . Redeem yourself!" Williams claimed the Cornerstone Speech revealed the flawed beliefs of a "people who with open eyes seek to found the edifice of their republic on a principle so hostile to the teachings of the Sermon on the Mount." Williams denounced Stephens for slandering the name of God by attaching it to a traitorous rebellion led by "cowards" and "blind men."[52]

Republicans accused Stephens of applying a false logic in his defense of slavery. If slavery was the natural condition of the African race, questioned the *Manhattan Express*, "surely there is no need to legalize that which is plainly established by natural laws. Human legislation cannot add to the legitimacy and strength of the immutable laws of God. . . . The fact is, Mr. Stephens, you know that this is all bosh." The newspaper accused Confederates of launching a rebellion to enact positive laws protecting slavery that violated natural laws that had placed the world on a path toward complete emancipation. No government, wrote editor James Humphrey, based on unnatural laws that enforced white supremacy could claim to be a model nation. The Confederate founders had formed a new government "[in]consistent with truth and the common sense of mankind."[53]

The Cornerstone Speech confirmed northern fears of a southern slave power conspiracy. The *New York Daily Tribune* appreciated that Stephens spoke the truth and threw "away all disguise and sets up the flag of the Slave Power in the full face of day." Stephens's opinions evidenced how the interests of southern enslavers had become so ingrained within the secession movement.[54]

The *Tribune* questioned Stephens's reputation as an intellectual statesman. "The warping effect of a belief in the justice of Negro Slavery, even upon a mind like that of Mr. Stephens, is plainly shown by this speech." Stephens had placed "the principle of the inequality of the African" on par with fundamental truths "enunciated by Galileo, Harvey, and Adam Smith." However, unlike those great minds who sought to enlighten humanity, Stephens "hurls everything backward into deepest darkness, reversing the wheels of progress with a violence which threatens eternal destruction to all its machinery."[55]

The Cornerstone Speech also offended many northern Christians. Stephens declared that black slaves required the example of white men to understand how to benefit from the fruits of their labor. Without white supervision, Africans would never develop productive civilizations. Northern Christians contested Stephens's efforts to use religion to excuse slavery. "The Negro," wrote the *Tribune*, "must earn the bread he is not allowed to eat, and the owner of the Negro, living not by his own labor, but the labor of others, shall eat the bread he does not earn!" Slavery had warped the minds of southern Christians into believing that the spoils taken from human bondage had benefited a downtrodden race. The *Tribune* and other newspapers mourned that the South's defense of slavery had blinded them to the horrors they had committed in the name of God.[56]

Stephens's condemnation of the Founding Fathers offended many Americans. The *Portsmouth Journal of Literature and Politics* thanked Stephens for reminding Americans that Jefferson and Madison viewed "the enslavement of the African [as a] violation of the laws of nature." Editors accused Stephens of misrepresenting American history to further a cause that until recently he had denounced. Many believed that Stephens's "devotion to the 'domestic institution'" had trumped his national loyalties. Unlike the Founding Fathers whom he criticized, Stephens had refused to serve in the vanguard of this revolution. Papers labeled him a Confederate "straggler" who wanted to avoid the stain of disunion, yet eagerly joined the rear guard of political opportunism.[57]

Some northern newspapers labeled Stephens a hypocrite. Stephens complained that federal tax revenues raised through protective tariffs and other measures had been unfairly allocated to northern states to fund internal improvements that accelerated westward expansion. The *Massachusetts Spy* reminded Stephens of the "over six hundred and seventeen millions of dollars" that the American government had spent to procure the lands the new Confederate government occupied. "This government," Allen Campbell, the newspaper's editor, declared, "for which the seceders have no words to express their contempt, bought their homes, for them, without a groan." Louisiana, Florida, Texas, and American Indian removal had cost taxpayers who lived outside of the South millions of dollars. Plus, the newspaper blamed the South for inciting the Mexican War as part of its larger effort to expand American slavery into Central and South America and the Caribbean Islands. According to editor Campbell, the Confederacy was just the latest plot hatched by the South to steal land from the federal government.[58]

Beyond commenting on slavery's importance to the Confederacy, the Cornerstone Speech assessed the new government's economic and military prospects. Stephens believed that the Cotton Kingdom had enough human and natural resources to fight for its independence. To bolster this position, Stephens pointed out that the Confederate States of America possessed more territory than France, Great Britain, and Spain—major global powers. The *Tribune* accused Stephens of misrepresenting some facts and omitting others. Stephens estimated that since the Confederacy had as many people as the thirteen colonies had in 1772 that the former possessed an equal chance of attaining independence than the latter. Stephens conveniently omitted, according to the *Tribune*, the fact that since 1776 the North's population had grown at a far greater pace than the "backward" South.[59]

The *Springfield Republican* commented that "one can hardly read [the Cornerstone Speech] without suspecting that Mr. Stephens is secretly ridiculing himself and his present associates, and artfully exposing the weakness and folly of the southern position while pretending to maintain it."⁶⁰ Northern newspapers often reminded readers that prior to Georgia's removal from the Union, Stephens had opposed secession. These newspaper writers hoped that Stephens had only agreed to join the Confederate government because he secretly wanted to destroy it before the nation was pushed into a bloody war. These editors were confused by Stephens's contradictory behavior, but they failed to recognize that his desire to play a role in shaping this new government overrode his staunch objections to secession. Stephens had always thought that secession was legal. He had only warned southerners of the dangers of using it to protest federal oppression.

Northern free labor advocates viewed the Cornerstone Speech as confirmation that slavery posed the greatest threat to American workers. Whereas Confederates, such as Stephens, claimed that secession had been necessary to protect slavery from northern abolitionists, free-labor promoters declared that enslavers had removed themselves from the Union because the American economy's profits received from free labor industries would soon eclipse the Cotton Kingdom's revenues. While Stephens barely mentioned tariffs, free-labor supporters reminded the nation that free trade agreements, such as those endorsed by the new Confederate government, had been designed "to degrade all labor to a level with that of slavery, and to make it subject to their demands and control." Free laborers rejected Stephens's assertion that racial inequality benefited all white men. Rather than elevate white men to a special status of citizenry, free-labor advocates argued that slavery restricted the financial compensation and political influence that wage earners had gained. The Cornerstone Speech, according to free laborers, "prov[ed] that the designs of the revolutionists at the South tend more to the establishment of the exploded dogmas of tyranny, than the recognition and preservation of civil and religious liberty."⁶¹

Republican Party supporters used the Cornerstone Speech to denounce northern Democrats as "Dough Faces" who sympathized with the Confederate States of America. "Dough Face" was a derogatory term that had been coined by Virginian John Randolph three decades earlier to slander northern Democrats who supported southern political positions. For Dough Faces, Stephens represented the ideal southern leader—opposed to secession and eager to foster compromise within a national party system. Dough Faces had urged northerners to seek out politicians like Stephens to restore the Union. Northern Democratic newspapers had provided many reasons for the South's secession that avoided any mention of slavery and tended to focus on various matters related to taxation and trade. Democrats blamed Republicans for pushing the South toward secession. The Cornerstone Speech provided Republicans with plenty of evidence that undermined those claims. "Whenever the Democratic press of the North," wrote a Republican newspaper editor, "seek[s] to give a different reason for this revolution, and essay to fore the responsibility on the Republican party, they utter the most malignant falsehoods, and render themselves amenable for the actions of the Southern allies." Republicans exposed Stephens as a leader whose rhetoric differed little from Confederate radicals who had "band[ed] themselves to destroy the fairest and greatest government on the globe" for the sole purpose of protecting slavery. Republicans cited the Cornerstone Speech as one of many reasons why the Federal government could not expect the Confederacy to compromise or negotiate their readmission into the Union. Even moderates, like Stephens, resolved to gain independence even if that meant war.[62]

At least one Republican wrote to Stephens expressing support for the Cornerstone Speech's analysis of race and the US Constitution. I. M. Hatch of Rochester, New York, contacted Stephens after reading the speech in his local Republican Party newspaper. Hatch believed that a slim majority of New York Republicans agreed with Stephens's pronouncements. He challenged Stephens's account of Jefferson's intentions behind the Declaration of Independence. Hatch claimed that Jefferson never intended to include African slaves among those who had been born equal. Emphasizing that America had been founded by white men for the benefit of white men, Hatch argued that any suggestion that Jefferson sought to include all races was "absurd." "I am glad to see you *found* a *Government* on the truthful idea that "all men" *are not* "created free and equal," wrote Hatch. Hatch depicted life as a "struggle" that pitted "each for himself, against all others, black or white, yellow or brown." Historically the strong have prevailed over the weak. Freedom, according to Hatch, derived from one group's ability to exert power over another. Like Stephens, Hatch believed that the African race had developed independently from the white race. He expressed support for the theory of polygenesis that hypothesized that humanity had been created in two distinct and separate Gardens of Eden—one for whites and one for blacks.[63]

Because of its open affirmation that the new nation depended upon slavery, the Cornerstone Speech weakened the position of northern Democrats who supported negotiating with Confederate leaders to restore the Union. When Stephens reported that the Confederate constitution included provisions for the admission of additional states and territories—both free and slave, Republican newspapers accused northern Democrats of collaborating with "Jeff Davis's oligarchy."[64]

Confederate newspapers expressed hope that Stephens's Cornerstone Speech would find a receptive audience across Europe. The *Des Arc Semi-Weekly Citizen* of Arkansas reported that copies of the speech had been reprinted and distributed across England and France. European governments, however, distanced themselves from Stephens's pro-slavery rhetoric. According to historian Donald Doyle, "use of the term cornerstone . . . became a shorthand method of reminding foreigners of the real purpose of the South's rebellion. Stephens's speech was a gift to the Union."[65] Newspapers across Great Britain, for instance, denounced the Cornerstone Speech. *The Caledonian Mercury* of Edinburgh, Scotland, declared that "if Mr. Stephens' conclusions be correct, the Southern States of this Republic are right, and the rest of the civilized world radically wrong." The newspaper predicted that Stephens's pronouncements would prevent the Confederacy from attracting public support among British philanthropists and statesmen.[66]

British writers and orators began using the Cornerstone Speech as an essential document that defined both the Confederate States of America government and the pro-slavery causes of the American Civil War.[67] British Member of Parliament and industrialist William Edward Forster delivered several lectures across Great Britain that offered explanations for the Civil War's principal causes. During a presentation given at the Bradford Mechanics Institute, Forster "conceived that it was a war to solve the problem, whether a nation of civilized men in this age of the world could, in peace and safety, keep millions of their fellow beings in slavery, and treat them as though they were beasts." Forster observed that America's support of slavery had created the conditions for this bloody conflict. "It appeared almost puerile to state any other cause except slavery as the cause of this war, when they had been wondering year after year that this state of things could go on without a convulsion," said Forster. After an extensive description of the various ways the American government had allowed slavery to continue despite its dubious moral standing, Forster turned his attention toward the Cornerstone Speech. Citing Stephens, Forster described the desperate position that American enslavers had occupied that forced their secession. Westward expansion, as Stephens had observed, had failed to neither spread nor entrench slavery in American society because the South lacked the surplus population needed to migrate to new western lands in large enough numbers to establish new slave societies. To resolve this problem, the South must reopen the African slave trade and devise public policies that limited democratic governments on the frontier. When the Republican Party successfully embraced a platform that called for western territories to be formed by free men and free laborers, the South had to either remove itself from the Union or accept slavery's inevitable demise. Forster viewed the Cornerstone

Speech as Stephens's attempt to provide an intellectual justification for an undemocratic government founded on limiting the political will of free laborers and promoting "the great truth that slavery—subordination to the superior race—was the negro's natural condition."[68]

As Forster read Stephens's remarks, the Bradford Mechanics Institute audience burst out in laughter as they mocked his "manifesto." Reformers had founded the Bradford Mechanics Institute to promote adult education among all of England's social classes. Industrial workers comprised the bulk of its membership. Although many workers held prejudiced views about Africans, they universally agreed that slavery's continued existence threatened the rights and privileges of free laborers worldwide. Whereas Stephens believed that the Confederacy had built a model government that would be emulated globally and that the British abolitionist movement was dwindling, Britain's industrial workers, many of whom worried about reductions in income due to slowing cotton imports, found Stephens's ideas to be baseless, irrational, and threatening. Like most enslavers, Forster commented, Stephens ignored the opinions of others. Industrial workers worried that if the Confederacy gained independence, Stephens and other enslavers would "tyrannise over others" as they sought to build a new global slave empire. When Forster urged his working-class audience to encourage British leaders to rebuke the Confederacy's cornerstone, they erupted in applause.[69]

The Leeds Mercury questioned Confederate efforts to claim the moral high ground. Editors found it incredible that enslavers such as Stephens and Jefferson Davis portrayed secession as an act of justice sanctified by a divine spirit when both men failed to consider how their actions had harmed enslaved laborers. If Confederate leaders could resort to revolution to secure "equal justice," "Could not the negroes of the Southern States, if they rose against their masters, say just as much with at least equal justice, for their own insurrection?" The paper recommended that Confederates avoid discussions of "justice and holiness" because it made their actions look foolish.[70]

Following the Cornerstone Speech, both foreign and domestic publications anticipated that Confederate leaders, especially Jefferson Davis, would respond to Stephens's statements. Davis never publicly criticized Stephens's speech. Decades later, Davis biographer Hudson Strode wrote that the president had rebuked the vice president's remarks, but no evidence survives that would confirm Strode's assertion.[71] Rather than condemn Stephens for his explicit support for white supremacy, Davis's words echoed the vice-president's sentiments. Instead of showing concern that public support for the Confederacy's white-supremacist origins might damage international support, Davis, like Stephens, believed that shared notions of white supremacy might inspire European sympathies.

Several weeks after the Cornerstone Speech and the Confederate's seizure of Fort Sumter, Davis laid out his own explanations for the causes of the Civil War in a speech before the Second Provisional Congress of the Confederacy. After blaming northern states for aiding abolitionists to spread fears of insurrection across the South, Davis declared that secession protected the mutual interests of southern white men and black enslaved laborers. "In moral and social condition," Davis proclaimed that "under the supervision of a superior white race . . . [enslaved laborers] had been elevated from brutal savages into docile, intelligent and civilized agricultural laborers." Davis acknowledged the central role that slaves had played in the development of the Cotton Kingdom. If slavery was preserved, Davis believed, the nation would continue to reap enormous economic benefits. The country's security depended upon strong federal laws protecting enslaver property and outlawing abolitionist activities. The election of Abraham Lincoln had so threatened to injure slavery's future that secession was necessary to preserve a distinctive southern society dependent upon preserving racial inequality. Davis never rebuked the Cornerstone Speech because, like Stephens, he believed that preserving white supremacy justified slavery and secession.[72]

Following President Abraham Lincoln's call for 75,000 volunteers to restore the Union, Stephens continued to use racism to inspire Confederate supporters. During a journey by rail, Stephens delivered speeches in numerous towns in Virginia and North Carolina, urging men and women to support the Confederacy. He spread fears that a Civil War would unleash a race war that would unfairly target the South's white population. Stephens pleaded with Virginians "to arm themselves to protect their wives, families and homes from the rapine, murder and incendiary torch of the black republican hordes whom President Lincoln had called upon to subjugate them." Stephens told the crowds that if the Confederacy could raise enough troops that their armies would soon invade Maryland and capture Washington, DC, before the Republican Party's "cowardly" race war began.[73]

The Cornerstone Speech promoted the CSA as an exceptional experiment in the history of national governance. Stephens proclaimed that the CSA had become the first nation to declare what nature and God had determined—the right of superior white people to control the lives of inferior black people. Stephens believed that he had helped create the most noble government in history. The new government had been necessary, Stephens exclaimed, because of the actions of a tyrannical North intent on trampling upon the rights of states to control their own destinies. Stephens's postwar writings reemphasized the role that defending states' rights had played in the CSA's formation.[74]

Ironically, Stephens's wartime record illustrates the numerous problems that the increasingly centralized CSA encountered upholding states' rights. The CSA discovered that managing a war required a strong central government with a chief executive that possessed broad powers. In the summer of 1861, the CSA enacted unprecedented laws to quell dissent stemming from the contentious secession conventions. These laws gave the government the power to deport political enemies, seize the property of disloyal citizens, and appoint executive branch officials to manage those acts. On February 27, 1862, the CSA Congress, at President Jefferson Davis's urging, suspended the writ of habeas corpus for one year, allowing the government to hold a prisoner indefinitely without justifying the arrest before a court. Later that year, the Confederacy passed laws restricting civilian movements. On April 16, 1862, after volunteer enlistments failed to provide enough soldiers for the CSA military, the government enacted a national draft of all white men between the ages of eighteen and thirty-five. Gradually, the CSA passed laws that gave the government enormous powers to seize personal property, nationalize critical wartime industries, and collect unprecedented taxes. Alexander H. Stephens opposed these measures, citing that "independence without liberty was of no virtue." He correctly predicted that the sum effect of these abusive policies would decimate the CSA's popular support. By 1863, Stephens had grown increasingly critical of the Davis administration for violating the very principles of decentralized government that secessionists had championed under the banner of states' rights prior to the war. During the war, Stephens worried that the CSA's internal divisions would prevent it from generating the kind of national loyalty needed to defeat a numerically superior opponent. He firmly believed that white southern men would fight and die to defend their principles. After the war, although he remained critical of the CSA's management of the conflict, Stephens largely downplayed those internal conflicts. Lost Cause proponents embraced Stephens's writings as evidence of the CSA's supposed steadfast defense of states' rights. Stephens's wartime record told a very different story.[75]

Stephens's Cornerstone Speech identified the defense of states' rights as a cause of the war, but he placed greater emphasis on slavery and white supremacy as determining factors. After the war, ex-Confederates strongly rejected accusations that the conflict had begun as a southern fight to preserve slavery. Sometimes Lost Cause advocates declared that both sides espoused racist ideas, and therefore it was unfair to cast the South as especially biased. Stephens's Cornerstone Speech firmly contested such arguments, because he clearly identified the South's unique brand of white supremacy as unprecedented in world history—and as a foundation for the creation of the nation itself. The Lost Cause had a difficult time deflecting the Cornerstone Speech's lucid white-supremacist pronouncements. Southern apologists gradually circulated back to the idea that black enslaved laborers had so enjoyed their lives as slaves that they offered enormous support for the Confederate cause throughout the war. Eventually that argument expanded as CSA heritage groups, such as the UDC and SCV, aggressively claimed that hundreds of thousands of black enslaved laborers had fought alongside their white enslavers in defense of liberty and the preservation of the region's way of life. The Cornerstone Speech had a complicated relationship with this oft-repeated mythology. Historical evidence disproved Lost Cause accounts of loyal slaves fighting in the CSA army. However, the Lost Cause successfully wove this falsehood into the tapestry of American Civil War memory, thanks in part to the white-supremacist ideologies espoused in documents such as the Cornerstone Speech. Stephens depicted black enslaved laborers as loyal members of an inferior race dependent upon the Christian charity of a superior white race for survival. Mirroring widely accepted notions of black inferiority held across many parts of America, the idea of a dependent black slave fighting to preserve a "benevolent" form of unfree labor seemed logical to many white people. The debate over what role black enslaved laborers played in the Confederate war effort became inseparable from discussions of the Cornerstone Speech.[76]

Some Lost Cause proponents later claimed that the Cornerstone Speech, in hindsight, was ill-advised and poorly timed because it ruined the CSA's chances of gaining foreign recognition and bolstered the rhetoric employed by northern abolitionists. Later historians would invent a narrative in which President Jefferson Davis chastises Stephens for his rash white-supremacist proclamations. However, no evidence exists that Davis ever reprimanded Stephens either publicly or privately. Others argued that the speech had a detrimental influence on CSA foreign relations. Although the speech shocked the British and French governments, both had already expressed opposition to the CSA because of its obvious connections to slavery. The speech only confirmed what foreign governments already knew about the CSA.[77]

White southerners inserted Alexander Stephens's wartime record and the Cornerstone Speech into postbellum debates about why the CSA had lost the war. Although proponents of the Lost Cause initially criticized President Jefferson Davis's administration, gradually southern apologists forgot his poor performance and rehabilitated his reputation. As Davis's legacy joined the ranks of other beloved Confederate heroes, like Robert E. Lee and Stonewall Jackson, Stephens remained a less popular figure because of his wartime opposition to many Confederate policies and open disdain for Davis. Lost Cause promoters downplayed internal conflicts among Confederate leaders but managed to remember Stephens's bickering. Some argued that Davis's record had been tarnished by backbiting subordinates like Stephens. The Lost Cause failed to connect Stephens's criticisms of conscription, impressment, suspensions of habeas corpus, and other complaints as signs of larger internal problems across the Confederacy. For later scholars who were less influenced by the Lost Cause, Stephens's wartime record provides an outline for identifying internal divisions that undermined Confederate independence.[78]

The Lost Cause found Stephens to be a useful tool for its propaganda campaign designed to cast the Union as warmonger capitalists bent on destroying the South's democratic government. Stephens helped Lost Cause promoters transform the hopelessly flawed Hampton Roads Peace Conference into a primary example of Union efforts to prolong the bloody war. On February 3, 1865, at Hampton Roads, Virginia, Alexander Stephens led a delegation of Confederate representatives who met with President Abraham Lincoln and Secretary of State William H. Seward. The conference had been initiated by New York journalists who encouraged Lincoln and Jefferson Davis to negotiate a peaceful end to the conflict. After negotiations to determine the meeting's location and agenda, Davis asked Stephens to head the delegation and gave him specific orders to not accept anything short of Confederate independence. During the meeting, Lincoln offered the Confederates lenient terms for their readmission into the Union. At one point, Lincoln and Seward suggested that the recently passed 13th Amendment might be set aside if the Confederacy surrendered. Lincoln expressed some support for compensating enslavers for the loss of their property. However, Lincoln insisted that the Confederacy surrender, rejoin the Union, and accept any actions the federal government had taken toward emancipation. After an unproductive four-hour meeting, the two sides reached an impasse and parted. After the war, Stephens and others failed to mention that few Confederate leaders believed that the peace conference would be successful. Stephens also mischaracterized Lincoln's response to their proposed terms and lied about their exertions to use the meeting to delay or prevent emancipation. Generations of Lost Cause proponents elevated the poorly planned, failed peace conference as the Confederacy was in the throes of its final collapse to a seminal event of the conflict.[79]

Lost Cause supporters also emphasized Stephens's postwar incarceration at Fort Warren to condemn the federal government as punitive, dishonorable warmongers. After the war, the federal government investigated the mistreatment of Union prisoners of war at Libby and Andersonville prisons, among others. The appalling conditions at those facilities shocked northern readers, who wanted to exact revenge for these crimes. In response to increased northern calls for trials and executions of Confederate officials associated with those deplorable prisons, southern apologists launched a counternarrative that included accusations of the mistreatment of Confederate leaders held in northern prisons.

The conditions Stephens experienced at Fort Warren may have wounded his pride and created some physical and emotional discomfort, but his situation paled in comparison to Union soldiers held at Andersonville. Nonetheless, Lost Cause writers exaggerated claims of Stephens's deteriorating health and supposed mistreatment at the hands of federal guards to distract from stories of southern war crimes.[80]

As Stephens sat in his cell at Fort Warren, the desire to explain the Confederacy's defeat weighed on his mind. Prior to Georgia's secession, he had warned the state's radical leaders that southern independence would fail due to a series of reasons that ultimately played out during the war. He had warned Georgians that the South lacked the necessary industrial manufacturing and transportation capacity to prosecute a war. Stephens also cautioned secession zealots that large numbers of white southern men did not share their politics. He also predicted that the rebellion would fail if any slave states remained in the Union. Stephens also questioned whether foreign powers would intervene on the South's behalf. His prior opposition to secession provided him with an opportunity to paint himself as a brilliant prognosticator whose counsel had been ignored by overly emotional zealots. Which version of himself did Stephens want history to remember? Did he want posterity to remember his last-ditch efforts to prevent the war and halt secession? Or did he want posterity to remember when he declared that the Confederacy had forged a new path for democracy and liberty in world history on the backs of inferior, black enslaved laborers? As Stephens transitioned from wartime Confederate executive to postwar intellectual, he initiated a dishonest rhetoric that purposely misconstrued his wartime experiences and pronouncements in defense of the Confederacy's legacy. Ultimately, Stephens wanted to convince future generations that he had always been on the right side of history, despite the overwhelming evidence that emancipation and Confederate defeat provided to the contrary.[81]

CHAPTER THREE

The Origins of a Dishonest Intellectual Tradition, 1865–1883

A fter the Civil War, Alexander H. Stephens played an important role in the development of a dishonest intellectual tradition that coalesced into the Lost Cause. As the former vice-president of the defeated CSA, Americans expected Stephens to offer some explanation of the war's causes, administration, and outcomes. The Cornerstone Speech explicitly identified Stephens's thoughts on the war's origins; however, for the remainder of his life he claimed that reports of the speech had been misunderstood. Lost Cause promoters ignored the speech because they believed that admitting that the war had been fought to preserve slavery would dishonor the heroic memory of the Confederate dead. Meanwhile, Stephens wrote several important commentaries and histories of the "War Between the States," a phrase that he coined, that turned the conflict from a war to defend slavery into a constitutional battle fought in defense of states' rights and liberty. Had Stephens retired from public life after the war and, instead of returning to politics, spent the remainder of his days writing history, he would have been largely forgotten, like most vice-presidents in American history. Stephens, however, remained in politics literally until the day he died. Stephens never wholeheartedly committed himself to the Democratic Party. Although he never renounced white supremacy and strongly opposed Reconstruction, Stephens disliked Georgia's conservative Bourbon Democrats and advocated for political alliances with moderate Republicans, African Americans, and poor white southerners. To build a more diverse Democratic Party, Stephens endorsed policies that would have seemed improbable prior to Confederate defeat and emancipation. Stephens remained a pragmatist, searching for peaceful ways to enhance southern prosperity while preserving as much of its white-supremacist social order as possible. He also remained an empathetic soul whose politics advocated for the poor, disabled, and uneducated masses who constituted a society that had been devastated physically and emotionally by the Civil War. Sometimes his policies overrode his white-supremacist beliefs if he believed those stances would attract black men into the Democratic Party. The former enslaver continued to believe that freedpeople would consent to be governed by their white superiors if the postbellum South could reestablish the kind of benign paternalistic master-slave relationship that Stephens thought had existed prior to emancipation. He never envisioned black men voting without white supervision or supporting political causes of their own making. Instead, Stephens's confidence that white supremacy was a pragmatic rather than an ideological view of race relations shaped his rhetoric. He believed that inferior freedpeople would serve the interests of white men if they were treated well. Even Stephens's contemporaries often struggled to understand what his politics were. This chapter examines how Stephens distorted history to advance the Lost Cause. Chapter 4 will analyze how emancipationists—a coalition of African Americans and Republicans who saw slavery and emancipation as the central experience of the Civil War—challenged Stephens's lies.

Alexander Stephens's first opportunity to reflect on the Civil War and the Cornerstone Speech came during his five-month incarceration at Fort Warren in Boston Harbor. From his cell, Stephens helped initiate a dishonest rhetoric that became a central part of Lost Cause doctrine. Arrested by Union Army cavalry at home in Crawfordville, Georgia, at Liberty Hall plantation, Stephens worried that he might be tried for treason and sent to the gallows. The damp conditions at Fort Warren aggravated Stephens's chronic respiratory ailments and placed him in a deep state of depression. Even for an introvert who lived within his own mind, the isolation of Fort Warren, the distance spent away from his beloved brother, Linton, and the absence of his best friend, Robert Toombs, made his imprisonment torturous. The poor food, bed bugs, and insolent guards troubled Stephens less than his persistent concern over his legacy. Plus, everyone that he contacted wanted to know why the South had seceded and why the Confederacy had lost the war. How would Americans remember the Confederate government he helped create?[1]

Stephens kept a journal during his imprisonment. Although the journal did not appear in print until decades later, this source provides important insights into how ex-Confederate leaders chose to remember the war. Stephens peddled falsehoods that soon became Lost Cause orthodoxy. Foremost among those lies, Stephens offered unsubstantiated claims that "the slavery question had but little influence with the masses." He also fabricated a myth that enslavers "were willing from the first years of the war to give up that institution for peace on recognition of the doctrine of ultimate Sovereignty of the separate States."[2] Both lies distorted Stephens's firsthand wartime experiences. During the spring of 1861, when provided several opportunities to explain why the newly formed CSA had seceded from the Union, Stephens delivered multiple versions of the Cornerstone Speech that touted the unprecedented virtues of a government founded on white supremacy. A few weeks later, Stephens delivered a similar message to the Virginia legislature, urging it to join the CSA. In numerous stump speeches delivered at rail depots between Alabama and Virginia, Stephens threw his heart and soul behind the Confederacy to motivate young white men to enlist to defend their homes, liberty, and white privilege. During the mobilization of CSA forces, Stephens never doubted whether "the slavery question" would inspire white men to fight to defend their way of life.[3]

Stephens's attitude might have changed during the war as Confederate public policies exacerbated tensions among white southerners. He protested conscription and exemptions for enslavers because he feared those policies would weaken Confederate support among non-slaveholders. When large numbers of white men either resisted conscription or deserted the army, Stephens likely realized that his belief that the South's slave society would create the best country for all white men in history, regardless of class or status, had been mistaken. Months after the CSA's collapse, Stephens invented the myth that the CSA's origins had little to do with protecting slavery and ignored the reality that privileging enslavers might have contributed to the rebellion's downfall.[4]

Stephens's claim that CSA leaders had been willing to sacrifice slavery to secure their independence contradicted his wartime record. During the winter of 1865, with the prospect of defeat and forced emancipation on the horizon, Stephens led a party of negotiators on a mission to negotiate a cessation of hostilities that might include southern independence or a continuation of slavery or both. Confederate officials who learned of Stephens's mission assumed that it had been undertaken "so that slavery be preserved." Few except Stephens's treaty party expected Lincoln to recognize CSA independence regardless of the South's offers. When Stephens met with President Abraham Lincoln at Hampton Roads, Virginia, Stephens's refusal to accept emancipation as part of the CSA's unconditional surrender dashed any prospects of a negotiated peace. He never presented Lincoln with a plan to emancipate slaves in exchange for southern independence or better terms following the CSA's surrender. Although the Confederate Senate narrowly passed a bill in the final weeks of the war to authorize the enlistment of free blacks and slaves who had been previously emancipated by their owners in the Confederate Army, the measure lacked support among Confederate soldiers and failed to lay out any long-term plans for emancipation. The status of southern slaves had remained the same throughout the CSA's existence. Stephens's claim that Confederates had been willing to negotiate an end to slavery was intended to distract observers from the hard truth that the CSA had never wavered from its commitment to slavery as laid out so clearly in the Cornerstone Speech. Stephens helped contribute to a Lost Cause mythology that depicted the North as uncompromising warmongers and profiteers who rejected any supposed efforts made by Confederates to halt the bloodshed.[5]

More than four years had passed since Stephens had delivered the Cornerstone Speech. Although the speech had appeared in several wartime collections of public addresses, the public had generally forgotten his remarks. Stephens knew that the Cornerstone Speech would be rediscovered as Americans sought to explain the Civil War's causes in the conflict's aftermath. Until this moment, Stephens had not expressed any concerns in public or private about the accuracy of the Cornerstone Speech's transcription. Explicating the Cornerstone Speech presented Stephens with several challenges. On the one hand, by denying that the CSA had been founded to preserve slavery and white supremacy, Stephens risked making pronouncements about southern race relations that might impact their post-emancipation reality. He did not wish to reject white supremacy nor to undermine the myth of slavery's benevolence. On the other hand, the speech left little room for alternative interpretations. The most powerful and emphatic statements found in the speech concerned black inequality. However, once Stephens had declared that slavery was the CSA's "cornerstone," he spent the rest of the speech identifying additional reasons behind secession, including a rejection of federal supremacy. The remarks that followed the "cornerstone" remarks provided Stephens with a useful cover after the war. Readers who wanted to find evidence that states' rights rather than slavery had caused the war could find what they needed in the Cornerstone Speech if they overlooked or rejected the accuracy of his "cornerstone" comments. In a clever move intended to undermine public confidence in the speech's transcript, Stephens accused reporters of misrepresenting his argument.[6]

Stephens's accusations of reporting errors were purposely misleading and confusing. Later generations of Lost Cause advocates would often quote the few lines from Stephens's diary that accused the reporter of misrepresenting his remarks without paying any attention to the additional explanations that followed. Stephens's prison journal reaffirmed unequivocally that "slavery was without a doubt the occasion of secession." Northern "disregard for all constitutional barriers and guarantees," according to Stephens, had violated the "compact" that had bound states together in the republic and forced most slave states to secede. The North's failure to comply with the Constitution, Stephens argued, had put at risk "the proper subordination of the inferior African race to the superior white." White supremacy, Stephens continued, had been "recognized" as "nature's great law." Confederate defeat and emancipation had done nothing to alter Stephens's defense of white supremacy. Stephens mourned that emancipation and "outside agitation" had ended the "great improvements [happening] in the condition of blacks in the South." Lost Cause mythmakers conveniently ignored how Stephens accused others of misunderstanding his words while following those accusations by reaffirming the Cornerstone Speech's white-supremacist proclamations. Stephens's explanations were purposely misleading and intended to confuse readers.[7]

Stephens's prison journal laid out many falsehoods that he repeated in several publications. Ironically, Stephens developed a national reputation as a great historian despite the numerous lies found throughout his politically motivated writings. The CSA might have lost the war on the battlefield, but Stephens intended to lend his intellect to ensure that the South would be remembered as principled martyrs. Had Stephens been allowed to resume his political career months after the CSA's surrender, he might have never written the works that helped influence Lost Cause rhetoric. In November of 1865, one month after his release from Fort Warren, the Georgia legislature elected Stephens to serve in the US Senate. When Stephens and several ex-Confederate officials arrived in Washington, DC, to take office, the Republican-dominated Congress refused to seat them. Disappointed at being denied his office, Stephens returned to Crawfordsville, Georgia, and began writing A *Constitutional View of the Late War Between the States*. The two-volume book, published in 1868, became Stephens's principal effort to defend his wartime record and silence his critics. Stephens neglected to include a transcript of the Cornerstone Speech in his massive work, yet he devoted considerable space to clarifying those remarks. Stephens claimed: "the war was inaugurated and waged by those at the head of the Federal Government against these states . . . [who] allied themselves in a common cause . . . maintained and carried on purely in defense of this great right, claimed by them, of State Sovereignty and Self-Government." Adding to confusion about what readers may have gleaned from the Cornerstone Speech, Stephens argued: "slavery, so-called, or that legal subordination of the black race to the white . . . was unquestionably the occasion of the war . . . [but slavery] was not the real cause."[8] Stephens's long-winded discussion of the US Constitution's origins and state sovereignty shrouded slavery. When he turned his attention toward slavery, Stephens always cast the institution as natural and moral. Throughout the tedious book, Stephens followed any mention of the word slavery with "so called." He explained that slavery was a natural reflection of white supremacy and black inferiority. Stephens saw slavery as an uplifting institution that advanced Africans toward civilization and Christianity and ensured that relations among southern white males were harmonious. While he refrained from repeating his cornerstone imagery, the book nonetheless

71

described a slave society based almost entirely on white supremacy. Even if Stephens had been correct that Confederate states had seceded to protect state sovereignty, his examples of federal tyranny centered on issues connected to protecting slavery. In sum, Stephens made a tremendous effort to disguise the Confederacy's origins.[9]

A Constitutional View of the Late War Between the States became one of the most influential commentaries on the Confederate States of America's origins. According to historian Gaines Foster, "Stephens's work became the most influential . . . in the development of the southern interpretation of the causes of the war." The book enhanced Stephens's reputation as a scholar both within the South and across the nation. Eventually, his writings would become preferred school textbooks that heritage organizations such as the United Daughters of the Confederacy lobbied southern school boards to adopt as "the" history of the Civil War. A Constitutional View ensured that Stephens, and by extension the Cornerstone Speech" would remain at the center of subsequent debates over the Civil War's origins.[10]

In the war's immediate aftermath, as Stephens distorted the Cornerstone Speech, Lost Cause advocates ignored the speech. Edward Pollard's epic, The Lost Cause (1866), does not mention it once. As the wartime co-editor of the Richmond Examiner, Pollard encountered Stephens's remarks and shared many of his criticisms of the Confederate government, especially their shared disdain for Jefferson Davis. Pollard's work portrayed the North as a region that envied the South's "superior refinements of scholarship and manners." Among slavery's many virtues, Pollard noted, in the South "capital . . . protected labour . . . starvation was unknown . . . order was preserved by an unpaid police [and] . . . the African . . . blessed the world with their production." According to Pollard, the "system of servitude in the South . . . was really the mildest in the world [and] . . . did not rest on acts of debasement and disenfranchisement, but elevated the African, and was in the interest of human improvement." Whereas Stephens had claimed that secession developed to defend slavery, Pollard defined the war as an ideological battle between opposing civilizations. While Stephens claimed that white supremacy and slavery had elevated southern society to a supreme position over its northern brethren, Pollard did not explicitly see slavery as foundational to the development of a southern civilization that possessed a level of wealth, intellect, and virtue that exceeded the inferior northern civilization. Unwilling to accept that slavery had caused the war, Pollard omitted any discussion of the Cornerstone Speech. Initially, Pollard and other Lost Cause proponents wanted little to do with it.[11]

Unlike his Lost Cause co-conspirators, Stephens appeared unwilling to let the Cornerstone Speech disappear from public memory. Rev. Henry

Cleveland, an Ohio-born minister, lawyer, and Confederate veteran, had befriended Stephens while training to become an attorney. As editor of the *Augusta Constitutionalist*, Cleveland had been among Stephens's ardent supporters. Before the war, Cleveland had shared his commitment to the Union and national political parties. When the vast majority of southern delegates to the 1860 Democratic National Convention in Charleston, South Carolina, removed themselves from the proceedings in protest of Stephen A. Douglas's platform, Cleveland was among the handful who remained at the convention.[12] During the war, Cleveland held many posts, including serving on the administrative staffs of both Georgia Governor Joseph E. Brown and President Jefferson Davis. Like Stephens and Brown, Cleveland grew critical of Davis's leadership. After the war, Cleveland collaborated with Stephens, while the latter was imprisoned at Fort Warren, to produce a biography. In 1866, with Stephens's assistance and endorsement, Cleveland published a massive eight-hundred-page work that included appendices containing the Cornerstone Speech and dozens of other speeches and letters. Cleveland's assessment of Stephens mirrored how the former vice-president saw himself—it portrayed a politically astute and intellectually gifted maverick, unafraid of challenging party allegiances to defend the Constitution. The book attracted considerable interest among northern readers who knew of Stephens's Confederate record and had been exposed to numerous stories of his imprisonment through newspaper reports.[13]

Cleveland's biography was a propaganda piece orchestrated by Stephens to pronounce to the world his opinions on the causes of the war, Confederate defeat, and his wartime record. Cleveland accepted without question Stephens's claims that the Cornerstone Speech had been an "impromptu" address that was "not reported with great accuracy." Nonetheless, the speech transcription included in Cleveland's biography was copied directly from the Savannah newspaper's original account. Interestingly, Stephens had the opportunity to alter the speech as he pleased and to prove to the world that he had been misquoted but chose to keep the existing transcription.[14]

Had Stephens chosen to retire from politics after the war, the Cornerstone Speech might have vanished from American public memory. His postbellum political career, however, breathed new life into a speech that now became a weapon wielded against him by Republicans. In 1873, Alexander Stephens stopped writing history and returned to Congress. His election to the US House of Representatives attracted criticism along numerous fronts. Foremost, many Republicans found the sight of the former Confederate vice-president occupying a seat in Congress insulting. They likely found the symbolism of Stephens's political return more threatening than his actual power and influence. Meanwhile, Stephens found few allies among Democrats. During the

1872 presidential election, Stephens had urged southern Democrats to withdraw their support for national candidate Horace Greeley, who had built a bipartisan coalition with some Liberal Republicans to challenge Republican Ulysses S. Grant's re-election bid. Stephens accused Greeley's coalition of pursuing policies detrimental to southern agrarian and racial interests. Despite Stephens's efforts, most Georgia voters cast ballots in support of Greeley as the Democratic Party lost in a landslide nationally. Stephens celebrated Greeley's defeat and ignored charges from Georgia Democrats that he had fractured the democracy.[15]

One month after the 1872 election, Ambrose R. Wright, Georgia's recently elected Eighth District congressman, died before taking office. The task of selecting a new congressional representative belonged to the Georgia General Assembly. Unlike Stephens, Wright had been a popular figure in the postbellum Georgia Democratic Party. In 1872, as a supporter of the Bourbon Democrats, Wright helped orchestrate the end of Republican Party rule and Reconstruction in Georgia.[16] Stephens, a former Whig Party member who never felt comfortable in the Democratic Party, accused Bourbon leaders of manipulating the party candidate nomination process to exclude Democrats who supported reforms that favored small farmers and Confederate veterans. Stephens cast himself as the defender of the common man. He also accused Bourbons of aligning themselves with northern politicians, such as Horace Greeley, and capitalists who sought to remake southern society. By 1872, Stephens stood on the periphery of his party, yet he remained among the most respected and recognized public figures in Georgia, especially in his congressional district. His 1873 congressional bid seemed unlikely to succeed as the Bourbons handpicked Gen. John B. Gordon for the office. During the final days of the Civil War, Gordon had become Gen. Robert E. Lee's most trusted general officer in the fledgling Army of Northern Virginia. After the war, Gordon helped organize the Ku Klux Klan in Georgia and played an important role in the sanctification of Lee. From Georgia's new capital in Atlanta, the Bourbon dominated legislature initially provided Gordon with a twenty-six-vote plurality. That night, Stephens's powerful friends, including his best friend Robert Toombs, convinced a few dozen Bourbons that the former vice-president posed no threat to the state party and would be a better legislator than the inexperienced Gordon. The following morning, enough legislators had changed their vote to elect Stephens. After a fifteen-year absence in Congress, Stephens returned to Washington in 1873. He was the highest-ranking ex-Confederate official to serve in the postbellum American government.[17]

Stephens's election had been akin to a retirement gift given to an elder statesman as a token of respect for his past accomplishments. According to

Stephens's biographer Thomas E. Schott, despite his popularity and celebrity status, "his influence was gone. People simply were no longer interested in arguing about the Constitution." Perhaps time had passed Stephens by. However, for Republicans and African Americans he remained an important figure in a prolonged debate concerning the civil status of African Americans. *The Christian Recorder*, an African American newspaper published in Philadelphia, mocked Stephens's return to Congress by pointing out that an enslaver had the gall to name his estate Liberty Hall.[18] Whenever Stephens delivered a speech in the House of Representatives, the long shadow of his brief time as Confederate vice-president followed him. As a symbol of a defeated nation that had embraced white supremacy as its cornerstone, Stephens remained a threat long after his political powers had declined.[19]

Despite Stephens's lukewarm support among Georgia Democrats, Republicans in Congress had good reason to fear his return. He staunchly opposed the Civil Rights Bill. In January 1874, Stephens blasted Republicans for crafting civil rights legislation that violated the Constitution's protections of individual liberty. In yet another effort to rehabilitate the Cornerstone Speech, Stephens reversed his earlier position and now declared that Thomas Jefferson had rightfully proclaimed that all men were created equal. Back in 1861, Stephens had described Jefferson's declaration to be a mistake and impossible to achieve due to black inferiority. Now Stephens claimed Jefferson had been correct but equal birth did not "warrant equal rights." His remarks referenced earlier constitutional violations that had caused the Civil War and warned that by pursuing civil rights legislation the nation might be causing future conflicts.[20]

Stephens aggressively resisted the Civil Rights Bill, and Republicans saw him as a key figure impeding the bill's passage. Meanwhile, southern Democrats who opposed the Civil Rights Bill found Stephens's remarks disappointing because instead of condemning the legislation for the threat it posed to white supremacy, he focused on the bill's constitutional violations. Southern Democrats wanted Stephens to recommit publicly to the explicit white-supremacist ideals expressed explicitly in the Cornerstone Speech. Rep. John T. Harris of Virginia responded to Stephens's intellectual haggling over constitutional questions and civil equality by delivering a more impassioned statement about the permanence of white supremacy in America. "I defy any man," Harris proclaimed, "to say that the black man is the equal of the white man." Harris's "old-time plantation swagger" prompted Alonzo Ransier, an African American Republican Congressman from South Carolina, to respond that he possessed the courage to declare "that the black man was the equal of the white man." As Ransier stood and glared across the aisle toward Harris, the Virginian fired back, "You sit down sir; I am not talking to you!" The Speaker of the House reprimanded Harris for violating congressional debate rules and ordered him to sit down and surrender the floor to the next speaker.[21]

Southern Democrats wanted Stephens to be more vocal and forceful in his opposition to Reconstruction. Stephens's rhetoric never satisfied those expectations.[22] Publicly, Stephens framed Reconstruction as a constitutional crisis rather than a crisis that would determine future southern race relations. His party questioned his allegiance to white supremacy. Stephens had stopped questioning the Founding Fathers' fallible opinions on race. He had de-emphasized white supremacy's supposed divine nature. Stephens had abandoned his explicit proclamations of the continuity of white supremacy. Political pragmatism contributed to Stephens's shifting rhetoric. He hoped to either end or weaken Reconstruction by negotiating compromises with moderate Republicans. He believed that Radical Republicans had lost control of the Grand Old Party, and moderate and conservative factions would check any radical civil rights legislation. Stephens also trusted President Ulysses S. Grant's moderate leadership.[23]

Stephens's words and actions often struck a conciliatory chord that emphasized the central role that preserving white supremacy would play in building a stronger nation. Stephens, like most Lost Cause advocates, believed that emancipation had weakened American society. On July 4, 1875, America celebrated its ninety-ninth birthday. A group of prominent Atlantans invited Stephens to deliver the city's Independence Day event's keynote address. Stephens's speech, like his other postbellum remarks, contained a series of conflicting messages that tried to reconcile Lost Cause inspired interpretations of liberty with his nationalist sympathies. After lauding the Founding Fathers for their wisdom and courage, Stephens subtly warned that the compact that had formed the nation could be ruined by an authoritarian state akin to the British Empire that had ruled the American colonies. He emphasized that the Declaration of Independence proclaimed the British colonies be "Free and Independent States." Independent states preceded the nation in this formulation, Stephens argued, and thus states could regulate federal powers. While celebrating American independence, Stephens delivered the Lost Cause's standard defense of states' rights and secession—the latter was justified and constitutional whenever the state compact had been violated.[24]

The Cornerstone Speech loomed in the background as Stephens analyzed the Declaration of Independence. Stephens questioned what Thomas Jefferson meant when he declared that "all men were created equal." Back in 1861, Stephens had claimed that Jefferson was mistaken. Stephens avoided directly criticizing Jefferson in his latest analysis, but his commentary reaffirmed the Cornerstone Speech. If men "are all equal in their individual and social relations," Stephens declared, "this meaning would destroy the very organization of society and defeat the objects for which all governments should be formed." The South's oppressive racial hierarchy had provided great security for its white male inhabitants. Stephens continued to believe that social equality was impractical and unnatural because of "black inferiority." Stephens argued that all men should enjoy an "equal right to justice in the administration of civil affairs, and that no one, however high, has any rightful power to wrong another, however low." Stephens believed that African Americans in 1875 enjoyed an "equal right to justice" thanks to a benevolent and moral white society whose paternalistic protection of enslaved laborers during the antebellum period had carried over into the postbellum era. Although numerous Lost Cause proponents held similar attitudes, Stephens's extensive writings and orations drew enormous attention and provided a pen and a voice to articulate evolving expressions of white supremacy.[25]

Whenever Stephens moved toward a conciliatory view of Civil War memory, Republicans challenged his sincerity and exposed his hypocrisies. In 1878, at the US Capitol, Stephens joined Ohio Congressman James Garfield, a Union veteran, on Lincoln's birthday to accept Francis Bicknell Carpenter's painting *First Reading of the Emancipation Proclamation of President Abraham Lincoln*. The ceremony was an ideal opportunity for Stephens to honor Lincoln while expressing opinions on the state of American race relations. Garfield opened the ceremony by recognizing donor Elizabeth Thompson's commitment to the "elevation of the laboring poor" and "the equal freedom of all its people." As Stephens listened from his desk, Garfield proclaimed that the Emancipation Proclamation marked "the third great act in the history of America, the fulfillment of the promise of the declaration." As Garfield explained the proclamation's origins, he handed Stephens a small symbolic victory, as he admitted "there have been, there are, and still will be great and honest differences of opinion" over what started the Civil War. After praising Lincoln's "unique" character, Garfield himself struck a conciliatory tone as he accepted the portrait on behalf of a "reunited nation."[26]

Stephens was less interested in reconciliation than Garfield. He used the event to peddle more Lost Cause mythologies before the numerous reporters, Republicans, and Union Army veterans who had gathered at the Capitol to honor the Great Emancipator. Supporters of the Lost Cause labored to tarnish Lincoln's legacy by reminding anyone willing to listen that the president was himself a white supremacist who only freed the slaves to punish the Confederacy. Confined to a wheelchair, due to an accident on his farm and declining health, Stephens claimed that Lincoln had only adopted emancipation "from the necessities of war" rather than "any purely humanitarian views." Stephens was convinced that most Americans now regretted how the federal government managed emancipation. He wanted to persuade others that slavery had been a virtuous institution hastily sacrificed to defeat the Confederacy. He urged Republicans to overcome its prejudices toward slavery since "it was not an unmitigated evil" or "without its compensations." In his mind, slavery had been a positive good that benefited all Americans, black and white.[27]

Stephens's employed a deliberately confusing rhetoric designed to obscure the Confederacy's attitudes toward slavery. He and other Lost Cause promoters liked to argue that they had wished to liberate slaves long before the Civil War but failed to do so out of a deep concern for the slaves' well-being. Repeating statements found throughout the Cornerstone Speech, Stephens admitted that slavery "was wrong and it ought to have been abolished" but "secession was resorted to as a remedy" to force free states to uphold "their constitutional obligations." Stephens's confusing rhetoric disguised his true feelings. By admitting that slavery "was wrong and it ought to have been abolished," Stephens believed he had occupied a moral high ground that expunged enslavers of any guilt. Stephens purposely failed to clarify his antebellum position on emancipation. Prior to the Civil War, Stephens believed that it would be possible in the distant unforeseeable future to liberate slaves if enslaved laborers advanced under the tutelage of white civilization. He never stipulated the exact achievements necessary to spark emancipation because his white-supremacist worldview could not imagine black people as anything more than wards of white society.[28]

Speaking before a crowd of Lincoln supporters, Stephens continued to proffer a series of Lost Cause lies. He also continued to contradict various parts of the Cornerstone Speech because many northern journalists and Republicans, especially African Americans and Union veterans, never forgot those controversial remarks. In trying to change the narrative that he started in the Cornerstone Speech, Stephens now dishonestly argued that states' rights, rather than slavery, had been "the basis and foundation of our fabric." Spreading yet another Lost Cause myth, Stephens argued that southerners were "doing the best we can for the colored people, hoping earnestly that they will fit themselves for higher civilization." Stephens claimed that northern interference in southern civil affairs had been responsible for slowing improvement for African Americans. He urged Republicans to allow white southern men to manage the future of the region's freedpeople without intrusions. The South knew best how to handle race relations, according to the ex-enslaver, because slavery had taught white southerners to be responsive to the needs of an inferior black race. After expressing some hope for a "nobler and grander future for these United States," he warned that if the "recent troubles and disasters" of Reconstruction carried into the future, "a deeper and more dreadful eclipse . . . will come upon this continent, blighting and blasting the brightest and best hopes of mankind." Stephens made clear that any sectional reconciliation would be defined in the Lost Cause's terms.[29]

Stephens's speech at the Lincoln portrait unveiling drew criticism from African American newspapers. The *Christian Recorder* reported that Stephens's speech "was liberal as could be expected from a man who gloried in proclaiming 'slavery to be the cornerstone' of the would-be Confederacy of the South." Finding agreement with Stephens's assertion that African Americans were "wards of the Almighty [and] not of the nation," the editor chastised Little Aleck for lacking faith that Christianity alone would be enough to accomplish "the adjustment of the two races." If "the two races cannot harmonize in this country," as Stephens doubted, then the failures of racial reconciliation would result from an underestimation of the powers of God. Emancipationists became increasingly frustrated by Stephens lack of vision for the future of American race relations.[30]

Despite Stephens's active role in promoting the Lost Cause, he maintained a strained relationship with southern Democrats. Throughout the 1870s, Republicans hoped that Stephens's divisive relationship with the Democratic Party might break up the "solid South." In 1878, Stephens broke ranks with House Democrats as they attempted to create investigatory hearings to oust Republican President Rutherford B. Hayes from office. Stephens felt that the investigations set a poor precedent and that "Hayes was doing more for the people of the South than Tilden could have done." Under Stephens's leadership more than a dozen Democratic congressmen joined the Republican minority to halt legislation that would have authorized the investigations. Stephens failed to prevent the resolution from reaching the House floor. As Stephens tried to raise his voice in opposition, Democrats shouted him down, forcing his silence.[31]

The Democratic Party of Georgia threatened to remove Stephens from the upcoming congressional election ballot. Across the state, newspapers labeled Stephens a traitor. For Republicans and African Americans, Stephens's defections from the Democratic Party gave them hope that he might lead a new biracial Independent political movement. The *Scranton Republican* optimistically reported that "the very best people of the South, with the colored people, will rally around Stephens and thus, we trust, divide the too solid South." Stephens's pride had been damaged by the Democratic representatives' actions, and he vowed to seek revenge upon those whose voices had silenced his protests. He remained committed to the right to voice one's opposition reasonably to any law. Democrats had robbed him of that privilege. When he returned to Georgia, Stephens pledged to "appeal to the people" if Democrats attempted to block his campaign. Before a biracial and bipartisan crowd in Augusta, Stephens appeared ready to declare war on the Democratic Party's leaders. He appealed to that portion of the electorate whom the state's ruling Bourbon Democrats had ignored. Several months later, Stephens led a slate of Independent Democrats that captured four of Georgia's nine congressional seats, while heavily contesting each district. During the 1878 election, black and white Republicans joined white yeoman farmers and Confederate veterans to build a statewide coalition that nearly toppled the reigning conservative order.[32]

Unfortunately for other Independent Democrats, Stephens inexplicably retreated into the clutches of the Bourbons. When other Independent leaders, most notably Dr. William Felton of northwest Georgia's infamous "Bloody Seventh" district, began openly calling for their supporters to caucus with Republicans, black and white, Stephens worried that the movement might permanently splinter the Democratic Party at a time when Republicans continued to exert enormous influence nationally. Stephens valued unity and compromise over division and provocation. By 1880, as he had done back in 1861 when he joined his secession enemies after initially opposing them at some political and personal cost, Stephens swallowed his pride and rejoined his opponents in the hopes of being a moderating influence. In his mind, it was better to be a moderate voice working among your bitter enemies than to be perceived by your opponents as a radical outsider who needed to be removed from power.[33]

Ironically, Stephens's former adversaries soon asked him to steady the Democratic Party of Georgia. In 1882, Stephens retired from Congress so he could run for the Georgia governor's office. He won a landslide victory. A series of corruption scandals involving the convict-lease system and the state penitentiary had divided the Democratic Party in Georgia, which turned to Stephens, the party's elder statesman, to restore public confidence. In office, he used his executive powers to undo many of the corrupt schemes that had upset the electorate. Stephens began pardoning convicted prisoners, black and white, whose prosecutions had been a grave miscarriage of justice and brought to life gross examples of the inhumane conditions in Georgia prisons. Pardoning convicts, especially African Americans, angered many Democrats, but Stephens continued to hope that future black voters would support the Democratic Party. Most Georgia Democrats rejected Stephens's efforts to forge biracial political coalitions. Stephens's controversial actions quickly eroded his popularity.[34]

On February 12, 1883, Alexander Stephens delivered his final public address at a ceremony honoring Savannah's history. Despite cold weather, Stephens delivered his speech and toured the city in a drafty carriage. He died two weeks later from a cold caught during the parade. Stephens's death marked the end of his efforts to distort the historical record and promote the Lost Cause.

Memorials and tributes to Alexander Stephens appeared in newspapers nationwide as well as in Great Britain, Canada, and France. Writers tried to capture Stephens's legacy. The memorials suggest that Stephens's campaign of dishonesty and myth making had been largely successful. Most articles that appeared in northern publications struck conciliatory chords that praised Stephens's intellect, work ethic, devotion to the Constitution, and public service. Most softly condemned Stephens's role in the Confederate government but applauded other aspects of his political career and personal life. Even fewer mentioned how Stephens had played a central role in the drafting of the Confederate Constitution—a role that ensured that his fingerprints were all over that document's explicit perpetual support for slavery and white supremacy. Writers sporadically mentioned the Cornerstone Speech. Few connected Stephens's white-supremacist statements with his postwar opposition to civil rights legislation. While Stephens's contemporaries credited him for being a moderating influence in the Confederate government, few recognized the central role that Stephens had played in shaping the Lost Cause.[35]

The numerous tributes to Stephens demonstrated how others perceived his messy legacy. The *Dunn County News* of Menomonie, Wisconsin, for example, described Stephens as "the ablest and most conspicuously honorable and honored surviving representatives of the Southern Confederacy."[36] The *Brooklyn Union* portrayed Stephens as a reluctant Confederate who refrained from joining secessionists "until overwhelmed by the popular voice." Had Stephens chosen to retire from public life once Georgia seceded from the Union, he might have "become a martyr for his convictions." Unfortunately, the editor wrote, Stephens "did not maintain a dignified loyalty in retirement" and instead did his best to strengthen the Confederate cause.[37] The *Boston Journal* described Stephens as an enterprising man who managed to gain a national reputation and personal wealth despite his humble origins and poor health—a politician who, regardless of his steadfast defense of slavery and territorial expansion, had advocated for peace and compromise within the Confederate government. Many editors highlighted Stephens's frayed relationship with Confederate President Jefferson Davis as evidence of the former's moderation. Surprisingly, even Republican Party–aligned newspaper editors, such as the *Boston Journal*, praised Stephens for his cooperative postwar relationships with Republicans.[38] Even newspapers such as the *Rutland Daily Herald* of Vermont, which struggled to understand why Stephens ultimately supported the Confederate government after devoting so much energy to preventing its creation, depicted Stephens as someone who "was never regarded with favor nor looked upon as altogether sound in heart for the confederacy." The *Herald*, as well as many other newspapers, devoted more attention to Stephens's short postwar incarceration at Fort Warren than his problematic Confederate record.[39]

Many northern newspapers, like their southern counterparts, echoed Stephens's postwar distortions of his supposed conflicted relationship with slavery. After the *Jasper Weekly Courier* (Jasper, Indiana) mourned the passing of "one of the most remarkable men of this century," the editor proclaimed that Stephens was "always outspoken in his opposition to the theory of slavery." Rather than deal with the Cornerstone Speech's explicit defense of slavery and white supremacy, the editor highlighted an 1845 speech Stephens had delivered in Texas. In that address Stephens had told the crowd that "I am no defender of slavery in the abstract; I would prefer to see all the sons and daughters of Adam's family in the full enjoyment of all the rights set forth in the Declaration of Independence." Sixteen years later in Savannah, Stephens told a different crowd that the Founding Fathers had been mistaken in their assertion that all men were created equal.[40]

In the Cornerstone Speech and many other speeches, Stephens had often claimed that he was "no defender of slavery in the abstract" as a means of appearing to soften his white-supremacist rhetoric. However, he believed that he lived in a practical world of observable realities. In his world, black enslaved laborers lacked the ability to achieve an equal footing with whites. At times, Stephens criticized enslavers for failing to educate their enslaved property so that they might, in some distant future, climb out of their current station. Meanwhile, Stephens doubted whether access to education and religious moral instruction could improve the condition of the black race in America due to the prevailing white supremacist attitudes held nationwide. Prior to the Civil War, Stephens never saw a future where the enslaved would be free and equal citizens in America. He did see a role for some chosen black men to be handpicked supporters of the Democratic Party. If enslaved laborers could be manipulated and coerced into serving the interests of their white enslavers, Stephens thought the Democratic Party might be able to create a loyal legion of freedmen. The 1845 Texas speech was often quoted out of context and without consideration for its deeper meaning as he explained the perpetual lack of opportunity for the black race in America.[41]

Seemingly, many white Americans at the time of Stephens death in 1883, embraced contradictory impulses that served to keep them in control of national politics. On one hand, the failures of Reconstruction to provide new opportunities for freedpeople had reaffirmed the lasting influence that white supremacy would have on the nation. On the other hand, white supremacist intellectuals, such as Stephens, clung to the false idea that racial equality could only be achieved in the abstract. Thus, racial equality was simultaneously possible and impossible. The abstract, yet improbable, potential for racial equality helped justify contemporary inequalities as practical realities.[42]

The *New York Tribune* published an account of Stephens's funeral, including a series of Atlanta City Council proclamations read by Gen. John B. Gordon. Death often heals old wounds. Gordon and Stephens had been political enemies throughout the previous decade. At one point, Stephens had accused Gordon of surrendering postbellum southern interests to northern capitalists. Now with Stephens's passing, the popular Gordon stood before a large crowd and read a series of resolutions honoring the fallen statesman. Those resolutions declared that Stephens's "catholic sympathies, embracing as they did all classes, colors and conditions—the whole family of man—render his life an aspiring example for the limitation of ourselves and of those who are to come after us." Gordon depicted Stephens as a maverick politician who often quarreled within his own political party. The city council asserted that "his brave support of the rights and privileges, as he conceived them, of all citizens, whether colored or of his own race . . . illustrates his courage of conviction, which never failed him, and which is worthy of emulation by the young men of his State and country." By southern standards, Stephens, who was a prominent white supremacist, stood out for his "friendly" opinions on African Americans. At the funeral Robert Toombs declared that Stephens "would have deserved all honor if he had done no act in his life except to advocate those principles of States rights which he had always held to." In death, Stephens, who had often found himself out of step with the postbellum Democratic Party, was washed of his many disagreements and rancorous relationships and elevated to the statue of a fallen Lost Cause icon, "worthy of emulation."[43]

Publisher Frank W. Norton also praised Stephens's career as worthy of emulation. A few months after Stephens's death, Norton published a biographical sketch of the deceased Confederate leader that included a near complete transcription of the Cornerstone Speech. Norton built an archival collection of Stephens's letters and speeches. He treated Stephens as an intellectual statesman whose "calm and dispassionate reasoning" contrasted sharply with Confederate leaders who had been "swept by a mad passion of excited self-confidence." According to Norton, Stephens believed white supremacy and slavery to be "fixed facts" and "divinely ordained." Norton cast Stephens as the most rational and reluctant Confederate leader. By joining the Confederate government, Norton claimed, Stephens had sacrificed his own desires to avoid secession and preserve the Union for the sake of the fledgling southern nation. Thus, his heart was never fully committed to Confederate independence. Although Norton challenged Stephens's description of the low intellectual capacity of northern people, he failed to challenge his white supremacist beliefs.[44]

Most southern newspapers neglected to mention the Cornerstone Speech in their eulogies to Stephens. Rather than dwell on his controversial career as Confederate vice-president, many editors chose to emphasize his statesmanship, intellect, and oratorical prowess. The *Telegraph-Bulletin* of Monroe, Louisiana, reported that Stephens "did not believe slavery to be the real issue of the late war, but only its immediate cause, the vital question being that of the right to the States to control their own affairs." The paper also described Stephens as a talented orator who always delivered addresses extemporaneously.[45] The *New Orleans Picayune*, for example, referred to Stephens as "an instructor of the people" who "has been great beyond the limits of ordinary human greatness." Southern editors also ignored Stephens's strained relationship with the Democratic Party and efforts during the mid-1870s to court political support from African Americans and Republicans. Few mentioned his difficult relationship with Jefferson Davis. Southern newspapers tended to turn a complicated public figure into a one-dimensional "great man" of superior intellect and "humble origins" who overcame significant disabilities to become a popular and "conscientious" southern leader.[46]

Rabbi Isaac P. Mendes of Alexandria, Louisiana, used Stephens's death as an opportunity to demonstrate Jewish patriotism for those who doubted their national loyalties. In Mendes's case, however, those national loyalties had to include a tribute to the fallen Confederacy. Mendes declared that Stephens's "great and noble soul . . . has been transplanted by angels upon sunbeams of immortal bliss and eternal honor." According to Mendes, Stephens was forever connected to a time "when might conquered right." The Rabbi chose to ignore Stephens's white supremacy and instead cast him as a victim of northern oppression whose liberties had been stolen after the war. Stephens's "dogged perseverance to the cause of right," Mendes continued, "and history will likewise show in the future that his hand and heart will be joined with his Christian brothers to defend the sanctity of his home and guard the safety of his domestic fireside." For some southerners, like Mendes, Stephens served as a useful martyr whose own death was secondary to the Confederate States of America's death.[47]

Alexander H. Stephens spent his postwar years crafting a dishonest and purposely misleading intellectual rhetoric that became a major component of Lost Cause mythology. Posing as amateur historian and political scientist, Stephens left behind several major works that gave a thoughtfully rationalized explanation of the Civil War. Unfortunately, Stephens willfully distorted the historical record by either ignoring or rejecting his firsthand wartime experiences. Although Lost Cause writers, especially in the immediate aftermath of the war, were not interested in revisiting the Cornerstone Speech, Stephens knew that his historical legacy might be forever tethered to that speech. Those who opposed the Lost Cause, on the other hand, never let him forget what he had said. Their activism forced Stephens to weave a complicated, messy, and often contradictory web of lies and misrepresentations that distorted, confused, and cast suspicions but never renounced his controversial statements. Despite Stephens's best efforts, the Cornerstone Speech remained part of American public discourse.

CHAPTER FOUR
Emancipationists Strike Back, 1865–1883

T oday, the Cornerstone Speech is often cited by scholars, journalists, activists, and more. The Cornerstone Speech never vanished from American public discourse because of the actions of postwar emancipationists, who held firm their belief that slavery and white supremacy had caused the Civil War—as firmly as Stephens himself believed when he delivered the speech. Some emancipationists, much like modern scholars, began carrying copies of the speech in their coat pockets prepared to wield its damning words if pressed to disprove Lost Cause fallacies. Emancipationists ensured that how later generations of Americans would remember Alexander H. Stephens would be forever linked to the Cornerstone Speech. Stephens and the speech became inseparable symbols of the CSA's racist origins.

As much as white southerners tried to diminish or revise the Cornerstone Speech, northern writers and Republicans, black and white, cited the speech as incontrovertible proof that slavery and secession were intertwined. According to historian David Blight, these groups coalesced to craft an emancipationist vision of Civil War memory that emphasized the central role that slavery and emancipation had played in shaping the conflict. Emancipationists argued that the Confederacy had fought to defend slavery and that the Union had evolved throughout the war toward an agenda designed to end slavery and extend civil rights to freedpeople. Emancipationists helped transform the Union war effort into a noble cause. By denying that slavery had motivated secession, ex-Confederates placed themselves in a difficult defensive stance that conceded that fighting a war to defend slavery would have been less noble than fighting to defend states' rights and to protect their families and homes from a northern invasion. Meanwhile, pro-slavery wartime statements made by Confederate officials, most notably the Cornerstone Speech, forced postwar defenders to balance de-emphasizing slavery's role while sustaining their white-supremacist beliefs and opposition to black civil equality. Ex-Confederates generally cloaked their defense of slavery and white supremacy in accusations that the North had caused the war by violating the Constitution and obstructing states' rights.

In addition to blaming Confederates for causing a bloody war to defend slavery, emancipationists accused postbellum white southern leaders of opposing black civil equality so their white-supremacist society could continue indefinitely. Emancipationists underestimated both the level of racism prevalent nationwide and the determination of white southerners to dominate Civil War memory. White southern males continued to connect their personal liberties with the oppression of the black race. Nonetheless, emancipationists kept inserting the Cornerstone Speech into the national debate at a time when ex-Confederates tried to forget it.[1]

The first attempts to situate the Cornerstone Speech into the emancipationist vision of Civil War memory began during the war. In 1863, historian John Stevens Cabot Abbott, a graduate of Bowdoin College who helped spread public interest in history through his entertaining biographies, published the first of his two-volume *History of the Civil War in America*. Abbott had recently spent time traveling through the American South and Cuba and had a visceral reaction to the aristocratic and anti-democratic slave society that dominated those places. During the Election of 1860, Abbott claimed that "slaveholders had resolved to change the character of our government, so that the United States should be the great bulwark of slavery. The great majority of the people resolved that the spirit of the government should not thus be changed." Lincoln's election had repudiated the slaveholder conspiracy that sought to corrupt the US Constitution. Abbott reminded readers that the Civil War was more than a fight to defend the US Constitution. The war sought to end the dominant influence that white southern enslavers held in national politics. Abbott feared that if secession succeeded, the horrors of slavery that he had witnessed across the Deep South would continue uncontested forever. A theologian as well as a historian, Abbott believed that God had ordained the war to combat the sins of slavery. Abbott included dozens of quoted passages penned by white southern enslavers proclaiming their defense of slavery. Buried in an abundance of evidence, Abbott included an extended quotation lifted from Alexander H. Stephens's Cornerstone Speech. Abbott claimed from his firsthand travels that only a "small band of slaveholders" truly endorsed the kind of white supremacy that Stephens espoused. Pro-slavery apologists like Stephens had manipulated "the masses of poor whites, who, in their extreme poverty and ignorance, took pride in contemplating a class still below them." Poor families who literally ate "dirt, were as hostile to emancipation as were the slaveholders." Like Stephens, who had even broader ambitions for the appeal of white supremacy, Abbott believed that the Cornerstone Speech would motivate white southern men of all social classes to unite under the banner of white supremacy in a war for independence. The lie behind white supremacy and black inferiority had been accepted across the South, thanks to a highly successful pro-slavery propaganda campaign. White southern men, argued Abbott, had accepted the lie that held together their white men's democracy.[2]

New York journalist Horace Greeley's large subscriber base exposed millions of Americans to his analysis of the Cornerstone Speech. Greeley contrasted Jefferson Davis's inaugural speech with it. Whereas Davis had avoided any explicit reference to slavery, Stephens, according to Greeley, "proved far less reticent and more candid." Greeley claimed that Stephens arrived in Savannah eager to celebrate the achievements of the new Confederate Constitution he had played a central role in drafting. Unlike many later commentators and historians, Greeley's history included a lengthy abridged version of the speech, rather than just the infamous cornerstone passage. Greeley pointed out that the Confederate Constitution included numerous measures that Stephens believed were superior to the US Constitution. The right of executive department cabinet members to hold seats in the national legislature, the abolishment of protective tariffs and federally funded internal improvements, and presidential term limits were all measures that Stephens expressed great personal pride in drafting. However, when he rose to speak in Savannah, his address almost immediately turned to the subject of slavery and the Confederate Constitution. The other accomplishments were buried deeper into the speech and were rarely discussed afterwards. Greeley hypothesized that had Stephens wished to minimize the subject of slavery in his remarks he could have either avoided the topic or de-emphasized them. Instead, because the subject meant so much to him and the new Confederate government's supporters, Stephens chose to lead with his thoughts on slavery and white supremacy. Greeley interpreted Stephens's choice as evidence that the defense of slavery and proclamations of white supremacy had motivated secession. What Davis had been reluctant to say was now laid bare for all to see by Stephens's Savannah speech. Clearly, Greeley found Stephens's speech to be indisputable evidence that the debate over slavery's future in America had been the paramount issue of the war.[3]

After the war, Alexander Stephens became a postbellum celebrity, as journalists sought his explanation for the war's causes and the Confederacy's defeat.[4] Reporters wanted Stephens's commentary because the war's results, defeat and emancipation, contrasted sharply with the ambitions outlined in the Cornerstone Speech, composed on the eve of conflict. In 1867, journalist George Alfred Townsend, who published articles under the pseudonym GATH, interviewed Alexander Stephens as the ex-Confederate prepared his history on

"The War Between the States." Prior to meeting face-to-face, Townsend had been told by his fellow reporters that Stephens was a "long winded invalid" who often quarreled with journalists. Townsend found Stephens to be a "serious man, kindling not to please anybody, but his inner enthusiasm and emotion. Something between the minister and the teacher." When Townsend asked Stephens to comment on black suffrage in the postbellum South, he responded that "if the negroes in the South were given suffrage, the whole of the Southern States would recur to a wilderness, and everybody would move out of it." Townsend recalled how, as Stephens spoke, an "ultra-Southern light flashed up in his eyes." After discussing the Cornerstone Speech at length, Townsend claimed that Stephens had delivered those remarks because he "could not reconcile it with his heart to break up the Union unless he could discover some great philosophical truth for his apology." Townsend predicted that, had the Confederacy succeeded, Stephens's belief in the "universality of slavery as the Creator's intention" would have led Confederate leaders to force slavery upon other nations like "Mohammed's Generals forced their religion at the point of the sword upon three continents."[5]

GATH judged Stephens to be a contradictory statesman who represented both the best and the worst example of southern temperament and racism. Here was a man who during his best moments had defended the oppressed, yet failed to see how enslavers, such as himself, had built a society based on racial oppression and exploitation. Townsend contested accounts of Stephens's superior wit, intellect, and statesmanship. "One of the meanest influences of slavery," wrote Townsend, "was the mental degradation it exerted over the mind of white genius." Much like John C. Calhoun, "the negro was his master all his life. He dreamed and feared and formulated for nothing but that negro." Stephens's obsession with white supremacy had misled him to believe that his spirited defenses of slavery amounted to the pinnacle of intellectual reason. Townsend felt sorry for Stephens because emancipation should have relieved him of this obsession, but instead it infected him with a new paranoia, black equality. To make matters worse, the Cornerstone Speech unleashed a "miserable heresy" when Stephens slandered God's name to condone slavery. In Townsend's opinion, the Cornerstone Speech had been a colossal failure that epitomized Stephens's poor judgment, weak rhetoric, and moral hypocrisy. Townsend claimed that Stephens had lost all credibility and influence in the aftermath of his infamous remarks.[6]

The Cornerstone Speech quickly became the favorite rhetorical arrow in the emancipationist's quiver. For example, the *Christian Recorder*, an African American newspaper published in Philadelphia, used Stephens's anti-secession Union Speech and the Cornerstone Speech to explain how a slaveowner conspiracy had resulted in the "horrors and desolations of war."[7] References to the speech can be found throughout Union Gen. Stephen Thomas's 1868 address delivered before a large crowd of Republican Party supporters in Norwich, Vermont. Invited to give some remarks in support of Ulysses S. Grant's presidential campaign, Thomas seemed primed to discredit remarks made by former Confederates. After thanking the locals for their dedicated support and personal sacrifice in support of restoring the Union, Thomas turned his attention toward explaining the war's causes. "Who inaugurated that rebellion?" asked Thomas. "Is it necessary for me to tell? . . . It was a premeditated plan on the part of one section of the country to break up this Government, and establish a great Southern Confederacy whose chief corner-stone should be perpetual slavery for all time to come?" Most biographies emphasized Stephens's humble origins, but Thomas recast him as a member of "a particular political class that inaugurated that rebellion." Whereas, Stephens had accused the North of violating the Constitution, Thomas accurately pointed out that he had once accused secession advocates of violating the Constitution by using secession to overturn Lincoln's lawful election. Thomas understood the need to defend the history of the Civil War from ex-Confederates, such as Stephens, who had launched a postbellum contest to frame the record from their perspective. Hence, the shots may have ceased and the flags had been furled, but a new campaign was needed to ensure that a true history of the war emerged victorious.[8]

Whereas many Republicans and African Americans feared that the Civil War had failed to change the southern society described in Stephens's Cornerstone Speech, northern laborers worried that growing white-supremacist rhetoric and the subordination of black workers threatened "the liberty of all other laboring men." Labor-friendly editors accused southern legislators of remaining wedded to the ideals expressed by Stephens. Without continued pressure applied by the federal government, the South would emerge from the Civil War and Reconstruction unchanged. While the Thirteenth Amendment had abolished slavery, the South had devised new forms of unfree labor because their devotion to white supremacy and notions of black inferiority made it impossible for ex-Confederates to either see black laborers as free men or competitors in the work force. Labor leaders expected that if the South successfully found new methods of controlling black labor, other state governments and private industry nationwide would endorse similar legislation to restrain all American workers. Capitalists across the nation might be inspired by the South's efforts to develop an unfree labor market that would enjoy the same level of control over its laborers as antebellum enslavers wielded over their enslaved property.[9]

By the early 1870s, emancipationists began criticizing Stephens's postbellum writings. Emancipationists accused Stephens of misrepresenting the Confederacy's origins to enhance the failed government's future legacy in American culture. If Stephens could convince American readers that the Confederacy died defending rights and ideas rather than slavery, future generations might embrace the "noble" rebellion free from the stain of white supremacy. When both volumes of Stephens's A Constitutional View were published, a writer using the pseudonym "Constitutionalist" penned a 179-page review of the ex-Confederate's history. "Constitutionalist" described Stephens as a "wise" and "good" man guilty of peddling "the delusion lying at the root of the great crime of the century." "Nothing," the critic claimed, "could have been more unfortunate for the future stability and peace of the country than Mr. Stephens's book." Stephens "knows that slavery is, and will be more odious to the civilized world . . . he seems to wish to shelter secessionists from the wrath to come of posterity, for warring to sustain the 'accursed institution,' and strives to present them as the champions of State Rights, rather than of slavery." The "Constitutionalist" accused Stephens of purposefully omitting any reference to his most explicit statement on slavery, the Cornerstone Speech. The critic accused Stephens of presenting lies when anyone could review secession convention debates and "find that nearly the whole of it is slavery, slavery, 'the nigger, the nigger,' from beginning to end." By offering such a far-ranging defense of secession that stretched across great lengths of time and space, Stephens, according to "Constitutionalist," had turned history into propaganda—a tactic that Lost Cause advocates mastered.[10]

Stephens's return to Congress helped emancipationists keep the Cornerstone Speech from disappearing from American public discourse. Although Stephens never again offered as explicit a defense of white supremacy as he did in Savannah, emancipationists never let the world forget that speech. As fierce debates raged in Congress over various civil rights bills, southern Democrats looked toward Stephens to help in their defense of white supremacy and local control that Reconstruction policies contested. Stephens largely disappointed Democrats because he generally softened his rhetoric, and, rather than appealing to white racial unity as a defense against black demands for civil equality, he framed the debate as a constitutional crisis. Stephens bored his colleagues with his extended lectures on the Constitution. They wanted him to be the firebrand who had rallied southern moderates in support of the CSA in the spring of 1861. Stephens never seized that mantle.

Whether in his postwar life Stephens wanted to soften his previous white-supremacist rhetoric did not matter because emancipationists in Congress used his historical record against him repeatedly to undermine southern opposition to Reconstruction. Emancipationists were insulted that Georgia had sent the former vice president of the CSA to Congress. Most thought that having served as vice-president should have disqualified Stephens from ever serving in federal office. To emancipationists, he became an important symbol of the postwar arrogance of the South, which failed to demonstrate any recognition of their recent catastrophic defeat. The fact that the South sent such a high-ranking member of their failed rebellion only supported emancipationist claims that the federal government had been too lenient on those traitors. Stephens's strained relationship among southern Democrats failed to attract any sympathy among emancipationists, who might have recognized him as a critical foe of the ultra-conservative Bourbon Democrats. Emancipationists exposed Stephens's complicated and misleading postbellum rhetoric as fraudulent and refused to allow him to escape from the Cornerstone Speech's long shadow.

Emancipationists in Congress took advantage of Stephens's presence among their legislative body to uncover the true motivations that lay at the center of white southern opposition to Reconstruction. Emancipationists firmly believed that, although slavery had ended, the white South remained as committed as ever to preserving white supremacy. Congressman Robert E. Elliott, a British-born and Eton College–educated African American Republican from South Carolina, was one of Stephens's most vocal critics. During the 1875 debates over the Civil Rights Act, several southern Congressmen made public appeals to their fellow members to oppose the legislation for the sake of preserving the South's existing social order. Stephens joined in opposition, but his speeches opposing the bill sounded more like a law school lecture than an impassioned plea to defend local control.[11]

Although several members of Congress had been far more personally insulting to black members of Congress, Elliott chose to focus his ire on Stephens because it was more important to discredit the former Confederate vice-president than rebuke lesser-known southern congressmen. Elliott reminded his fellow congress-men that they should not "take lessons in matters touching human rights or the joint relations of the State and National Governments" from someone who "has done his utmost to destroy" the United States. Whereas Stephens claimed that civil rights laws would disturb the cooperative relations that African Americans and white southerners enjoyed, Elliott declared that the supposed loyal slaves that Little Aleck referenced had lifted "their earnest prayers for the success" of the Union to remove themselves from the "burdens and oppressions" of their owners. "Even in the darkness of slavery," Elliott claimed, the enslaved had "kept their allegiance true to freedom and the Union." Only thirteen years had passed since Stephens had delivered the Cornerstone Speech. According to Elliott, Stephens had "shocked the civilized world by announcing the birth of a government which rested on human slavery as its cornerstone." Elliott described the Confederacy as a "pseudo government" whose foundations "rested on greed, pride and tyranny." Elliott wondered how Stephens felt today as he sat in Congress, engaged in a debate with a man whose race he had proclaimed as naturally inferior. Yet, Elliott told Stephens that freedpeople were "forgetful of their inhuman and brutalizing servitude at the South" as well as "their degradation and ostracism at the North." Elliott asked Stephens to "put away entirely the false and fatal theories which have so greatly marred an otherwise enviable record . . . and accept in its fullness" the expansion of American citizenship to those who only ask to enjoy the same rights and constitutional privileges that Stephens himself had spent a lifetime defending. After directing his remarks at Stephens, who quietly observed from a nearby seat, Elliott turned his attention to the other House members, who had gathered and offered a new cornerstone for American democracy. Elliott proclaimed: "Emancipation and Reconstruction have settled forever the political status of my race. . . . [N]ot only of the negro, but of all other classes of citizens who feel themselves discriminated against. . . . [B]uilding the grandest [nation] the world has ever seen, realizing the most sanguine expectations and the highest hopes of those who, in the name of equal, impartial and universal liberty, laid the foundation stones."[12] Elliott's address consciously repurposed Stephens's imagery to declare that universal liberty was the new foundation for "the grandest [nation] the world has ever seen." As Stephens listened to a black man lecture him on how emancipation and Reconstruction had transformed American society, the scene itself was evidence enough that some things had changed.[13]

Emancipationists struggled to cast Stephens's legacy and politics as being permanently wed to white supremacy because his actions defied simple explanations. At times, Republicans and northern Democrats praised Stephens's willingness to break with party or regional interests. In 1875, President Ulysses S. Grant asked Congress to pass legislation that would provide executive powers to resolve the racial violence and voter fraud that had impeded Louisiana's readmission to the Union. Much to the chagrin of southern Democrats, Stephens, who labeled himself as an Independent Democrat, supported the federal intervention bill. A New Orleans newspaper called Stephens "the Benedict Arnold of the South, as a man who, physically and morally rotten, like [William] Brownlow, has finally succeeded in sinking deeper into the Radical cesspool than even that festering specimen of malignant scalawaggery." The *Chicago Tribune* applauded Stephens's "honest vote in favor of restoring peace and order in Louisiana" and claimed that he had rejected the class of "fire-eaters" who had dominated the South before, during, and after the Civil War. Stephens's Cornerstone Speech, according to the *Tribune*, "exposed the real meaning of the Southern secession movement . . . [and] prevented the South from going into the War of the Rebellion under false pretenses." The newspaper claimed that southern secession zealots remembered how Stephens's explicit embrace of slavery as foundational had ruined the Confederacy's chances to receive additional foreign aid.[14] According to this idiosyncratic interpretation, Stephens had revealed the "actual character of the struggle" because he had never supported secession zealots. Due to his "solitary" vote for intervention, "the people of the United States will applaud his manliness and sterling courage which enabled him to stand true to his convictions of right in the face of Bourbon dough-faces . . . [this vote] will outlive him and stand to his credit in history."[15]

Emancipationists continued to expose Stephens as a dedicated white supremacist whose fight with Bourbon Democrats would prove short lived because ultimately, he and the Bourbon Democrats agreed on limiting federal intervention into southern racial affairs. Emancipationists expressed concern that the ideals and arrogance expressed in the Cornerstone Speech had not only inspired the rebellion but also had undermined Reconstruction and threatened the Civil War's legacy. As the presidential election of 1876 approached, Republican Party leaders, such as Edward Stoughton of Vermont, implored voters to recommit themselves to supporting the civil rights of African Americans in the South as a bulwark to prevent ex-Confederates from dominating the South, and the nation, forever. Stoughton, who had served as US ambassador to Russia during the Grant administration, argued that despite Confederate defeat, Republicans had surrendered "over the entire colored race to the mercies" of their former enslavers. Asking the crowd to imagine an America governed by ex-Confederate leaders, Stoughton unfolded a piece of paper from his pocket and began to read extracts from the Cornerstone Speech. Only "God in His mercy" had restored the Union so "the principles of eternal justice" could rise above "the cornerstone of the Confederacy" that had "crumbled away." Stoughton warned that ex-Confederates, generally, and Stephens, specifically, were poised to take control of the federal government if Democratic presidential candidate Samuel Tilden won the November election. Tilden, Stoughton warned, might help ex-Confederates repair their "crumbled" society.[16]

Emancipationists never forgot the Cornerstone Speech. After Stephens's death, they continued to remind Americans of its importance to the Civil War's legacy. They carried the speech around in their coat pockets ready to quote it whenever it became necessary to counter the Lost Cause's failure to acknowledge the CSA's racist origins. In an era when Lost Cause promoters and Stephens sought to minimize or explain away the speech's significance, emancipationists never let the Cornerstone Speech go.

CHAPTER FIVE

Different Things to Different People, 1883–1911

I n the decades that followed Alexander H. Stephens's death, his memory and how Americans remembered the Cornerstone Speech lacked consensus and meant different things to different people. Stephens's legacy included a lengthy political career and voluminous speeches and writings on a broad range of subjects. He defied simple characterizations and, like other major public figures, created a contradictory record. Therefore, some could applaud his intellect while others questioned if his dedication to white supremacy clouded his mental abilities. Some cast him as the "great commoner" while others placed him among the ranks of elite enslavers. Many Confederate veterans and historians hypothesized that the South would have been more successful had Stephens been selected as president instead of Jefferson Davis. Meanwhile, among the pantheon of Confederate figures memorialized across the South, Stephens occupied a secondary position. During the decades that preceded the Civil War semicentennial, multiple versions of Stephens were established, including the following: abused prisoner of war; great compromiser; white supremacist; Christian philanthropist; benevolent enslaver; prognosticator of southern race relations; great commoner; free-thinking political maverick; devotee of loyal slaves and freedpeople; intellectual statesman; revisionist historian. The Cornerstone Speech influenced the many facets of Stephens's legacy and, in some cases, helped contemporary figures find pragmatic or convenient meaning in those memories. In an era filled with racial violence, white-supremacist attitudes and public policies, and a vibrant public debate over the Civil War's history and memory, Stephens and the Cornerstone Speech remained at the core. How one chose to remember Stephens revealed much about one's stand on these issues at the dawn of the Jim Crow South.[1]

The creators of the Lost Cause waged what was, in effect, a second civil war to influence how Americans remembered the conflict. Alexander Stephens's postbellum writings provided an intellectual justification for secession that became part of the Lost Cause's central arguments. Col. Richard Henry Lee of Virginia delivered an address at the dedication of the Confederate monument at Old Chapel, in Clarke County, Virginia, where he explained this version of the causes of the Civil War.

> It is stated in books and papers that Southern children read and study that all the blood shedding and destruction of property of that conflict was because the South rebelled without cause against the best govern-ment the world ever saw; that although Southern soldiers were heroes in the field, skillfully massed and led, they and their leaders were rebels and traitors, who fought to overthrow the Union and to preserve human slavery, and that their defeat was necessary for free government and the welfare of the human family. . . . We did not fight to perpetuate human slavery, but for our rights and privileges under a government established over us by our father and in defense of our homes. . . . Those Southern States believed that the powers granted to the Federal Government had been used to their injury and oppression, and therefore they decided to abandon the Union. In taking this step slavery was not the cause, but the occasion, of the separation.[2]

Lee claimed that the federal government had placed limits on slavery that weakened "the integrity of the Constitution of the United States and the equality of the people of the Southern States." "Although African slavery was not the cause, it was the occasion of our war. It was useful and valuable in its day. It lifted a people who, in the land of their nativity, were savages, out of barbarism and animalism to such a plan of Christian civilization as to qualify them, in the judgement of the conquerors of the South, to participate in the government of the great republic. What a tribute to the much-abused South! What a monument to Southern Christian men and women!" Lee proclaimed that slavery resulted in one of the most successful Christian missionary efforts in history. Lee's argument leaned heavily on Stephens's postbellum writings, while ignoring the Cornerstone Speech.[3]

Lost Cause defenders promoted Stephens as a states' rights crusader. Adelia Dunovant, historian of the Texas Divisions of the United Daughters of the Confederacy, chided the history committee of the United Sons of Confederate Veterans for publishing a report admitting that the causes of the Civil War "were open to honest differences of opinion." Dunovant explained that the North had violated the US Constitution and that abolitionist lawlessness had "resulted in the most deplorable loss of life and in the virtual transfer of the wealth of the South to the North." The South seceded to uphold both biblical and constitutional values. To honor Union soldiers, Dunovant argued, "is impossible" because "two opposing principles cannot each be right." God had forbidden humanity from serving two masters, Dunovant continued, "it is Christlike to forgive wrong, but it is not Christlike to honor wrong. . . . If the combatants on the Northern side . . . were Christian like, why their continued denunciation and misrepresentation? If they were heroic and honest, why no truthful histories." Where could southerners find a truthful history of the Civil War? Dunovant pointed toward the writings of Alexander H. Stephens, whose interpretation of the war as a constitutional crisis put aside slavery and white supremacy as causal factors. They claimed that Stephens represented the "general character of the antebellum Southerners, who . . . [were] too high-minded to be governed by money considerations" and thus could not have been motivated to secede merely to protect their personal property. "The issue decided by the sword," wrote Stephens "was the attempt on the part of the Confederates to maintain this principle and right (State sovereignty) by physical force."[4]

During the early twentieth century, many remembered Alexander H. Stephens as a leader who tried to broker a compromise that might have avoided the conflict. Biographical sketches of him regularly appeared in newspapers across the nation. Most biographies stressed his humble origins, physical disabilities, and steadfast devotion to the Constitution. Stephens represented the prototypical reluctant Confederate, who only embraced secession when all other options had been exhausted. Consequently, none of these works devoted much attention to the Cornerstone Speech or acknowledged Stephens's important role in drafting the Confederate Constitution. The only mention of slavery in these works praised Stephens for his generous treatment of his enslaved laborers. Above all else, writers cast Stephens as an underappreciated moderate voice of reason, caught in the maelstrom of sectional strife.[5] The plaque installed in the Botanical Gardens in Washington, DC, told visitors that a mossy overcup oak had been planted by John J. Crittenden, a Kentucky politician who tried to broker a last-minute compromise on the eve of the Civil War, in order to "commemorate his unsuccessful efforts for peace between the North and South—between the Republicans on one side and Alexander Stephens of Georgia on the other."[6] Likewise, the *Catholic Advance* of Wichita, Kansas, remembered Stephens as a leader who denounced all forms of political extremism, including abolitionists, fire-eaters, and nativists.[7] Others applauded Stephens's willingness to resist demagogues, such as John C. Calhoun, whenever they threatened the Constitution.[8] Some listed Stephens as one of the most accomplished congressmen to have ever occupied the US Capitol.[9] A Chicago newspaper praised Stephens's wartime record of opposition to the policies of President Jefferson Davis and assured readers that Little Aleck treated everyone "high and low, black and white" equally.[10] Stephens had become an exemplar of political moderation that many felt was missing in early-twentieth-century American politics.

Simultaneously, some Americans continued to connect Stephens to various expressions of white supremacy. In 1902, Thomas Dixon Jr. author of an extremely popular racist novel, *The Leopard's Spots: A Romance of the White Man's Burden, 1865–1900*, and a college roommate of President Woodrow Wilson, toured the country delivering lectures on the past, present, and future of the Anglo-Saxon race in America. Enthusiastic crowds attended Dixon's lectures. During a Tampa, Florida, event, Dixon, a leading proponent of white supremacy, said "The Anglo-Saxon race . . . had reached its position of world-supremacy by backbone. Some men take a stand, right or wrong, and maintain it, refusing to be convinced that they are wrong." Before moving on to an extended discussion of Stephens's career, Dixon compared those who sought to end white-supremacist ideologies with ancient Jews who had initially welcomed Jesus Christ only to later demand his crucifixion. According to Dixon, Stephens had possessed the "backbone" needed to defend white supremacy. Dixon mourned that the nation had ignored Stephens's supposedly moderate stances but equated white supremacy with moderate politics because black inferiority had been divinely ordained. Plus, Dixon interpreted Stephens's disabilities as further proof of white supremacy, since he overcame them due to his Anglo-Saxon lineage. Dixon likely referenced Stephens because of the Cornerstone Speech's white-supremacist rhetoric.[11]

White southern men were not the only ones who used the Cornerstone Speech to remind Americans of white supremacy's enduring influence. In 1902, a situation erupted in Boston that elicited memories within the African American community of the nation's former fugitive slave laws. Monroe Rogers, a young black man and industrial worker from Durham, North Carolina, had fled to Boston to escape a lynch mob that falsely accused him of plotting to burn down the home of his girlfriend's white employer. When North Carolina authorities discovered Rogers's whereabouts, they petitioned Massachusetts Governor Winthrop M. Crane to return the young man to the Durham police department. Boston police arrested Rogers and held him as they considered North Carolina's extradition petition. When the governor ordered a hearing to determine Rogers's fate, Boston's black community organized to protest his potential deportation. They predicted that Durham police would surrender Rogers to the lynch mob once he returned to North Carolina. More than 32,000 black Bostonians gathered in protest of the extradition. During the hearing, several black leaders spoke in Rogers's defense.[12]

Rev. William Henry Scott of Boston Cavalry Baptist Church played a leading role in organizing the protests. He had firsthand experience as a fugitive slave. Born a slave in Virginia, Scott ran away during the Civil War and enlisted in the 12th Massachusetts Infantry Regiment. After the war, he graduated from the Howard University School of Law and returned to Virginia where he worked as a schoolteacher before an armed mob of white men forced him to flee the state. In 1892, after running a successful bookstore, Scott became pastor of Calvary Baptist Church in Boston. A few years later, Scott was among the founders of the Massachusetts Racial Protective Association and Niagara Movement. He was one of the most outspoken black advocates for civil equality in America. Monroe Rogers's situation reminded Scott of his encounters with southern lynch mobs. Georgia Gov. William J. Northen criticized Scott's interference and accused the revered preacher of leading a pack of "incendiary northern Negroes."[13]

On the second day of Monroe Rogers's extradition hearing, Scott delivered a powerful condemnation of America's long history of racial discrimination and violence. Scott blamed the American government for caving to the interests of the enslaver "oligarchy" and white supremacists who had defiled the nation. "Foreigners," observed Scott, "have regarded our form of government a paradox. It is crying freedom for all the oppressed nations of the earth; yet the most loyal and true citizen is denied an absolute existence." Scott's piercing knowledge of American history shone brightly as he referenced Thomas Jefferson's sexual liaisons with enslaved female laborers, Preston Brooks's violent assault on Sen. Charles Sumner, Supreme Court Justice Roger Taney's decision denying black people American citizenship, and the federal government's active role in helping southern enslavers retrieve runaway slaves. He reminded the Massachusetts judge that one of the North Carolina men seeking Rogers's return had been a postwar leader of the Ku Klux Klan. Scott described the South as a "land of anarchy" that undermined American democracy.[14]

As Scott's address exposed the underlying roots of these American injustices, he arrived at Alexander H. Stephens's Cornerstone Speech. Scott described Stephens as a false intellect whose white-supremacist statements proved that "slavery cursed the master as much as the slave." According to Scott, by slandering black people as naturally inferior, white supremacists like Stephens were in "violation of all of the higher laws of Christianity." Scott accused white supremacists like Stephens of peddling theories that Africans had been cursed by God and imposed them upon white people. Ideas of black subordination had left such an indelible stain of prejudice on the white southern mind that African Americans could hold out little hope of receiving justice from the descendants of enslavers. Scott warned the court that no African American could rightfully trust the southern judicial system. If Rogers were released into North Carolina custody, Scott guaranteed that he would die in the hands of an angry mob eager to vent its frustrations of black efforts to seek protection and justice from the law. North Carolina persisted with its extradition request. The governor of Massachusetts released Rogers into the Durham police's custody. Back in North Carolina, after months of sensational stories about the supposed horrors of his crime, Rogers was tried and convicted on a misdemeanor charge, attempted arson, and sentenced to ten years in the state penitentiary. North Carolina bragged that Monroe's "light sentence" had disproved Scott's claims that no black person could receive a fair trial in the South.[15]

The South's response to Monroe Rogers's extradition proved Reverend Scott's point that the white supremacy extolled by Alexander Stephens had cast a permanent shadow on present race relations. Stephens had claimed that slavery benefited the black race. Twentieth-century white supremacists argued that racial segregation and incarceration benefited the black race by protecting them from white aggressors and by removing criminals from their communities. Stephens argued that God had created black people as inferior examples of humanity. His descendants portrayed African Americans in subhuman terms that emphasized racist stereotypical behaviors, such as cannibalism and voo-doo spiritualism. Stephens vaguely predicted that enslaved laborers might one day qualify for the civil liberties enjoyed by white men. His descendants also claimed that African Americans might earn civil liberties if they met expecta-tions that were both purposely vague and unattainable. Stephens had declared that the Founding Fathers had erred when they proclaimed that all men were created equal. His descendants continued and enhanced public policies based on the assumed inequality of the races. Stephens depicted relations between enslavers and enslaved laborers as benevolent and reflective of a paternalistic bond forged through an imagined shared understanding of black inferiority. His descendants also viewed themselves as benevolent protectors whose sole crime was caring too much about the black race's present and future. Both Stephens and his descendants viewed anyone who tried to assist black southerners in their struggle for equality as interlopers incapable of managing black behavior. No one claimed to know and understand African Americans more than the white southerners, who relentlessly reinforced and defended white supremacy for generations. In 1902, Rev. William Scott interpreted the South's history as one continuous theme of racial oppression articulated by men such as Alexander Stephens and carried on by their damaged descendants. According to Scott, sectional reconciliation had re-energized white supremacy. "The Love Feast Period when the North and South were gathered around one large soup bowl, feeding with one large spoon to the martial music, 'I wish I were in Dixie'."[16]

White speakers often used Stephens as an example of Christian charity and philanthropy. At the 1902 Alabama Sunday School Convention meeting in Troy, Alabama, George Legare Comer, a local politician and educator, told the crowd a story from Stephens's youth to inspire them to donate additional funds for youth education initiatives. According to Comer, an unnamed woman had provided Stephens "food and shelter while he was a boy en route to an orphanage . . . [and] invaluable legal aid afterward when he became a man." Without her Christian charity, said Comer, Stephens would have never inspired so many others to engage in similar acts of kindness. Comer recalled that Stephens supported orphans and youth education for the rest of his life. His actions had inspired others, especially the United Daughters of the Confederacy, to fund similar causes.[17]

Efforts to erect a statue honoring Alexander Stephens had been afoot since the early 1890s. At that time, heritage organizations in Atlanta had successfully raised funds to commission statues to honor Benjamin H. Hill, a Civil War–era politician, and Henry Grady, a newspaper editor and New South proponent. Supporters of Stephens in Augusta unsuccessfully lobbied various Atlanta organizations to launch a fundraising campaign to honor Little Aleck with a statue.[18]

Those who sought to create a lasting memorial in honor of Stephens's life turned their attention toward Liberty Hall in Crawfordville, Georgia. The site proved to be the perfect place to celebrate Stephens's rags-to-riches story. In 1812, Stephens had been born about two miles from Liberty Hall. By age fourteen, Stephens was an orphan who depended on the charity of family and friends. At that time, Stephens lost ownership of the property, as it passed into the hands of some distant relatives. In 1845, Stephens purchased the property and began modest renovations to the house and grounds. Between 1872 and 1875, Stephens tore down most of the original home, except for a pair of rooms that housed his library and temporary living quarters, and built the extant two-story building known as Liberty Hall. In 1883, following Stephens's death, the house and surrounding property passed into the hands of his extended family, who turned it into a profitable boarding house. Originally, Stephens's family chose to bury his remains at Oakland Cemetery in Atlanta. Two years later, the family reinterred Stephens's remains next to the remains of his beloved brother, Linton Stephens, who had died in 1872, in a small cemetery located in front of Liberty Hall. Reportedly, descendants kept Stephens's bedroom precisely as it had looked at the time of his death. Even with the home's numerous tenants,

Liberty Hall gradually became a living memorial, as items that had belonged to Stephens were either preserved or restored to be displayed on site. Located a short distance from the local rail depot, Crawfordville visitors often took advantage of their train stopping for fuel and water to make a short pilgrimage to the home of the only vice-president of the Confederate States of America.[19]

In the decades that followed Stephens's death, many remembered him as the "Great Commoner" because of his humble origins. Liberty Hall represented the best portions of Stephens's life that his admirers wanted the world to see. The large two-story home, surrounded by extensive grounds, orchards, and fields evidenced just how far the impoverished Stephens had ascended despite his physical ailments. Stephens, however, was not Liberty Hall's sole occupant. Before the Civil War, Stephens owned thirty-four black enslaved laborers. After the war, most of Stephens's former enslaved laborers remained on the property employed as wage laborers. According to all surviving accounts, Stephens had an amicable relationship with the black families at Liberty Hall. Most of those families chose to take his surname following emancipation. Many remained on the property long after Stephens died, thanks to the terms of his will. A small cemetery on the property contains the remains of the many enslaved and freedpersons who lived at Liberty Hall.[20]

Defenders of Stephens's reputation often refer to his close relationship with Harry and Eliza Stephens as evidence of his benevolence. Born into slavery and later acquired by Stephens, Harry Stephens became the most trusted black man at Liberty Hall. During Stephens's prolonged absences, Harry assisted in the management of the plantation, greeted visitors, and extended to them the comforts that Liberty Hall offered. Meanwhile, Eliza Stephens, Harry's wife, performed a wide variety of domestic duties, including cooking and cleaning and taking care of the property's white and black family members and guests. The married couple lived with their children in a modest two-room cabin located near Liberty Hall. Visitors often commented that Harry and Eliza "ruled the domestic life at Liberty Hall."[21]

Surviving evidence suggests that Alexander Stephens might have been among a rare group of enslavers who treated their black slaves with as much sympathy as could be generated within an inhumane institution, and those seeking to cleanse the stain of slavery from the Confederate States of America and its leaders and followers often celebrated Harry and Eliza Stephens as model examples of the loyal slave. In the years following Stephens's death, Lost Cause memorialists labored to transform Liberty Hall into a Confederate shrine. Memorialists seeking to turn Liberty Hall into a hallowed Lost Cause commemorative landscape simultaneously diminished, distorted, and ignored Alexander Stephens's white-supremacist rhetoric.[22]

One month after Stephens's death, the Stephens Memorial Association formed to raise funds to erect a statue of him at Liberty Hall. They planned to place the monument next to Stephens's grave. The memorial association benefited from support received by Mary Gay of Decatur, Georgia. After the Civil War, Gay played an instrumental role in creating Confederate cemeteries across the state. She raised thousands of dollars to create new Confederate cemeteries that contained the remains of hundreds of unknown soldiers who perished in battlefields and hospitals throughout Georgia. Fundraising for the Stephens memorial coincided with Gay's publication of her wartime memoir, *Life in Dixie During the War.* The book contains a harrowing first-person account of the Battle of Atlanta as well as vivid descriptions of the Confederate home front and various hospitals. Gay's endorsement of the Stephens monument helped to shroud Stephens further in the cloak of Lost Cause sentimentalism. Over the course of a decade, with Gay's assistance, the association raised over $2,200 in small individual donations. After a short search, the association hired sculptor Theodore Markwalter of Augusta to create the monument. Markwalter, a German-born immigrant and Confederate veteran, had become a leading sculptor of Confederate monuments. During the late 1870s, Markwalter created some of the first Confederate memorials to be erected across Georgia.[23]

With funds in hand, the Stephens Memorial Association had to decide what kind of monument would best represent Alexander Stephens's legacy. Association members engaged in a lively debate over whether to depict Stephens as a man "in his prime" or an aging statesman confined to a wheelchair. Members who advocated for the wheelchair-bound Stephens argued that his disabilities only accentuated his reputation as the "Great Commoner." Stephens's physician, C. A. Beasley, shared with the committee what he claimed to be Stephens's own opinions on his physical appearance. According to Beasley, Stephens "disliked to have his picture taken as a cripple, for he hated to go down to the memory of his fellow men as a maimed, crippled public man." Stephens rejected "people's pity" and preferred that he "be remembered—at his best." Markwalter's sculpture attempted to capture Stephens's physical prowess as an orator. Although physical descriptions of Stephens tended to emphasize his slender build and low body weight, Stephens's height, at five foot, seven inches, would have been average among American men at that time. Markwalter's carving depicts Stephens standing upright with his left hand resting on a stack of books atop a small table as his right-hand gestures across his midriff, as if the artist has frozen his body mid-sentence. Markwalter based his work on a late 1850s engraving created by Mathew Brady that Stephens had purchased while in Congress. Supposedly, Stephens hired Brady to celebrate what he considered to be one of his greatest oratorical triumphs. Known as the *Georgia and Ohio Again* speech, in 1855, Stephens had engaged in a debate with Ohio Congressman Lewis D. Campbell. The Ohio congressman had made some disparaging remarks about the declining future of slavery in the South. Campbell had predicted the Cotton Kingdom's future collapse. Intent on disproving Campbell's observations, Stephens exhausted himself preparing detailed tables and charts to demonstrate the vibrancy and sustainability of slavery and cotton. He ultimately demonstrated that, despite having less than half of Ohio's population, Georgia's annual agricultural products exceeded those of the Buckeye state by over $250,000. Stephens later told his biographer, Henry Cleveland, that the *Georgia and Ohio Again* speech had been his most impassioned speech.[24]

The first statue erected in honor of Alexander Stephens celebrated his *Georgia and Ohio Again* speech and ignored the Cornerstone Speech. The former consisted of an impassioned defense of antebellum slavery while the latter declared white supremacy to be the cornerstone of the Confederate States of America and southern civilization. The Lost Cause impulse to include one and disregard the other had much to do with how the commemoration treated plantation life at Liberty Hall. News reports of the statue included numerous recollections of faithful slaves whose loyalties remained steadfast after emancipation and beyond their former enslaver's natural life. According to an Atlanta reporter, Eliza Stephens, known locally as Old Aunt 'Liza, "stands half the day beside the marble image of 'Marse Alec,' and nobody ever asks her why the corner of her big red handkerchief is ever moist, while standing on that particular spot 'whar Marse Alec's eyes seem to look down sorter sad, like.'" The reporter claimed that Eliza "used to wait upon her owner in the time of slavery" with "the love of a mother." After emancipation, Eliza chose to remain at Liberty Hall so that she could continue to care for her former "master." As Eliza stood in "de shadder of Marse Alec's monument," the reporter claimed that her "big red handkerchief makes frequent visits to her tearful eyes with the statue there to make those recollections all the more vivid."[25]

Lost Cause promoters stressed the familial relations between Stephens and his enslaved house servants, Eliza and Harry. Memorialists cast Eliza as Stephens's adoptive mother and her husband, Harry, as his "ministering brother." Based on the writings of Lost Cause proponents, if readers did not know Harry's complete story, they would have thought that he had been born a free man who enjoyed the same civil rights and privileges as his white owner. Writers emphasized that Harry had complete authority in managing Stephens's estate during the owner's numerous absences. Like his owner, Harry earned a reputation for being "thrifty," having saved more than twenty thousand dollars in wages. When Harry died of typhoid in 1881, Stephens placed an obituary in an Atlanta newspaper that commemorated his "faithful body servant" as an "obedient, trustworthy, and faithful" slave and an "orderly, industrious, respectful in demeanor, and blameless in conduct" freedman. The obituary's tone cemented Harry's memory as the quintessential loyal slave who even in freedom remained in his owner's service. Lost Cause writers turned stories such as Harry's into representative examples of the master-slave relationship. Writers made no effort to include stories of other enslaved laborers who were held in bondage at Liberty Hall. Writers accepted without further examination that Harry and Eliza's story was accurate and representative of all enslaved laborers who toiled under Alexander Stephens's ownership. Loyal slave narratives evolved into a body of evidence that, according to Lost Cause adherents, proved that slavery had been a benevolent, charitable, and humane institution that benefited everyone's interests. Back in 1861, Stephens had made this exact argument in the Cornerstone Speech. Three decades later, Lost Cause supporters continued to echo the speech's central ideas while ignoring its explanations for secession. The Lost Cause had fashioned a revisionist history that distorted Alexander Stephens.[26]

The reporter's description of the eternal loyalties of Stephens's former enslaved laborers echoed how the Lost Cause and Stephens himself interpreted slavery. Stephens had defended slavery because black inferiority had required white men to provide for the weaker race. He had predicted that without slavery the black race would vanish from the Earth. He had urged enslavers to treat their black laborers humanely and provide for their spiritual needs, but never used his full influence as a leading statesman to improve the lives of black enslaved laborers beyond those he and his family owned. Lost Cause proponents had tried to diminish slavery's role in the birth of the Confederacy by claiming that southern enslavers had planned to abolish the institution even if the war's outcome had not forced them to do so. Accounts of Liberty Hall's enslaved laborers obscured the realities of American slavery by ignoring the fact that even the most benevolent enslaver deprived their human property of liberty, personal choice, and the enjoyment of the fruits of their labor. Nor did any Confederate leader seriously consider a time when the South's economy would not depend on slave labor. Lost Cause promoters celebrated Stephens as "the defender of civil and religious liberty" because their white-supremacist beliefs defined those rights as the exclusive domain of white men. Owning slaves, in their view, evidenced Stephens's benevolent attitude toward uplifting a divinely inferior race in the name of Christian charity and human philanthropy. Without mentioning the Cornerstone Speech, Lost Cause advocates confirmed that the ideals of white supremacy had survived Confederate defeat and emancipation to help white southerners to justify modern society's race problem.[27]

After months of planning and advertising, on May 24, 1893, the Stephens Memorial Association officially dedicated the Alexander H. Stephens statue in a ceremony attended by more than two thousand visitors. Mary Carry, Stephens's grand-niece, unveiled the large granite monument. Although the service included many individuals who knew and admired Stephens, several prominent Georgia leaders missed the event, including Senators Joseph E. Brown and John B. Gordon. Few prominent Democratic Party members attended the dedication. During his postbellum political career, Stephens had alienated many Georgia Democrats and former Confederate leaders. Shortly before his death, for example, Stephens accused former Confederate Gen. John B. Gordon of abusing the convict-lease system. Earlier, Stephens blasted Joseph E. Brown, and his family, for using their political clout to profit from the private lease of the state-owned Western and Atlantic Railroad. Personal and political rivalries prevented some Lost Cause figures, such as Brown and Gordon, from lending their voices to honor the vice-president of the Confederate States of America's memory.[28]

The dedication event suffered from poor timing as an extended tour of the last remains of President Jefferson Davis, who died in 1889, attracted significant attention. Davis had passed away and was originally interred in New Orleans. Richmond, Virginia, and many other southern cities, lobbied Davis's widow, Varina Davis, to host his final resting place. After several years of fundraising and lobbying, the Davis family agreed to reinter Jefferson Davis's remains in Richmond. Four years after his death, Davis's casket was carried on board a special train and displayed in various cities along the route from New Orleans to Richmond. At the time of the Stephens's monument dedication, Davis's casket was on display at the Alabama State Capitol, which had also served as the first capital of the Confederate States of America. At each stop along the multi-state procession, former Confederate leaders and contemporary southern dignitaries honored Davis. Given the opportunity to decide whether to attend the Stephens statue dedication or the Davis processional, most Lost Cause figures chose Jefferson Davis.[29]

Newspapers from New York to Los Angeles reprinted reports of Stephens and Davis memorials. The celebrations drew little commentary. Only a handful of Republican Party newspapers criticized the memorials. The *Omaha Daily Bee* called it "preposterous to assume that the name of Jefferson Davis will occupy in history an equally honorable place with those of Lincoln and Grant." Edward Rosewater, the *Omaha Daily Bee's* renowned Republican editor, urged Americans to remember what the Union had achieved in victory and the threat that men like Davis and Stephens had posed to the nation.[30] The *Seattle Post-Intelligencer* declared that recent Confederate memorials "will be viewed with profound regret, because they are avowedly intended to impress the growing generation of the youth of the South that secession was right" and that the North started the war.[31]

A few weeks after the statue dedication ceremony, communities across the nation assembled to mark Decoration Day, an event in which locals decorated the graves of their Civil War dead. Such ceremonies provided ample opportunities for northern communities to challenge the Lost Cause. In Middlebury, Vermont, former Vermont Gov. William Dillingham's keynote speech accused antebellum southern enslavers of violating "the right of individual liberty." Rather than promote the ideals of American democracy, southern enslavers "assailed" those "principles" when they attempted to use secession to impose "absolutism" so that slavery would be preserved. Dillingham immediately turned his attention to the Cornerstone Speech as the single greatest piece of evidence that contradicts Lost Cause revisionist histories of the war. "Although it had been often maintained that the Rebellion did not grow out of slavery," commented Dillingham, "Alexander H. Stephens, vice-president of the Confederate States, had himself proclaimed that that was the very cause and reason for the Rebellion." According to Dillingham, by trying to preserve the "subordinate" position of enslaved laborers the Confederacy chose to "assault . . . the individual liberty of man that the soldiers of the North . . . had fought so long and so bravely and with so many and so great sacrifices, to put an end to the slavery idea forever." Dillingham questioned the veracity of the historical accounts that leavened most of the Lost Cause's ideology. Those that celebrated Stephens and the Confederacy, Dillingham argued, ignored the serious threat that the Confederacy posed to the future of American democracy and civil liberties.[32]

In Great Bend, Kansas, members of the Sons of Union Veterans and Grand Army of the Republic organized a large program to honor their Union war dead. The event's first speaker urged Americans to remember the sacrifices of the Union war dead, whose actions had saved the Union from destruction and preserved American democracy. Republican politician George L. Douglass closed the ceremony with a detailed account of the Civil War's causes. He described secession as a desperate, undemocratic plot hatched by enslavers after their efforts to expand slavery failed. Douglass reminded the audience that those who wondered why the Confederacy tried to leave the Union only had to read Alexander H. Stephens's Cornerstone Speech, which "proclaimed that slavery was to be the chief cornerstone." He implored the audience to study history so that they could refute the Lost Cause's false narratives. Douglass mourned a prospective future when America might elevate the deeds of the Confederate dead above their Union counterparts.[33]

While some northern leaders criticized the growing number of Confederate memorials and various aspects of Lost Cause historical revisionism, most newspapers accepted and helped promote the South's interests. Across the nation, writers presented Stephens and Davis as model examples of statesmanship, leadership, and citizenship. Many articles stressed their moral character and religious devotion. Others interpreted Confederate memorials as an opportunity to heal sectional wounds while promoting the study of history, something that many considered critical to preserving American democracy.[34]

In many places across the nation, Stephens's revisionist legacy as an idealistic enslaver and defender of civil and religious liberty meshed with stories of white southern men murdering African Americans. Americans did not need to look back to slavery and the Civil War to find stories of racial violence. In May 1893, as newspapers commented on events honoring notable Confederate leaders, they also reported on a growing number of lynching tragedies. News of the Stephens statue dedication ceremony published in the *Staunton Spectator and General Advertiser*, for example, was followed by a separate article on a recent lynching in Smyth County, Virginia. George Halsey, a black man, had been accused of raping a white woman near Marion, Virginia. The paper provided a detailed account of the woman's injuries and claimed that "such heinous outrages are becoming fearfully common." Local white men worried that area courts might fail to deliver justice commiserate with Halsey's supposed crimes. Hours after his arrest and confinement in the county jail, a white mob stormed his cell and hanged "him to a tree on the outskirts of the town [and] fired more than one hundred bullets into his body."[35] More than one dozen lynchings were reported in May 1893 alone. Newspaper editors never connected the wave of racial violence to the long history of racial violence and oppression in America represented by the many Confederate leaders who were being honored at that time. However, reports of lynchings and accounts of Confederate memorials shared a common theme. Both events led many Americans to long for a mythical past when benevolent enslavers, such as Alexander H. Stephens, and loyal enslaved laborers, such as Harry Stephens, peacefully coexisted under the guidance of a social order founded upon white supremacy and black inferiority. As fears of black-on-white violence spread and actual episodes of white-on-black extralegal murder increased, Stephens's Cornerstone Speech and other writings produced by antebellum white supremacists became self-fulfilling prophecies that had predicted the level of racial violence that would follow emancipation. This combination of mythical history and self-fulfilling prophecy motivated white southern men to enact stronger Jim Crow laws, supposedly to protect society from an inferior race. From the perspective of Stephens, a view gleaned from his voluminous writings, secession, like subsequent Jim Crow laws, had been necessary to defend the rights of a superior race that depended on their ability to control enslaved black laborers. The continuity of white supremacy's influence on the minds of white southern men had limited the potential for change in the region. Ultimately, the threat of change might have been their greatest fear.[36]

Proposals for an additional Alexander Stephens statue arose at the turn of the twentieth century when Georgia considered placing his likeness at Statuary Hall in the US Capitol. Since 1864, Congress had allowed each state to donate up to two statues to be displayed at Statuary Hall that represented major figures in a state's history. For decades, Georgia failed to raise the funds necessary to commission, transport, and donate the statues. Many states had been slow to place statues at the capitol.[37] In 1902, Georgia Gov. Allen D. Candler formed a committee within the state legislature to solicit and review nominations for the erection of two statues of prominent Georgians at the US Capitol. The committee recommended Alexander H. Stephens and Crawford Long, a noted nineteenth-century surgeon. Both men appeared to be odd choices for this honor. Stephens was an intellectual statesman and Long was a pioneering physician. Unlike many honored at Statuary Hall, neither of these men were among America's Founding Fathers nor combat leaders. Also, Long's inclusion proved controversial, because some physicians contested the claim that the Georgian surgeon had performed the first surgical procedure using anesthesia. Although Stephens spent many years in Congress, the nominating committee noted that "no great deed of legislation or administration can be assigned to his initiative or execution."[38]

Stephens appealed to many Georgia legislators because of his rags-to-riches story of overcoming family tragedy and physical disabilities, as well as his work as a postbellum historian of the American Civil War. "As a historian," declared the *Atlanta Constitution*, "he seized and enjoyed a great and novel opportunity. The causes, events, and resultants of the unique civil 'war between the states' found in him a delineator of rare truthfulness, impartiality, and fullness of knowledge." Stephens's writings defended the Confederacy's account of secession and explained how the South's defeat had regrettably changed postbellum America. He provided readers with a firsthand account of the Confederacy's actions and motivations. The nominating committee ignored obvious contradictions that existed between Stephens's postbellum writings and his wartime rhetoric. Whereas his history of the "war between the states" tried to reconcile the Confederacy's defense of states-rights with its desire to protect slavery, the Cornerstone Speech centered the rebellion on a foundation built upon slavery and white supremacy. The statue committee never directly addressed Stephens's record on slavery and white supremacy, but by endorsing his historical writings, its members implicitly acknowledged that the statue would represent Lost Cause ideology. While Stephens may have lacked the military credentials or legislative accomplishments that others honored at Statuary Hall possessed, his defense and promotion of the Lost Cause made him an attractive candidate for inclusion at a time when many southerners shared his version of the past.[39]

As Georgia began a modest fundraising campaign for the Stephens statue, John E. Bruce, an African American civil rights activist and newspaper editor, chastised their choice. Georgia had explained that Stephens deserved to be recognized because of his superior intellect. Bruce pointed out the danger of honoring former Confederate leaders as intellectuals. According to Bruce, Southern writers, such as Stephens, "assumed to be endowed with a superior kind of wisdom" and "thank[ed] God that they are not as obtuse in their intellectuals as the Yankees, who in their superior judgment, have committed the unpardonable sin by admitting that the negro is not only a man, but that he is also a citizen." Bruce placed Stephens in the long tradition of southern white supremacists who had used their proximity to and ownership of enslaved laborers to declare some special understanding of the nation's "negro problem." According to Bruce, Stephens's infamous Cornerstone Speech had "set the pace" within this tradition by declaring that the depths to which white southern men were willing to go to defend the civilization that white supremacy had created. Stephens and others had transformed black inferiority into a self-serving "philosophical and moral truth" that only southern enslavers were mentally equipped to understand. Bruce asked white Americans to choose between Stephens's false truths and the "true expression of the sentiments of the American people on the equality of man" laid out in the Declaration of Independence. He urged Americans to reject depictions of Stephens as a moderate compromiser who only reluctantly joined the Confederate fray. According to Bruce, Stephens "did nothing to save the Union when treason wound its slimy form around the altar of liberty." The Confederacy could only muster a "feeble and futile" effort to defend white supremacy because the wartime actions of enslaved laborers and freedpeople proved without a doubt that they were "much more entitled to citizenship" than white southern men. The Confederacy's foundation rested upon a series of falsehoods fostered by intellectual statesmen such as Stephens. Unfortunately, said Bruce, the collapse of slavery had failed to erode white supremacy. The Confederacy's defeat left the region in the hands of white men who passed new laws intended to reinforce the truths that Stephens espoused despite abundant evidence that rejected black inferiority.[40]

During the early twentieth century, a debate raged in Congress over whether statues honoring former Confederate leaders would be accepted in Statuary

Hall. The 1909 addition of Gen. Robert E. Lee of Virginia sparked heated debate within Congress over whether former Confederate leaders should be included in this national hall of fame. The sight of Lee's statue standing beside a statue of George Washington upset many Republicans, who accused the South of using the hall to celebrate the vanquished Confederate States of America. One Republican Senator referred to Lee's statue as a "desecration." Another said, "I think it is a disgrace. He was a traitor to his country, and I will not sanction an official honor for a traitor." Kansas Republicans threatened to erect a statue of abolitionist John Brown. Members of the Grand Army of the Republic in Chicago, a Union Army veterans' organization, exclaimed that the statue went "against the honor and integrity of veterans who nobly gave up life and home to preserve the country Robert E. Lee tried to destroy."[41] A divided Republican Party failed to prevent the installation of the Lee statue. Ultimately, Congress decided it would not interfere with each state's choices.

Congress's capitulation opened the door for the installation of a wave of Confederate statues at the US Capitol. Fundraising for the proposed Alexander H. Stephens statue failed in part due to the enormous production and cost of Confederate monuments across Georgia during the first quarter of the twentieth century. In addition, by the early 1910s, heritage organizations, such as the United Daughters of the Confederacy, had committed enormous resources and attention to the development of a permanent Confederate memorial carving on the face of Stone Mountain. Plans for the carving were revised several times before planners decided that the memorial should feature the likenesses of Jefferson Davis, Robert E. Lee, and Stonewall Jackson on horseback leading a legion of Confederate soldiers into battle. Planners never seriously considered including Stephens, despite his popularity among white Georgians. Stephens's lack of military service before, during, or after the Civil War likely prevented his inclusion on Stone Mountain. Those who supported the commission of a Stephens monument would have to wait until the early 1920s before their efforts gained traction.[42]

Unable to raise funds for a Stephens statue, the Georgia General Assembly found another means to honor Alexander H. Stephens. In 1905, legislators created eight new counties across the state. Seven of the eight counties would be named in honor of men associated with the Confederate States of America. Those honored included President Jefferson Davis and Sen. Robert Toombs, Stephens's best friend. This marked Georgia's first wave of naming or renaming counties in honor of Confederate leaders. Previously, the sole county named in honor of a Confederate leader had been Bartow County, which had been changed from Cass County during the war in honor of fallen Confederate Col. Francis S. Bartow of Savannah. In the forty years that followed the Civil

War, no additional counties were named in honor of Confederate leaders. The creation of new counties was commonplace in Georgia. Eventually, the state comprised 159 counties, more than any state except for Texas. Traditionally, Georgia's government believed that citizens should have close access to local officials. Georgia officials believed that the creation of new smaller counties produced a more democratic government.[43]

One of the new counties was in the northeastern corner of the state that had previously been part of Stephens's congressional district. Like Stephens, the mountainous region had a reputation for expressing dissent against the state's ruling Democratic Party. Naming the county in honor of Stephens was the popular choice. Debate over the proposed naming of the county offered legislators an opportunity to reflect on Stephens's place in history. Several lawmakers proudly recalled that they had known Stephens personally and testified that he was an honorable man worthy of recognition. They lauded Stephens as a voice of reason during a tumultuous period of Georgia history. Several recognized that Stephens had correctly predicted that secession would instigate a devastating war that would strip the South of its wealth and national power. In 1861, like Stephens, most white men from the north Georgia mountains had opposed secession. After the war, many of those same men cast ballots in support of Stephens's Independent Party efforts to challenge Democratic Party rule. Mostly, they remembered Stephens as a principled statesman and intellectual who had served as the only vice-president in the Confederate States of America's brief history. Neither the Cornerstone Speech nor his central role in the writing of the Confederate Constitution were mentioned.[44]

As various legislators expressed support for the bill to name a new county in honor of Stephens, Rep. Martin V. Calvin of Augusta mourned the poor state of history in America. Calvin complained that northern writers had ignored the "the lives of the southerners who made their section more than notable and the union great." Writers had produced favorable biographies of Abraham Lincoln, Charles Sumner, and William Seward that "exploited" southern and northern youth and purposely omitted tales of the "great men" of the South, such as Stephens, who possessed "high character" and "patriotism." Calvin believed that more southern white men should write American history as Stephens had done. Without those histories, erecting memorials and naming places in their honor would have to suffice as a means of keeping their memory alive. Many white southern men shared Calvin's criticism. They turned to the production and dedication of Confederate monuments to correct what they perceived to be an absence of southern history in America's historical memory.[45]

Efforts to honor Stephens's memory stirred up lingering disagreements over his role in the rise and fall of the Confederate States of America. In the decades that followed the Civil War, Stephens had become a favorite example of southern wisdom and moderation because of his initial opposition to secession. Those who sought to elevate Stephens to the role of an underappreciated voice of reason tended to reference his anti-secession Union Speech delivered before the Georgia legislature in November of 1860 as evidence of his sage prognostic abilities. Most articles about Stephens produced by northern writers possessed a common theme that events might have happened differently had the South listened to Stephens. He became one of the great "what might have been" stories of American lore.[46]

Stephens became a symbol for the internal divisions that undermined the Confederate government. Some writers pointed to Stephens's turbulent relationship with Jefferson Davis as one major factor in the Confederacy's demise. In 1905, a *Washington Post* article penned by an unknown writer who used the pseudonym of Savoyard offered a favorable account of Stephens's wartime record. Savoyard claimed that Davis lacked the necessary talents to administer the Confederate government. He picked the wrong men to serve in specific cabinet positions and had equally poor luck in judging the capabilities of his commanding officers. Conversely, Stephens, a leader known for his moderate stances and intellectual acumen, struggled to have his voice heard as Davis ignored his counsel. Specifically, Davis chose to keep millions of bales of cotton off the international market following secession despite Stephens's recommendation to stuff the treasury before the Union blockade organized. Davis also decided to fire on Fort Sumter without seeking Stephens's advice. Plus, according to Savoyard, Stephens warned Davis that Confederate conscription and impressment policies would lower the fledgling nation's morale. Thanks to Davis's mismanagement, Savoyard believed that the Confederacy would have failed even without a war due to his inadequacies. Savoyard also argued that the Civil War would have turned out quite differently had all sides devoted more attention to leaders such as Alexander Stephens. Likewise, the *Weekly Pioneer-Times* of Deadwood, South Dakota, speculated that "there were not a few who thought that [Stephens] more conciliatory methods and sounder practical judgment would have been better calculated to pilot the secession movement to success than the arbitrary and unyielding spirit of Jefferson Davis."[47]

Many Americans remembered Stephens's role in the Confederate government far more favorably than they recollected Jefferson Davis's performance. Stephens had benefited from decades of sympathetic and revisionist media coverage that emphasized his intellect, honesty, and patriotism and ignored his white-supremacist rhetoric. By the early twentieth century, however, many Americans believed that the Confederacy had chosen the wrong man to lead their rebellion.[48]

Stephens's popularity surged across the nation as memorials tended to exaggerate his character and role in the Confederate government. In 1905, an Atlanta newspaper published a retrospective article that highlighted various aspects of postbellum life in the booming railroad city. The publication memorialized Alexander Stephens's role in the fusion of two local newspapers to form the Atlanta Constitution—the South's largest newspaper. The newspaper, like Stephens, had a complicated relationship with the Lost Cause. It helped shape the Lost Cause by publishing numerous favorable accounts of the rise and fall of the Confederacy and the supposed horrors of Reconstruction. The Atlanta Constitution regularly referred to Reconstruction as Georgia's "darkest hour." The paper covered every major Confederate veteran reunion and devoted special attention to the erection of monuments and memorials as well as the passing of various anniversaries and memorial days. Its editors openly endorsed white supremacy and encouraged white-on-black extralegal violence as a means of demonstrating white authority. Henry Grady, the newspaper's famous editor and co-owner, once wrote: "the supremacy of the white race of the South must be maintained forever, and the domination of the negro race resisted at all points and at all hazards, because the white race is the superior race."[49]

The Atlanta Constitution also promoted a new vision for the South that contrasted with many Lost Cause proponents. Published in a city that claimed to be the epicenter of postbellum southern economic development, the newspaper urged southerners to embrace a "New South," where industry and capital investment would supplant agriculture to become a driving force for change. The Atlanta Constitution stood firmly with one foot entrenched in the region's Confederate past and one foot seeking a new foundation that would provide renewed prosperity for southern white men.[50]

In addition to Henry Grady, whom the newspaper cast as a representative example of the blending of old and new, the Atlanta Constitution lionized Alexander Stephens as a historical figure worthy of contemporary emulation. One story by Clark Howell, owner and editor of the paper, compared Stephens's triumph over his physical disabilities to Atlanta's postwar resurgence following the city's mass destruction. Stephens possessed "the intellect of a giant" and was "the embodiment of the genius of constructive statecraft." Despite his impairments, Stephens had earned the moniker "the brains of the Confederacy." Unlike so many other former Confederates, according to the newspaper, Stephens had remained "the faithful servant of his people in the bitter days of the south's reconstructive agonies." Stephens proved willing to sacrifice his popularity by defending positions taken "in the face of real dangers" to protect the South's interests.[51]

This *Atlanta Constitution* article reflects how revisionist interpretations of Stephens's life had emerged as an orthodox history of the Civil War era. Throughout his antebellum political career, Stephens had sided with national positions on issues that led many southerners to question his loyalty to the region. During Reconstruction, unlike many conservative Democrats, Stephens had urged the Democratic Party to court black voters openly so that an environment of justice could overcome the period's racial violence. He imagined the postbellum Democratic Party preserving the paternalistic role once held by enslavers in overseeing the lives of freedpeople. Stephens spent most of that period fighting against many of the former Confederates, whose actions and words helped define Lost Cause interpretations of the war. Also, the paper glossed over Stephens's accusations that Grady's New South agenda was a plot to surrender the region's interests to northern capitalists. Stephens worried that New South boosters might sacrifice laws and customs that had preserved white supremacy for the sake of economic development. In the decades that followed Stephens's death, memories of him evolved, as he emerged as a symbol of the kind of national leader needed during a time of national reconciliation—intelligent, reserved, honest, pragmatic, but committed to preserving white supremacy.[52]

Lost Cause supporters wanted the nation to recommit to "the natural inferiority of the Negro race" as a matter of public policy and historical truth. Among Lost Cause proponents were men whose views differed, and like Alexander Stephens, some tried to reconcile white-supremacist assertions of black inferiority with a belief that black inferiority was not eternal. Unlike Stephens, these individuals believed that white supremacy was not an indelible circumstance granted for all time to white southern men. Instead, expressions of white supremacy recognized the reality of black life in America before and after emancipation. Ultimately, these men argued that it was possible that African Americans could find an equitable place within southern society if certain vague, ever-distant conditions were satisfied. Their arguments mirrored similar statements made by Stephens that proclaimed slavery to be temporary yet provided no concrete path for its eradication. By proclaiming that white supremacy was not a permanent right guaranteed for the enjoyment of all southern white men forever, the fate of African Americans appeared to be in the hands of white trustees, responsible for guiding them towards equality. Unfortunately, this journey toward justice and civil rights was conducted by the very people whose power, prosperity, and notions of white supremacy depended on depriving black people of adequate legal protections and economic opportunities. Nonetheless, moderate white supremacists attempted to perform duplicitous acts of intellectual gymnastics that, on one hand, reasserted the need for the preservation of white supremacy, while on the other hand acknowledged its unnatural foundations. From this perspective, white southerners had adopted racial segregation laws for the protection and preservation of an inferior black race.[53]

William H. Fleming ranked among the most prolific writers and orators that espoused this brand of supposedly moderate white supremacy. His writings and speeches illustrated the uneasy relationship between how some chose to remember Stephens and the Lost Cause. In 1906, the alumni association of the University of Georgia invited Fleming to comment on the state of American race relations. Fleming, an Augusta, Georgia native and a former US congressmen, had once received a one-hundred-dollar gift from Alexander H. Stephens that helped the young educator launch his career. He deeply admired Stephens and often referenced the vice-president and the Cornerstone Speech during his numerous public orations. After quoting the famous lines from Stephens's Savannah speech, Fleming proclaimed that "the fact of race inequality . . . cannot well be denied. But there is still a fatal flaw in the logic. That flaw lies in the assumption that a superior race has the right to hold an inferior race in slavery." White supremacy, according to Fleming, did not grant white people a right to enslave black people, but it did extend an "obligation of the superior to lead and direct" their racial inferiors. Fleming admitted that the "judgment of a great intellect like that of Alexander Stephens" had been "warped" by centuries of slavery in America that had reinforced "the right of a superior race to enslave an inferior race." Although Fleming remained committed to defending the morality of slavery, he, unlike most Lost Cause proponents, admitted that the assumption among white southerners that slavery would last forever was immoral. The moral and political certainty that rested behind the South's defense of slavery, according to Fleming, "was the particular irritating cause that forced on the conflict of arms between the sections." Fleming, unlike most Lost Cause adherents, found little reason to question the role that slavery and white supremacy had played in the Confederacy's creation because in 1861 both had been "undeniable" facts in American race relations.[54]

Urged by the audience to connect lessons learned from slavery to race relations in the Jim Crow South, Fleming channeled contemporary adaptations of Stephens's complicated opinions. Like Stephens, Fleming empathized with the plight of African Americans, who had been denied the civil liberties that all white men enjoyed. Fleming wondered how society could expect a race to be anything but inferior if its members had been denied access to rights that had been fundamental to American liberty. He acknowledged that African Americans possessed a constitutional right to vote that had to be exercised to "protect itself against reduction to slavery in many of its substantial forms."

Whereas southern governments had taken enormous steps to limit the application of the civil liberties identified in the Fourteenth and Fifteenth Constitutional Amendments, Fleming urged his audience to see these amendments as a foundation for creating equal justice for all Americans.[55]

Fleming also rejected the popular idea held during the antebellum period that God had created African Americans and white people as distinctive forms of humanity. Unlike Stephens, Fleming did not interpret slavery as a curse placed on certain descendants of the biblical Noah. Fleming accepted that economic demand and differences in "blood" had promoted slavery's growth. He urged southerners to seek out God's hand in accepting the "Brotherhood of Man" and extending justice to African Americans. According to Fleming, "God knows the South wants no more" of the "curse" of slavery that had plagued all aspects of society. "God did not so ordain" racial prejudice in "His universe."[56]

But Fleming's sense of justice had its limitations. African Americans, according to him, continued to require the close supervision and guidance provided by white southerners. Without the continued aid of white southerners, Fleming suggested, the future population of African Americans would decline sharply, reducing their influence on American society. "An ineradicable race pride" would prevent any assimilation of the white and black races and thus restrict the potential for universal justice. The sole hope rested in white southerners' willful extension of justice to African Americans. Like Stephens—who never articulated a proposal for ending slavery despite professing to believe in its impermanence—Fleming offered no plan for resolving the period's racial animosities and white-on-black violence. As white supremacy had helped antebellum white southern men to convince themselves that slavery was both divine and benevolent, those same ideals provided a path for postbellum moderates, such as Fleming, to simultaneously shun racial prejudice while reinforcing its foundational principles. During the early twentieth century, some white southerners saw white supremacy as a necessary evil that protected both white and black interests.[57]

Most Lost Cause advocates would have rejected Fleming's calls for racial justice. The distinctions within the Lost Cause demonstrates how Stephens's Cornerstone Speech could mean different things to different people, especially when interpreting the Civil War's origins and slavery's place in American society. Judge George Christian, a Georgia native who had previously helped found the United Confederate Veterans in 1878, chaired the UCV's historical committee in 1907 and prepared a lengthy report that identified the "true" causes of the Civil War. While Christian tried to debunk the notion that slavery had been the cause, he nonetheless devoted the bulk of his lengthy essay to the history of slavery in America. Christian blamed England for imposing slavery upon America. The profits from the colonial trade had inspired New England to develop a prosperous shipbuilding industry that expanded the slave trade. Slavery in the North, according to Christian, lasted until the Civil War and "the treatment of slaves by the people of that section was as harsh, if not more so, than was ever known in any part of the South." Christian accused northerners of treating the enslaved as merely "property" in contrast to southerners, who felt a moral and religious obligation to uplift Africans. Slavery, claimed Christian, had been "brought [to the South] against its will" and it had been maintained because of a lack of better options. Christian, like most Lost Cause defenders, believed that abolitionists and the northern press had been responsible for writing an inaccurate history of slavery in America that placed too much blame on the South for its perpetuation.[58]

After spending several pages detailing the supposed failed efforts launched by southern states, especially Virginia, to abolish slavery, Christian finally turned to Alexander Stephens and the Cornerstone Speech. The popularity of this speech, according to Christian, was due to the anxieties of "our former enemies to convince the world that the South did fight for the perpetuation of slavery." The South's "enemies" had "either wittingly or unwittingly, resorted to misrepresentation or misinterpretations of some of the sayings of our representative men, to try to establish this as a fact." Christian walked a fine line between rejecting accusations that Stephens's speech represented Confederate motives and asserting that white supremacy was a fundamental belief that undergirded American race relations. "Isn't [white supremacy]," questioned Christian, "recognized as true to-day in every part of this land?"[59]

Eager to use America's problems with race to shed the Confederacy's guilt, Christian turned the reader's attention toward racist comments made by northern men. Historian Charles Francis Adams II, the son of John Quincy Adams and grandson of John Adams, had written an essay titled "The Modern Conception of History" that speculated that "Africans are distinctly an inferior order of being not only in the South, or former slave States, but throughout the North also, not entitled to unrestricted pursuit, on equal terms of life, liberty, and happiness."[60] The following year, Adams had delivered a speech in Charleston, South Carolina, that defended secession and white supremacy. "The Southern people have the dead-weight of Africanism tied to them," declared Adams. He described freedpeople as a "handicap" that had burdened white southerners since emancipation.[61] Christian selectively chose quotations from well-known northern men that indicated white supremacy was a national fact rather than a Confederate cornerstone.

Christian and other Lost Cause promoters often compared Stephens's Cornerstone Speech with Abraham Lincoln's address at Charleston, Illinois, delivered during the famous Lincoln–Douglas debates. During those remarks, Lincoln stated, "there is a physical difference between the white and black races, which, I believe, will forever forbid the two races living together on terms of social and political equality. . . . I, as much as any other man, am in favor of having the superior position assigned to the white man." According to Christian, Stephens's and Lincoln's pronouncements on the issue of slavery were so similar that the Confederacy would have had little reason to secede from the union had the central cause been differing views on slavery. Supposedly, Confederate leaders understood that Lincoln never intended to abolish slavery. During the war, Christian claimed, no Confederate soldier discussed the issue of slavery. "Do men fight for a thing, or a cause, they never speak of or discuss," questioned Christian. Rather than Lincoln's policies regarding slavery, Confederate leaders found the incoming president's violations of the US Constitution to be most troubling and the cause for secession. "History shows," wrote Christian, "that in every respect and in every instance the aggressions and violations of the law were committed by the North."[62]

Christian attempted to transform the Cornerstone Speech from an address delivered on the eve of the Civil War into a declaration of the continuity of white supremacy in America. Christian reminded readers that all Americans believed that white supremacy "is just as true today as it was" during the Civil War era. However, slavery had offered African Americans an opportunity, claimed Christian, to be "treated as members of the families to which they severally belonged [and treated] with kindness and consideration." Before the arrival of "mean and designing white men" in the Union Army, "both the white and the black people of the South regarded the Confederate cause alike as their cause, and looked to its success with almost, if not quite equal anxiety and delight." Christian argued that, had the South been willing to arm slaves earlier, slaves would have been willing to fight alongside their masters in a war to protect southern society. Most Lost Cause writers implied that emancipation had broken the bond between master and slave in ways that had led to the racial violence found across the turn-of-the-twentieth-century South. Contemporary history, Christian believed, had proved that Stephens was correct—the Founding Fathers had erred when they declared that all men were created equal.[63]

The growing ranks of professional historians kept the Cornerstone Speech part of public discourse. Many of these historians held doctoral degrees from programs such as Columbia University and Johns Hopkins University. Others had received some training in history in college before attending law school. These historians usually referenced primary source materials and verified whether a figure's postwar writings matched their wartime statements and actions. During the late nineteenth and early twentieth century, public and academic audiences had a strong interest in the history of the American Civil War. At the time of his death, Alexander Stephens, due to his monumental *A Constitutional View of the Late War between the States*, ranked among the most successful historians in American history. Stephens had played a central role in writing what later historians referred to as the "southern point of view" of the Civil War. His book became a widely adopted public school textbook and his general history of America found a popular audience domestically and internationally. Subsequent historians who researched the American Civil War had to deal with Stephens as both a historical actor and a successful historian.[64] Harvard Professor of History Albert Bushnell Hart's *Sourcebook of American History* included an extended analysis of the causes of the American Civil War. Hart concluded that Alexander Stephens never intended the Cornerstone Speech to be a declaration of the war's causes. Instead, Stephens "never meant to imply anything more than that a superior race will inevitably rule an inferior one." Hart argued that the Confederacy was more committed to preserving white supremacy than to defending slavery.[65]

Likewise, University of the South Prof. William Peterfield Trent described Stephens as an "idealistic statesman" whose Cornerstone Speech was "madness." Trent hinted that Stephens's declarations of white supremacy had been necessary because of President Jefferson Davis's "weak and chimerical" inaugural address failed to be explicit enough on the issue to bolster support for the new government.[66] Like Trent, Edgar Sanderson suggested that Stephens's words and actions might have been intended to emphasize the Confederacy's strengths to force the Union to negotiate their readmission.[67] Oliver Perry Temple, a Knoxville attorney who helped organize wartime Unionist opposition to the Confederate government, wrote histories that countered the Lost Cause narrative and exposed a fratricidal side of the Civil War that few discussed at that time. Temple explained that east Tennesseans had to make the difficult choice of whether to remain committed to a Union "with the peculiar thoughts, prejudices, ways and isms of its people, and with their deadly hatred of slavery" and a rebellion that identified "slavery as the cornerstone of the Confederacy." Large numbers of white southern men refused to "accept a despotic public opinion on the subject of the righteousness and the economic benefits of slavery which would permit no one to question it or discuss it; with the degradation of free white labor." In contrast to Lost Cause histories, Temple claimed that divisions among white southern men critically damaged the Confederate rebellion.[68] Other historians, most notably Benson John Lossing of *Harper's Magazine*, criticized Stephens's usage of the phrase "War between the States" to describe what Lossing argued "was a war between the national government and insurgents in several states." Lossing warned readers that Stephens's antebellum opposition to secession should not overshadow his wartime declarations "that slavery was the true cornerstone of the Confederate government."[69]

As white southern men affirmed their commitment to white supremacy, the Cornerstone Speech appeared in numerous works, speeches, and sermons prepared by African American writers, organizers, and ministers during the early twentieth century to counter that ideology. Most drew connections be-tween the ideals that underpinned Jim Crow segregation and Stephens's 1861 speech. Rev. Francis J. Grimke, an American Presbyterian Church minister in Washington, DC, often used his pulpit to analyze and critique American race relations. In 1909, on the eve of President William H. Taft's inauguration, Grimke took a moment to reflect on the American Civil War's legacy in con-temporary society. The war, he claimed, ended forever the threat of secession among southern states. "The ghost of secession," Grimke argued, "will never again arise to disturb the peace of the Union." Grimke saw slavery as the key factor motivating southern secession. The South "insisted upon its right, not only to hold slaves, but the right to carry them in any part of the country, and to have their property right in their slaves respected in every part of the country. . . . The war . . . was begun on the part of the South, with the idea of perpetuating slavery." The war, however, left many issues unresolved. While the Thirteenth Amendment had eradicated slavery, great disagreement remained, especially in the South, concerning the status of African Americans. Grimke traced these modern problems back to the beliefs espoused in Stephens's speech. Stephens had declared in public what most southerners believed in private. Although more than forty years had passed since Stephens's address, according to Grimke, he had set "forth clearly the proslavery idea of citizenship in this country. In this scheme of citizenship the Negro has no part; and he has no part because he is looked upon as in inferior . . . this is exactly the Southern view today; and is exactly the programme to which it is committed." Grimke traced a direct line between the ideals found in the Cornerstone Speech and the Ku Klux Klan, White Caps, Red Shirt Brigade, segregation constitutions, Jim Crow laws, and black disfranchisement. "All these things," Grimke said, "have grown out of the idea that the rightful place of the Negro is that of subordination to the white man, that he has no rightful place in the body politic." While Stephens's generation had failed to create a new nation whose cornerstone rested upon white-supremacist ideals, according to Grimke, Jim Crow represented a renewed effort by southerners to expand white supremacy's influence throughout the United States.[70]

Union Army veterans also helped keep the Cornerstone Speech in public conversations about the American Civil War. Kentucky native and Union veteran John McElroy survived a lengthy confinement at Andersonville prison camp to become a popular printer, memoirist, and journalist. In addition to writing a best-selling autobiographical account of his experiences as a prisoner of war, McElroy penned a serial history of the war that appeared in dozens of early-twentieth-century newspapers. His account of "The Southern Confederacy" shined a bright light on the Cornerstone Speech. McElroy rejected Confederate explanations that secession had been carried out to protect states' rights. He concluded that foreign powers would have been more likely to support the Confederacy and its free trade commercial policies had Stephens never delivered the Cornerstone Speech. Confident that Stephens's words were powerful enough evidence to condemn the Confederacy's motives, McElroy included a long section of the speech so that his readers could interpret the South's motives for themselves.[71]

Interpreting for themselves had been a major part of defining how Americans would remember Alexander Stephens at the dawn of the Jim Crow South. Although many tried to present various forms of Stephens throughout the years, the words found in the Cornerstone Speech continued to define his ultimate legacy. Stephens's very essence rested upon his staunch belief in black inferiority and white supremacy. One of the major reasons Americans continued to revisit Stephens decades after he drew his final breath was because his central identity closely resembled the nation's identity during a period of widespread racially motivated violence and racially discriminatory public policies. By the early twentieth century, Stephens's legacy resembled the harsh realities of America's "race problem."

Alexander H. Stephens with unidentified attendant, c. 1880. Brady-Handy
Photograph Collection, Library of Congress, Prints and Photographs Division.

Alexander H. Stephens, c. 1870. Brady-Handy Collection, Library of Congress, Prints and Photographs Division.

Statue of Alexander H. Stephens at US Capitol, 1932. Harris and Ewing
Collection, Library of Congress, Prints and Photographs Division.

Alexander H. Stephens, c. 1860. Civil War Photographs, 1861–1865,
Library of Congress, Prints and Photographs Division.

Liberty Hall and Alexander H. Stephens statue, Crawfordville, Georgia, 1936. Historic American Buildings Survey, L. D. Andrews, photographer, Library of Congress, Prints and Photographs Division.

Black enslaved laborer quarters, Liberty Hall, Alexander H. Stephens Memorial State Park, Crawfordville, Georgia, 1932. Historic American Buildings Survey, L. D. Andrews, photographer, Library of Congress, Prints and Photographs Division.

Alexander H. Stephens, c. 1857. Sculptors used this photograph of Stephens as the model for a statue erected in his honor at Liberty Hall in Crawfordville, Georgia. Brady-Handy Collection, Library of Congress, Prints and Photographs Division.

Alexander H. Stephens statue, Alexander H. Stephens Memorial State Park, Crawfordville, Georgia. Ezra Trumpet, photographer.

CHAPTER SIX

Civil War Semicentennial, 1911–1915

During the Civil War Semicentennial, the Cornerstone Speech and Alexander H. Stephens remained part of American discussions of the war's history, legacy, and relevance to contemporary life. The man and his speech stood at the center of heated debates over the war's causes and the nature of southern race relations. Interpretations varied widely, as did efforts to contextualize the speech's meaning. White supremacists drew an enduring connection between antebellum slavery and contemporary race problems. In their opinion, the speech was an important reminder of white supremacy's continuity in American life. Few white southern men questioned whether the Confederacy's defeat had undermined white supremacy's legitimacy. The Cornerstone Speech hampered efforts by many southern and northern factions to reconcile the nation's sectional animosities. Complete reconciliation with emancipationists was impossible if white southerners continued to dispute slavery's role in the Civil War. Reconciliation hinged on northern groups acquiescing to Lost Cause–inspired histories that either ignored the speech or questioned its legitimacy. Emancipationists, who continued to play a role in shaping Civil War memory, remained opposed the Lost Cause's distortions. White southerners were only willing to embrace reconciliation on their terms. They had lost the war but dominated its memory.[1] They had failed in their bid for independence but managed to build a New South that was as equally committed to the ideals of white supremacy as the fallen Confederate States of America. Despite the period's racist public policies and distorted historic commemorations, the Cornerstone Speech remained a potent weapon for an outnumbered minority who challenged Lost Cause orthodoxy.[2]

According to historian David Blight, by the early twentieth century most Americans had adopted a reconciliationist memory of the Civil War. Reconciliationists emphasized the common bonds that white Americans shared.

They extolled the heroic actions of soldiers and statesmen on both sides of the conflict and rarely probed into the war's causes. Reconciliationists also agreed that Reconstruction had been a tragic failure and blamed the nation's white on black racial violence on emancipation. This point of view played an important role in the codification of white supremacy as expressed in the nation's Jim Crow laws.[3]

Today, many historians have argued that although the Confederacy lost the war on the battlefield, the South dominated how Americans would remember the nation's defining conflict. Black scholar W.E.B. DuBois, whose academic career spanned the Jim Crow-era and both the Civil War semicentennial and centennial commemorations, wrote "The slave went free; stood for a brief moment in the sun; then moved back again toward slavery."[4] The reconciliation of white Americans directly influenced the declining civil liberties of African Americans in the postbellum period. In 1861, Alexander Stephens believed that shared beliefs in white supremacy would overcome the nation's sectional divisions and forge a stronger country explicitly dedicated to preserving black inferiority. During the Civil War, Stephens's predictions of a global white man's movement never materialized, but fifty years later his words seemed prophetic. Thanks to the US Supreme Court's *Plessy v. Ferguson* decision that declared racial segregation constitutional and allowed states to create new stringent racial segregation laws without fear of federal intervention, Stephens's dreams of a nation founded upon explicit declarations of white supremacy had been realized. If, as Blight argues, reconciliation emerged as the dominant expression of Civil War memory, it did so on southern terms. The rhetoric of reconciliation and white supremacy shared so much in common that it was difficult to identify where one ended and one began. Alexander Stephens had been correct. White supremacy was the glue that bound together white Americans.[5]

The Civil War Semicentennial (1911–1915) both reflected and shaped how Americans remembered the nation's central conflict. Americans commemorated the fiftieth anniversary by organizing memorial-day ceremonies, veterans' reunions, and monument dedications. Before and during the semicentennial, numerous histories, biographies, and memoirs appeared in print as public interest remained high. Many newspapers included daily features highlighting various Civil War anniversaries. While the 1913 reunion at Gettysburg was the semicentennial's culminating event, hundreds of memorials and reunions were well attended across the nation. Most of those events included speakers who reflected on the Civil War's origins, results, and consequences. Those discussions often included references to the Cornerstone Speech.

Some white supremacists and Lost Cause proponents turned Alexander Stephens into a scapegoat who helped explain why the Confederate States of America had failed to gain independence. Louis Beauregard Pendleton's *Alexander H. Stephens* (1908) accepted that the newspaper transcription of the Cornerstone Speech had been correct. Pendleton, a Georgia-born author who primarily wrote children's books, claimed that the Cornerstone Speech misrepresented the Confederate government's motivations. Supposedly, Stephens had gotten carried away trying to entertain an excited crowd of supporters when he delivered "the damage done at the outset by his speech." Like other Lost Cause writers, Pendleton refused to accept that the Confederacy's "valiant" military would have succumbed to inferior Union soldiers had not the misdeeds of Confederate politicians had prevented the rebel army from achieving its full power. The same Lost Cause rhetoric that described Robert E. Lee as infallible sometimes sought out civilian figures like Stephens to blame for the Confederacy's widespread failures. Most notably, in this interpretation, Stephens's careless Cornerstone Speech had cost the Confederacy any hope of striking a negotiated alliance with Great Britain. "In a sense," wrote Pendleton, Stephens "was in his own person one of the Confederacy's heavy handicaps." If "the cause was lost by our own dissensions . . . no other man contributed to those dissensions in so large a measure as Stephens." Pendleton referenced unsubstantiated stories of British citizens responding in "horror" to Stephens's declaration that slavery was the cornerstone of the Confederacy. Ironically, claimed Pendleton, "Stephens was the very last of the Southern leaders that one would expect to make slavery the all-important question." Instead, a "confused" Stephens had obscured "the fundamental issue of State rights" and wrought "incalculable damage to the Confederate cause."[6]

Louis Pendleton claimed that Stephens's public declaration of white supremacy had been unnecessary. "Nothing is more certain even in our time," Pendleton argued, "that such a race as the negro, when placed in association with Americans or Europeans, must inevitably occupy a subordinate position." The author asserted that slavery had been a pragmatic solution to manage an inferior race rather than a divine or natural law. According to Pendleton, the world accepted that slavery was a necessary institution, but wanted the Confederacy to refrain from making their quest for independence hinge on slavery's permanent preservation. Without any supporting evidence, Pendleton speculated that Stephens's "corner-stone speech no doubt brought thousands of recruits to the Northern standard and was not the least of the factors concerned in the prevention of the recognition of the Confederacy by the governments of Europe." The massive four-hundred-page biography had largely praised Stephens for his intellect, statesmanship, and leadership. In Pendleton's opinion, the Cornerstone Speech had been Stephens's worst, and perhaps sole, mistake.[7]

Meanwhile, some white supremacists celebrated the Cornerstone Speech. On the eve of the Civil War Semicentennial, journalist John Temple Graves published the co-edited volume *Eloquent Sons of the South: A Handbook of Southern Oratory*, which included a complete copy of the Cornerstone Speech.[8] A descendent of South Carolina Sen. John C. Calhoun and the son of a Confederate general, Graves had emerged as a major voice in the defense of white supremacy. During a 1903 meeting in Chautauqua, New York, Graves openly defended the lynching of black men by white mobs as "the most potential bulwark between the women of the South and such a carnival of crime as would infuriate the world and precipitate the annihilation of the negro race." Graves claimed that "black rapists" had to be lynched because they did not fear the legal forms of justice in America. He recommended that the best solution to end the violence would be to force African Americans to return to Africa. Three years later, Graves played an important role in inciting white Atlanta men to assault African Americans during the infamous 1906 Atlanta Race Riots. Whereas some Lost Cause writers blamed Stephens for ruining the Confederacy's chances of receiving additional foreign support, Graves believed that he had been correct when he argued that other nations would eventually join in the new government's defense of white supremacy. According to Graves, the Confederacy might have gained additional support from white men across the world if other southern leaders had more assertively espoused their white-supremacist beliefs. Graves dreamed of a global empire dominated by white men who would use other territories to relocate America's black populace.[9]

In 1914, Graves was among the first Atlantans to propose transforming Stone Mountain into a Confederate memorial park "to the great cause 'fought without shame and lost with honor.'" He suggested that funds be raised to carve a statue of Gen. Robert E. Lee on the face of the granite mountain located about twenty miles west of Atlanta. Graves claimed that such a monument would compare to the Lion of Lucerne, the Sphinx, and the Taj Mahal. He believed that Stone Mountain would remain "an object of artistic, romantic and sentimental interest unique among the wonders of the age." Publicly, he hoped the monument would inspire greater awareness of and sympathy for the Confederate cause. Privately, he and other Stone Mountain supporters, most notably UDC leader Helen Plane, sought to transform the natural beauty of the mountain into a symbol of the enduring strength of white supremacy in America. In fact, in 1915, during the Civil War semicentennial, the second Ku Klux Klan was founded during an elaborate cross burning ceremony atop Stone Mountain. This version of the Klan imitated the attire and rituals depicted in the film *Birth of a Nation*, which also appeared during the semi-centennial.

Alexander H. Stephens's Cornerstone Speech had played a small role in shaping how white southern men like Graves remembered white supremacy's past.[10] Whereas Stephens's speech declared slavery to be an enormous asset to the South, Berkeley Minor, a Confederate veteran who had served in the famed Stonewall Brigade, argued that in hindsight slavery had played a major role in the Confederacy's defeat. Foremost, he argued, no foreign power would come to the South's aid if slavery remained. Minor, who suggested that Gen. Robert E. Lee might have been more sympathetic to ending slavery than Jefferson Davis, wished that the Confederacy had traded "the right of self-government" in exchange for emancipation. Minor repeated a common myth perpetuated by the Lost Cause that major Confederate leaders and enslavers were moving toward emancipation on their own accord prior to the rebellion's defeat. Like Stephens, Lost Cause writers who attempted to transform rebellious enslavers into aspirational abolitionists struggled to envision what emancipation on their terms might resemble. Minor only vaguely suggested that enslavers should have gotten "rid of it gradually, and in the way least hurtful to both races" rather than "have our conquerors . . . settle it for us and carry out their plan of emancipation as they think best." Minor's counterfactual history of the war contradicted what Stephens and other Confederate leaders said in the spring of 1861. Stephens viewed slavery as a critical component that united white southerners under a banner of economic prosperity and Christian charity. He believed that other states and nations around the world would recognize slavery's virtues and decide to join the Confederacy in its fight against "Black Republicans." Minor fantasized that had Lee urged Davis to end the "evil" of slavery, the Confederacy could have played an important role in a global abolition movement. This fantasy derived from a common falsehood peddled among Lost Cause writers: "The institution of slavery was in large measure forced upon us." In a narrative that defied all historical evidence, Minor posited that since slavery had been forced upon the South, then enslavers would have been willing to shed that burden under the leadership of Lee, whom the author compared to Moses leading the Jews out of bondage.[11]

Minor believed that white supremacy could survive without slavery if an independent Confederate States of America could have managed African Americans' transition from slavery to freedom. Had Lee and others been willing to abandon slavery, Minor concluded, Europeans powers would have thrown their support behind the Confederate war effort and guaranteed their independence. However, Minor admitted that Confederate leaders stubbornly clung to their defense of slavery even as their hopes for independence dwindled.[12]

In 1911, as the fiftieth anniversary of the Cornerstone Speech passed, excerpts from the speech and analysis of its contents appeared in several newspapers. The analysis that accompanied the speech reflected the emancipationists' continued effort to define Civil War memory. Unlike their Lost Cause and reconciliationist counterparts, emancipationists rejected Stephens's postbellum explanations of the Cornerstone Speech. However, like their counterparts, emancipationists also ignored the complexities of Stephens's life and legacy, especially his postbellum courting of black and Republican Party voters and the conflicts he had with Confederate and Democratic Party leaders. Stephens remained a polarizing figure in American public memory. How one remembered Stephens had more to do with one's politics and sectional partisanship than the historical record.

Emancipationist newspapers, such as The Citizen (Honesdale, Pennsylvania), proclaimed that the Cornerstone Speech explained "the cause of secession" and used the speech to celebrate the war's greatest accomplishments, emancipation, and the ruin of southern enslavers. According to the editor, after four years of war, the Confederacy's "corner stone was ground to dust and the edifice built on it was rent asunder and prostrated."[13] Other emancipationist writers blamed the South's determination "to take its slaves into any of the territories of the country" as the driving force behind secession and war.[14]

During the Civil War Semicentennial, some writers shined a spotlight on the Cornerstone Speech to reveal truths obscured by supporters of the Lost Cause. The Boston Globe published an article marking the speech's fiftieth anniversary. The article's subtitle read "The Constitution of the Confederate States, Founded on Human Slavery, Was Adopted at Montgomery, Ala." Beneath the subtitle, the paper included a large photograph of Stephens with the following caption: "Vice President of the Confederate States of America. He Declared Without Reservation That Slavery Was the Cornerstone of the Confederate Constitution." Confederate founders, according to the author, arrived in Montgomery anxious to establish a new government and constitution dedicated to "establishing slavery forever in the south." Stephens had played a central role in the Confederacy's creation. Known throughout the country as a frank and honest statesman, Stephens's speech in Savannah tried to explain how the Confederacy had improved the old US Constitution. As he spoke, "he swept away all the fallacious reasoning of those who declared the principle of states' rights, and not slavery, was bringing on the war." Rather than reject Stephens's pronouncements, according to the Boston Globe, the South applauded his remarks and confirmed their determination to "rest upon the great truth that the negro is not equal to the white man: that slavery—subordination to the superior—is his natural and normal condition."[15] Aware that many white southern men and historians rejected the assertion that protecting slavery had been central to secession and the development of the Confederate States of America, this article urged Americans to read the Cornerstone Speech to discover what had motivated these men. "Mr. Stephens' earnest indorsement of the confederate constitution . . . show[s] the present generation the strength of slavery's hold on even the most conservative men of the south. Only war could defend such opinions as they held." Whereas some southern newspapers and Lost Cause historians had argued that Stephens was neither representative of the Confederacy nor the government's official spokesperson, the *Boston Globe* reminded its readers that southerners at the time lauded Stephens for his candid rhetoric. Plus, according to the newspaper, in the weeks that followed the Cornerstone Speech, no Confederate leader opposed Stephens's declarations. The newspaper demonstrated that even moderate voices such as Stephens clung steadfast to their defense of slavery.[16]

Only a handful of newspapers devoted special attention to the Cornerstone Speech's fiftieth anniversary. Emancipationists were more likely to use various anniversaries connected with the war's opening battles to remind Americans what had caused the bloodshed. At a Decoration Day event held in Ottumwa, Iowa, Dr. T. W. Jeffrey, a Methodist Episcopal minister, told a crowd filled with Grand Army of the Republic members that the Union dead had given their lives for a "good purpose." "Our victories have been moral victories," claimed Jeffrey. "Our fathers fought for principle and America is their apotheosis." Critical of those who misrepresented the war's causes and outcomes, Jeffrey asked the crowd "what are we to tell those who come after us was the cause of this war? Are we to sit dumb when all the blame is thrown back upon those who fought for the Union? Secession was the pretext of the war but slavery was its cause." Rather than being founded by a people who valued liberty, as the Lost Cause claimed, Jeffrey accused the South of launching a pro-slavery crusade that threatened to unleash tyranny upon American soil. Both the living and the dead, said Jeffrey, could be proud that "slavery is dead" and that millions of Americans fought to defend freedom.[17]

As Jeffrey's remarks tried to find some contemporary meaning for the audience to glean from the Union dead's sacrifices, his emancipationist message found unexpected common ground with Alexander Stephens's Cornerstone Speech. Although Jeffrey praised Union veterans for ending slavery, he did so because ending slavery had protected American democracy from the ravages of tyrannical enslavers. But he also believed that Confederate defeat was never intended to usher in a new era of racial equality or power for freedpeople. For Jeffrey, the Union victory marked yet another chapter in the Anglo-Saxon race's unique role in human history. The white man "has made the land of the Pharaoh's bloom. He has brought the ends of the earth together in civilization.

Out of his brain have come the greatest inventions." According to Jeffrey, white men have been given "a mission to all people and all the world . . . to bring about peace." Like Stephens, Jeffrey acknowledged that white supremacy could survive in a world without black slavery and that inferior races would always require white supervision. Whereas Stephens had predicted that slavery would overcome various abolitionist movements to spread across the globe, Jeffrey claimed that the white man's role in ending slavery had given him a new responsibility of extending his influence wherever America's influence could reach. In Jeffrey's mind, Union soldiers died to end slavery and to preserve the supremacy of the Anglo-Saxon race.[18]

Like Jeffrey, some commentators blurred the lines between emancipationists, reconciliationists, and white supremacists. Charles E. Stowe, the son of *Uncle Tom's Cabin* author Harriet Beecher Stowe, promoted legal segregation to resolve America's racial problems. As a member of one of the nation's most prominent abolitionist families, Lost Cause advocates used his opinions as evidence that even those who had opposed slavery lacked any commitment to racial equality. Stowe delivered a speech at Fisk University, a black university in Nashville, Tennessee, that southern journalists proclaimed had "treat[ed] the causes leading up to the war with surprising accuracy and fairness." The event raised funds to support the university by honoring the one-hundredth anniversary of Harriet Beecher Stowe's birth. Other notable speakers included Booker T. Washington, founder of Tuskegee Institute. Stowe was invited because his rhetoric of race appealed to Lost Cause promoters and a segment of the black population who agreed with Washington's views on the subject. Southern newspapers noted the irony of the son of one of the most hated abolitionists in the South applauding various aspects of slavery, secession, and white supremacy before a black audience. Some referred to Stowe's speech as an "Abolitionist's Confession."[19]

Echoing the white supremacist rhetoric of Lost Cause advocates, Stowe declared "we can truly say that the underlying efficient cause of our Civil War was the compromises of the constitution, utterly irreconcilable principles existing there side by side, covered only by compromises that could in the end satisfy neither party." Stowe described Thomas Jefferson's declaration that "all men were created equal" as a "great" but "vague" idea that was never intended "to abolish human nature." Stowe called on Fisk students to "not look back upon slavery as a reign of unalleviated wickedness and horror, but remember that it had within itself, in spite of its many abuses and intolerable horrors, much that was good." Among slavery's attributes, claimed Stowe, was the introduction of Christianity to a race that hailed from "barbarous Africa." He disingenuously claimed that his mother's novel *Uncle Tom's Cabin* had described many positive views of slavery. If slavery had produced some advancements for black people, Stowe predicted that racial segregation would also lead to similar improvements. Stowe echoed the popular Lost Cause charge "that the Northern States were just as responsible for the existence of slavery as were the Southern States." Plus, pious enslavers rightfully defended slavery because "the South found abundant authority for his beloved institution . . . [in] the Bible." When the war came, claimed Stowe, "many patriotic Southern men who cared little or nothing about slavery were stirred with the deepest indignation at the suggestion of the national government subduing a Sovereign State by force of arms." Stowe maintained that white southern men came to the defense of the Confederacy not because of their determination to preserve slavery but in protest of "a union that could only be held together by bayonets." White southern men "fought with a holy ardor . . . that covered even defeat with imperishable glory." Stowe urged the nation to put aside any festering sectional divisions since all sides had just reasons for fighting.[20]

Stowe's views on the Cornerstone Speech were complicated. The Confederacy's "slave power" had "flagrantly violated . . . the proposition, we believe that men are created equal." Stowe criticized Stephens's declaration that the Confederacy "had made slavery its foundation stone" based on "the undeniable fact of the inferiority of the negro to the white man, and that his only possible relation to the white man must be that of slavery or subordination of the inferior to the superior race." Rather than denouncing the fallacies of white supremacy, Stowe urged his African American audience to view Stephens's remarks as a challenge that should motivate their drive for civil equality. Claiming that racial segregation laws were "inevitable," Stowe counseled Fisk University faculty and students to "develop their own peculiar culture, their own peculiar race pride, and remove prejudice, not by protest, but by doing away with all worthy cause for such prejudice." Stowe speculated that African Americans could solve the race problem by working harder, saving their earnings, abiding by existing laws, and seeking to improve their education. Through their efforts, African Americans could take advantage of "the open door of opportunity" that could forever put "behind them, barbarious Africa, the slave ship, the slave pen, the auction box, the plantation and the lash." Stowe reminded the audience that "millions of the white race" would be "watching your progress." He placed the burden of dismantling white supremacy on the shoulders of African Americans, whose every action would be carried out under the white society's gaze. As Stowe concluded his remarks, Dr. Reuben Lindsay Cave, chaplain and historian of the Tennessee Division of United Confederate Veterans, took the stage and "heartily agreed with the sentiments of the speaker" before closing with program with a prayer for peace.[21]

Most northern newspapers adopted a reconciliationist vision of Civil War memory. Those papers tended to de-emphasize the Cornerstone Speech and celebrate various aspects of Stephens's national loyalties. Reconciliationists cast Stephens as a prime example of a reluctant Confederate who believed that joining and exerting a moderating influence on the rebellion was his national duty. Reconciliationists also forgot Stephens's postbellum political career. The *Bemidji Daily Pioneer* (Minnesota) published a glowing account of members of their congressional delegation participating in a Richmond, Virginia, ceremony to mark Alexander Stephens's wartime residence.[22] The *Evening Journal* (Wilmington, Delaware) focused on Stephens's failed endeavors to end the war through compromise. Stories retelling Stephens's actions during the Hampton Roads Conference always neglected to mention that the Confederacy's unwillingness to accept emancipation caused those meetings to fail.[23] Historian Charles N. Lurie's "State of the Union Half a Century Ago" article provided a detailed account of the secession crisis but never once mentioned slavery or tried to explain the Confederacy's motives. Lurie's writing, which appeared in several newspapers, stripped the Civil War of any ideological meaning turning the fighting into nothing more than a political spat that cost 100,000s of lives.[24]

Although northern newspapers rarely mentioned the Cornerstone Speech, they often commemorated the speeches Alexander Stephens delivered that opposed secession. In distorted hindsight, Stephens became the favorite moderate voice of southern reason. He seemed to provide evidence that most southerners had been rational men who only reluctantly accepted secession when their state's removal from the Union forced their hand. The *Quad-City Times* of Davenport, Iowa, declared that Stephens's Union Speech proved that the Civil War lacked any central cause. In that speech, Stephens had tried to convince secession supporters that the North had done very little that required such a rash reaction as secession. Fifty-plus years later, newspapers printed extended sections of the speech because, like the semicentennial commemorations themselves, in this speech Stephens had downplayed the role that slavery had contributed to the late antebellum period's sectional strife. Stephens had warned the Georgia legislature that secession "can never be recalled, and all the baleful and withering consequences that must follow (as you will see) will rest upon this convention for all coming time. When we and our posterity shall see our lovely South desolated by the demon of war . . . and every horror and desolation upon us, who but this convention will be held responsible for it." Stephens called secession a "suicidal act." Slavery, according to Stephens, had national support and would be protected because of its economic value to the global economy. Time and time again, declared Stephens, the nation had capitulated to the interests of southern enslavers. Unlike the Cornerstone

Speech, the Union Speech lacked any specific declarations of white supremacy, but clearly identified southern fears of abolition as the secession movement's primary concern. Stephens's list of potentially divisive sectional issues began with several that pertained to slavery: reopening of the slave trade; the three-fifths compromise, Fugitive Slave Act, and territorial expansion of slavery. Stephens claimed that the worst outcome of the "unwise and impolitic act" of secession would be to "have your last slave wrenched from you by stern military rule, or by vindictive decree of universal emancipation." The North would only resort to emancipation, predicted Stephens, if the South seceded.[25]

The Union Speech, read with fifty years of hindsight, transformed Stephens into a prognostic compromiser who foresaw secession's potential impact on the South, but failed to convince enough of his peers to follow his lead. In 1911, newspapers presented this moment as a lesson in contemporary leadership. Writers expected modern-day leaders to glean from Stephens's heroic defeat in the face of radicalism examples of the value of moderation and compromise. The world seemed to need statesmen like Stephens regardless of his role in the Confederate government after his anti-secession protests failed. To embrace Stephens's as an example of exceptional leadership, writers had to conveniently forget that after Georgia seceded Stephens abandoned his anti-secession rhetoric and launched a more explicit defense of slavery and white supremacy.[26]

Meanwhile, Daniel Cremin, a graduating student at Willimantic Normal Training School in Connecticut, chose to honor Alexander Stephens's contributions to American history by reciting portions of his January 1861 Union Speech during the school's annual graduation ceremony.[27] In Ohio, the state school commissioner administered exams to prospective educators that asked them to identify Alexander Stephens. Among the many historical figures included on the exam study guide, Stephens was the sole representative associated with the Confederate States of America. The only other material teachers needed to know about the Civil War was the Battle of Gettysburg. Stephens remained part of what educators thought American students needed to know about the Civil War.[28]

Most stories published in 1911 in the North cast Alexander Stephens as an enviable example of traits that contemporary Americans should emulate. As Americans consumed firsthand memories of the Civil War and descriptions of its major figures, Stephens's unforgettable physical appearance pushed stories of various encounters to the front pages of national and international newspapers. Stephens's physical disabilities garnered much interest and helped his legacy gain sympathy among northern audiences who might have otherwise condemned his actions as Confederate vice-president. In an age when most Americans who suffered from disabilities that limited their mobility led restricted, often isolated lives, Stephens's disabilities played a central role in drawing Americans to his story.

A Pittsburgh newspaper chose to mark Stephens's role in the Civil War by publishing a sympathetic account of Stephens's final postbellum years in Congress. As Congress convened, its members ceased "the buzz which char acterizes the House of Representatives" as the door near the Speaker's desk "opened disclosing a sort of invalid's chair which several House attendants pushed" into place. "In the chair sat the figure of a man [who] might have passed for a little dummy but for the wonderous luster of the large, dark eyes." House members recognized the "pale corpse" as Alexander H. Stephens. Journalist Elisha Jay Edwards reported how the representatives stood in silent reverence, a sort of "involuntary tribute" to Stephens's celebrity status among his peers. Stephens acknowledged their admiration with a simple bow of the head before the House's business resumed. Several days later, Edwards asked Stephens why he had chosen to remain in Congress despite his failing health. Stephens responded, "I keep fighting on, for my life's work is not yet done. . . . I hope to come back to Congress for a good many years yet." He wanted to complete several histories that he had started and believed that his continued public service would keep his mind sharp enough to finish those manuscripts. Edwards's account of Stephens appeared decades after the actual event. Published in newspapers across the nation as part of Edwards's series on major historical figures, its appearance on the eve of the Civil War Semicentennial gave audiences a conciliatory view of Stephens. Rather than examining either the context of Stephens's "life's work," which at that time included opposing civil rights legislation, or his writings, tracts defending the Confederacy's actions, Edwards painted the former vice-president as a sympathetic figure weakened by a life of hardship brought on by extensive public service and intellectual rigor. Writers such as Edwards who sought to reduce sectional animosities cast Stephens exactly how he saw himself: as a brilliant and well-respected mind, undeterred by physical disabilities.[29]

The Cornerstone Speech exposed the limits of sectional reconciliation. For decades, local chapters of the Grand Army of the Republic had organized special Decoration Day ceremonies to honor the Union dead and celebrate veterans who had survived the war. The 1913 event in Stafford, Kansas, offered a vision of America's past and present that contrasted sharply with Alexander H. Stephens's Cornerstone Speech. Maj. A. M. Harvey, a veteran of the Spanish-American War, challenged the Lost Cause mythology that depicted Confederate soldiers as honorable heroes and argued that this misinterpretation obscured the war's causes and meaning. He systematically repudiated the Cornerstone Speech by exposing how Stephens and the Confederacy had perverted many ideals central to American identity. Harvey warned that groups who spread false histories of war posed a serious threat to the nation and desecrated the Union dead. The Confederacy had been founded by tyrants, exclaimed Harvey, who ignored that "our nation was founded upon the foundation principle of the equality of men." The Union dead had laid down their lives to preserve a nation founded on those lofty ideals whereas the Confederacy sent their youth into battle to defend slavery.[30]

Whereas some Lost Cause advocates and reconciliationists had described the Civil War as unnecessary and avoidable, Harvey proclaimed that "no one can contemplate the great loss of life and the sorrow and suffering of the Civil War without deep regret that such a war was necessary." Harvey held up Stephens as a prime example of slavery's hold on the white southern mind. Without question, Stephens was an intelligent leader who knew right from wrong—except for when the debate involved slavery. Harvey questioned how a man so kind and generous to so many could devote his energies to the preservation of a "wicked" and "immoral" institution like slavery. Harvey speculated that Stephens and others had become so obsessed with the need to preserve slavery that they allowed their minds to be overcome by passions that betrayed the nation's founding ideals. Those men had placed slavery above all else, including God and the United States of America. Fortunately, Harvey declared, despite the courage demonstrated by the Confederate military and its leaders, "you and I can well rejoice in the fact that the great political questions involved were determined on the side of right, humanity, and justice." Harvey told the crowd that "no man can be as good a citizen as he ought to be unless he knows and understands the sacrifices that were made for us by men who made up the Union Army and carried our flag to victory." The Confederacy may have been defeated, but its memory and how white southerners distorted the war's causes and legacy posed an enduring threat to the nation. Harvey castigated Lost Cause writers who had transformed the Confederacy's leaders from men who fought to preserve slavery into noble crusaders, motivated by fears of federal supremacy.[31]

Harvey thanked the Grand Army of the Republic for organizing so many memorial services and erecting numerous monuments that honored the sacrifices of Union soldiers, but he reminded the crowd that the Union dead would want this generation to fight for "a government where every man is a man, free to do all he can with no privileged class to prevent and where men are not only born free and equal, but have equal rights and equal opportunity. . . . It is our duty as a nation, and our duty as good citizens, to build toward the perfect realization of this idea. A great civil war was fought to the end that we might climb higher and closer to this perfect state." Harvey acknowledged that America had failed to achieve the ideals of its founders but stressed that the

Civil War had placed the nation on a better path. All that stood in the way of those ideals, according to Harvey, were lingering ideals of inequality that stemmed from leaders who followed Stephens's poor example.[32]

Decoration Day memories often sharply contrasted with the Lost Cause ideology. The Cornerstone Speech served as an incontrovertible reminder of the Confederacy's true motivations. On May 29, 1914, the city of Indianapolis hosted its annual Memorial Day commemorations. That year remaining members of the Grand Army of the Republic invited local Confederate veterans to join the celebration in a display of national unity. The ceremony included a series of speeches delivered by Union and Confederate orators. All speakers pronounced the arrival of a new America forged from lessons learned during the war and praised those who had fallen. Dispersed among the symbolic blue and gray handshakes, however, was a polite debate over the war's memory. Without explicitly mentioning Alexander Stephens, Indiana Juvenile Court Judge Newton M. Taylor declared that southern "slaveholders resolved to secede from the Union and form a government of their own, whose cornerstone would be slavery." Taylor, who had read the Cornerstone Speech as well as *A Constitutional View of the Late War Between the States*, refuted Stephens's decades-old efforts to defend states' rights. Taylor shared the stage with the memory of a man who had died thirty-one years earlier. As evidenced by the Northwest Ordinance, the Founding Fathers, claimed Taylor, had always intended to prohibit slavery in some American territories. Only the federal government held the authority to determine slavery's future. Whereas Stephens had argued in the Cornerstone Speech that states predated the nation and thus held supreme authority to determine which laws should be upheld locally, Taylor countered that most of the states that joined the Confederacy were formed after the Constitution had been ratified and thus only became states because the federal government gave them that right. Speaking before a bipartisan crowd filled with elderly white men in blue and gray uniforms, Taylor used Stephens's anti-secession Union Speech to identify multiple reasons why secession had been unnecessary. Using Stephens's own words to undermine the Lost Cause and his own Cornerstone Speech, Taylor asserted "that the movement for secession was a matter of personal ambition on the part of the slaveholding politicians of the south to establish a government wherein they could reign supreme." The ceremony honored dead soldiers killed in a "slaveholder's rebellion" conspired to protect slavery.[33]

The Cornerstone Speech made many appearances in various ceremonies honoring Union Army veterans. In Santa Ana, California, Judge Curtis D. Wilbur, whose father had served in the 66th Ohio Infantry Regiment, told a crowd of Grand Army of the Republic and Sons of Union Veterans of the Civil War members that the Union Army had laid the foundation for America's postbellum prosperity. Wilbur declared that "a moral issue" had caused the war. After reading a selection from President Abraham Lincoln's Cooper Union Speech that reminded southern pro-slavery supporters that the US Constitution lacked any specific language that protected human property, Wilbur began quoting the Cornerstone Speech. Ultimately, both speeches, according to Wilbur, proved that all sides understood "that the south believed African slavery to be a legal right and that God had made the black race an inferior race." Stephens had provided future generations ample evidence to determine Confederate motivations. Unfortunately, despite the heroism of Union soldiers, "the problems" that caused the war "are not all settled." Modern-day Americans, according to Wilbur, must resist the immoral assertions found in the Cornerstone Speech and the South's pro-slavery crusade. "It is of the utmost importance today," implored Wilbur, "that we as a nation have right ideas on moral issues." He urged the crowd to remember Union veterans who "when they close their eyes, they now see a marvelous land, stretching from sea to sea, showing that their work and warfare were not in vain. It will always be true that these men fought on the side that was eternally right, and however valiantly those who wore grey fought, it will always be true that they fought for a wrong principle." If the nation followed the example set by Union veterans, America could be "clothed in clothes of righteousness" and worthy of receiving God's redemption. In contrast, if America allowed itself to revert to the "wrong principle(s)" espoused by immoral men, such as Alexander Stephens, the nation would never take its rightful place in the lead of nations around the globe.[34]

At least one southerner used the Cornerstone Speech as evidence of her emancipationist views of Civil War memory. In an editorial published in the *Times Dispatch* (Richmond), an author identified as "A Virginia Woman" criticized the editor for ignoring the "horrors of slavery" during the semicentennial. One week earlier, the editor had criticized an English abolitionist's account of American slavery. "It is time that Southern papers should not shrink from letting the truth be known to this generation, yet, as one of this generation I know that it is always hidden," wrote "A Virginia Woman." She questioned how southerners had forgotten slavery's horrors when Alexander Stephens said that "slavery is the corner-stone of the Confederacy." Southerners had also overlooked Jefferson Davis's statement that "the idea of slavery is repellant to the moral sense of mankind in general." Had the Confederacy abandoned slavery, she speculated, Great Britain would have allied itself with the fledgling nation. "A Virginia Woman" implored the *Times Dispatch* editor to quit "trying to pull the wool over the eyes of the coming generation" by printing stories of benevolent masters and faithful slaves. The editorial presented the most historically accurate depiction of slavery to appear in the newspaper's history. She even chastised enslavers for breaking apart enslaved families and marriages and broached the taboo subject of interracial sexual exploitation: "the negro girl was at the mercy of the master's lust." Despite "A Virginia Woman's" criticisms, her editorial failed to change how most white southerners remembered slavery. Her editorial was one of a handful of publications that appeared in the South during the semicentennial that recognized the Cornerstone Speech's central truths.[35]

The Cornerstone Speech also attracted some comment from British writers during the semicentennial era. As Europe plunged into World War I, Maj. Evan R. Jones, editor to the *Shipping World*, a British periodical, drew a comparison between Kaiser Wilhelm II and Alexander Stephens. After paraphrasing the Cornerstone Speech, Jones claimed that "Alexander Stephens fought for the subjugation of the colored race as the first principle of government under the Confederacy." Likewise, "the Kaiser is waging war for nothing less than the subjugation of the world." Lost Cause authors had cast the American Civil War as a struggle to defend their liberty from an oppressive northern-dominated federal government. Jones, a well-educated Brit whose views likely were representative of many of his fellow citizens, rejected that claim and accused the Confederacy of harboring more sinister ambitions—the global expansion of the South's slave society.[36]

Historian James Ford Rhodes also urged audiences to pay more attention to the Cornerstone Speech. In 1912, during the Civil War Semicentennial, Rhodes delivered a series of Civil War lectures at the University of Oxford in England. Considered by many of his peers to be one of the first nonpartisan writers to examine the conflict, Rhodes explained to British audiences that there was only one "notable" difference between the North and the South. "The difference," according to Rhodes, "was frankly stated by the Vice-President of the Southern Confederacy, Alexander H. Stephens, who said: The foundations of our new government are laid; 'its corner-stone rests upon the great truth that the negro is not equal to the white man; that slavery is his natural and normal condition. . . . This stone [the doctrine that negro slavery is right] which was rejected by the first builders [the fathers of the republic] 'has become the chief of the corner'—the real 'corner-stone' in our new edifice." Rhodes explained that modern audiences should avoid condemning enslavers for seeking to hold onto their human property because slavery had evolved into an overarching institution that dominated the South's social, cultural, and political life. Stephens's speech merely expressed what had become ingrained across an entire society of like-minded enslavers and white supremacists, who could not bring themselves to imagine what a South without slavery would resemble. Rhodes agreed with Stephens that slavery had been a curse imposed on the South rather than an institution embraced and developed in the region. Thus, even as Rhodes accurately accused the Confederacy of seceding to defend slavery, the scholar also absolved southern enslavers of any responsibility for slavery's development.[37] Externally, the region appeared to be affluent and advanced, but internally, slavery and their sincere belief in black inferiority had stunted their growth. Attacks against slavery were met with inflamed passions that prevented otherwise intelligent white men from acting in a reasonable fashion as secession turned into war. Rhodes described a South addicted to the power and influence that slavery had provided for white men to lord over their black enslaved laborers. Shedding that addiction required a bloody war.[38]

During the Civil War Semicentennial, writers rarely sought to be objective when producing biographies of Stephens. His story attracted writers' attention because his story could be used to support their views on the war. Those who lacked an apparent partisan view often got caught up in the romantic stories of the war that were produced by all sides. The heroism and sacrifice of Civil War soldiers and the rise and fall of the Confederate government became powerful and popular narrative devices. Writers who might have supported emancipation and civil rights for freedpeople sometimes succumbed to romanticism to pen flattering histories of major Confederate leaders. American and British readers eagerly consumed those romantic biographies. Inadvertently, some of those works became major contributors to Lost Cause mythology.[39]

Gamaliel Bradford Jr., known as the "Dean of American Biographers," wrote a popular romantic biography of Stephens that offered some objective assessments of the vice-president's life and legacy. Bradford, a descendant of Gov. William Bradford of the Plymouth Colony, penned 114 biographies over a twenty-year period. His father had been an early abolitionist leader in Massachusetts.[40] Unlike most early-twentieth-century biographers, Bradford adopted a psychographic style of writing that attempted to describe for readers their subject's personality, values, opinions, and attitudes. Bradford tried to answer the eternal historical question—what were they thinking?—and the less obvious question for historical discussion, how should contemporary people remember the past? Bradford believed that consumers of biographies wanted to emulate many of the core values and heroic actions found in these romantic accounts. Bradford also tried to use his pen to heal sectional animosities by transforming Confederate rebels into affable national heroes. He felt that all Americans, North and South, black and white, male and female, could find something within the biographies of prominent Confederates that could have a positive impact on their lives. In 1912, before studying Stephens, Bradford wrote a bestselling biography of Gen. Robert E. Lee that ranked the commander as one of the greatest Americans alongside George Washington and Abraham Lincoln. According to Bradford, Lee represented an ideal version of American masculinity who deserved to be revered in both the North and the South. Bradford's praise of Lee hinted that the Confederate States of America would have had a better chance at attaining independence if the general had been in complete control of all matters civil and military. Modern-day America, in Bradford's opinion, needed more leaders and men of character like Robert E. Lee. In his effort to build a national hero, Bradford committed several mistakes that tainted the biography's claims of objectivity. Foremost, Bradford relied almost exclusively on histories written by prominent Lost Cause writers to build his psychographic portrayal of Lee. Bradford frequently referenced the works of J. William Jones, whom many considered to be the "evangelist of the Lost Cause." Audiences paid little attention to Bradford's sources. The Lee biography became a bestseller and catapulted Bradford's literary career.[41]

During the Civil War Semicentennial, Bradford wrote several biographical sketches of Union and Confederate leaders that appeared in national periodicals and newspapers, including the *Atlantic Monthly*. In 1914, Bradford published a book entitled *Confederate Portraits*, in which the preface declared "that the net result of careful study of Lee's companions in arms is to bring out more than ever the serene elevation of his greatness. . . . Not one approaches him in those moral qualities." Lee's legacy, like that of George Washington, ranked "far above those who aided him in his terrible struggle." Lee became the standard by which all other Confederate leaders were measured and found wanting in character. In addition to Lee, *Confederate Portraits* included detailed biographies of Joseph E. Johnston, J. E. B. Stuart, P. G. T. Beauregard, James Longstreet, Judah P. Benjamin, Robert Toombs, Raphael Semmes, and Alexander Stephens. The book also contained an account of the Battle of Gettysburg that released Lee from any blame for that critical defeat. Bradford did not include a biography of Jefferson Davis, although the embattled Confederate president appeared throughout each sketch as a foil that undermined the nation's independence.[42]

More than any previous Stephens biography, Bradford's analysis probed into his psyche. Bradford referred to Stephens as "the most curious and interesting figure in the lightning-lit panorama of Confederate history."[43] Stephens's contradictions fascinated Bradford because they proved difficult to explain. For example, despite having served in Congress for decades, Stephens, according to Bradford, had no major legislative accomplishments. Furthermore, regardless of the respect Stephens received from his peers, he had proved to be "politically ineffectual" and incapable of swaying his opponents to his side. Prior to the war, Stephens had failed to prevent Georgia's secession and could not use his relationship with President Abraham Lincoln to end the war at the failed Hampton Roads Conference. Bradford pointed out so many of Stephens's contradictions that Stephens came across as someone who suffered from a multiple personality disorder. He was a mass of contradictions intelligent but stubborn; high achieving but terminally depressed; friendly but reclusive; kind but abusive; against slavery's westward expansion but for protecting slavery; compromising but partisan; submissive but rebellious; frail but strong; spiritual but atheistic; and logical but emotional. Stephens was the "great common man" who "was probably one of the most logical, clear-headed, determined defenders of slavery and of the thorough subordination of black to white. Yet few men have been more sensitively humane, more tenderly sympathetic with suffering in either white or black." The "benevolent" enslaver whom "negroes loved . . . and on one occasion after the war three thousand freedman gathered on his lawn and serenaded him with passionate admiration and devotion." Stephens was a politician who upheld the Constitution as the model of enlightened government, yet he joined a rebellion whose victory would have seriously undermined those principles. Bradford described a man who, on one hand, ignored popular mandates while, on the other hand, tried to be all things to all people.[44]

Confederate Portraits reached a mass audience of American readers. Bradford's psychographic biography purposely omitted any mention of specific bills, speeches, and other details of Stephens's political career, including the Cornerstone Speech. Bradford, who was the son of a noted abolitionist and a supporter of civil equality, identified the protection of slavery and the extension of white supremacy as primary motives for secession and factors that contributed to Stephens's reluctance to remain permanently wedded to the Union and its beloved Constitution. By casting Stephens as an indecisive leader whose moral compass failed to determine his ultimate stances on controversial issues, Bradford incidentally helped Lost Cause supporters who claimed that the Cornerstone Speech had been been misinterpreted or possibly mistranscribed. Lost Cause proponents constantly tried to discredit the speech by either claiming that Stephens had been misquoted or that Little Aleck had never really meant what he had said in Savannah. Bradford's psychographic depiction of Stephens added much support for the latter criticism. Bradford left the impression that anyone who examined Stephens's record would be frustrated by his numerous contradictions and outright reversals of opinions that led him to make stances on issues that seemed to contrast with his moral compass, if such a thing ever existed. Stephens, who saw himself as a principled politician, would have rejected Bradford's interpretation. Bradford claimed that Stephens distrusted speeches and preferred other means of delivering public policy statements when Stephens actually adored the limelight of that public orations provided. Bradford mistook Stephens's lack of prepared notes as evidence of his lackluster commitment to a speech's content. Stephens, however, repeatedly defended his public remarks and took great care to say exactly what he meant. The mental exercise of preparing for a public speech was a taxing part of Stephens's daily life—a reclusive ritual that he tended to relish in lieu of other more social activities. Those who wanted to dismiss the Cornerstone Speech as the rantings of a madman who lacked conviction could find a great deal of value in Bradford's account. Gradually, Bradford's Confederate biographies became recommended reading for supporters of the Lost Cause, and eventually, neo-Confederates, who wished to present an untarnished image of Robert E. Lee, while convincing readers to not take Stephens's words too seriously.[45]

During the semicentennial, the strong public demand for Civil War histories and memoirs led to the publication of Alexander H. Stephens's postwar prison journal. The journal had appeared in the *Confederate Veteran Magazine* and newspapers decades earlier. In 1910, UDC leader Myrta Lockett Avary, the widow of Stephens's chief of staff, Col. Isaac W. Avary, published the journal. The diary reinforced Lost Cause visions of Civil War memory. Like many Confederate publications, the journal added to an existing narrative that sought to slander the Union victory by painting its government as inhumane, especially in its treatment of Confederate prisoners of war. As the semicentennial approached, northern newspapers had published haunting narratives of Union prisoners of war held at Andersonville, Georgia. If the Lost Cause wanted to maintain its aura of nobility, it had to accuse the North of similar crimes against humanity.[46]

Imprisonment humiliated Stephens, who believed that his initial opposition to secession and wartime efforts to end the fighting through a political compromise should have been enough to demonstrate his loyalty to the Union. False rumors spread that Stephens's poor health had been caused by the supposed horrible conditions at Fort Warren. One commonly repeated falsehood was that "when he went to Fort Warren his hair was a glossy chestnut. When released five months later it was snow white." Avary and others purposefully distorted Stephens's antebellum medical history so that his health made him one of many martyrs claimed by the war. Writers used the memory of his imprisonment to paint Stephens as a sympathetic historical figure whose incarceration represented the North's vengeful spirit. *Goodwin's Weekly* of Salt Lake City, Utah, touted Stephens's postwar efforts to reconcile the bitter sectional feelings that had been created by the war's devastation. "This diary," claimed the editor, "shows no bitterness of soul, but rather a vast anxiety that the while country might be restored and re-united" because "he had been a Union man up to the last and only went to the confederacy when there was no other place on the continent that he could go." The article exaggerated supposed exceptional traits that set Stephens apart from other Civil War leaders. Many writers accepted at face value Avary's disingenuous claim that Stephens "was the one public man of the day who remained throughout the war neither northern not southern, but American."[47]

Many writers drew additional attention to Stephens's innocence by repeating several passages in the journal in which the "great commoner" displayed kindness to animals. Subject to fits of loneliness and melancholy, Stephens "tried to make friends with a mouse." When guards killed several bed bugs that had infested Stephens's cell, the former vice-president mourned for their needless deaths. The commentary's tone tried to suggest that if Stephens had been unwilling to harm animals then he could not be blamed for the war's human toll.[48]

Lost in the campaign to wash Stephens's legacy clean of his active role in the Confederate government was the journal's commentary on the Cornerstone Speech. While at Fort Warren, Stephens for the first time claimed that reporters had misquoted several passages of the Cornerstone Speech. Stephens's efforts in his journal to discredit the speech transcript seemed odd given that he had not previously criticized their reporting, nor did he point which passages had been misquoted. Throughout his career Stephens had often quarreled with reporters who he claimed had inaccurately transcribed his remarks on other occasions. Stephens published plenty of letters in newspapers that corrected the errors. In the years after the Cornerstone Speech, Stephens never once publicly complained about the transcription's accuracy. By 1911, however, writers did not seem concerned with what he had either said or had not said back in March of 1861. Instead, Stephens's proclamation that God had given white men the right to preserve, expand, and defend the inhumane institution of human slavery because of black inferiority vanished from most accounts of his wartime record. Rather than remember Stephens as a leader who worked tirelessly to withhold rights and privileges from an entire race of people, writers mourned that more Americans had not heeded his pre-Cornerstone Speech warnings about the consequences of secession.

During the semicentennial, Stephens became one of the great "what ifs" and martyrs of conscience commemorated by Lost Cause supporters, who chose to ignore his role in identifying the war's true causes. Instead, writers insisted that "the whole pitiable story ought to fix more deeply the impression upon every American that whatever the future may bring, there must never be any sectional quarrel in our country that must not be peaceably settled." For a nation concerned by its "race problem," Stephens's greatest failure was not that he helped lead a failed rebellion to preserve white supremacy. His greatest failure might have been that he had failed to prevent a war whose results produced emancipation and challenged white supremacy's hold on American life.[49]

Nearly thirty years after Stephens's death, southern politicians continued to find ways to insert his name into contemporary debates. As part of a series of events designed to mark the centenary of Stephens's birth, the Georgia General Assembly, in collaboration with the United Daughters of the Confederacy, the

Confederate Memorial Literary Society, and the United Confederate Veterans, passed a resolution to install a bronze tablet to mark his wartime residence in Richmond.[50] Georgia Congressman William Gordon Brantley delivered a keynote address that blended current events with Lost Cause memory. Inspired by Horatio Alger's children's books, Brantley noted that Stephens had overcome poverty and disease to serve his "country and humanity." According to Brantley, the results of the Civil War and its aftermath had vindicated Stephens's "conservatism." During the secession crisis, Stephens "urged moderation" only to be ignored. Likewise, he implored the nation to defend the Constitution, but an abusive majority used their powers to force secession upon the South. After the war, the South found itself weakened by war, defeat, and emancipation and unable to fend off a tyrannical federal government determined to reconstruct the region. As Brantley's Lost Cause history lesson ended, he accused the modern federal government of committing "political heresies" that abused the Constitution by interfering with the judiciary. Brantley warned that "a similar arrogant assumption of power by the majority which a half century ago, plunged the nation into internecine war" was on the horizon if the majority remained unchallenged.[51]

During the semicentennial, most southern newspapers refrained from mentioning the Cornerstone Speech. The *Athens Banner* published numerous full-page histories of the Civil War between 1911 and 1915. In an article detailing the secession crisis in Georgia, the paper portrayed Stephens as a moderate voice who had urged Georgia to remain in the Union. No reason was given for why Stephens accepted a position in the Confederate government after secession. The article, penned by United Daughters of the Confederacy historian Ruth Rodgers, omitted any mention of the Cornerstone Speech in its detailed account of the events of 1861. The word slavery did not appear anywhere in the text. Rodgers described secession as a necessary counteraction to the North's constitutional abuses and the election of Republican President Abraham Lincoln. A later article stated that "it was not abolition of slavery that was so agitating the Northern mind before the sixties . . . it was a desire for a centralized government." Other articles that mentioned Stephens tended to focus on the Hampton Roads Conference or his incarceration at Fort Warren.[52]

Southern newspapers may have ignored the Cornerstone Speech, but white southern schoolchildren helped keep the speech in public conversations about the war. In 1914, the state of Louisiana Board of Education, in collaboration with the United Daughters of the Confederacy, sponsored an essay-writing contest that, among other topics, encouraged students to write a biographical sketch of Alexander Stephens. No higher-ranking Civil War–era official wrote more during the postbellum period than Stephens. At the start of the semicentennial, public and private funds were collected across the South to purchase history books written from a southern perspective. Sales of three of Stephens's books, *Constitutional View of the Late War Between the States, A Comprehensive and Popular History of the United States,* and *Recollections of Alexander H. Stephens,* skyrocketed as libraries across the South purchased copies. His reputation as an intellectual statesman led many to believe that he was also a great historian. On one hand, Stephens's writings helped shape aspects of Civil War memory. On the other hand, most audiences seemed to ignore the substance of those writings and relied on more popular (public) sources of information to ground their views. Therefore, when Daisy St. Germain, an eighth-grader from New Orleans, wrote her sketch of Stephens's life, she likely had access to his historical writings, but ignored them. Instead of refuting the Cornerstone Speech, St. Germain accused Stephens of "greatly weakening the position of the Confederacy by a speech delivered at Savannah in 1861, in which he declared that slavery was its cornerstone." She further blamed Stephens for failing to convince sympathetic northerners that the Confederacy was fighting "to preserve constitutional government." After the war, according to St. Germain, Stephen "exercised a beneficent influence on the negroes . . . and promoted reconciliation between the North and the South." Stephens remained a respected, yet flawed, historical figure whose actions as Confederate vice-president damaged the fledgling nation's fight for independence. Alexander Stephens landed somewhere between hero and scapegoat.[53]

During the semicentennial, the Cornerstone Speech usually turned up whenever white southerners believed they had discovered some evidence that invalidated Stephens's claim that slavery was the foundation of the new nation. One common argument was that by the late antebellum era slavery's place in southern society had declined. Lost Cause authors often paired that flawed history with another falsehood—the assertion that few Confederate leaders owned enslaved laborers. The fiftieth anniversary of President Abraham Lincoln's Emancipation Proclamation sparked renewed interest in the Cornerstone Speech among those who peddled those lies. Some white southerners doubted the need for the proclamation because they claimed that slavery had been on the verge of extinction on the eve of the war. In a letter to the editor published in the *New York Tribune,* a white southern male identified as "W. N.," argued that slavery could not have been the cornerstone of the Confederacy because so few Confederate generals and soldiers owned enslaved laborers. If slavery had been the Confederacy's cornerstone, the writer questioned, "why [did] Gen. Robert E. Lee . . . [free] his own slaves just fifty years ago?" The writer speculated that Lee had supposedly freed his slaves "to show his dissent from Stephens' declaration." Sidney Blan, a newspaper editor who reprinted this *New York Tribune* letter in his *Troy Messenger,* added some additional editorial remarks, arguing that "the illusion that African slavery was the issue upon which the War Between the States was fought, will probably never die, because false teachers have been allowed to hold sway over minds which knew no better." Blan included below his comments a list of Confederate leaders who either did not own enslaved laborers or owned a handful of enslaved laborers. His cherry-picked list failed to include notable leaders who owned considerable numbers of human property, such as Jefferson Davis, Robert Toombs, Howell Cobb, Alfred H. Colquitt, Samuel Cooper, Judah P. Benjamin, Braxton Bragg, Wade Hampton, and Alexander Stephens himself, to name just a few.[54]

The Civil War Semicentennial failed to resolve the major debates that shaped how Americans remembered the Confederate States of America. Those memories would be further complicated by the 1915 premiere of D. W. Griffith's *The Birth of a Nation*. The highly successful and controversial film, based on Thomas Dixon Jr.'s 1905 novel *The Clansmen*, portrayed the Civil War and Reconstruction eras as a tragic period when a nefarious coalition of northern abolitionists and carpet baggers conspired with black enslaved laborers and freedpeople to overthrow southern civilization. Using white actors donning blackface paint, the film depicted black men as rapists whose primary goal in obtaining freedom was to sexually assault white women. Through the heroic actions of the Ku Klux Klan, the story's protagonists, the South was able to defeat those internal and external threats and preserve its white-supremacist social order. The NAACP condemned the film. President Woodrow Wilson, a historian, praised the movie's historical accuracy.[55]

The Cornerstone Speech remained a part of a contentious public discourse throughout the semicentennial. Americans who wanted to discredit the Lost Cause found the speech to be quite useful. Their opponents devoted much time to undermining Stephens's credibility and legacy. The speech drew immediate comparison with the values found in the Declaration of Independence. For some, the message espoused in the Cornerstone Speech was un-American and tyrannical. At times, Stephens emerged as a scapegoat who helped explain Confederate defeat, while both recognizing and obscuring the Cornerstone Speech. Some writers chose to greatly exaggerate the speech's influence on Confederate lack of success in foreign affairs. In other instances, the speech was omitted entirely, as Stephens became a symbol of the mistreatment of Confederate leaders in the hands of a vengeful federal government. In the hands of white supremacists, such as John Temple Graves, the Cornerstone Speech served as an unofficial manifesto that outlined the historical development and rationale behind white supremacy. Alexander Stephens and the Cornerstone Speech would continue to influence how Americans remembered the Civil War for decades to come.

CHAPTER SEVEN

Old Times There Are Not Forgotten, 1915–1965

In the decades that followed the Civil War Semicentennial, white supremacists and Lost Cause proponents dominated how Americans remembered the war, but opposition to their views forced them to continue defending their position. The persistent need to defend their views led Lost Cause followers to continue producing distorted partisan histories that made it difficult for some to differentiate history from propaganda.

The Lost Cause remained committed to disproving that defending slavery had been central to secession. Lost Cause publications tried to mislead readers into believing that President Abraham Lincoln and Confederate leaders such as Alexander H. Stephens shared similar racial prejudices. Supporters of the Lost Cause argued that the war could not have been about slavery if the American president was not a devout abolitionist. They refused to take into consideration that Lincoln's views on race and slavery might have evolved over time and in response to pro-slavery partisans. Lost Cause advocates fixated on highly selective examples of Lincoln's voluminous writings and speeches, bringing attention to only those statements that confirmed his support for enslavers. Lincoln and Stephens's brief antebellum friendship had long played a small part in the Lost Cause. During Lincoln's single term in Congress (1847–1849), he befriended fellow Whig Party member Alexander H. Stephens. After Lincoln left Congress, the two men did not communicate with each other until after the election of 1860. Lincoln admired Stephens's intellect and remembered their relationship, but neither sought advice from the other.[1]

In 1917, the *Montgomery Advertiser* published an article that used Ida Tarbell's *Life of Abraham Lincoln* to sully Lincoln's reputation. The article focused on a single passage taken from a January 19, 1860, letter that Lincoln had sent in reply to Alexander Stephens's earlier message. Trying to convince Stephens that southern states should remain under the protection of the

Constitution rather than secede and abandon those rights, Lincoln wrote "All the States' rights which they wish to retain are now and forever retained, including slavery." The newspaper expressed surprise that "Lincoln's admirers" had been "surprised at this curious sentence" because "the modern idea of Lincoln devoting his life to the abolition of slavery as a political and economic necessity, is due to biographers and commentators who have advanced far beyond the record." After admitting to slavery's indirect role in the war, the newspaper reminded everyone that "the North, led by Lincoln, did not, in 1861, set out to abolish slavery, but to preserve the Union at all costs." The war had been caused by abolitionist "agitators" who failed to recognize that "slavery itself would have passed out of human customs, even as it had been abolished in every other civilized country, without a war." Supposedly, southern efforts to end slavery initiated by Thomas Jefferson's generation had ceased in response to "the hot passions of [abolitionist] agitators."[2]

After World War I, the United Daughters of the Confederacy, with the help of the Ku Klux Klan, raised the $18,000 needed to produce a large marble statue of Stephens. Harriet Harwell Wilson High, a prominent Atlanta art collector, UDC member, and wife of an affluent department store owner, donated the funds for the Stephens statue. To reduce the monument's cost, the Georgia Marble Company generously sold the marble to planners at cost.[3] Unexpectedly, renowned sculptor Gutzom Borglum agreed to carve the monument for free. Borglum had a long and rocky relationship with the UDC. In 1915, UDC leaders first approached Borglum to solicit his ideas for a Confederate memorial at Stone Mountain. That same year, the KKK had relaunched its organization at a cross burning ceremony held atop Stone Mountain. UDC leader Helen Plane wanted the memorial to honor both the Confederacy and the KKK, whom she credited for saving "us from Negro domination and carpetbag rule" during Reconstruction. At one point, Borglum joined the KKK to gain favor with his project's sponsors. In 1923, Borglum began carving Stone Mountain, but his work ended less than two years later after several disagreements with the UDC and KKK. Borglum and his white supremacist sponsors disagreed over the monument's design and the artist's management of the project. During a fit of rage, Borglum destroyed the models that he had created for the carving and left Georgia, determined never to return. Newspaper editorials denounced Borglum's resignation for weeks.[4]

A few months after Borglum's resignation, the Georgia General Assembly formed a statuary committee to select an artist to produce the Stephens statue as Georgia's contribution to the US Capitol's Statuary Hall. To everyone's surprise, Borglum responded positively to the committee's solicitations and agreed to donate his labor if the state could cover all other expenses. Georgia shipped a large block of marble to Borglum's studio in San Antonio, Texas. Borglum completed the statue in less than two years.[5]

Some Americans chastised Georgia and its congressional delegation for honoring Alexander H. Stephens—and the US government for allowing its installation. Neval Thomas, an African American educator and leader of the Washington, DC, Chapter of the National Association for the Advancement of Colored People (NAACP), published a letter of protest sent to the Architect of the United States Capitol, the official in charge of Statuary Hall. A few years earlier, Thomas played a central role in the Washington Riots, known as the Red Summer. As racial violence spread across the capitol, Thomas met with Washington, DC, leaders to demand police protection for the black community. When the city ignored his request, Thomas urged the city's black residents to arm and defend themselves. Through his actions, Thomas earned a reputation as a leader who was willing to stand up against white authorities for black rights despite considerable risk.[6]

Thomas questioned why the US government had allowed the placement of statues at the capitol "in honor of men who gave their supreme effort to destroy this nation." He pondered why a statue of Confederate Gen. Robert E. Lee had been placed at the Capitol when he "rewarded the splendid gift [of] training in the Union Military Academy at West Point . . . with treason." The legacy of Alexander H. Stephens proved to be more offensive to African Americans than that of Lee. Stephens wore "the stain of helping to found the only government in the history of the world whose sole purpose was the perpetuation of slavery." Any "genius" that he possessed was exhausted solely for the purpose of "champion[ing] every demand of the slave power." Stephens and the South had shown their arrogance by returning the ex-Confederate to Congress after the Civil War. Most nations, Thomas speculated, would have tried and convicted traitors like Stephens and Lee, but America gave them the chance to retire in peace. Instead, the "ungrateful South sent [Stephens] to Congress again, where he obstructed every wise measure of Reconstruction statesmanship." Whereas Lee had been defeated on the battlefield, Stephens had suffered a far more humiliating defeat in the halls of Congress. Stephens's "foolish and wicked notions of racial inferiority" had been exposed and disproved by African American Congressman Robert Elliott of South Carolina. The sight of a black man lecturing Stephens in the House of Representatives on the virtues of American democracy confirmed for all to see the fallacies of white supremacy.[7]

After eviscerating Stephens's legacy, Thomas launched a set of criticisms against the American government that connected the memorialization of Confederates with contemporary racial divisions. Thomas argued that Statuary Hall had been created to honor the memory of Americans whose legacy would inspire future generations to advance the nation's lofty ideals. "The urge for the admission for these two statues," Thomas exclaimed, "springs from the unrepentant spirit that wants the Nation to admit that the South was right in seeking to wreck the Union." Lost Cause and white-supremacist forces understood "that the cold marble can proclaim its cause, especially when it is placed in the very center and heart of government." The nation should be ashamed to revere traitors at the US Capitol while "the many illustrious Negroes who have rendered distinguished service in every noble endeavor in our country's history have no place there." By omitting memorials of notable African Americans at Statuary Hall, Thomas accused the nation of stripping away the black race's patriotism by encouraging them to forget their contributions. Thomas demanded that the statues of Lee and Stephens be prohibited from Statuary Hall.[8]

Congress ignored Thomas's demands. On December 8, 1927, Congress unveiled the Stephens statue during a ceremony attended by approximately fifteen hundred Georgia elected officials, business leaders, and heritage association officers. The long shadow of the Lost Cause hung over the proceedings. At the start of the ceremony, a special decorative wreath was placed in front of the nearby statue of Gen. Robert E. Lee. The ceremony recognized Stephens's reluctant role in helping form and govern the Confederacy but treated the Civil War as a painful mistake that had damaged the nation. Speakers drew a firm connection between Stephens and national reconciliation but steadfastly remained committed to the idea that any healing required some consensus that the defense of states' rights and not protecting slavery had caused the war. In the eyes of the supporters of the monument, recognizing Stephens, and by extension legitimizing the complaints of the Confederacy, proved that the Civil War had been both necessary and just and offered contemporary audiences meaningful lessons about the proper relation between state and federal governments.[9]

Dora Stephens, the last living enslaved laborer owned by Stephens, also attended the event at the invitation of Stephens's descendants. Although she was recognized during the ceremony by several speakers, she did not speak. Her appearance was largely used as an example of Stephens's reputed charitable relations with his formerly enslaved laborers. Throughout the program, orators cast Stephens as a racial moderate who shunned extremism on all sides in favor of enacting meaningful legislation that benefited white and black men. If speakers included any mention of Stephens's enslaved human property, the institution served as a foil that highlighted his benevolence. Most speakers agreed that Stephens believed slavery to be a problem in antebellum society that lacked any easy solutions but should remain intact if enslavers treated their enslaved laborers humanely. Event speakers tried to reconcile Stephens's role as

Confederate vice-president with his inclusion at Statuary Hall, considered to be a national hall of fame. They could not avoid the irony of honoring a man whose actions as Confederate vice-president were treasonous. Weeks prior to the ceremony, Congress passed a resolution that recognized Stephens's "distinguished humanitarian service" and omitted any mention of the Confederacy.[10]

The addition of a statue at the US Capitol honoring the former vice-president of the Confederate States of America was met with approval across the nation. Southern newspaper editors memorialized Stephens as a hardworking statesman who rose from poverty to become a major politician and intellectual. Southern editors stressed how the addition of a monument honoring a former Confederate leader had "served to bring closer together, if that could be possible, all the sections of this country into a great brotherhood of man and of government."[11] The UDC regularly published monthly news and announcements in local newspapers. After the statue's unveiling, the UDC promoted another essay-writing contest to honor Stephens's legacy. Women donated funds to purchase books about Stephens for local libraries across the region and encouraged teachers to publicize the contest. The UDC promoted Stephens as a major literary figure in southern history whose legacy as a historian that "defended the South" outweighed his political career. Stephens appealed to UDC leaders because his lifelong pursuit of education and self-improvement reflected the organization's charitable work.[12]

Northern newspapers emphasized Stephens's opposition to secession and postbellum role in healing the nation's sectional discord. Few questioned Stephens's Confederate credentials. They seemed more concerned by how the addition of new monuments had left little room in Statuary Hall for future memorials.[13]

In addition to being remembered as a champion of education, newspapers also celebrated Stephens as a defender of religious toleration. During the Election of 1828, New York Gov. Al Smith became the first Roman Catholic to win the Democratic Party's presidential nomination. Smith's victory sent shockwaves throughout the nation, as some Democrats threatened to withdraw their support in protest of his Catholic faith. White southerners, in a region where protestant denominations were predominate and anti-Catholic animus predated the nation's founding, debated whether to remain committed to a national party that had endorsed a Catholic for president but worried that any defections from the party might lead to a Republican Party victory. In 1928, southern politicians still saw the Democratic Party as defenders of the region's interests. As the Democratic Party splintered, the *Atlanta Constitution*, Georgia's primary news organ for the party, published an editorial calling for Georgia voters to follow in Alexander Stephens's footsteps. Stephens's name had been in the news thanks to the recent Statuary Hall celebration. In 1855, Stephens had delivered a speech that criticized the Know Nothing Party's nativist rhetoric. Stephens advised Americans to resist "mixing religion and politics." From the House chamber, Stephens had proclaimed that "In American every citizen, wherever he might be born, or whatever may be his religion, is to be measured and weighed in the civil scales according to his merits and conduct, deserts and worth."[14] Urging readers to continue their support for the Democratic Party, editors warned voters, much like Stephens had done during the Election of 1860 when he condemned pro-slavery radicals for destroying party unity, that the Democratic Party was the sole national party devoted to preserving the South's interests. During Reconstruction, the party had provided "the shelter of which the white people of the south escaped from negro domination, and from laws enforced by 'carpetbaggers' with federal bayonets at their back." The newspaper accused modern-day Republicans of once again plotting to assault the South's racially segregated social order.[15]

On February 11, 1928, the City of Atlanta and the State of Georgia organized an "Alexander Stephens memorial parade . . . through the downtown canyons of Atlanta" to honor his 116th birthday. UDC leaders Elizabeth Venable Mason and Harriet Harwell Wilson High organized the event program. The event drew thousands of spectators to witness the unveiling of a bronze replica of the Alexander Stephens Statuary Hall statue to be displayed at the Georgia Capitol. Gov. L. G. Hardman accepted the statue on "behalf of the youths of Georgia, whose futures have been brightened by the principles [Stephens] advocated." The parade included a procession of cadets from Emory University and the Georgia Military Academy (GMA). A single car occupied by the last surviving Confederate veterans brought up the parade's rear. US and Confederate flags lined the buildings and light posts as the GMA cadet band serenaded the procession with renditions of "Dixie" and the "Star-Spangled Banner."

Inside the packed Atlanta Auditorium, speakers lauded Stephens's life. A former personal secretary told the crowd that "the most searching scrutiny . . . can not discover anything unworthy, anything inconsistent with true greatness, in the life of him in whose honor we are here assembled. His private life no less than his public acts conformed to the highest standards." Former Gov. Nat E. Harris retold the story of how Stephens had helped the Confederate veteran afford an education after his forced relocation from east Tennessee. Harris portrayed Stephens as a kind man who never refused to help a stranger in need. Beyond the inclusion of Confederate veterans, flags, and songs, the event did not reflect on Stephens's role as Confederate vice-president. For the moment, Stephens's admirable character traits appeared to overshadow his role in the Civil War. The sole assessment of his wartime record accurately claimed that, although Stephens had opposed the act of secession, he had been fully convinced of secession's constitutionality. Stephens, according to one speaker, supported secession as a means of protecting the "old constitution," which during the 1850s had been assaulted by northern partisans.[16]

Perhaps the greatest change in how Georgians chose to remember Stephens came from ninety-two-year-old Rebecca L. Felton. Felton and her husband, William H. Felton, had once been close political allies of Stephens during their postwar bid to challenge the Democratic Party's Bourbon faction rulers. When Stephens betrayed the Feltons by eventually aligning with his old Bourbon adversaries, Rebecca Felton condemned Stephens's perceived cowardness and placed him on a list of enemies that included Gen. John B. Gordon. Decades had helped to heal those old wounds. By 1928, Felton referred to Stephens as an "intimate friend" and "great Georgian." Her remarks emphasized the mutual respect that Stephens and Lincoln had shared. According to Felton, Lincoln "referred to Congressman Stephens as the most powerful orator in the house of representatives. . . . The president knew and loved him, recognizing in the Georgia representative a leading statesman without fear or prejudice." One of Stephens's loudest critics had now cast Stephens as a "marble man" absolved of criticism. In sum, the speakers celebrated Stephens's "stainless fame" as worthy of being immortalized in "an enduring marble statue." Neither the statue's marble nor Stephens's reputation would change.[17]

Among the many dignitaries and Confederate veterans who joined the dais that day were "three darkie retainers, formerly in the employ of Alexander Stephens." Reporters omitted the African American guests' names, and none spoke during the event. Prof. Linton S. Ingram, one of Stephens's last surviving former enslaved laborers who after emancipation taught and administered the Sparta Agricultural and Industrial Institute in Sparta, Georgia, did not receive an invitation. For decades Ingram had been held up as a stellar example of Stephens's benevolence. While enslaved Ingram learned to read and write with Stephens's encouragement. After emancipation, Stephens provided Ingram financial support to attend Atlanta University. Ingram often spoke fondly of Stephens and used his connection to the deceased statesman to lobby the Georgia legislature to finance his institute.[18] The Stephens's birthday celebration speakers ignored slavery except for a passing reference to the unconstitutionality of emancipation and the repeated assertions that Stephens treated all persons equally. Lost Cause advocates no longer felt the need to defend Stephens's record or acknowledge the Cornerstone Speech because in the decades that followed the Civil War Semicentennial they dominated how white southerners remembered the war.

In 1929, Alexander Stephens's Cornerstone Speech became embroiled in a controversy stemming from a series of forged letters that Abraham Lincoln had supposedly written to Stephens following the Election of 1860. The forged letters had been purchased by Lincolniana collector Judd Stewart and later donated to Huntingdon Library in California. Originally, the letters were thought to be a series of communications among Lincoln, Stephens, and Kentucky Sen. John J. Crittenden as the men tried to find a political solution to avoid secession. A letter dated January 19, 1860, was purported to be Lincoln's response to an earlier letter from Stephens that urged the president-elect to protect slavery. In the lengthy forged reply, Lincoln supposedly wrote "you say that slavery is the corner stone of the south and if separated, would be that of a new Republic; God forbid." A fake Lincoln shared with Stephens his memories of encountering slavery along the Mississippi River as a young man and how he had prayed that various emancipation schemes might succeed. The letter made it seem as if Stephens had communicated to Lincoln portions of the Cornerstone Speech months prior to its delivery in Savannah. The unidentified forger who sold the letters to Stewart also forged a letter of authenticity supposedly penned by Stephens to his biographer Henry Cleveland, verifying the document's origins. The forger skillfully addressed the letter from Stephens to "Henry Whitney Cleveland" rather than Henry Cleveland. Henry Whitney Cleveland did not exist and was not Stephens's trusted friend and biographer. The false letters had appeared in a 1909 pamphlet published by Stewart that supposedly provided evidence that neither Lincoln nor Stephens was willing to compromise on the future of slavery and that both men despised the radical elements that had pushed the nation toward secession. The forged letters were important because Lost Cause proponents sometimes used them to portray Lincoln as an uncompromising ideologue whose leadership pushed the South toward secession. Today, the forged letters continue to be trafficked on the internet and referenced by Civil War enthusiasts, despite their fraudulent origins.[19]

Federal programs created during the Great Depression helped preserve Stephens's legacy. Since Stephens's death in 1883, his admirers dreamed of creating a lasting memorial at Liberty Hall, the vice-president's home in Crawfordville, Georgia. Two years after his death, the Alexander H. Stephens Memorial Association formed and purchased Liberty Hall. Most of the property that comprised Stephens's plantation passed into private ownership. Some of the property was sold or deeded to several formerly enslaved laborer families who had remained with Stephens after emancipation. The association was headed by Dr. and Mrs. Horace M. Holden and Mary Corry Holden, Stephens's grandniece. Together, they lobbied local and state leaders for decades on behalf of Liberty Hall. They received a great deal of assistance from the United Daughters of the Confederacy, which sponsored numerous scholarships and essay contests and supplied Georgia libraries with free copies of Stephens's writings. The association hatched numerous schemes to fund their memorial. Foremost, the group transformed Liberty Hall from a residence into a school that continued Stephens's lifelong passion for learning. The school made efforts to provide free or reduced cost educational opportunities for poor white children in the region. In 1916, the association lobbied the state to create a unit of the state university system at Crawfordsville. Ultimately, the association could not raise enough donations to fund the school. By the 1930s, Liberty Hall's future use remained uncertain.[20]

In 1932, the creation of the Georgia Department of Forestry and Geological Development breathed new life into plans for a Stephens memorial. The new agency replaced the existing Department of Forestry, which had been woefully underfunded during its brief seven-year existence. Due to sharp declines in state funds caused by the Great Depression, Georgia Gov. Richard B. Russell consolidated the state's 117 agencies into 17 departments. As part of the state's consolidation program, leaders gave forestry agents responsibilities for establishing and managing memorial parks that promoted a combination of natural and cultural resources.[21]

Stephens Memorial Association Director Mary Corry Holden approached Burley M. Lufburrow, the state forester, to consider transforming Liberty Hall into a state memorial park. The UDC also sent lobbyists to encourage his support. After Lufburrow toured the property, the memorial association voted unanimously to donate the house and twelve acres of land to the state. A few weeks later, the Department of Forestry and Geological Development commission passed a resolution to accept the property. Commissioners embraced Stephens's reputation as one of Georgia's greatest statesmen. Discussions of Stephens's life tended to emphasize his "flawless character." Plans for the park soon included discussions of erecting a Confederate history museum on the property. With plans for a Confederate Memorial Park at Stone Mountain stalled, Georgia's government decided that Liberty Hall could memorialize the state's role in the Confederate States of America. Alexander H. Stephens Memorial Park was Georgia's first memorial park. Meanwhile, as Liberty Hall passed into state ownership, the commission held meetings with President-elect Franklin D. Roosevelt at his Warm Springs, Georgia, retreat to discuss potential state and federal partnerships to expand Georgia's protected forests and to build new recreational facilities.[22]

On March 31, 1933, Congress established the Civilian Conservation Corps (CCC) to recruit unemployed young men for forestry, flood prevention, erosion control, and parks development. The CCC created work camps across the nation to house crews of young men who received a dollar-a-day wage and food and housing in exchange for their labor. Between 1933 and 1942, the CCC built 127 camps across Georgia, employing more than 78,000 white men. Among the 127 camps in Georgia, the CCC played a direct role in the development of 10 state parks, including A. H. Stephens Memorial State Park. On June 24, 1933, a train pulled into Crawfordville carrying 200 young white men from Fort McClellan, Alabama, whose assignment was to transform the land into a recreation facility and to manage the local forest.[23] The initial Stephens Memorial Association donation of land only included 12 acres of property that surrounded Liberty Hall. In 1933, the National Park Service created the Recreation Demonstration Area (RDA) to employ young men across the nation to build new parks near urban centers. Located halfway between Atlanta and Augusta on the Georgia Railroad (now CSX), Crawfordville represented an ideal site to develop recreational facilities that would provide respite for residents of two urban areas. The RDA provided Georgia with funds to purchase an additional 200 acres of park property. The RDA's involvement also ensured that the development of a public park would be the federal government's primary mission in Crawfordville. From its inception, however, Alexander Stephens Memorial State Park was designed for the exclusive use of white people despite the area's large African American population. The federal government also did nothing to discourage Georgia from using national funds to build a recreation facility that would also serve as a memorial to the Confederacy. Of the 46 parks that the RDA created, Alexander Stephens Memorial State Park would be the only sole facility dedicated to the memory of the Confederate States of America. The decision to use federal funds to build a Confederate memorial drew no comment across the country because park promoters emphasized Stephens's faultless character, generous philanthropy, and steadfast loyalty to the Constitution.[24]

Between 1933 and 1935, the CCC and RDA dramatically changed the landscape surrounding Liberty Hall. The CCC built a children's wading pool, a 2.3-acre lake, a bathhouse, granite benches, barbeque pits, shelters, 13 miles of roads, and hiking trails. Perhaps the most visible addition was a 60-foot fire tower that offered a 30-mile panoramic view of the area. As the park took shape, Mary Corry Holden supervised CCC workers as they restored Liberty Hall to its 1875 appearance. A fundraising campaign raised money to purchase period appropriate furniture. Holden, who was an active leader in Georgia's Chapter of the UDC, predicted that "thousands of tourists [will] visit Liberty Hall annually to see the place where the traditions of the old south are being carried on to enlighten a more modern world."[25] Holden failed to specify which Old South traditions Liberty Hall exemplified, but she regarded the Confederacy's loss and emancipation as destabilizing forces in southern history. After the CCC disbanded Camp Liberty in November 1935, the Works

Progress Administration (WPA) continued to add recreational facilities to the park, including a 23-acre lake, rustic cabins, a dining hall, a ranger's residence, and other buildings. The WPA purchased an additional 900 acres of land for the park and spent five years clearing overgrown forests to produce a managed landscape that appealed to visitors.[26]

On July 18, 1935, after two years of CCC labor, Alexander Stephens Memorial State Park supporters gathered to dedicate the park to "one of Georgia's most famous statesmen." The Georgia Chapter of the UDC planned the event. Poor weather in Washington, DC, had prevented Gov. Eugene Talmadge from attending the ceremony. In his stead, Georgia Attorney General M. J. Yeomans delivered the keynote address proclaiming that Stephens's life was "absolutely perfect he did no wrong." Judge Horace Holden, the husband of Mary Holden, director of the Alexander H. Stephens Memorial Association, declared that Stephens was "all any man could be." State Sen. V. M. Lester of Augusta told the crowd that "he was thankful that southerners were no longer rabidly sectional." Despite Lester's comments, the program reflected the UDC's continued commitment to the Lost Cause. Various speakers acknowledged Stephens's critical role in providing a southern interpretation of the "War Between the States." UDC leader and Georgia poet laureate Helen Rogers Franklin of Tennille, Georgia, organized a moving portion of the ceremony that involved members of the Children of the Confederacy—a Confederate heritage youth group—dedicating a special granite bench in honor of Georgia's two greatest historians, Stephens and Mildred Rutherford, both of whom had played a critical part in building and defending the Lost Cause. The Children of the Confederacy then saluted Stephens by singing Franklin's poem "Alexander Stephens Georgia's Own" to the tune of the "Bonnie Blue Flag." Lost Cause beliefs and rituals saturated the day's events.[27]

Despite spending several weeks prior to the event acquiring the final resting place of Dora Stephens, Alexander Stephens's beloved African American cook, the ceremony's planners failed to include any African American speakers, even though many descendants of his enslaved laborers lived in the immediate area. The ceremony also ignored the park's former history as a plantation. Although CCC workers had reconstructed a slave cabin as part of their work, no attention seemed to paid to slavery at Liberty Hall. Surviving accounts suggest that no African Americans were invited to the event due to prevailing Jim Crow laws, which prohibited their use of whites only public parks in Georgia.[28]

Alexander Stephens's legacy was also impacted by a program of the Federal Writers' Project (FWP) that interviewed hundreds of former slaves across the South. On August 4, 1938, FWP interviewer Sadie Hornsby, a white thirty-seven-year-old widow and single mother who often took in boarders to make ends meet, interviewed Georgia Baker, a black eighty-seven-year-old woman who lived with her daughter at 369 Meigs Street in Athens, Georgia. For more than three hours, Baker proudly recalled that she had been "borne on de plantation of a great man. . . . Marse Alec Stephens." When asked how Stephens treated his enslaved laborers, Baker proclaimed that "dere warn't no Marster no whar no better dan our Marse Alec Stephens, but he never stayed home enough to tend to things hisself much 'cause he was all de time busy on de outside." However, when Stephens was at home, "he used to walk down to de cabins and laugh and talk to his Niggers. He used to sing a song for de slave chillum." Baker portrayed Stephens as a kind and generous enslaver who provided his human chattel with ample amounts of food and eschewed physical violence. Unlike most slaves, Baker reported that Stephens's slaves had passes that allowed them to regularly travel to neighboring plantations to visit their friends and family. According to Baker, "folks in Crawfordville called us 'Stephens' Free Niggers.'" Stephens also disliked slave patrols and banned them from his property. She regaled Hornsby with the exceptional story of Stephens helping one of his slaves escape the region following a violent altercation with a local white woman. When asked if she preferred her life as an enslaved laborer compared to her current situation, Baker replied "I sho would ruther have slavery days back if I could have my same good Marsters 'cause I never had no hard times den lak I went through atter dey give us freedom. I ain't never got over no bein' able to see Marse Alec no more. . . . If ever a man went to Heaven, Marse Alec did. I sho does wish our good old Marster was livin' now." Hornsby found Baker to be so interesting that she returned for a second shorter interview. At the end of the first interview, Baker had complimented a yellow dress that Hornsby wore. When Hornsby returned, she gave Baker a yellow dress[29]

The FWP's slave narratives are problematic sources for many reasons. White interviewers intruded into the lives of elderly former slaves during the depths of the Great Depression. Most of the interviews were conducted in cities, where poverty was often more acute. Many of the black narrators lived in poverty at a time when Americans were unsure if the nation's economy would recover from the depression. Narrators, like Baker, had been children at the time of their emancipation and might have been shielded from some of the horrors of slavery. White interviewers often asked leading questions, such as "how good was your master?" No attention was given to the fact that these black narrators had lived through the worst period of white-on-black violence in American history. Historians understand the slave narratives' problems, but the public, and especially those who endorse the Lost Cause, eagerly consume narratives like Georgia Baker's that depict slavery as a benevolent institution that benefited enslaver and enslaved laborers equally. Stories of Stephens's kind-hearted relations with his enslaved laborers were already commonplace prior to the FWP's slave narratives project. Nonetheless, the narratives, especially with the advent of the internet in the late twentieth century, provide latter-day believers in the Lost Cause with abundant amounts of evidence to support their partisan beliefs. For decades, Georgia Baker's recorded affinity for her master played a major role in shaping public perceptions of Alexander Stephens and antebellum slavery.[30]

During the Great Depression, as Georgia memorialized Alexander Stephens's memory, the placement of Confederate monuments continued to spark controversy. In 1935, New York Republican Congressman Hamilton Fish III proposed to erect a statue of Gen. Robert E. Lee near Arlington House at Arlington National Cemetery. Fish believed that the statue would "cement the feelings of unity between North and South engendered by both the Spanish and World War."[31] The United Daughters of the Confederacy (UDC) backed Fish's legislation, while the Grand Army of the Republic (GAR) urged Congress to reject the proposal on the grounds that Lee had been an American traitor. The GAR argued that if a contemporary American military officer left the ranks to lead an army against the United States, that individual would be considered a traitor. According to Boston writer Norman Hesseltine, Lee's "friends think that he wasn't [a traitor] because, they say, he was honest in his convictions." If Lee had followed his convictions out of the Union, what did his actions say about his views on slavery, asked Hesseltine. Lee "devoted his talents," remarked Hesseltine, "not to the cause of freedom but slavery. Never in history was the line so clearly drawn between right and wrong as in the Civil War."[32]

Hesseltine argued that by the time Virginia seceded from the Union following President Abraham Lincoln's call for 75,000 volunteers to put down the southern rebellion, Confederate Vice-President Alexander H. Stephens had already delivered his much-publicized Cornerstone Speech. Richmond newspapers, which Lee read, widely reported Stephens's remarks. Lee had firsthand knowledge of the remarks that Stephens and others had presented to the Virginia legislature, urging them to secede to defend slavery. Hesseltine questioned one of the Lost Cause's most sacred claims: that Lee resigned from the federal army because his loyalties to Virginia prevented him from following her out of the Union. Hesseltine, citing the Cornerstone Speech, forcefully argued that all Confederate leaders had endorsed Stephens's pro-slavery manifesto. Rather than commit himself to defending his beloved state, Hesseltine accused the venerable Lee of devoting "his life to the curse of civilization." Echoing the sentiments of past and present emancipationists, Hesseltine claimed that erecting a statue of Lee at Arlington National Cemetery would desecrate "the bodies of those who gave their lives to freedom." He urged Americans not to "forget" that Lee "direct[ed] plans to kill those whose bodies lie buried below." Whereas Lost Cause proponents yearned for a new generation of leaders to emulate the examples set by Lee and Stephens, Hesseltine and other emancipationists proclaimed that "it was fortunate that in the nation's greatest stress [World War I] there were no more like" them. Thanks to the GAR's opposition, Fish's proposed Lee statue never materialized.[33]

Some parts of Stephens's legacy were less controversial and epitomized the complexities of his political career. Oregon, for example, honored Stephens as a "founding father." In 1936, the Sons and Daughters of the Pioneers of Oregon organized a celebration to mark Oregon's admission to the Union. In 1859, Sen. Stephen A. Douglas had sponsored a bill to admit Oregon to the Union. Vigorous debate ensued concerning whether slavery would be prohibited in the Pacific Northwest. Oregon's territorial legislature had banned African Americans from the state in its "white's only" constitution to discourage enslaver migration. After a heated debate, the bill passed the Senate. Among the bill's most vocal critics, Mississippi Sen. Jefferson Davis vehemently opposed the admission of any northern state regardless of whether that territory met the conditions for statehood. In the House, the bill met staunch resistance from southern Democrats, who demanded that Oregon's admission be accompanied by the opening of the southwest territories to slavery. Congress recessed for more than six months, further delaying any decisive on Oregon's admission. For thirty-nine weeks Oregon's admission languished in the House.[34]

On January 7, 1859, Alexander Stephens breathed new life into the stalemated legislation. Stephens moved the bill through the House Committee on Territories to the House floor, where a contentious debate ensued. Southern Democrats called Stephens a traitor for supporting Oregon's admission. They accused him of upsetting the national balance of power by agreeing to admit a free state without the admission of a new slave state. Stephens defended his position by stating that the South had already lost its dominance in the national government. However, if the South remained committed to the Constitution, "principles, not numbers, are our protection." Stephens urged Democrats to do the right thing and not stand in the way of the nation's growth. Twentieth-century Oregonians remembered Stephens not for his role in the Confederate government, but because of his heroic defense of American nationalism in the face of southern obstructionists.[35]

During the Great Depression, the Cornerstone Speech continued to be involved in controversies surrounding grade school history textbook adoptions. Many white Americans, North and South, expressed opposition to history textbooks suspected of being written by sectional partisans. In 1938, Indiana adopted Fremont Wirth's *The Development of America* as the state's official high school history textbook. Members of the Indiana Chapter of the Grand Army of the Republic accused Wirth, a professor of history at George Peabody College for Teachers in Nashville, Tennessee, of being "a Southern sympathizer whose ignorance of the Civil War, its cause, men and the measures used to put down the rebellion is inexcusable." Likewise, the Daughters of Union Veterans of the Civil War claimed that the book's pro-Confederate bias perpetuated "through the teaching of children a disrespect or disregard of the high purpose of the Union cause, the Union Army and the great Northern leaders." The book's tone and content disturbed northern audiences. For example, Wirth repeatedly emphasized that undermanned Confederate armies defeated numerically superior Union armies. Confederate soldiers were cast as heroic men who endured numerous hardships, especially those who had been held in northern prisons, while Union soldiers received no credit for neither their valor nor their sufferings. Meanwhile, Wirth accused Lincoln of secretly supporting slavery. Wirth declared falsely that the war had resulted from northern greed and "that slavery was not an issue in 1861." Indianans were incensed that Wirth's book failed to mention that Alexander Stephens had proclaimed that "slavery is the 'cornerstone of the Confederacy' and that he was proud of the fact that the Southern Confederacy was founded upon the principle that the Negroes should always remain in slavery, and that Jefferson Davis stood for slavery and was elected with the understanding that he would uphold slavery." In retrospect, Indiana Union Army heritage organizations believed that their ancestors had fought a noble cause to emancipate black enslaved laborers because slavery represented the biggest threat to America's future. Those beliefs had been handed down through the memories of their ancestors and transformed into contemporary views about the war that continued to elicit emotionally charged contestations to opposing opinions as if they were firsthand experiences. For those who espoused emancipationist tinted memories, no honest assessment of the Civil War could ignore the assertions found in the Cornerstone Speech.[36]

Following World War II, Alexander H. Stephens appeared in editorials that questioned the white South's opposition to African American civil equality. Ralph McGill, editor of *Atlanta Constitution*, believed that southern Dixiecrats should have learned a valuable lesson from Stephens's initial resistance to secession. During the 1948 presidential election, a faction of white conservative southern Democrats stormed out of their national convention in opposition to President Harry S. Truman's support for the extension of certain civil rights to African Americans. The group, referring to themselves as Dixiecrats, nominated staunch white-supremacist and segregationist Strom Thurmond, the governor of South Carolina, for president. The defection of large numbers of white southern Democrats threatened to split the national Democratic

Party vote and help elect the Republican nominee, Thomas E. Dewey. Prior to exiting the party, white conservative southern Democrats issued threats, hoping to force the national party to abandon prospective civil rights legislation. McGill, a supporter of civil rights reforms, cautioned conservatives that their threats had little impact because everyone knew they lacked any practical way of strengthening existing segregation practices. The award-winning editor, who received death threats for his support for civil equality, had been inspired by Alexander H. Stephens's anti-secession Union Speech. Echoing Stephens's argument that, by removing themselves from the umbrella of the national party, white southerners had weakened themselves and emboldened their enemies to outright ignore their demands, McGill urged leaders "not to oversimplify the present complex problem." In 1860, Stephens told those who supported secession that they had greatly overestimated the strength of their position while dangerously underestimating their enemy's resolve. Eighty-eight years later, McGill observed that "nothing has been more disturbing than the apparent inability of . . . Southern governors . . . to admit what they are up against." McGill compared post-World War II Dixiecrats to late antebellum fire-eaters who convinced everyone that their loud voices represented most white southern men when their actual numbers remained small. The editor urged his readers to hear moderate voices, such as Alexander Stephens's in the Union Speech, rather than "listen only to the hotheads, or to hold Klan meetings."[37] For his purposes, McGill left out any mention of the Cornerstone Speech, in which Stephens's had embraced secession wholeheartedly.

In 1955, University of Alabama English Professor Hudson Strode made several assertions that significantly influenced future discussions of the Cornerstone Speech. Strode had earned a national reputation as a writer of popular travel books and a mentor of several University of Alabama alumni who published award-winning works of fiction. Between 1955 and 1967, Strode produced a three-volume biography of CSA President Jefferson Davis, as well as an edited collection of his letters. The bestselling biographies appealed to academic and popular audiences. Strode offered readers a sympathetic account of Davis's wartime record that placed blame for the Confederacy's defeat elsewhere, including upon Vice-President Alexander H. Stephens. Strode described the "rabble-rousing" Cornerstone Speech as "ill-advised," "foolish," and "inopportune." According to Strode, Davis must have wondered "could anything . . . have been more calculated to damage the Confederate cause both in the North and abroad than his Vice-President's unfortunate speech?" Portions of Strode's account derived from often-repeated Lost Cause mythologies that stressed that had Stephens not so openly declared the Confederacy's support for preserving slavery that the infant nation would have received foreign recognition. Strode claimed that without the Cornerstone Speech England and France would have aided the Confederacy by using their navies to disrupt the blockade of southern ports. Domestically, Stephens's speech, claimed Strode, inspired abolitionists to demand the Lincoln administration to adopt "drastic measures" to combat slavery. "Alexander Stephens's ill-advised speech," claimed Strode, "helped launch the Sumter relief ships that were to start the war." Ignoring other examples of proslavery rhetoric expressed throughout the secession crisis, Strode argued that Stephens misrepresented the views of "millions of people, the majority of whom had nothing to do with slavery."[38] Strode fabricated Davis's response, indicating that Davis had been extremely upset by the Cornerstone Speech and implying that he had been farsighted enough to know that Stephens's words would be enough to gain foreign support for the new nation. To be sure, Lost Cause writers had claimed that Stephens's speech ruined the Confederacy's chance of receiving foreign recognition, but no prior work had claimed that Jefferson Davis had such a visceral reaction to the speech. Stephens's part in the creation of the Confederate government had been satisfactory enough for Davis to dispatch him to Virginia right after the Cornerstone Speech to persuade its legislature to join the rebellion. Stephens's important mission to Virginia included several speeches that reaffirmed the vice-president's earlier white-supremacist pronouncements.

Jefferson Davis never delivered a public statement refuting the Cornerstone Speech or questioning Stephens's actions. On the contrary, one month after the Cornerstone Speech, Davis told the Confederate Congress that "Fanatical organizations . . . were assiduously engaged in exciting amongst the slaves a spirit of discontent and revolt; means were furnished for their escape from their owners; and agents secretly employed to entice them to abscond." Davis accused Republicans of embracing "a spirit of fanaticism" and denying slavery's westward expansion. Davis described enslavers as members of a "superior race" who transformed "brutal savages into docile, intelligent, and civilized agricultural laborers." "With interests of such overwhelming magnitude imperiled, the people of the Southern State were driven by the conduct of the North to the adoption of some course of action to avert the danger with which they were openly menaced," declared Davis.[39]

Moreover, Davis's *Rise and Fall of the Confederate Government* (1881) never refuted the Cornerstone Speech. Nevertheless, Davis claimed that "slavery may have served as an occasion" for the war, but "it was far from being the cause of the conflict." Like Stephens's history of the Civil War, Davis's writings offered a convoluted explanation of the principal importance that the Confederate government had placed on securing states' rights, yet never fully explained how most of the identified grievances were linked to the defense of slavery.[40]

Strode supplied no evidence to support his assertion that Davis had re-sponded negatively to the Cornerstone Speech. He also provided no evidence of the Cornerstone Speech's alleged negative impact in Europe. Nonetheless, Strode's entertaining biography became a bestseller that continues to be read by a wide array of Civil War enthusiasts. His own views on race are unclear. His maternal grandfather had served as a colonel in the Confederate Army. For a period, Strode developed a close friendship with British author Rudyard Kipling, author of the poem "The White Man's Burden." A native of Alabama, Strode taught popular courses in Shakespeare and creative writing between 1916 and 1963, retiring in his early seventies before the University of Alabama was integrated. Strode traveled widely and held a deep respect for the peoples and cultures beyond America's shores. Clearly, Strode revered Davis and sought to defend the controversial former president from his many detractors. Like many biographers, perhaps, Strode grew a bit too fond of his subject. Maybe Strode's fondness for Shakespearean drama spilled over into his Davis biography as the embattled Confederate president mirrored the lives of many of Shakespeare's protagonists.[41]

Regardless of his motives, Strode's biography had several direct impacts on how Americans remembered the Cornerstone Speech. Foremost, Strode er-roneously proclaimed that Stephens's remarks concerning the importance of slavery to the Confederacy failed to represent anything more than his personal feelings rather than any agreed-upon Confederate public policy. Secondly, Strode falsely claimed that Stephens never really meant what he said and that he had allowed himself to get worked up by the exuberant crowd; therefore, we should ignore the speech. Finally, without presenting any evidence, Strode declared that Davis had reacted negatively to the speech because the Confeder-ate government's true cornerstone had been defending states' rights, rather than slavery. Lots of available evidence in Davis's own speeches, on the contrary, shows that he had views about slavery that echo the Cornerstone Speech and reflect Stephens's own views. Strode's biography gave Lost Cause advocates a popular and reputable source that confirmed many of their central tenets.[42]

As the Civil War Centennial approached, articles about the Civil War began appearing in large numbers. Unlike the semicentennial, the centennial marked the passing of Civil War memory from those who had experienced war and reconstruction to a new generation of Americans who lacked any direct personal connection to this cataclysmic event. Lost Cause depictions of the war continued to garner recognition, but the centennial also witnessed a rise of nonpartisan examinations of the war's origins, outcomes, and memories. In the May 11, 1960, edition of the *Montgomery Advertiser*, a frank, nonpartisan account of the events that led to secession appeared. The newspaper reprinted an article written by D. W. Brogan for *Harper's* magazine, a national monthly periodical that had discussed literature, politics, culture, finance, history, and the arts since its launch in 1850. Brogan challenged several facets of Lost Cause memory. He chided southerners for continuing to label the Civil War as the "War Between the States." He preferred Civil War, because the conflict pitted "brother against brother, father against son" in a "savage" struggle in which "murder and rapine [were] rampant." Brogan asked "did slavery really start the war? That this was so nobody, I suspect, doubted when the war was on." How do contemporary Americans know that slavery was central to the war? Brogan directed them to read Alexander H. Stephens's Cornerstone Speech. "Stephens, who was against secession before it happened and not enthusiastic about it even when he was vice-president of the Confederacy, let the cat out of the bag." Brogan insisted that Stephens's declaration that the Confederacy's "cornerstone rests upon the great truth that the Negro is not equal to the white man" disapproved many previous claims that only radicals (fire-eaters and abolitionists) believed the war to be a fight over slavery. Brogan cast Stephens as a representative moderate voice of reason who nonetheless saw secession as an opportunity to preserve white supremacy in perpetuity. To achieve this goal, the South had been willing to break apart the last surviving national political body capable of forging a compromise to hold the Union together, the Democratic Party. When Stephens delivered the Cornerstone Speech he acknowledged the factual basis—the South's desire to preserve slavery and white supremacy—upon which the Confederate government had formed. The Confederacy ultimately failed because its vision of a nation built upon permanent enslaved laborers proved to be the last remnant of a dying labor system that Europeans powers had already discarded. Brogan's concluding remarks also took aim at one of the Lost Cause's most often-repeated myths—slavery would have ended without the Civil War. Again referring to the Cornerstone Speech, Brogan argued that "in no other way could the America experiment have been purged of the poisonous infection of slavery in the country 'dedicated to the proposition that all men are created equal.'" The Civil War, thanks to the "high price" paid by Union Army soldiers, had "saved 'the last best hope of earth'" from destruction. After suggesting that the struggle for equality had yet to be won, Brogan declared that the price of liberty and equality were "still being paid" a century later.[43]

Brogan's article appeared in the *Montgomery Advertiser* without any additional editorial commentary challenging its interpretations. During prior commemorations of the Civil War, whenever a view of history appeared to contrast with the Lost Cause, southern editors would accompany that piece with some critical remarks. Brogan's article appeared without additional explanation. The newspaper seemed more concerned with the rising conservatism of President Dwight D. Eisenhower than with refighting the Civil War. The Lost Cause remained strong in the South, but the Civil War Centennial showed some cracks in its foundation.[44]

As with many national commemorations, some Americans expressed concerns that the Civil War Centennial would further aggravate sectional tensions at a time when the Civil Rights Movement appeared to be testing the South's relationship with the federal government. Jones Osborn, owner and editor the *Yuma Daily Sun* (Arizona), opposed the federal government's centennial plans. He worried that the federal government would privilege some stories and perspectives while ignoring others. Osborn claimed that the "bitter, bloody" Civil War and "shameless carpetbagging which followed left deep scars" across the South that "are tender to this day." Any commemoration of a painful and unresolved past, Osborn argued, "seems likely to make more ill-will than good-will." Osborn decided to publish several sections of the Cornerstone Speech, including Stephens's white supremacist declarations, as a representative example of the "bitter" feelings that might result from resurrecting the nation's past. The editor failed to see how commemorating the Civil War could help the nation during a period of mounting racial strife.[45]

Osborn had a point. Commemorations often produce unexpected results. The official memory of the war as communicated by local, state, and federal governments conflicted and failed to achieve a consensus interpretation. The process of commemorating a war that centered on slavery during a period of equally enormous social strife in America led many participants to seek out those views which only confirmed their pre-existing prejudices. During the Civil War, Vermont had sent thousands of young men into the Union Army and fostered a growing community of abolitionists. A century later, the romantic image of the Confederacy found among Lost Cause proponents, bestselling historians, and some academics led some to sympathize with the enslavers and traitors who caused the war. In a review of Bruce Catton's award-winning and bestselling *The Coming Fury*, Brattleboro, Vermont, book critic Ruth Hard Bonner shared a revelation inspired by recent commemorations and Catton's stirring narrative. Southern enslavers were "reasoned," "thoughtful" men of "moral conviction" who believed "that slavery was right and proper." Although "when they stopped to think, they realized it was wrong," the enslavers who led the nation into a bloody Civil War "were fighting for . . . states rights not slavery." Bonner revealed that although modern readers might find slavery to be inhumane, "it was obvious . . . that to the sober, gentle, Christian gentleman as much as the fire-eating extremist, there was nothing remotely unethical about slavery." Bonner urged Americans to recognize slavery's virtues to better "appreciate the bitter plight of the average Georgian or South Carolinian." Rather than judge enslavers as immoral, advised Bonner, contemporary Americans should put themselves in their shoes. Bonner claimed that secession was justified because abolitionists had damaged the "knightly code of chivalry" upheld by "honorable Christian gentlemen." Bonner referred readers to a quotation from Alexander Stephens that Catton highlighted in his work in order to describe the exceptional qualities of Confederate leaders. Secession, according to Stephens, had avoided bringing "such men as revolution of civil commotions usually bring to the surface. They were men of such substance as we of solid character. . . . Their object was not to tear down so much as it was to build up with the greater security and permanency." The more virtuous men lost the war, implied Bonner.[46]

Bruce Catton's writings inspired Bonner to think about how the current Civil Rights Movement compared with the Civil War. She claimed that pride prevented contemporary white southerners from recognizing civil equality. "If it took decades for the Southerner to become convinced that slavery was wrong," wrote Bonner, "it is likely to take as long for him to learn that the Negro is his equal." Bonner suggested that white southerners would become more aggressive in their defense of racial segregation if the nation committed the same mistakes that it made during the Civil War—undermining the honor of white southern men. White southern men, intimated Bonner, understood how to best lead the region toward civil equality, even if it took longer. In her mind, the lessons she learned from reading about the Civil War confirmed her distrust of federal intervention and provided her with a more sympathetic view of southern enslavers.[47]

During the Civil War Centennial, sympathy for the Confederate States of America came from unexpected quarters. New Jersey native Edmund Wilson ranks among the greatest authors of the twentieth century. In 1962, the sometimes playwright, literary critic, poet, and historian published *Patriotic Gore*, one of the most memorable histories of the Civil War ever written. The book's twenty-six chapters examine the lives of thirty prominent Civil War–era writers chosen by Wilson for their exceptional insights into the period. In *Patriotic Gore*, readers encountered familiar voices, such as Ulysses S. Grant, Abraham Lincoln, Harriet Beecher Stowe, Walt Whitman, Nathaniel Hawthorne, and Mark Twain, situated among writers who at that time were less familiar, including Mary Boykin Chesnut, Richard "Dick" Taylor, Albion W. Tourgée, Frederick Law Olmsted, and John William De Forest. According to many of the book's reviewers, Wilson became infatuated with Alexander H. Stephens because he had offered the most convincing defense of the Confederacy. By 1962, Wilson and the Lost Cause had become strange bedfellows due to their shared disdain for the centralized authority of the federal government. The Cold War influenced Wilson's view that depicted American leaders as warmongers, intent on demonstrating their might through nuclear weapons. Wilson sympathized with people throughout history who, despite impossible odds, had resisted those who trampled upon their freedoms. According to historian David Blight, Wilson "needed the Confederacy to play the role of the devoured in his drama—the little, misguided David to the huge and imperialistic Goliath of the United States, preparing for its 20th-century career of war and expansion."[48]

If Wilson came to the Civil War in search of a David, he found one in the writings of Alexander H. Stephens. Wilson purposely ignored the Cornerstone Address because he accepted Stephens's postbellum assertions that he had been misquoted and misunderstood. Also, Wilson rejected the idea that slavery had caused the war. In the North, Wilson claimed that anti-slavery sentiment was too weak to push the nation toward war. Wilson echoed claims made by Lost Cause writers when he argued that the North fought to expand its imperialist-oriented capitalist economy in a drive to seize the South's wealth. Meanwhile, Wilson wrote that secession had been a necessary act to preserve southern liberties from an abusive centralized federal regime. Rather than provide readers with a glimpse into Stephens's white-supremacist views, ideas that clearly demonstrated slavery's role in southern secession, Wilson found Stephens at one of the lowest points in his life imprisoned at Fort Warren in Boston harbor. From Wilson's perspective, Stephens evolved into a martyr who had risked everything for his defense of the constitution. Wilson used Stephens weakened health to build sympathy among readers who were led to believe that his imprisonment had been a gross miscarriage of justice. Isolated and deprived of his normal routine and comforts, Stephens rallied to create a diary and begin writing what would become *A Constitutional View of the Late War Between the States*. Wilson's *Patriotic Gore* became a national bestseller thanks to its engaging narrative style and sentimentalism. Few readers noted the contradictions of the author's earlier praise for the intellectual origins of social justice and socialism as they devoured a history that Lost Cause disciples declared to be a rejection of emancipationist interpretations of the war. Wilson effectively recast Confederates, especially Alexander H. Stephens, as victims of federal tyranny.[49]

During the Civil War Centennial, Wilson's explanations of the war's causes shared much in common with numerous writers across the South, although others sometimes portrayed Alexander H. Stephens's in a less positive light. Writer Earle Bowden of Pensacola, Florida, asked his readers to pause and to reflect on the "independent nation that almost was. . . . For the Southern imagination [the war] was the great single event in Dixie history." Hailing the conflict as "the forerunner of modern war," Bowden proclaimed that Confederate soldier had "fought for what he believed right and proper—preservation of the order of government by states, which had originally formed the Union and delegated to it a portion . . . of their sovereignty." Bowden claimed that although the causes of the war were "rarely stated or clearly formulated," southerners "will remember that slavery or its abolition was not the cause for which the soldiers of the sixties fought." As Bowden regaled the heroic actions of Confederate generals, such as Robert E. Lee, "Stonewall" Jackson, Nathan Bedford Forrest, and "Fighting" Joe Wheeler, he reserved criticism for Alexander H. Stephens, whose quarrels with Jefferson Davis undermined the war effort. Despite dismissing slavery's role in the war, Bowden, unlike most Lost Cause writers, admitted that internal divisions within the Confederacy contributed to the government's failures. Most notably, Bowden pointed out that many southern soldiers "resented their engagement in what they considered to be a rich man's war and a poor man's fight." Had white southerners united in support of the Confederate government, wrote Bowden, victory could have been achieved. Stephens represented one of many instigators of internal disagreements that wrecked Confederate independence.[50]

As part of the Civil War Centennial commemorations, the Library of Congress developed a large exhibit that examined the war's causes, major events, and outcomes. An introductory panel greeted visitors and declared that "underlying the dispute was the obvious issue of slavery." The exhibit incorporated the writings of Harriet Beecher Stowe, Jefferson Davis, and Abraham Lincoln to help the public understand how antebellum-era leaders viewed the conflict's causes. Missing from the exhibition, however, was Stephens's Cornerstone Address. The speech's absence likely resulted from the controversies that surrounded the address. At the time curators were planning the exhibit, scholars, most notably Hudson Strode, believed (based in part on Stephens's own postwar assertions) that the speech had been inaccurately transcribed. Other popular historians, such as Bruce Catton and Shelby Foote, ignored the speech entirely. Those questions and omissions contributed to the speech's reduced place within the centennial celebrations.[51]

In March 1961, newspapers across America marked the Cornerstone Speech's one-hundredth anniversary. Many printed a brief "on this day" summary of the speech without additional commentary. The frequent mention of the Cornerstone Speech's centennial evidenced the speech's continued contested status in American memory. Interpretations of the speech remained in flux as various groups continued to find distinctive ways to assign meaning to this controversial event.

This description of the speech appeared in dozens of newspapers:

100 YEARS AGO

Also on March 21, 1861, in Savannah, Georgia, the vice-president of the Confederate States, Alexander H. Stephens, made his famous "corner-stone" speech, not directly related to the Fort Sumter issue, but important for the adverse effect it may have had on the cause of the South. The "corner-stone" of the new Confederate government, Stephens reportedly said, rested upon "the great truth that the Negro is not equal to the white man; that slavery –subordination to the superior race—is his natural and normal condition."[52]

Although the widely syndicated account omitted any accompanying editorial commentary, the brief piece included some choice language that reflected Lost Cause ideas. For example, the speech was not important for what it revealed about Confederate motivations, "but important for the adverse effect it may have had on the cause of the South." Furthermore, despite overwhelming evidence to the contrary, the article cast doubt on the speech's authenticity by claiming that "Stephens reportedly said"—suggesting that reporters may have misquoted Stephens's remarks.[53]

Further muddying the waters, some writers referred to the speech as the "disputed cornerstone." Sergeant Dalzell, a World War II veteran who published many articles about the Civil War, repeated Hudson Strode's assertion "that some of [Stephens] Confederate colleagues deplored" the speech and that "Stephens later disagreed with himself." Dalzell doubted whether Stephens had said "that slavery was the very cornerstone of the Confederate government." He claimed that many Confederate leaders publicly condemned Stephens, fearing "the effect of such a speech on foreign relations." Although Dalzell did not explicitly reject the premise that slavery had been a central cause of the war, his repudiation of the Cornerstone Speech implied that Stephens had either been mistaken or misquoted.[54]

The *Atlanta Journal-Constitution* writers Norman Shavin and Mike Edwards collaborated with Willard Wright, a professor of history at the Georgia Institute of Technology (now Georgia Tech), to produce "A Non-Partisan Account of Events of This Week 100 Years Ago." Together they reported on the events of the Civil War as if they were current breaking news. The headline and subheading chosen for the Cornerstone Speech's centennial read: "Stephens Sees Great Future for C.S.A.: Inequality Held As the Cornerstone: Georgia Adopts New Constitution." Shavin, Edwards, and Wright omitted any editorial commentary on the speech. Instead, they let Stephens's word speak for themselves. Most articles included the speech's most famous line, "Our new government is founded—its foundations are laid, its cornerstone rests upon the great truth that the Negro is not equal to the white man," but they included a less often yet important passage that proclaimed that white supremacy was divinely sanctioned. "The substratum of our society is made of the material best fitted by nature for it, and by experience we know that it is the best, not only for the superior but for the inferior race, that it should be so. It is, indeed, in conformity with the Creator. It is not for us to inquire into the wisdom of His ordinances or to question them." By the time of the centennial, the *Atlanta Journal* and *Atlanta Constitution* had positioned itself as a supporter of the Civil Rights Movement. The paper's award-winning editor, Ralph McGill, had long urged his white southern readers to acknowledge and reject the illogical premises that supported racial segregation. McGill and his staff viewed the Cornerstone Speech as an important piece of evidence that had helped articulate white-supremacist beliefs. Throughout the Civil War Centennial, the *Atlanta Journal* and *Atlanta Constitution*'s writers syndicated numerous articles that reminded their readers that racial segregation and the Confederate States of America shared a common foundation.[55]

By 1963, newspaper writers across the country began to draw connections between the Civil War Centennial and the Civil Rights Movement. Associated Press writer Jules Loh published a series of articles that firmly situated the roots of the Civil Rights Movement in the white-supremacist beliefs that girded slavery in America. Loh had spent the previous few months covering various civil rights demonstrations for the Associated Press, including the Freedom Rides, Albany Movement, and the Birmingham Campaign. The New Jersey native and Korean War veteran empathized with the plight of African Americans. Initially unfamiliar with the origins of racial segregation, Loh looked to the South's history to contextualize contemporary problems.[56] He argued that over the course of centuries, white enslavers, with the aid of the federal government, had tried to stripped black enslaved laborers of their humanity by depriving them of basic human rights, such as the right to care for their families or the right to control their labor. Opposition to slavery was as old as the institution itself, claimed Loh, but in America before the war, the voices of abolitionists and critics of slavery had been routinely silenced by the government and angry mobs. Slavery became such a vital part of southern life, "it appeared obvious that slavery was a positive good, and practicing it was simply following the natural order of things." No other statesmen had more effectively described white southern attitudes on slavery than Alexander H. Stephens. According to Loh, the Cornerstone Speech articulated what the South thought was the "natural order" On the eve of the Civil War. Stephens did not have to choose his words carefully because his message voiced beliefs that were shared by millions of white men across the globe—but nowhere more than in his own region.

Stephens had good reason to believe that other white men would come to the Confederacy's aid if the new government staked a claim as defenders of white supremacy. Stephens's ideas proved to be far more powerful than the Confederacy as many white Americans rallied to the defense of white supremacy in the decades that followed emancipation. Loh argued that the Confederacy's cornerstone continued to define modern-day American race relations. Civil rights leaders faced the challenge of sweeping away a cornerstone that had been laid centuries earlier and strengthened over the years by white supremacists, such as Alexander H. Stephens of Georgia.[57]

Jules Loh's syndicated articles appeared in newspapers across the country. They usually appeared alongside a graphic illustration of the horrors of the Middle Passage. In the South, local editors often included a brief introduction for readers, urging them think about the current problems in America from a historical perspective. The editor of the Greenville News in South Carolina wrote: "The struggle for integration of the races in American started quietly. But a historical perspective reveals its inexorable progress to this critical summer of sporadic violence, frustration and discord—a forward march of events predestined to occur from the moment the first slave ship dropped anchor on our shores."[58] Loh's article marked one of the first times in history that an interpretation of the war that sharply contrasted with Lost Cause orthodoxy appeared in numerous southern newspapers without any accompanying rebuttals from local editors. Southern readers in every corner of the former Confederacy had access to Loh's nuanced views on the war. If many white southerners remained tethered to the Lost Cause, newspaper editors appeared ready to explore alternative interpretations.

As the Civil War Centennial wrapped up, news from Alexander H. Stephens's hometown of Crawfordville, Georgia, reminded Americans that the white-supremacist ideals expressed in the Cornerstone Speech continued to negatively impact the lives of African Americans. Lost Cause writers had always emphasized that Stephens had a good relationship with his black enslaved laborers that continued after emancipation. Writers painted a portrait of black life in and around Liberty Hall as happy, carefree, and accepting of the region's racial inequalities. Lost Cause proponents suggested that Stephens's benevolence was carried on by subsequent generations of white residents who kept the peace in rural Taliaferro County.[59] In May 1965, the Southern Christian Leadership Conference (SCLC) launched a voter-registration drive in Crawfordville, Georgia. SCLC's director of voter registration, Hosea Williams, had targeted Taliaferro County because more than half of its residents were African American. The demonstrations were part of SCLC's Summer Community Organization and Political Education (SCOPE) Project, launched in

1965 to register black voters in 120 counties in six states. Stephens's estate is in one of Georgia's smallest counties and ranks among its poorest. SCLC organizers admitted that the county's association with Alexander H. Stephens, the vice-president of the Confederate States of America, drew their attention to the area. Integrating businesses and public accommodations in a town that had been transformed into a Confederate memorial would be a symbolic victory over white supremacy.

Events in the county also attracted the SCLC's attention. At the end of the 1964–65 school year, the Taliaferro County Board of Education fired six teachers and the principal at the county's sole black school, the Murden School. African Americans accused the board of hatching a scheme to close public schools in the upcoming fall semester rather than integrate. By 1965, most Georgia counties had created integration plans that had been approved by the state. Taliaferro County was among the last counties to develop one.

The SCLC's Taliaferro County voter-registration drive successfully registered over 75 percent of black voters. Efforts to integrate local businesses and public services drew staunch resistance from the area's white residents. The protests attracted national attention, as reporters from the Associated Press and United Press International covered events as they unfolded. Reports from Crawfordville appeared in newspapers from coast to coast. On Wednesday, May 26, 1965, a group of SCLC protestors tried to integrate the Liberty Café, Crawfordsville's sole restaurant. After a group of local white males blocked the restaurant's entrance, four brothers assaulted Tony Scruton, a twenty-five-year-old white minister's son from Chewelah, Washington, who had participated in several SCLC-led demonstrations. Police arrested and charged two SCLC workers with trespassing for trying to enter the restaurant with a black male. That same day, a mixed-race group of SCLC protestors successfully entered the town's segregated laundromat and began washing loads of clothes before being forcibly removed by local police. An Augusta, Georgia, journalist covering the protests was confronted by angry white men, who told him to "get out of Crawfordville, and stay out."[60]

The next day, SCLC Field Secretary Willie Bolden pledged to remain in Crawfordville until Liberty Café's integration. Bolden planned to test whether the Liberty Café would comply with the 1960 US Supreme Court ruling *Boynton v. Virginia*, which prohibited racial discrimination in interstate passenger transportation. Every Thursday a bus stopped in Crawfordville and allowed passengers the chance to eat at the Liberty Café. Bolden planned to pack the bus with African American passengers who would force their way into the restaurant. Rather than confront the black passengers, the Liberty Café chose to close its doors. Unable to enter the restaurant, Bolden led a group of demonstrators on a march around the Taliaferro County Courthouse, located across from the restaurant. The next day, the restaurant and laundromat remained closed as owners hoped that protestors would leave town. Undeterred, demonstrators picketed the courthouse, resulting in the arrests of ten marchers, who were charged with obstructing a public sidewalk. Given the choice between paying a forty-dollar fine or spending fifteen days in the local jail, the protestors chose incarceration. As a closed-door hearing for the arrested demonstrators proceeded, Crawfordville rang with the sounds of freedom songs.[61]

On Saturday, May 29, the public swimming pool at Alexander H. Stephens Memorial State Park opened for the summer 1965 season. Although the director said that the park had integrated in 1964, the SCLC challenged those claims and launched a "swim-in" protest. Over one hundred demonstrators, many of them small children, entered the park immediately after it opened. A group of black and white children occupied the playground without incident. Meanwhile, a mixed-race group of swimmers quickly changed into bathing suits and entered the pool. No arrests were made. No one was asked to leave the park. According to most reports, a handful of local whites chose to remain in the park after its integration.[62]

Following the racial integration of Georgia's first Confederate memorial park, the SCLC turned its attention to Taliaferro County's all-white high school, the Alexander Stephens Institute. When eighty-seven black students attempted to register for the start of the fall semester, the county's entire white student population chose to enroll in segregated schools located in neighboring counties. Taliaferro County provided white students with bus transportation. Five new segregated academies opened, further ensuring that no white student would remain in the county's public schools. Alexander Stephens Institute's all-white faculty and staff resigned and found new jobs elsewhere, as the local school board refused to hire replacements.[63]

In the fall of 1965, African American students boycotted the Murden School to protest the county's closing of Alexander Stephens Institute. Students laid down on the state highway to block white school buses from exiting the county. They also organized sit-ins at neighboring all-white county schools. After several months of protests, the federal government forced the neighboring all-white schools to enroll black students from Taliaferro County. In 1966, the first black students enrolled in Alexander Stephens Institute.[64]

At the end of the Civil War Centennial, Alexander H. Stephens's name could be found in newspaper stories across the nation. As civil rights activists sought to end racial segregation, Alexander H. Stephens Memorial State Park and Alexander Stephens Institute became symbols of the enormous changes that were afoot across America. The centennial offered a more complicated view of Stephens's legacy, but failed to erase the numerous memorials that prior generations had erected in his honor. Following integration, Alexander H. Stephens Memorial State Park remained a Confederate memorial. Stephens's statue remained at Statuary Hall in the US Capitol. Portraits of Stephens continued to hang in the Georgia State Capitol. The most popular works of history largely ignored the Cornerstone Speech and continued to honor Stephens for his intellect and compassion. The Civil War Centennial and Civil Rights Movement failed to define Alexander H. Stephens's legacy.

CHAPTER EIGHT
Heritage and Hate, 1990–2019

Since the early 1990s, the Cornerstone Speech has become one of the most widely quoted orations associated with the American Civil War. After the Civil War Centennial, the speech remained in American public discourse, but was not as prevalent during the 1970s and 1980s. Despite the Civil Rights Movement's gains for African American civil equality, emancipationists lost momentum during the two decades that followed the movement as conservatives slowed those reforms. Generally, Americans' interest in the Civil War had declined after the centennial. The Cornerstone Speech found new life and meaning during the 1990s as it became embroiled in America's growing culture wars. Passages from the speech can be found in every newspaper in the country as well as numerous magazines. Mention of the speech on social media sparks intense debates over the war's meaning and the legacy of white supremacy in America. The speech provides ample proof that a broad and diverse range of Americans are engaged in historical interpretation. They are eager to engage in conversations about history as part of a robust national public discourse to shape how Americans remember their past. Interest in the Cornerstone Speech remains high both within academia and across the broad public spectrum. In academic circles, references to the speech provide clear evidence of the Confederacy's link to white-supremacist ideals. Abridged selections of the speech appear in countless published volumes of primary sources and have become a standard part of most American history survey textbooks. Outside of academia, opinions differ. On one side, there are many educators, civil equality activists, and others who have drawn connections between the speech and contemporary racial biases in America. Whenever a major event occurs that demonstrates how America has failed to resolve the problem of white supremacy, such as the deaths caused by white supremacists in Charleston, Charlottesville, or Ferguson, the Cornerstone Speech resurfaces across various media platforms as evidence of the historical origins of white America's long-standing racial bigotry. The speech has found an eager audience among what historian David Blight has called the emancipationist interpretation of Civil War memory.[1] Meanwhile, a consortium of Neo-Confederates, white suprema-cists, hate groups, and libertarians object to academia's constant references to the speech as evidence of a conspiracy to slander Confederate heritage, and by extension, white southern male history.[2] Generally, these groups accuse others of misrepresenting the Cornerstone Speech in order to promote what some refer to as the Righteous Cause Myth—the belief that the North fought the war to emancipate enslaved laborers, which they contest. Neo-Confederates have continued the dishonest intellectual rhetoric established by their Lost Cause predecessors by obscuring, confusing, oversimplifying, distorting, and misleading Americans about their sources, lack of objectivity, and political motivations. Neo-Confederates, like advocates for the Lost Cause before them, have tapped into the period's divisive political culture, helping expand their numbers by appealing to right-of-center-conservatives, who often share their conspiratorial views of federal supremacy and fears of national cultural degra-dation. Neo-Confederates interpret the Cornerstone Speech's proliferation in public discourse as another symptom of a progressive/liberal/Marxist /"politi-cally correct" conspiracy to undermine the freedoms and liberties of white men in America. Neo-Confederates believe that civil rights earned by minorities result in a loss of rights among white men. They, like Alexander Stephens, see liberty as the domain of white men to be handed out to others on a case-by-case basis based on vague qualifications established by the ruling majority. Rather than acknowledge the role that white privilege has played in perpetuating racial disparities in America, Neo-Confederates identity themselves as abused mi-norities whose rights have been trampled upon by a politically correct culture.

Among Neo-Confederates, however, differences of opinion exist concern-ing whether slavery had caused the war. Some Libertarians, for example, reject Neo-Confederate and Secessionist-Libertarian assertions that slavery did not cause the war. Anti-Neo-Confederate Libertarians interpret the Confederate States of America as an elite political movement designed to infringe upon the rights of individual citizens. Rather than celebrate the Confederacy as a bas-tion of individual liberty and states' rights, Anti-Neo-Confederate Libertarians criticize that government's abusive conscription, impressment, coerced labor practices, centralized government, and taxation policies as a negative episode in the history of American freedom. Moreover, they tend to extend these criti-cisms of the Confederacy to the current federal government. The Cornerstone Speech provides a lens through which to examine how Americans remember the Civil War and, perhaps more importantly, how white supremacy in America has persisted despite emancipation, civil equality, hate-crime legislation, and other measures intended to reduce its influence. America's inability to eradicate white supremacy has kept scholars and audiences returning to the speech. Discussions of the Cornerstone Speech have transformed Alexander Stephens, especially in non-academic discussions of history, into a central and polarizing figure in the nation's struggle to combat racism.

On the evening of September 23, 1990, Ken Burns's *The Civil War* miniseries premiered on the Public Broadcasting Service. Over thirty-nine million viewers watched at least one or more of the nine episodes that aired for five consecutive nights. Episode one examined the war's causes. About forty-five minutes into the series, Burns introduced viewers to the Cornerstone Speech as the writer-director proclaimed what most historians had already accepted—slavery caused the Civil War. Burns summed up Stephens's two-hour speech with a single impactful quote: "Our new government is founded upon the great truth that the negro is not equal to the white man." While the film aired Stephens's white-supremacist statements, Burns failed to emphasize how representative those beliefs were throughout the new Confederate government. By providing very little analysis or nuance on this point, *The Civil War* portrayed white supremacy as a nearly invisible part of the larger political fight over slavery and thus missed why so many white southern men cared about preserving the institution beyond possible economic motivations. Burns followed the quotation from the Cornerstone Speech with a selection from the diary of Mary Boykin Chesnut that "described slavery as a monstrous system" that reinforced white male privilege and patriarchy. Chesnut's words condemned a system that had become central to the fabric of southern society but gave the audience a false impression that many white southerners shared her disdain. Even Stephens could be critical of slavery's influence on southern society, but those criticisms never questioned the institution's righteousness. Burns also ignored the central role that Stephens's white-supremacist beliefs had played in the Confederate Constitution's creation. The filmmaker told viewers that little distinguished the Confederate Constitution from the US Constitution. That interpretation obscured the fact that the Confederate Constitution included new provisions intended to guarantee the right to own slaves and to make emancipation virtually impossible. Ironically, a government supposedly founded on states' rights stripped states of the power to regulate slavery within their own jurisdictions.[3]

For millions of Americans, *The Civil War* provided their first exposure to the Cornerstone Speech. Unfortunately, the wildly successful documentary devoted far more attention to the heroics of noted white supremacists, such as General Nathan Bedford Forrest, and to popular writers who waxed poetically about the Lost Cause, such as Shelby Foote, than it did to the underlying roots of America's slavery crisis. Influenced by the teary-eyed Foote, many viewers empathized with the embattled Confederates who appeared to have lost so much in their noble defeat and failed to grasp that neither secession nor defeat could erase the South's cornerstone built on white supremacy.[4]

On July 22, 1993, Confederate States of America Vice-President Alexander H. Stephens returned to the US Capitol as the invited guest of an unexpected host. Sen. Carol Moseley-Braun had heard enough. The newly elected senator from Illinois had listened in disgust as North Carolina Sen. Jesse Helms and South Carolina Sen. Strom Thurmond proposed a bill that would have renewed the patent for the United Daughters of the Confederacy (UDC) insignia—the Confederate flag (Stars and Bars national flag, not to be confused with the St. Andrew's Cross battle flag). Both Helms and Thurmond had connections to the Council of Conservative Citizens, a white-supremacist organization that endorsed the Lost Cause. Previously, the Senate had passed similar measures honoring various Confederate leaders and symbols, but Moseley-Braun, the first black woman to serve in the US Senate, had promised her supporters that when the opportunity arose, she would oppose Helms and others who sought to use their elected office to glorify the Confederate States of America. From the Senate chamber, Moseley-Braun "spoke with tears running down her face" as she chided "her fellow senators for not paying attention to the vote they had cast." "I have to tell you," Moseley-Braun argued: "this vote is about race. It is about racial symbols, the racial past, and the single most painful episode in American history. . . . If there is anybody in this chamber—anybody—indeed anybody in the world—that has a doubt that the Confederate effort was about preserving the institution of slavery, I am prepared—and I believe history is prepared—to dispute them to the nth degree." When Wyoming Sen. Alan Simpson questioned why she had chosen this day to protest what he considered to be an inconsequential vote, Moseley-Braun gave him a history lesson. "To suggest as a matter of revisionist history," Moseley-Braun spoke with her eyes fixed on Simpson, "that this flag is not about slavery flies in the face of history."[5]

Moseley-Braun reminded senators of the numerous statues of Confederate military and civil leaders that southern states had put on display in the Capitol. Men whose zeal for defending slavery ruptured the Union and had led to the deaths of 100,000s. Moseley-Braun questioned why men who had betrayed the United States of America should be honored in the nation's Capitol. Since 1927, a statue of Confederate Vice-President Alexander H. Stephens had been one of two monuments that Georgia had chosen to display as representative examples of the Empire State's history. As Moseley-Braun took the Senate floor, wiping tears from her cheeks, she evoked the words of Stephens to help her cause. The Confederacy's cornerstone, according to Stephens back in 1861, "rests upon the great truth that the Negro is not equal to the white man, that slavery, subordination to the superior race is his natural and moral condition." Passing any measure that honored the Confederacy, Moseley-Braun argued, "is absolutely unacceptable to me and to millions of Americans, black or white, that we would put the imprimatur of the U.S. Senate on a symbol of this kind." She proclaimed that while millions of Americans might revere the Confederate flag, the symbol remained nonetheless a symbol of slavery and racial oppression for millions.[6]

Despite Moseley-Braun's eloquence, Helms's bill passed 52 to 48 with bipartisan support. Moseley-Braun rejected the vote and returned to the Senate floor, demanding the body reconsider. She implored them to consider the message that celebrating the Confederacy sent in modern-day America. Moseley-Braun argued that glorifying the Confederacy and upholding the ideals of racial equality were incompatible ideals and that the former had no place in the halls of Congress. Again, referencing Stephens's 1861 Cornerstone Speech, Moseley-Braun asked if the Confederate flag should be commemorated by the US Congress, a body that should stand as the cornerstone of democracy. In an unprecedented move, one by one several senators who had initially supported Helms's amendment reversed their votes. Daniel Patrick Moynihan of New York claimed that during his entire career he had never been "so moved as by her statement." Surprisingly, Alabama Sen. Howell Heflin, a conservative Democrat and a Helms ally, changed his vote. The son of arch-segregationist and Jim Crow legislator "Cotton" Tom Heflin, Howell lived in a new political era in Alabama, where conservative Democrats were defecting to the Republican Party and those who remained depended on the support of African American voters to hold their elected offices. Reluctant to condemn the Confederate flag outright and risk losing his few remaining white conservative supporters, Heflin tried to walk a fine line between expressing empathy for Moseley-Braun's position and maintaining his personal pride in his own Confederate ancestors. Like most members of Confederate heritage organizations, such as the Sons of Confederate Veterans and the United Daughters of the Confederacy, Heflin refuted charges that the Confederacy had waged a war to protect white supremacy and slavery. Heflin explained that he "strongly" felt that if his Confederate ancestors "were alive today they would stand for what is right and honorable and they would agree with me that it is time to move forward in our nation's history." Heflin's reversal provided political cover for several conservative southern senators, Democrat and Republican, to change their vote. On a second vote, Helms's bill failed by a 76 to 24 vote. A defeated and embarrassed Helms, according to reporters, "slunk off snarling." Under Moseley-Braun's leadership, the Senate failed to renew the UDC's patent.[7]

Moseley-Braun's protest was the culmination of a larger NAACP initiative, launched six years before in 1987. That year the NAACP campaigned to remove Confederate symbols from public properties in South Carolina, Alabama, Mississippi, and Georgia. Moseley-Braun's high-profile speeches in Congress were significant because previous arguments for removing Confederate symbols had failed to mention the Cornerstone Speech. After she quoted Stephens's words from the Senate Chamber floor, editorial writers across the country began to regularly reference the Cornerstone Speech; in 1993, the Cornerstone Speech received more attention across the nation thanks to Moseley-Braun than it had back in March of 1861. After Moseley-Braun's protests, the Cornerstone Speech played a pivotal role as those who advocated for the removal of Confederate symbols from public properties began to argue that a direct line existed connecting Stephens's white-supremacist ideals with those symbols. For the NAACP, the battle flag and various monuments represented pride in the Confederacy's racist past and defiance toward modern-day civil rights movements. The NAACP accused contemporary governments of southern states of displaying the flag as a symbol of white supremacy and resistance to the federal government's attempts to dismantle racial segregation.[8]

African American journalist Gregory P. Kane of the *Baltimore Sun* declared that "all claims given by Confederate sympathizers that secession was inspired by the noble goals of freedom and independence do not erase Mr. Stephens's words from history." Challenging assertions made by Sons of Confederate Veterans leaders that the Confederate battle flag was "an honorable part of this nation's past and deserve[s] the respect of all of us," Kane reminded readers that the battle flag had flown over Fort Pillow when Confederate soldiers under the command of Gen. Nathan Bedford Forrest murdered black Union soldiers who had surrendered their arms. Wherever the Confederate battle flag flew during the war, it helped rally white southern men to fight to preserve slavery. As writers connected Stephens's speech with actual events describing the black experience during the Civil War, readers were exposed to a more complicated version of the war than had been traditionally part of the nation's public discourse. Through the Cornerstone Speech, Americans learned more about the massacres at Fort Pillow and the mistreatment of enslaved laborers before and during the war. Readers discovered that hundreds of thousands of black enslaved laborers ran away from their white enslavers in search of freedom at tremendous risk to their lives. Given a chance to demonstrate the fallacies of white supremacy, over 179,000 black men enlisted in the Union Army so that they could fight against their white enslavers. The NAACP campaign used the Cornerstone Speech to transform the interpretation of the Civil War from a Lost Cause waged by noble white southern men into the world's largest slave uprising. The Cornerstone Speech became the NAACP's most effective interpretative weapon in its struggle to topple the Lost Cause's stranglehold on Civil War memory.[9]

The NAACP's fight attracted support from historians, as the Lost Cause's influence on academia faded. Scholars wrote numerous editorials that offered some historical context in defense of the NAACP's campaign. Purdue University historian Robert E. May declared without reservation that slavery played a central part in the Confederacy's development. Citing the Cornerstone Speech, May wrote that although white southern men might have joined the Confederate Army to defend states' rights, the government they served had dedicated itself to preserving slavery and white supremacy. "Flying a Confederate flag from a state capitol," May argued, "prioritizes the Confederacy. It gives a modern state government's implicit endorsement to a prior government's defense of slavery." If southern states continued to display Confederate flags, the nation could not resolve its racial divisions.[10]

The NAACP campaign sparked a national conversation on Confederate memorials. While many applauded Senator Carol Moseley-Braun's stand, some questioned if removing Confederate symbols from public commemorations would achieve any tangible improvements in race relations. Citizens, politicians, and historians engaged in a historical debate citing an array of facts, opinions, and, sometimes, mistruths. Outside academia, an individuals' personal politics tended to influence their rhetoric and choice of source materials. Michael W. Pierce of Lemay, Missouri, penned a letter to the editor opposing Moseley-Braun's rhetoric. "To deny renewal of this symbol to a group of a few thousand patriotic ladies is an insult to them," wrote Pierce. "To see it as a great step forward in race relations is downright ridiculous. The senator needs to practice what she preaches: tolerance." Pierce, who like Alexander H. Stephens, referred to the Civil War as the "War Between the States," urged Moseley-Braun to revisit the war's history. He reminded her that although Alexander Stephens had declared that slavery was the cornerstone of the Confederacy, President Abraham Lincoln had only emancipated slaves when it became a necessary step to preserve the Union. Pierce speculated that had the Confederacy been defeated during the war's first months, slavery would have been preserved. Robert L. Hawkins III of Jefferson City, Missouri, accused Moseley-Braun of distorting history by insinuating that all Confederates owned slaves—a statement that she did not make. Hawkins felt that Moseley-Braun and others who opposed Confederate symbols were guilty of depriving Americans of "that special part of American heritage that was the Confederate States of America." Rather than fighting to preserve slavery, wrote Hawkins, Confederates fought "to establish their own government; to retain local control over their own affairs; or simply because an invading army was coming down the road toward their home." Hawkins encouraged Americans to celebrate Confederate values, such as "fidelity," "courage," "sacrifice," and "tenacity." He represented an opinion held by many white Americans, who viewed Moseley-Braun's protest as an attack on their heritage.[12]

The Cornerstone Speech developed into the favorite counterpoint used against conservatives who argued that American values had declined because of a failure to acknowledge history, especially the Confederate States of America. During the 2000 presidential election, conservatives rallied behind Texas Gov. George W. Bush, whose evangelical beliefs and conservative principles appealed to voters who sought to halt the nation's supposed moral decay. Conservatives sought to restore the powers of the states to determine many issues that the federal government had resolved, such as abortion, school prayer, and voter registration. Some conservatives openly saw themselves as modern-day Confederates who, like their ancestors, had launched a political movement to defend states' rights. Bush won the election by a razor-thin margin that ignited accusations of potential voter fraud. Americans voiced concerns about the vulnerability of their elections. In 2001, Republican Sen. John Ashcroft of Missouri, Bush's nominee for US attorney general, an office responsible for enforcing the nation's civil rights laws, offered praise for "patriots" like Robert E. Lee, Stonewall Jackson, and Jefferson Davis. Ashcroft urged conservatives to "stand up and speak . . . or else we'll be taught that these people were giving their lives, subscribing their sacred fortunes and their honor to some perverted agenda." Ashcroft blasted "liberal revisionist" historians for, in his view, rewriting American history. African Americans voiced concerns that Ashcroft's admiration for the Confederacy might lead him to ignore the needs of the nation's minorities. The *Chicago Tribune* called Ashcroft the "Confederacy's favorite cabinet nominee." Editorials questioned how Ashcroft could "love a nation whose vice president Alexander Stephens said the 'cornerstone' of the Confederacy rests upon the great truth that the Negro is not equal to the white man." They asked if Ashcroft would emulate Stephens and other Confederate leaders, who during Reconstruction endorsed the use of violence to suppress African American voters and ignored widespread voter fraud. Liberals suspected anyone who offered praise for Confederate leaders of harboring racist sentiments that would limit the federal government's powers to protect endangered minorities.[11]

African Americans' views on the Cornerstone Speech and Confederate symbols also varied. A research group at the Nation of Islam, an organization that the Southern Poverty Law Center has identified as a hate group, claimed that the Cornerstone Speech proved that "the Confederate flag was raised in

1861 by white slave-owners in their violent attempt to preserve Black slavery." In the group's opinion, the Confederacy's white-supremacist revolution received considerable help from Jewish investors, most notably Emile Erlanger.[13] Meanwhile, according to the Nation of Islam, the Lincoln administration made numerous efforts to avoid emancipation and did nothing during the war to help freed slaves enter the postwar period with any resources or ability to defend themselves against the violence orchestrated by their former enslavers. The NAACP, according to this analysis, had initiated a "false flag controversy" that obscured the fact that America was as committed to white supremacy in 1865 as it had been in 1861—and as it would always be. Whereas Stephens claimed that enslaver paternalism protected and guided black enslaved laborers, the Nation of Islam accused the federal government of using social welfare systems and public housing programs to keep African Americans dependent upon the white man for their survival. Some Nation of Islam members have urged African Americans to abandon efforts to remove Confederate flags and monuments because they are effective reminders to all that America has always defined itself as a white man's country, dedicated to white supremacy. Removing those symbols would only hide the reality of white supremacy's permanent hold on American life.[14]

The Cornerstone Speech had always been contested ground in America's culture wars. Supporters of the Lost Cause attempted to dismiss or selectively edit the speech, while refusing to dishonor the Confederacy's legacy by admitting the truth about its claims. During the late twentieth century, the rise of a new brand of cultural conservativism in American politics transformed the speech from a disputed piece of evidence concerning the Civil War's origins into a claim that it constituted one of many examples of historical revisionism carried out by liberal elites in academia intent on slandering American heritage. The rise of this new brand of American conservativism led to the widespread desertion of the "liberal" Democratic Party by white southern conservatives as the Republican Party began to dominate local and state elections in the South. The solid Democratic South, which had once been the stalwart of racial segregation and included renowned conservatives as Strom Thurmond, George Wallace, and Richard B. Russell, vanished as the national party diversified along racial lines and adopted support for progressive issues, such as abortion and gun control. Within a generation, most white southerners who espoused pride in their Confederate heritage became diehard Republican Party supporters who expected their elected officials to preserve and celebrate their history.[15]

As debates over the public display of Confederate flags raged, a new group emerged that combined the historical distortions perpetuated with the Lost Cause with contemporary right-wing conservative values: Neo-Confederates.

Neo-Confederates traced their origins to the founding of the Southern League on June 25, 1994, in Tuscaloosa, Alabama. The Southern League soon thereafter changed its name to the League of the South (LOS) after a minor league baseball organization sued for copyright infringement. On October 29, 1995, LOS co-founders Thomas Fleming and Michael Hill published a declaration of principles titled the "New Dixie Manifesto" in the *Washington Post*. LOS leaders accused hypocritical, prejudicial northerners of destroying the South's unique culture and undermining Christianity's influence on American culture. "The war that is being waged against the Southern identity and its traditional symbols must cease," wrote Fleming and Hill. They advised southerners to establish home rule to restore the US Constitution to what they claimed was its original meaning so that "black and white Southerners of good will" could be "left alone to work out their destinies, avoiding, before it is too late, the urban hell that has been created by the lawyers, social engineers and imperial bureaucrats who have grown rich on programs that have done nothing to help anyone but themselves." The LOS claimed that southern history had been rewritten so that a northern-based "mythology" had been forced "upon generations of students, who have come to believe that their ancestors were uniquely guilty in the annals of inhumanity. . . . This is not scholarship but propaganda." The LOS warned that if things did not change the South would fall victim of a "cultural genocide" that would destroy its "cultural identity."[16]

Neo-Confederates shared much in common with their Lost Cause predecessors. Foremost, both viewpoints endorsed white supremacy and portrayed African Americans as an inferior race that needed the guidance of their Caucasian or Anglo-Celtic superiors. The desire of local white men to control the destiny of the black race formed the core of their beliefs. Secession tried to preserve slavery. The Lost Cause justified racial segregation. Neo-Confederates blamed hostile northerners and an overreaching federal government for thrusting civil rights legislation upon the South. Author Tony Horwitz described Neo-Confederate discourse as "little more than a clever glide around race and slavery, rather like the slick-tongued defense of the Southern 'way of life' made by antebellum orators."[17]

While united on some points of ideology, Neo-Confederates, however, held diverse views. Distinctions among them demonstrate how some of these groups have diverged from their Lost Cause origins. For example, Neo-Confederates hold a diverse array of opinions concerning Alexander Stephens's Cornerstone Speech. The LOS, an organization that the Southern Poverty Law Center has identified as a hate group since 2000, celebrates Little Aleck's white-supremacist manifesto. Initially, the LOS tried to conceal its white-supremacist rhetoric by posing as an association of academic scholars and journalists dedicated to defending southern culture. The group's founder, Michael Hill, received a PhD in history from the University of Alabama under the direction of conservative historians and future LOS members Grady McWhiney and Forrest McDonald. Hill taught British history at Stillman College, a historically black college and university located in Tuscaloosa, for eighteen years. Several LOS members held tenured faculty positions at major southern universities. At its pre-9/11 peak, the LOS had over nine thousand members. Conspiracies peddled by Hill in the aftermath of 9/11 led to a mass exodus from the organization. During recent conventions and protests, the LOS has struggled to attract more than a few dozen attendees. Despite its declining numbers, Hill and the LOS remain active Neo-Confederate ideologues who use the internet and social media to flame alt-right conspiracy theories. Like many hate groups across America, their influence rose following the 2008 election of President Barack Obama and continued to grow during President Donald J. Trump's 2016 election campaign.[18]

Today, the LOS openly celebrates Alexander H. Stephens's Cornerstone Speech for its white-supremacist declarations. Whereas the Lost Cause and many Neo-Confederate organizations, such as the Sons of Confederate Veterans, disputed how scholars have interpreted Stephens's remarks, the LOS applauded Stephens for recognizing "the importance of keeping the South under firm control of whites." LOS founder Michael Hill routinely argued that Confederate leaders like Stephens had predicted the damage that emancipation and civil equality would create in America. According to Hill, Confederate leaders, like Stephens, Henry Benning, Jefferson Davis, and Robert E. Lee, defended "the proper status of the negro in our form of civilization." Like Stephens, the LOS criticized the supposed negative influence that Enlightenment ideals of equality had on undermining white supremacy. Although the LOS admitted that the South's past was imperfect, when compared to post-emancipation and post-civil rights–era America, the Old South represented an ideal civilization that conformed to natural and divine laws. Hill's white-supremacist writings borrowed heavily on ideas found throughout Stephens's Cornerstone Speech.[19]

Like other Neo-Confederate groups, the LOS blamed a consortium of "Deep State" bureaucrats, liberals, Marxists, homosexuals, non-Aryan peoples, Muslims, leftist scholars, atheists, civil rights advocates, journalists, and corporations for launching an assault upon southern culture. The LOS often depicted African Americans as ignorant or innocent victims of these outside influences who have been manipulated into believing that white southerners are racists. Like Stephens, the LOS has perpetuated a long-held dishonest belief that Confederates could not have been racists because they believed that black people could attain the full rights of citizenship and enjoy the same fruits of liberty as white men *if* their race could meet certain vague conditions. Hill and Stephens asked black southerners to trust their white counterparts to know when those vague conditions had been met. These white supremacists blamed any tensions or violence between white and black southerners on outside agitators.

The LOS embrace of the Cornerstone Speech has led the group to criticize other Neo-Confederate organizations that continue to deny the CSA's racist origins as reflected in Cornerstone Speech. Hill referred to the Sons of Confederate Veterans (SCV) as "Rainbow Confederates" because of the heritage organization's efforts to deny the central role that white supremacy played in secession. Rather than celebrate the Confederacy's supposed righteous defense of white supremacy, the SCV, according to Hill, has taken positions to "placate the Cultural Marxists and to justify the Southern cause in the name of political correctness." The LOS has referred to the SCV's "Heritage Not Hate" slogan as the "effeminate, limp-wristed, apologetic battle cry of Rainbow Confederates." The LOS's rhetoric is a reminder that, in addition to promoting white supremacy, the organization espouses extremely homophobic positions. Like "any modern liberal utopia," chastised Hill, the SCV has dishonestly argued that "the historic South was not really 'racist' but was a society that valued multiculturalism, diversity, and tolerance." The SCV has lost "the courage to proclaim that their ancestors" fought to defend the white race from northern efforts to usurp the South's natural and divine social order. The LOS has criticized SCV campaigns to promote the role that mythical black Confederates played in defending the South. Likewise, SCV attempts to depict the Confederacy as more tolerant than the North because of the cabinet positions that Catholics and Jews held in its administration have been rejected by the LOS. According to the LOS, Stephens's Cornerstone Speech told people all they needed to know about the Confederacy and how and why it came about. It was a white men's government founded by white men for the benefit of white men and in recognition of white supremacy and black inferiority. The LOS claimed that efforts to contest what Stephens had so plainly explained was not only dishonest but served the conspiratorial interests of liberals who refuted white supremacy's legitimacy. Without white supremacy, the LOS would find little reason to celebrate the Confederate States of America. Except for the large exuberant crowd that witnessed the Cornerstone Speech, Stephens never found a more approving audience for his speech than Michael Hill and the LOS.[20]

The Sons of Confederate Veterans (SCV) is among the oldest Neo-Confederate organizations. Founded on July 1, 1896, in Richmond, Virginia, to "encourage the preservation of history, perpetuate the hallowed memories of brave men, to assist in the observance of Memorial Day, and to perpetuate the record of the services of every Southern soldier." The SCV strove to "hand down to posterity the story of the glory of the men who wore the gray." From its inception, the SCV dedicated itself to promoting the Lost Cause. Like modern-day Neo-Confederate organizations, such as the LOS, the SCV presents a public façade designed to validate its beliefs through historical research, serial publications, public programs, monument dedications, and anniversary observances. Between 1893 and 1932, Confederate heritage groups published the popular *Confederate Veteran* magazine to promote Lost Cause interpretations and organize various commemorative activities. After a fifty-two-year hiatus, the SCV revived the *Confederate Veteran* in 1984. Today, in addition to the six editions of the magazine published annually, the SCV maintains an active blog and Facebook page that provides public access to their activities and opinions. The SCV has always supported an education/historical committee that promotes, explains, and defends the Lost Cause. They have also formed several institutes, such as the Stephen Dill Lee Institute, that present their ideology in a format resembling academic scholarship but ignores vast amounts of available historical evidence and professional scholarship. The group's website proclaims that they are "preserving the history and legacy of [Confederate] heroes so that future generations can understand the motives that animated the Southern Cause." They also claim to be a "non-political organization" although their website displays their affiliation with the political activist group "Make Dixie Great Again"—an obvious reference to the SCV's support for President Donald J. Trump.[21]

The SCV has evolved over time as members sought to modernize the organization and distance themselves from Neo-Confederate hate groups. During the 1980s and 1990s, SCV membership numbers soared as public interest in genealogy drew thousands of men into the group, spawning new camps nationwide. Most of those new members were more interested in commemorating their Confederate ancestors than extolling Lost Cause virtues. The SCV's new members pushed the organization to differentiate itself from hate groups, which had adopted Confederate symbols. In 1989, SCV members passed a resolution condemning groups and individuals who used the Confederate flag when espousing "political extremism and racial superiority." Three years later, the SCV's leaders denounced "the KKK and all others who promote hate among our people."[22]

Efforts to reform the SCV sparked a civil war among its members as moderates clashed with extremists over the group's future. The SCV's extremist wing followed the leadership of North Carolina attorney Kirk Lyons, a white supremacist with ties to Aryan Nation organizations. Lyons represented SCV members who opposed the group's anti-KKK statements and disavowals of Neo-Confederate hate groups. By the early 2000s, Lyons had successfully reversed the SCV's moderation movement, thanks to what Southern Poverty

Law Center (SPCL) attorney Heidi Beirich has referred to as an "infiltration" movement orchestrated by the LOS. During the 2002 SCV annual reunion held in Dalton, Georgia, the extremist wing's influence was on full display as white supremacists forcibly ousted Walter Hilderman III, a politically conservative SCV moderate, who demanded the organization publicly disavow hate groups by removing its leaders with known ties to hate groups. After Hilderman's removal, the SCV voted to renounce his membership and passed a new anti-hate resolution criticizing "racial and political extremists." This time, however, the proclamation targeted the NAACP and Jesse Jackson rather than the KKK.[23]

Today, according to the SPLC, the SCV is "a Southern heritage group that has been largely dominated by racial extremists since 2002."[24] The SPLC does not consider the SCV to be among the hate groups, but acknowledges that "in their effort to gloss over the legacy of slavery in the South, these groups strengthen the appeal of Lost Cause mythology, opening the door for violent incidents spurred by the rhetoric of cynical individuals like Michael Hill."[25] As "right-wing radicals" wrestled over control of the Confederate heritage organization, many existing SCV members left the group. "I have no desire to be associated with neo-Nazis and white trash," wrote Henry Seale, a former SCV camp leader commander. "With great sadness, I concede that this is what the SCV has become."[26]

Since the early 2000s, the SCV has adopted contradictory public statements that reject accusations of racism while failing to disavow known hate groups. SCV publications and social media regularly trafficked in white-supremacist conspiracy theories alongside aged Lost Cause myths. Compared with other Neo-Confederate organizations and hate groups, the SCV made a greater public effort to present Confederate heritage as multicultural.[27] The SCV often identified exceptional examples of African Americans, Jews, Catholics, Hispanics, and American Indians who served or were forced to serve in the Confederacy and presented them to the public as representative case studies of the rebel government's racial tolerance.[28] The SCV has made a concerted effort to insert celebrations of mythical black Confederates into national Black History Month programs. SCV members who have argued that black history is Confederate history are oblivious to why many African Americans might find such an assertion to be highly offensive as well as historically inaccurate. The SCV devoted much of its intellectual energy and propaganda tools trying to deceive the world that Confederates were simply patriots dedicated to personal liberty and not white supremacists. The prominent role that slavery played in the secession crisis and Confederate public policy, however, invalidates their efforts to shed the rebel government of its inherent white-supremacist origins and actions.[29]

SCV publications regularly engaged with Alexander H. Stephens's Cornerstone Speech. If, as they contend, the CSA was not founded to preserve slavery and white supremacy, the SCV must discredit the Cornerstone Speech. The SCV rejected Stephens's assertion that slavery and white supremacy were the primary factors that influenced secession. The SCV has borrowed heavily from longstanding Lost Cause ideologies to create a complex set of defenses that sought to repudiate the Cornerstone Speech. Foremost, the SCV often claimed that Stephens had been misquoted and that readers should pay more attention to what he wrote after the Civil War than his 1861 Cornerstone Speech. This defense is problematic because it treated the Cornerstone Speech as an exceptional and unreliable example of Stephens's, and by extension the Confederacy's, rhetoric. Missing from the SCV's defense was any discussion of Stephens's prior white-supremacist speeches in Montgomery, Atlanta, or Augusta. Absent from the discussion were the speeches that Stephens and other Confederate emissaries delivered to southern states, pleading with them to join their new government to preserve their civilization, a slave society whose cornerstone was black inferiority. The SCV, for example, ignored Charles Dew's award-winning *Apostles of Disunion* because its well-documented claims refute Neo-Confederate distortions of the Confederacy's founding.

The SCV also ignores the prominent role that Stephens played in the development of the CSA Constitution. Every Constitution Day, the SCV and Make Dixie Great Again launch numerous criticisms toward the contemporary federal government, which they claim has been ruined by judicial activism and political correctness. Neo-Confederates offer the CSA Constitution and government as a shining articulation of individual liberty, Christian nationalism, and states' rights. They suggest that we could "Make America Great Again" by rediscovering America's lost heritage. While the SCV does not refer to the decline in Confederate celebrations as a sign of an impending white cultural genocide, the messages posted by supporters on social media often warn of an impending extermination campaign. Liberals and "Cultural Vandals," according to SCV supporters, want to take their guns and then erase their history in advance of creating a socialist utopia in America. The SCV describes itself as an organization dedicated to personal liberty, yet its resistance to federal civil rights legislation, especially minority voting rights and LGBTQ protections, reveals a different reality. SCV and Make Dixie Great Again conveniently ignore provisions in the CSA Constitution that protected slavery by prohibiting local governments from interfering with its existence. The right to own slaves found in the constitution that Stephens helped draft ensured that the most basic of civil liberties would be permanently denied to black enslaved laborers. Like Lost Cause followers who depicted the CSA as a unified government with broad popular support among white and black southerners, the SCV continued a dishonest narrative spun by Stephens's Cornerstone Speech, namely, that white supremacy united all southerners, white and black, under a banner of security, prosperity, natural law, and divine sanction.[30]

Social media posts found on the W. F. Jenkins SCV Camp #690 Facebook page are representative of SCV treatments of Stephens's Cornerstone Speech. In a post chastising the new signage at Piedmont Park in Atlanta, Georgia, that explains the missing context behind why the Confederate monument was originally erected, a lively conversation erupted over the "real story" behind "such bullshit and Yankee lies." SCV sympathizer Jim Armour expressed his frustration that "no matter what the subject is of our posts someone will crawl out of the woodwork and comment, 'But, but, but the Cornerstone Speech.'" Armour promptly resumed a dishonest rhetorical strategy that had been employed by several generations of Lost Cause believers—the North was just as racist as the South. Armour claims that Stephens's was quoting passages from an obscure 1830s US Supreme Court case. Armour then repeated the conspiratorial falsehoods that had transformed the Lost Cause into the modern-day Neo-Confederate political movement. Armour claimed that: "our enemies operate under a heavy, thick, dark cloud or ignorance, both historical and Constitutional, sickening self-righteousness, and an abject lack of understanding of the original intent of our fathers the Founders and our Fathers the Confederate citizen-soldier. They only know what they are told and/or taught by others who are just as ignorant and confused as they are. . . . They are nothing more than parrots with letters of the alphabet after their names." Armour called upon southern heritage advocates to educate themselves to "understand the finger-pointing at the South is unfair, unjust, and NOT historically accurate. Not at all."[31]

Using Facebook as a platform to expound on his views, Armour lectured readers about the Cornerstone Speech's true origins. As Armour laid out a prodigious Neo-Confederate rant countering liberal interpretations of the speech, he followed with great precision a series of falsehoods and distortions that had originated among Stephens and Lost Cause creators over a 150 years ago. Armour accused Stephens of "engaging in hyperbole" as he pontificated on the Confederacy's origins. Rather than being a sincere expression of white-supremacist ideology, Armour claimed that Stephens's speech had been merely "toying" with the idea that "slavery is the Cornerstone of the Constitution." Armour condemned "newcomers, outsiders, and the abjectly ignorant" for not understanding that Stephens's contemporaries would have understood that his "cornerstone" metaphor was a reference to a three-decades-old Supreme Court decision. In the countless number of commentaries written about the

Cornerstone Speech, no one, including Stephens, had claimed that he was parroting the words of a northern slavery advocate. As Lost Cause proponents had done, Armour admitted that Stephens might have been a racist "as we understand it in our day." The suggestion that slavery was not an expression of racism was an argument that Stephens had made repeatedly as he celebrated the institution's benevolent paternalism and positive impact on the black and white southerners.

Neo-Confederates also continued another Lost Cause rhetorical tactic: the art of distraction. The best strategy for a debater to shore up an indefensible position is to change the subject or redefine the argument on his own terms. Neo-Confederates turned the question of "was slavery the cornerstone of the CSA" into "was the North just as racist as the South?" A critique of Stephens's speech would not be complete without a condemnation of President Abraham Lincoln's racism. Neo-Confederates repeatedly point out that "Alexander Stephens was no more 'racist' than Abraham Lincoln or any other Northern man in a leadership position in the 1860s." The SCV is correct in pointing out that racism was a national problem, but they purposely obscure Lincoln's evolving position as he rose to power within the nascent antebellum-era Republican Party. Armour resorted to a common rhetorical tactic employed by the Lost Cause and Neo-Confederates alike. Rather than address the CSA's obvious racist origins, Armour and countless others seek to distort the truth by tearing down Lincoln's legacy. Whether Lincoln was a racist had little to do with the CSA's origins or Stephens's speech. As Armour explained Stephens's white-supremacist ideals, he wrote:

> [T]here is an elephant in the room regarding any supremacy discussion anyway. The elephant is this: with all fairness to the people in the 1860s, can anyone blame them for thinking their culture superior to others in their day? Look at Africa and South America in the 1860s. For whatever reason, be it environment, luck or happenstance, the cultures these men came from were the ones mapping oceans, building buildings and engaging in science in their day. . . . [P]retty much everyone of the time was "racist" in some capacity, due to the differences of cultures and the ones making a mark on the world. Racism is a heart problem, not a Confederate problem.

As Armour's rant fizzled, he drew upon one last Lost Cause myth. "The truth is all those in servitude, black, white, brown and red were being manumitted and taught to thrive in western style culture." The myth that slavery would have ended without the catastrophic Civil War had the North permitted secession to proceed ignores an avalanche of evidence that proves that white enslavers were as committed to slavery as ever in American history on the eve of the conflict. So dedicated were these white men to preserving slavery that they risked everything by seceding from the Union to preserve slavery in a new government founded for that explicit purpose, as the Cornerstone Speech explicitly states.[32]

James Armour and other SCV members have used new social media and digital publishing platforms to achieve what historian Carl Becker warned about in his 1935 American Historical Association speech "Everyman His Own Historian." Humans use history in their everyday lives whether they consciously understand those acts to be part of some larger historical consciousness. The SCV's prolonged war against so-called political correctness and "cultural vandals" has thrust followers like Armour into a role of perpetrating myths that were formed long before he and other SCV members were born. Although social media and digital publishing has made it easier for Neo-Confederates to share their distorted interpretations with broad audiences of like-minded conservatives, the potency and adaptability of those Lost Cause ideals had established deep roots in American culture long before the internet revolution. For the public, determining which sources of information are reputable and trustworthy will remain an increasingly difficult process as Neo-Confederates continue to undermine the credibility of "leftist" historians and the sources they rely on such as the Cornerstone Speech.

Neo-Confederates, like the SCV, have exerted tremendous influence on American society. Historian David Goldfield has warned that Neo-Confederates "are not fringe people." Neo-Confederate ideologies have become so mainstream that, according to scholar Peter Applebome, it is "hard to know these days where the Confederacy ends and the Republican Party begins."[33]

A lucrative industry has developed to sell clothing, flags, and other items that mix Confederate symbols and leaders with contemporary right-wing and alt-right political stances related to protecting the Second Amendment, halting foreign immigration, preserving a Christian nation, persecuting homosexuals, and opposing supposed judicial tyranny. Images of the controversial AR-15 assault rifle, for example, are commonly placed over the Confederate Battle Flag alongside phrases such as "come and get it." In 1997, entrepreneur and Neo-Confederate Dewey Barber founded Dixie Outfitters to honor "our ancestors who fought and died in the War for Southern Independence" and to resist those who "have distorted the real meaning of the Confederate Flag for their own purposes." Some described Barber as "an evangelist for a Southern heritage revival."[34] The business proclaims to represent "all Southern, and even Northern, Confederates regardless of race or religion" who support "less government, less taxes, and the right of the people to govern themselves." Dixie Outfitters's website includes several mission statements and history lessons that reflect contemporary Neo-Confederate explanations of the Civil War and the Cornerstone Speech. Dixie Outfitters interprets the Civil War as a plot hatched by northern industrialists who elected President Abraham Lincoln to act as their puppet in a scheme to rob the South of its wealth through exorbitant tariffs on European imported goods. The "War for Southern Independence of 1861 was fought over 'taxation without representation.' . . . Slavery was not the issue. . . . The truth about the Confederate Flag is that it has nothing to do with racism or hate." Americans who believe that the war resulted from conflicts over slavery, according to the company, are ignorant and unduly influenced by their emotions.[35]

Dixie Outfitters makes a concerted effort to portray Confederate heritage as an inclusive belief system founded on a certain view of civil liberties rather than white supremacy. Like the SCV, it tries to defend against charges that the Confederacy was racist by promoting examples of its supposed ethnic diversity and tolerance. The company produces merchandise with text that reads:

White Confederates
Black Confederates
Red Confederates
Brown Confederates
Yellow Confederates
All Deserve Honor

Dixie Outfitters also claim that since many northern-born and African American customers purchase its goods that the company's prodigious use of the Confederate Battle Flag could not be associated with racism or any lingering sectional hostilities. Like most Neo-Confederates, the company makes a concerted effort to highlight any African Americans who might purchase their apparel as evidence of widespread support for their cause among the black community. H. K. Edgerton, an African American whom Dixie Outfitters describes as an "activist for Southern Heritage and a member of the Sons of Confederate Veterans," is prominently featured in the company website's "in-the-news" section. Edgerton touts his former role in the NAACP and his interest in Confederate heritage as evidence of the racial tolerance of Neo-Confederates.[36]

Despite the company's claims of its popularity among northern customers, it also claims that the history of the "War of Northern Aggression" had been distorted by northern writers and liberals who are plotting to destroy southern civilization. Apparently, there are good and bad northerners. That line of demarcation roughly correlates with an individual's politics, as libertarian-leaning conservatives are attracted to the Confederacy as a supposed bastion of individual liberty, a myth that had been promoted by supporters of the Lost Cause for over a century. Dixie Outfitters often labels those who support the removal of Confederate symbols from American public life as Marxists. Although company publications accuse northern interests of misrepresenting Confederate history, they fail to provide any evidence of who precisely would benefit from such a conspiracy. The rhetoric often resembles that employed by 1930s era anti-Semitic German Fascists. Most Neo-Confederates are not overtly anti-Semitic, but they use many of the same rhetorical devices to spread fear of a looming, hidden enemy intent on destroying their way of life. The company, like other Neo-Confederates, has created an imagined enemy that has effectively galvanized followers under a cohesive white-supremacist ideology disguised as a protest of federal tyranny.[37]

Initially, Dixie Outfitters sold its goods through mail order and flea market vendors scattered across the nation. Sales tended to increase as the NAACP's campaign to remove Confederate flags from public buildings and parks gained momentum. In 2001, Georgia chose to change its flag from a design that had prominently featured the Confederate Battle Flag to a new design that reduced the controversial symbol's size and now included the phrase in God we trust. Critics of the new flag claimed that Georgia had caved under pressure from the NAACP and the "politically correct" media. The controversy sparked renewed interest in Confederate-themed apparel, especially among young white southern males. Dixie Outfitters's sales climbed to more than three million dollars annually. The brand became so popular that school systems began banning their products to prevent the escalation of racial violence after some African Americans complained that the white-supremacist symbols "made them uncomfortable." The company, with the help of an unusual alliance between a Neo-Confederate legal defense fund and the American Civil Liberties Union, mounted a vigorous attack on these bans, claiming that schools had infringed upon their students' First Amendment rights. The bans failed to diminish Dixie Outfitters's popularity and inspired a new generation of creative Confederate-themed designs that circumvented the prohibitions. By the late 2000s, Dixie Outfitters was a flourishing company that had expanded by opening several franchises in Georgia, South Carolina, and Florida and developing a lucrative retail website. Buyers who visited the company's website found more than clothing. They encountered Dixie Outfitters's Neo-Confederate explanations of the Civil War, including its extensive efforts to counter academic interpretations of the Cornerstone Speech.[38]

Why would a successful retailer that peddles Confederate-inspired clothing care how Americans remember the Cornerstone Speech? Neo-Confederate evangelists, such as Dixie Outfitters, have assumed the mantle of defending the Confederacy's legacy that originated among Lost Cause believers. The consumers of Confederate heritage refute any assertions that the defense of slavery and white supremacy had inspired eleven southern states to secede from the Union. Dixie Outfitters claims that a Righteous Cause Myth has emerged among northern writers and Marxists who have reached the "superficial, narrow, and adolescent conclusion" that slavery was the "reason (singular) the South seceded."[39]

Modern-day American conservatives hold differing opinions of the Cornerstone Speech's meaning. The conservative evangelical Christian non-profit organization WallBuilders formed to present "America's forgotten history and heroes, with an emphasis on the moral, religious, and constitutional foundation on which America was built." Like Neo-Confederates, WallBuilders believes that American values are threatened by liberal activists and judicial activists, whose stances on abortion, gay marriage, and religion have supposedly undermined the nation's families and morality.[40]

WallBuilders has produced numerous historical essays examining various topics in American history. The group has expressed deep concerns that revisionist distortions of history have spread among an undereducated populace unaware that the history they receive in classrooms and from the media has been altered to serve a liberal political agenda. WallBuilders, for example, criticizes scholars who contend that the Founding Fathers were "deists and atheists" who intended to build a secular society that precluded a substantial place for organized religion in the public sphere. Like Neo-Confederates, WallBuilders often exaggerates or oversimplifies the arguments of academic scholars to spread fears among the public of a widespread conspiracy among liberals to destroy American Christianity. Surprisingly, however, WallBuilders rejects the validity of Lost Cause interpretations of the Civil War. The organization argues that numerous Confederate documents, including Alexander Stephens's Cornerstone Speech, "indisputably show that the South's desire to preserve slavery was indisputably *the* driving reason for the formation of the Confederacy." According to Wall-Builders, Stephens used the speech to differentiate the Confederate government from its American primogenitor. Stephens depicted the Founding Fathers as fallible men who failed to see slavery as a permanent part of American life. He condemned their inability to build a government upon a cornerstone based on the lasting acknowledgment that white men were created to govern an inferior black race. WallBuilders found Stephens's criticism of the Founding Fathers unacceptable and the Lost Cause's efforts to minimize slavery as a cause of the Civil War illegitimate.[41]

Like WallBuilders, RenewAmerica describes itself as an organization dedicated to "one unifying premise: *America must return to its founding principles if it is to survive.*" Founded in 2002 to promote the ideas of African American conservative commentator Alan Keyes, the group "has evolved into a significant Christian political vehicle" that champions "the core issues of moral conservatism." RenewAmerica's primary mission is to unify American moral conservatives. Its website includes editorials penned by a broad range of conservatives who offer commentary on current events and promote America's supposedly more moral past. Commentators often lament that today's leaders have failed to follow President Ronald Reagan's moral example and condemn efforts among progressives to legalize gay marriage, protect abortion, and promote multiculturalism. Articles range from Rev. Jerry Falwell–inspired defenses of America's moral majority to celebrations of Ayn Rand–inspired objectivism.[42]

RenewAmerica's editorials reveal that explaining the causes of the American Civil War has created fissures among American libertarians. Like WallBuilders, RenewAmerica followers reject Neo-Confederate efforts to merge Lost Cause ideology with modern-day Libertarian Party platforms. Together they represent a growing number of Anti-Neo-Confederate libertarians who oppose Neo-Confederate efforts to obfuscate libertarian politics. Jake Jacobs, a RenewAmerica writer, argues that the CSA abused national power by censoring the press, seizing private property, nationalizing private industries, conscripting citizens into military service, and denying its citizens the right to a fair and speedy trial. Jacobs claims that contemporary libertarians would have opposed the CSA because of their contrasting views on individual liberty. RenewAmerica questions how Neo-Confederates can suggest that enslavers would be good role models for contemporary libertarians, since slavery denied millions of African Americans liberty based solely on the color of their skin. RenewAmerica worries that Neo-Confederates will do to libertarian organizations what they did to the SCV. Jacobs and others argue that libertarians who celebrate the CSA as a model government are purposely distorting the historical record. Libertarians, by-and-large, believe that secession was a valid right exercised by the South, but reject how the CSA chose to administer its rebellion.[43]

On the opposing side of the issue stands secessionist-libertarian groups, such as the Young Americans for Liberty who have been inspired by libertarian politician Ron Paul. The Republican Texas Congressman finds common ground between the southern slave states who seceded in 1861 and contemporary libertarians who feel threatened by the federal government's growing power. Paul often criticizes the "tyrannical" President Abraham Lincoln for destroying individual freedom in America. Founded after President Barack Obama's 2008 election victory, Young Americans for Liberty expanded to over 78 chapters across 32 states from Hawaii to Maine. The group is especially popular on private Christian-affiliated college campuses, such as Shorter University in Rome, Georgia, and Liberty University in Lynchburg, Virginia, but it has also started new chapters at major public universities, including Georgia Tech and the University of Virginia.[44]

Today, Young Americans for Liberty has advocated for the view that states possess the right to secede to resist perceived federal abuses. Libertarians have labeled those who espouse this view as secessionist libertarians. Young Americans for Liberty has collaborated with members of the League of the South, Sons of Confederate Veterans, and Abbeville Institute to build a grassroots political movement to place leaders in local elected offices that share their views. The youthful appearance of the Young Americans for Liberty's members hides its dark connections to recognized American hate groups. The group's lobbying for Republican and Libertarian Party candidates also helps blur the lines between student activism, Neo-Confederate ideology, and conservative Republican Party politics. The example of the Young Americans for Liberty provides ample evidence of the mainstreaming of hate in American public discourse.

Another libertarian-inspired Neo-Confederate group is the New Confederate States of America (NCSA). The NCSA argues that "the original confederacy was founded to fight for freedom from tyranny, over taxation by the federal government on goods produced/grown in the south, and about states rights." Rather than fight to defend slavery and white supremacy, the NCSA urges "brothers and sisters from all ethnic backgrounds" to join its movement to "uphold the values from our ancestors" and "to learn true history of America."[45] Although the NCSA does not explicitly reference the Cornerstone Speech, its message reflects Stephens's influence on the Lost Cause and Neo-Confederate movements. Like Stephens, NCSA believes that all Americans, as well as various ethnic groups across the globe, will join their cause because of their dedication to personal liberty. In the Cornerstone Speech, Stephens predicted that the Confederacy's global appeal would play a critical role in helping it gain independence—only he based that potential global appeal on white supremacy. NCSA and Stephens both proclaimed the existence of a southern civilization that was under attack from outside interests. Both portrayed themselves as moderates surrounded by radical elements. Publicly, NCSA differentiates itself from other Neo-Confederate organizations because of its supposed ethnic inclusivity. NCSA, however, fails to acknowledge that most Neo-Confederate groups claim to be racially inclusive. Stephens also tried to convince observers that the Confederacy's concern for the lives of black enslaved laborers had transformed secession into a multiethnic revolution based on ideals and principles but grounded in the pragmatic recognition of black inferiority.[46]

Neo-Confederates and hate groups are not the sole parties interested in shaping contemporary public memory of Alexander H. Stephens's Cornerstone Speech. A broad coalition has adopted the Cornerstone Speech as the central piece of evidence required to understand the Civil War's origins and shed light on white supremacy's persistence in American culture. This Emancipationist coalition lacks any formal organizational body, leadership, or manifestos and includes a broad spectrum of actors ranging from academics to activists. The lines between emancipationist nonpartisan scholars and partisan activists are often blurred. Emancipationists wholeheartedly believe that the Cornerstone Speech proves beyond a doubt that slavery and white supremacy motivated secession and laid the foundation for the new Confederate States of America. Emancipationist interpretations have become the official, federally sanctioned memory of the Civil War as articulated by the National Park Service, Library of Congress, National Archives and Records Administration, and Smithsonian Institution, as well as the standard view taught in university classrooms and published in academic peer-reviewed scholarship. In an era filled with mounting racial violence and alt-right politics, journalists and political activists have rediscovered the Cornerstone Speech.[47] Today, the speech remains such a widely cited speech of the Civil War era because of its undeniably racist message. The speech is used to invalidate Neo-Confederate and alt-right claims on a regular basis in newspapers, social media outlets, cable news, late-night television shows, YouTube videos, and more. Stephens has become one of the most recognizable vice-presidents in history and, alongside ex-KKK leader David Duke, the symbol of white supremacy in America. Whenever Neo-Confederate racism emerges in American life, the analysis turns to the Cornerstone Speech to remind readers of white supremacy's continuity.

Much to the chagrin of many Civil War historians and Confederate heritage groups, emancipationists often conflate or fail to explain several major questions that have been central to this debate since 1861. To what degree did the defense of slavery contribute to the creation of the Confederate States of America? Why did soldiers on either side of the conflict fight? If protecting slavery motivated the actions of southern leaders, how did these men convince non-slaveholders to join their rebellion? Also, if the Confederacy sought to destroy the Union to preserve slavery, did the Union seek to preserve the nation by destroying slavery? Each question has been thoroughly addressed by nonpartisan scholars for decades, but large segments of white Americans distrust their objectivity and remain convinced that academics are part of a conspiracy to rewrite history in a way that undermines American pride and diminishes the role of white people in building America. Most Neo-Confederates appear reluctant to accept that the average Confederate soldier fought to preserve slavery because of the racial prejudices they shared with their more affluent enslaver neighbors. Likewise, emancipationists rarely explore other possible factors that, in addition to slavery and white supremacy, might have motivated Confederates to fight. To be sure, slavery is central to those discussions, but additional factors also played a supporting role. History is complicated. Public debates of history are messy, emotional, and influenced by a broad range of partisan beliefs.

As this book goes to press, Americans remain at an impasse as a coalition of Neo-Confederates, mainstream conservatives, and alt-right activists continue to discredit academic research, often portraying it as driven by a desire to build a liberal utopia founded on political correctness and multiculturalism. The most extreme of these views share much in common with Confederate fears on the eve of the Civil War—that they would become the North's slaves if they remained in a government ruled by Black Republicans. Modern secession advocates and white supremacists fear that our supposedly declining society is on the verge of a white cultural genocide. Meanwhile, a coalition of scholars, activists, and media remain committed to exposing the racist ideologies that have been proffered by generations of Neo-Confederates and white supremacists. Generally, they believe that acknowledging America's troubled past would be a major step toward achieving some form of reconciliation for those who have been most impacted by these corrosive ideologies. They draw a direct line from the rhetoric of Alexander Stephens and other Confederate leaders to modern-day alt-right white supremacists and Neo-Confederates. Racism has been a central theme in American history that this country has never adequately acknowledged, in their opinion.[48] These groups believe that removing Confederate symbols and memorials from public sites and commemorations, especially in the wake of the 2015 Emanuel AME Church murders in Charleston, South Carolina, and the 2020 murder of George Floyd in Minneapolis, Minnesota, are central to changing the course of American race relations so that future generations of Americans can escape the cycle of white supremacy. Emancipationists fear that racism is on the rise in American society. Members of both sides predict a bleak future for America. Alexander H. Stephens's Cornerstone Speech stands at the intersection of the battle for the past, present, and future of American culture. How we interpret and remember the Cornerstone Speech tells us much about where we stand in this contested struggle for equality and justice in America. Who says the Civil War ended in 1865?

CONCLUSION
Colfax in the Mourning

In February 2020, I traveled to central Louisiana to present my Cornerstone Speech research to the Central Louisiana Civil War Roundtable. That morning as I sat in my Alexandria, Louisiana, hotel room I used Google Maps to search the area for nearby historic sites. I realized that Colfax, Louisiana, was nearby. I jumped in my car, eager to see a place as connected to the defense of white supremacy as Alexander Stephens's Cornerstone Speech.

In 1873, white southern men committed one of the worst episodes of domestic terrorism in American history in the small rural town of Colfax. After emancipation, the region's freedpeople had provided enormous support for the Republican Party. In Grant Parish, where Colfax was the county seat, black Republicans held most seats in county government but faced mounting political opposition from white Democrats. Fearful that mobs aligned with the Democratic Party would seize and overthrow the elected local government, armed black militia occupied the courthouse, hoping to preserve the local Republican-controlled government. For nearly three weeks, tensions in the area rose as armed white men began to lay siege to the courthouse and its armed black militia occupants. On Easter Sunday 1873, 150 white armed men, many of whom belonged to the Ku Klux Klan and White League, surrounded the courthouse and ordered the black militia to surrender and disarm. When the black militia refused, the white mob fired a canon on the black militia. After a brief firefight, the black militia agreed to surrender, hoping to prevent any further escalation of violence. Following their surrender, the white mob opened fire on the disarmed black militia, ultimately killing around 150 African Americans. Fear spread across the area as armed white men seized the opportunity to exert their dominance by launching a coordinated terrorism campaign that targeted freedpeople households.[1]

News of the violence spread nationwide. Colfax's white population claimed that the murders had been necessary to restore local order. They blamed the armed black militia for instigating the entire tragedy. Federal prosecutors brought charges against ninety-seven white men accused of participating in the massacre. However, only nine of those men would be prosecuted for violating the Ku Klux Klan Acts. In 1875, after some initial success prosecuting the white men on federal conspiracy charges, the US Supreme Court decision *United States v. Cruikshank* overturned those convictions and sent a strong message to the nation: the federal government would neither prosecute perpetrators of white-on-black violence nor protect victims of domestic terrorism. The campaign of racial violence waged by white men across the South, combined with northern ambivalence about black civil liberties, contributed to Reconstruction's failures. The Colfax Massacre was just one of many violent episodes that emboldened white supremacists as they sought to restrict black civil liberties in post-emancipation America. Decades of racial violence followed, as the nation sunk into the "nadir" of southern race relations. Lynching became an oft-repeated tragedy as white supremacists continued to use violence to bolster their distorted ideology in the name of justice.[2]

In 1920, a group of white citizens in Colfax erected a monument in the town cemetery that honored the three white men who had been killed during the "Colfax Riot." The monument's inscription reads:

Erected to the memory of the Heroes
Stephen Decatur Parish
James West Hadnot
Sidney Harris
Who fell in the Colfax Riot fighting for White Supremacy

Decades after the Colfax Massacre, white supremacists continued to deceive the public about the terroristic acts their ancestors had committed during and since Reconstruction. The monument laid bare for all to read precisely what locals thought their ancestors had been fighting for: "White Supremacy." Further legitimizing this warped interpretation of the Colfax Massacre, in 1950 the state of Louisiana erected a bronze historical marker at the Grant Parish Courthouse to commemorate the violence in Colfax. That marker's text read: "On this site occurred the Colfax Riot, in which three white men and 150 negroes were slain. This event on April 13, 1873, marked the end of carpetbag misrule in the South." The official memory of one of the most significant acts of domestic terrorism in American history had been interpreted by the state as a "riot" that had resulted in the deaths of "three white men and 150 negroes" for the sake of ending "carpetbag misrule in the South." By the middle of the twentieth century in Louisiana, the Lost Cause indoctrination of American history had achieved more than its originators could have ever hoped. While the Confederate government that Stephens had so proudly proclaimed as the greatest nation ever conceived had been swept aside, the motivating factors behind its revolution continued to pulsate throughout the American commemorative landscape.[3]

Having learned of the history of the Colfax Massacre as an undergraduate student, I knew that visiting this historic site might reveal some connection to my Cornerstone Speech research. Driving to Colfax from Alexandria revealed that the landscape contained numerous other clues about how locals remembered the Old South. Numerous self-identified "plantations" lined the small state highway. Beside the driveway that led into one of those plantations was a cannon that supposedly had been used by the white mob during the Colfax Massacre. Later, when I asked a local white man why so many places in the region continued to be identified as plantations, he responded "don't get your pitchforks out because plantations here just don't mean what you think they mean or what they mean elsewhere." Interested in learning more about local perceptions of historical memory, I did not challenge that individual's claim but upon further conversation it became clear that the history of slavery and racial violence, which in my mind is connected to the unfree labor practices and white-supremacist ideologies rooted in southern plantations, was something local whites did not want to remember.

As I entered the small rural town of Colfax, Louisiana, I immediately encountered the 1950 state historical marker that now stood in front of the modern Grant Parish Courthouse. I hoped an additional marker had been erected, explaining what the historical record revealed about this tragic incident. I was deeply saddened to discover that no additional marker existed. The sole voice on the history of the massacre remained white. Until that moment the optimist within me had always hoped that maybe a campaign could be launched to contextual Confederate and white-supremacist monuments so that the public could weigh alternate perspectives. The absence of any signs of the actual history of what happened there on Easter Sunday 1873 crushed those hopes. If no effort to counter Lost Cause lies could be made at one of the most notorious sites of domestic terrorism in American history, what hope do we as historians have of challenging similar distortions found elsewhere?

After snapping a few images of the "Colfax Riot" historical marker, I sought out the infamous white-supremacy monument. Colfax is a small town. The cemetery that contains the monument is within walking distance of the courthouse. As I entered the cemetery, an unidentified white man immediately sought me out. He questioned what I was doing at the cemetery. I responded that I was a Civil War historian interested in the town's monument. At that moment I realized that I was not the first random white man to show up in that town looking for this monument. Clearly, in addition to the number of historians who might have journeyed to this out-of-the way destination, many modern-day white supremacists have made pilgrimages to this site to honor the white-supremacy monument. Naively, despite spending many years researching white-supremacist groups, I had not thought about white-supremacist pilgrimages to Colfax until that moment.

After I explained why I was in Colfax, he immediately pointed out the monument's location and began complaining about how "local black leaders" had purposely ignored the cemetery for decades, resulting in its poor condition. To be sure, the cemetery was in rough shape, and many of its concrete pathways had sunken into the ground. Many gravestones appeared to have been broken. Clearly, no one had trimmed the property in years, as weeds covered many graves. As I took out my phone to snap some photographs of the cemetery, the man looked me in the eye and said, "If you are going to take photographs of our monument to put on the internet, I am going to kick to your ass because we don't want folks to know about our monument. We are trying to keep our monument and not let others remove it." As a native southerner I was not shocked by this man's threats. He was not the first white supremacist to threaten me. Plus, I knew that the threat was hollow and represented his casual manner of communicating as much as it represented a sincere threat to my safety. Yet, this man was clearly threatened by my appearance.

Eager to learn more about this individual's perceptions of what happened in Colfax back in 1873, I innocently asked "what happened here?" I got a Neo-Confederate lesson in history as the man retold the false story that armed black men had formed a mob and seized the courthouse by force. Those armed black men, according to this man, then attacked white men and began assaulting white women in the area. A band of ex-Confederate veterans and local white men retaliated with violence, killing at least 150 black people to "restore order" in Colfax. When I asked how so few white men died in such a large gun battle, he joked that the freedpeople were not used to firearms and were no match for the experienced Confederate veterans. As we ended our conversation, he reminded me that the black leaders of Colfax were not interested in telling the true story. He politely asked that I keep my photographs of their monuments to myself so that outsiders would not be tempted to come here and desecrate their sacred memorials. We shook hands and parted ways.

As I left Colfax to return to Alexandria, I was overwhelmed by the contemporary relevance of Alexander H. Stephens's Cornerstone Speech. Back in March of 1861, Stephens had proudly stood before a jubilant crowd and declared that the CSA had been founded to defend white supremacy. Today, numerous monuments, especially the one in Colfax, exist across the nation that also declare similar support for the preservation of white supremacy. Meanwhile, much like the many generations of emancipationists who wielded the Cornerstone Speech as prime evidence of the incontrovertible truth of the CSA's origins, a new generation of activists and scholars has taken up the fight to question the motivations of those who in the past erected those monuments and those in modern society who continue to defend them. Much of the story of the Cornerstone Speech's lasting impact on American historical memory remains to be written.

Despite uncertainty about the speech's future role in American memory, there are several concrete conclusions that can be drawn through a critical analysis of the Cornerstone Speech. First, although white-supremacist political rhetoric did not mature until the eve of the American Civil War, the origins of those ideas, as well as many of the numerous metaphors used to construct the white-supremacist imagination, were a major part of antebellum pro-slavery discourse. Despite subsequent claims by Lost Cause defenders and many historians, Stephens's Cornerstone Speech was accepted by Confederate leaders as representative of their beliefs and motivations. After the Civil War, the speech contradicted claims made by Lost Cause promoters that the war had been fought to defend states' rights and for far more noble reasons than defending slavery. After the war, generations of emancipationists—those who viewed the war as a crusade to end slavery—literally carried the speech in their pockets, ready to wield its contents like a sword drawn in battle, in order to remind an audience about the true cause of secession. Despite overwhelming evidence that undermined any white-supremacist interpretations of history, until the last decades of the twentieth century, emancipationists struggled to overcome the powerful grip that Lost Cause ideology and propaganda held on American historical memory. Today, a vigorous public debate remains between those who can largely be grouped into two major categories based on their interpretation of the Cornerstone Speech. Much to Stephens's chagrin, the one speech of thousands that he delivered in his long career that remains in American public discourse is the Cornerstone Speech. Historians are of course poor predictors of future events, but the future of white-supremacist rhetoric and influence on American historical memory appears to lack any immediate resolution.

Appendix: The Cornerstone Speech

"THE CORNER STONE SPEECH"
BY ALEXANDER H. STEPHENS
MARCH 21, 1861, SAVANNAH, GEORGIA

The Mayor, who presided, introduced the speaker with a few pertinent re-marks, and Mr. Stephens was greeted with deafening rounds of applause, after which he spoke as follows:

Mr. Mayor and Gentlemen of the Committee, and Fellow-Citizens—For this reception, you will please accept my profound and sincere thanks. The compliment is doubtless intended as much, or more perhaps, in honor of the occasion, and my public position in connection with the great events now crowding upon us, then to me personally and individually. It is, however, none the less appreciated epochs in our history. The last ninety days will mark one of the most memorable eras in the history of modern civilization.

[There was a general call from outside of the building for the speaker to go out; that there were more outside than in. The Mayor rose and requested silence at the doors; said Mr. Stephens's health would not permit him to speak in the open air. Mr. Stephens said he would leave it to the audience whether he should proceed indoors or out. There was a general cry indoors, as the ladies—a large number of whom were present—could not hear outside. Mr. Stephens said that the accommodation of the ladies would determine the question, and he would proceed where he was. At this point the uproar and clamor outside were greater still for the speaker to go out on the steps. This was quieted by Col. Lawton, Col. Foreman, Judge Jackson, and Mr. J.W. Owens, going out and stating the facts of the case to the dense mass of men, women, and children who were outside, and entertaining them in short, brief speeches, Mr. Stephens all this time quietly sitting down until the furor subsided.]

Mr. Stephens rose and said—When perfect quiet is restored, I shall proceed.

This transcription is from one of the first published versions of the speech, *Garrett Davis, Hon. Garrett Davis, of Kentucky. African slavery the cornerstone of the Southern confederacy. Speech by Hon. Alex. H. Stephens, of Georgia* (New York: E. D. Barker, 1862), 65–78. While this transcription has been formatted to accord more closely with the rest of the book, the original spelling and style have been preserved. As discussed in the text, there is no definitive transcript of the Cornerstone Speech, which Stephens apparently delivered extemporaneously, but this is one of the most complete versions.

I cannot speak so long as there is any noise or confusion. I shall take my time. I feel as though I could spend the night with you, if necessary. [Loud applause.] I very much regret that everyone who desires cannot hear what I have to say. Not that I have any display to make, or anything very entertaining to present, but such views as I have to give, I wish all, not only in this city, but in this State, and throughout our Confederated Republic, could hear, who have a desire to hear them.

I was remarking, that we are passing through one of the greatest revolutions in the annals of the world. Seven States have within the last three months thrown off an old government and formed a new. This revolution has been signally marked, up to this time, by the fact of its having been accomplished without the loss of a single drop of blood. [Applause.] This new constitution, or form of government, constitutes the subject to which your attention will be partly invited.

In reference to it, I make this first general remark. It amply secures all our ancient rights, franchises, and liberties. All the great principles of Magna Carta are retained in it. No citizen is deprived of life, liberty, or property, but by the judgment of his peers under the laws of the land. The great principle of religious liberty, which was the honor and pride of the old constitution, is still maintained and secured. All the essentials of the old constitution, which have endeared it to the hearts of the American people, have been preserved and perpetuated. [Applause.] Some changes have been made. Of these I shall speak presently. Some of these I should have preferred not to have been made; but these, perhaps, meet the cordial approbation of a majority of this audience, if not an overwhelming majority of the people of this Confederacy. Of them, therefore, I will not speak. But other important changes do meet my cordial approbation. They form great improvements on the old constitution. So, taking the whole new constitution, I have no hesitancy in giving it as my judgment that it is decidedly better than the old. [Applause.] Allow me briefly to allude to some of these improvements. The question of building up class interests, or fostering one branch of industry to the prejudice of another under the exercise of the revenue power, which gave us so much trouble under the old constitution, is put at rest forever under the new. We allow the imposition of no duty with a view of giving advantages to one class of persons, in any trade or business, over those of another. All, under our system, stand upon the same broad principles of perfect equality. Honest labor and enterprise are left free and unrestricted in whatever pursuit they may be engaged. This subject came well nigh causing a rupture of the old Union, under the lead of the gallant Palmetto State, which lies on our border, in 1833.

This old thorn of the tariff, which was the cause of so much irritation in the old body politic, is removed forever from the new. [Applause.] Again, the subject of internal improvements, under the power of Congress to regulate commerce, is put at rest under our system. The power claimed by construction under the old constitution was, at least, a doubtful one—it rested solely upon construction. We, of the South, generally apart from considerations of constitutional principles, opposed its exercise upon grounds of expediency and justice. Notwithstanding this opposition, millions of money in the common treasury had been drawn for such purposes. Our opposition sprung from no hostility to commerce, or all necessary aids for facilitating it. With us it was simply a question upon whom the burden should fall. In Georgia, for instance, we have done as much for the cause of internal improvements as any other portion of the country, according to population and means. We have stretched out lines of railroads from the seaboard to the mountains; dug down the hills, and filled up the valleys at a cost of not less than twenty-five millions of dollars. All this was done to open an outlet for our products of the interior, and those to the west of use, to reach the marts of the world. No State was in greater need of such facilities than Georgia, but we had not asked that these works should be made by appropriations out of the common treasury. The cost of the grading, the superstructure, and equipments of our roads, was borne by those who entered upon the enterprise. Nay, more—not only the cost of the iron, no small item in the aggregate cost, was borne in the same way—but we were compelled to pay into the common treasury several millions of dollars for the privilege of importing the iron, after the price was paid for it abroad. What justice was there in taking this money, which our people paid into the common treasury on the importation of our iron, and applying it to the improvement of rivers and harbors elsewhere?

The true principle is to subject the commerce of every locality, to whatever burdens may be necessary to facilitate it. If Charleston harbor needs improvement, let the commerce of Charleston bear the burden. If the mouth of the Savannah river has to be cleared out, let the sea-going navigation which is benefitted by it, bear the burden. So with the mouths of the Alabama and Mississippi river. Just as the products of the interior, our cotton, wheat, corn, and other articles, have to bear the necessary rates of freight over our railroads to reach the seas. This is again the broad principle of perfect equality and justice. [Applause.] And it is especially set forth and established in our new constitution.

Another feature to which I will allude, is that the new constitution provides that cabinet ministers and heads of departments shall have the privilege of seats upon the floor of the Senate and House of Representatives—shall have the right to participate in the debates and discussions upon the various subjects of administration. I should have preferred that this provision should have gone further, and allowed the President to select his constitutional advisers from the

Senate and House of Representatives. That would have conformed entirely to the practice in the British Parliament, which, in my judgment, is one of the wisest provisions in the British Parliament. It is the only feature that saves that government. It is that which gives it stability in its facility to change its administration. Ours, as it is, is a great approximation to the right principle.

Under the old constitution, a secretary of the treasury for instance, had no opportunity, save by his annual reports, of presenting any scheme or plan of finance or other matter. He had no opportunity of explaining, expounding, enforcing, or defending his views of policy; his only resort was through the medium of an organ. In the British parliament, the premier brings in his budget and stands before the nation responsible for its every item. If it is indefensible, he falls before the attacks upon it, as he ought to. This will now be the case to a limited extent under our system. Our heads of departments can speak for themselves and the administration, in behalf of its entire policy, without resorting to the indirect and highly objectionable medium of a newspaper. It is to be greatly hoped that under our system we shall never have what is known as a government organ. [Rapturous applause.]

[A noise again arose from the clamor of the crowd outside, who wished to hear Mr. Stephens, and for some moments interrupted him. The mayor rose and called on the police to preserve order. Quiet being restored, Mr. S. proceeded.]

Another change in the constitution relates to the length of the tenure of the presidential office. In the new constitution it is six years instead of four, and the President rendered ineligible for re-election. This is certainly a decidedly conservative change. It will remove from the incumbent all temptation to use his office or exert the powers confided to him for any objects of personal ambition. The only incentive to that higher ambition which should move and actuate one holding such high trusts in his hands, will be the good of the people, the advancement, prosperity, happiness, safety, honor, and true glory of the confederacy. [Applause.]

But not to be tedious in enumerating the numerous changes for the better, allow me to allude to one other —though last, not least. The new constitution has put at rest, forever, all agitating questions relating to our peculiar institution—African slavery as it exists among us—the proper status of the negro in our form of civilization. This was the immediate cause of the late rupture and present revolution. Jefferson in his forecast, had anticipated this, as the "rock upon which the old Union would split." He was right. What was conjecture with him, is now a realized fact. But whether he fully comprehended the great truth upon which that rock stood and stands, may be doubted. The prevailing ideas entertained by him and most of the leading statesmen at the time of the formation of the old constitution were, that the enslavement of the African was in violation of the laws of nature; that it was wrong in principle, socially, morally, and politically. It was an evil they knew not well how to deal with, but the general opinion of the men of that day was that, somehow or other in the order of Providence, the institution would be evanescent and pass away. This idea, though not incorporated in the constitution, was the prevailing idea at that time. The constitution, it is true, secured every essential guarantee to the institution while it should last and hence no argument can be justly urged against the constitutional guarantees thus secured, because of the common sentiment of the day. Those ideas, however, were fundamentally wrong. They rested upon the assumption of the equality of races. This was an error. It was a sandy foundation, and the idea of a government built upon it fell when the "storm came and the wind blew, it fell."

Our new government is founded upon exactly the opposite idea; its foundations are laid, its corner-stone rests upon the great truth, that the negro is not equal to the white man. That slavery—subordination to the superior race—is his natural and moral condition. [Applause.]

This, our new government, is the first, in the history of the world, based upon this great physical, philosophical, and moral truth. This truth has been slow in the process of its development, like all other truths in the various departments of science. It has been so even amongst us. Many who hear me, perhaps, can recollect well, that this truth was not generally admitted, even within their day. The errors of the past generation still clung to many as late as twenty years ago. Those at the North, who still cling to these errors, with a zeal above knowledge, we justly denominate fanatics. All fanaticism springs from an aberration of the mind—from a defect in reasoning. It is a species of insanity. One of the most striking characteristics of insanity, in many instances, is forming correct conclusions from fancied or erroneous premises; so with the anti-slavery fanatics; their conclusions are right if their premises are. They assume that the negro is equal, and hence conclude that he is entitled to equal privileges and rights with the white man. If their premises were correct, their conclusions would be logical and just—but their premise being wrong, their whole argument fails. I recollect once of having heard a gentleman from one of the northern States, of great power and ability, announce in the House of Representatives, with imposing effect, that we of the South would be compelled, ultimately, to yield upon this subject of slavery, that it was as impossible to war successfully against a principle in politics, as it was in physics or mechanics. That the principle would ultimately prevail. That we, in maintaining slavery as it exists with us, were warring against a principle, a principle founded in nature, the principle of the equality of men. The reply I made to him was, that he and his associates, in their crusades against our institutions, would ultimately fail. The truth announced, that it was as impossible to war successfully against a principle in politics as in physics and mechanics, I admitted; but told him that it was he, and those acting with him, who were warring against a principle. They were attempting to make things equal which the Creator had made unequal.

In the conflict thus far, success has been on our side, complete throughout the length and breadth of the Confederate States. It is upon this, as I have stated, our social fabric is firmly planted; and I cannot permit myself to doubt the ultimate success of a full recognition of this principle throughout the civilized and enlightened world.

As I have stated, the truth of this principle may be slow in development, as all truths are and ever have been, in the various branches of science. It was so with the principles announced by Galileo—it was so with Adam Smith and his principles of political economy. It was so with Harvey, and his theory of the circulation of the blood. It is stated that not a single one of the medical profession, living at the time of the announcement of the truths made by him, admitted them. Now, they are universally acknowledged. May we not, therefore, look with confidence to the ultimate universal acknowledgment of the truths upon which our system rests? It is the first government ever instituted upon the principles in strict conformity to nature, and the ordination of Providence, in furnishing the materials of human society. Many governments have been founded upon the principle of the enslavement of certain classes but the classes thus enslaved were of the same race and violation of the laws of nature. Our system commits no such violation of nature's laws. The negro by nature, or by the curse against Canaan, is fitted for that condition which he occupies in our system. The architect in the construction of buildings, lays the foundation with proper materials—the granite—then comes the brick or the marble. The substratum of our society is made of the material fitted by nature for it, and by experience we know, that it is best, not only for the superior, but for the inferior race, that it should be so. It is, indeed, in conformity with the ordinance of the Creator. It is not for us to inquire into the wisdom of his ordinances, or to question them. For his own purposes, he has made one race to differ from another, as he has made "one star to differ from another star in glory."

The great objects of humanity are best attained when conformed to his laws and decrees, in the formation of governments as well as in all things else. Our confederacy is founded upon principles in strict conformity with these laws. This stone which was rejected by the first builders "is become the chief stone of the corner" in our new edifice. [Applause.]

I have been asked, what of the future? It has been apprehended by some that we would have arrayed against us the civilized world. I care not who or how many they may be, when we stand upon the eternal principles of truth we are obliged and must triumph. [Immense applause.]

Thousands of people who begin to understand these truths are not yet completely out of the shell. They do not see them in their length and breadth. We hear much of the civilization and Christianization of the barbarous tribes of Africa. In my judgment, those ends will never be attained, but by first teaching them the lesson taught to Adam, that "in the sweat of his brow he should eat his bread," [applause,] and teaching them to work, and feed, and clothe themselves. But to pass on: some have propounded the inquiry whether it is practicable for us to go on with the confederacy without further accessions? Have we the means and ability to maintain nationality among the powers of the earth? On this point I would barely say, that as anxiously as we all have been, and are, for the border States, with institutions similar with ours, to join us, still we are abundantly able to maintain our position, even if they should ultimately make up their minds not to cast their destiny with us. That they ultimately will join us—be compelled to do it—is my confident belief; but we can get on very well without them, even if they should not.

We have all the essential elements of a high national career. The idea has been given out at the North, and even in the border States, that we are too small and too weak to maintain a separate nationality. This is a great mistake. In extent of territory we embrace five hundred and sixty-four thousand square miles and upward. This is upward of two hundred thousand square miles more than was included within the limits of the original thirteen States. It is an area of country more than double the territory of France or the Austrian empire. France, in round numbers, has but two hundred and twelve thousand square miles. Austria, in round numbers, has two hundred and forty-eight thousand square miles. Ours is greater than both combined. It is greater than all France, Spain, Portugal, and Great Britain, including England, Ireland, and Scotland, together. In population we have upward of eight millions, according to the census of 1860; this includes white and black. The entire population, including white and black, of the original thirteen States, was less than four millions in 1790, and still less in '76, when the independence of our fathers was achieved. If they, with a less population, dared maintain their independence against the greatest power on earth, shall we have any apprehension of maintaining ours now?

In point of material wealth and resources, we are greatly in advance of them. The taxable property of the Confederate States cannot be less than twenty-two hundred billions of dollars. This, I think I venture but little in saying, may be considered as five times more than the colonies possessed at the time they achieved their independence. Georgia, alone, possessed last year, according to the report of our comptroller-general, six hundred and seventy-two millions of taxable property. The debts of the seven confederate States sum up in the aggregate less than eighteen millions, while the existing debts of the other of the late United States sum up in the aggregate the enormous amount of one hundred and seventy-four millions of dollars. This is without taking into the account the heavy city debts, corporation debts, and railroad debts, which press, and will continue to press, as a heavy incubus upon the resources of those States. These debts, added to others, make a sum total not much under five hundred millions of dollars. With such an area of territory—with such an amount of population—with a climate and soil unsurpassed by any on the fact of the earth—with such resources already at our command—with productions which control the commerce of the world, who can entertain any apprehensions as to our ability to succeed, whether others join us or not?

It is true, I believe I state but the common sentiment, when I declare my earnest desire that the border States should join us. The differences of opinion that existed among us anterior to secession, related more to the policy in securing that result by co-operation than from any difference upon the ultimate security we all looked to in common.

These differences of opinion were more in reference to policy than principle, and as Mr. Jefferson said in his inaugural, in 1801, after the heated contest preceding his election , there might be differences of opinion without differences in principle, and that all, to some extent, had been Federalists and all Republicans; so it may now be said of us, that whatever differences of opinion as to the best policy in having a co-operation with our border sister slave states, if the worst come to the worst, that as we were all co-operationists, we are now all for independence, whether they come or not. [Continued applause.]

In this connection I take this occasion to state that I was not without grave and serious apprehensions, that if the worst came to the worst, and cutting loose from the old government would be the only remedy for our safety and security, it would be attended with much more serious ills than it has been as yet. Thus far we have seen none of those incidents which usually attend revolutions. No such material as such convulsions usually throw up has been seen. Wisdom, prudence, and patriotism, have marked every step of our progress thus far. This augurs well for the future, and it is a matter of sincere gratification to me, that I am enabled to make the declaration of the men I met in the Congress at Montgomery (I may be pardoned for saying this), an abler, wiser, a more conservative, deliberate, determined, resolute, and patriotic body of men, I never met in my life. [Great applause.] Their works speak for them; the provisional government speaks for them; the constitution of the permanent government will be a lasting monument of their worth, merit, and statesmanship. [Applause.]

But to return to the question of the future. What is to be the result of this revolution?

Will everything, commenced so well, continue as it has begun? In reply to this anxious inquiry, I can only say it all depends upon ourselves. A young man starting out in life on his majority, with health, talent, and ability, under a favoring Providence, may be said to be the architect of his own fortunes. His destinies are in his own hands. He may make for himself a name of honor or dishonor, according to his own acts. If he plants himself upon truth, integrity, honor and uprightness, with industry, patience and energy, he cannot fail of success. So it is with us. We are a young republic, just entering upon the arena of nations; we will be the architect of our own fortunes. Our destiny, under Providence, is in our own hands. With wisdom, prudence, and statesmanship on the part of our public men, and intelligence, virtue and patriotism on the apart of the people, success, to the full measures of our most sanguine hopes, may be looked for. But if we become divided—if schisms arise—if dissensions spring up—if factions are endangered—if party spirit, nourished by unholy personal ambition shall rear its hydra head, I have no good to prophesy for you, Without intelligence, virtue, integrity, and patriotism on the part of the people, no republic or representative government can be durable or stable.

We have intelligence, and virtue, and patriotism. All that is required is to cultivate and perpetuate these. Intelligence will not do without virtue. France was a nation of philosophers. These philosophers become Jacobins. They lacked that virtue, that devotion to moral principle, and that patriotism which is essential to good government. Organized upon principles of perfect justice and right—seeking amity and friendship with all other powers—I see no obstacle in the way of our upward and onward progress. Our growth, by accessions from other States, will depend greatly upon whether we present to the world, as I trust we shall, a better government than that to which they belong. If we do this, North Carolina, Tennessee, and Arkansas cannot hesitate long; neither can Virginia, Kentucky, and Missouri. They will necessarily gravitate to us by an imperious law. We made ample provision in our constitution for the admission of other States; it is more guarded, and wisely so, I think, than the old constitution on the same subject, but not too guarded to receive them as fast as it may be proper. Looking to the distant future, and, perhaps, not very far distant either, it is not beyond the range of possibility, and even probability, that all the great States of the north-west will gravitate this way, as well as Tennessee, Kentucky, Missouri, Arkansas, etc. Should they do so, our doors are wide enough to receive them, but not until they are ready to assimilate with us in principle.

The process of disintegration in the old Union may be expected to go on with almost absolute certainty. We are now the nucleus of a growing power which, if we are true to ourselves, our destiny, and high mission, will become the controlling power on this continent. To what extent accessions will go on in the process of time, or where it will end, the future will determine. So far as it concerns States of the old Union, they will be upon no such principle of reconstruction as now spoken of, but upon reorganization and new assimilation. [Loud applause.] Such are some of the glimpses of the future as I catch them.

But at first we must necessarily meet with the inconveniences and difficulties and embarrassments incident to all changes of government. These will be felt in our postal affairs and changes in the channel of trade. These inconveniences, it is to be hoped, will be but temporary, and must be borne with patience and forbearance.

As to whether we shall have war with our late confederates, or whether all matters of differences between us shall be amicably settled, I can only say that the prospect for a peaceful adjustment is better, so far as I am informed, than it has been.

The prospect of war is, at least, not so threatening as it has been. The idea of coercion, shadowed forth in President Lincoln's inaugural, seems not to be followed up thus far so vigorously as was expected. Fort Sumter, it is believed, will soon be evacuated. What course will be pursued toward Fort Pickens, and the other forts on the gulf, is not so well understood. It is to be greatly desired that all of them should be surrendered. Our object is peace, not only with the North, but with the world. All matters relating to the public property, public liabilities of the Union when we were members of it, we are ready and willing to adjust and settle upon the principles of right, equality, and good faith. War can be of no more benefit to the North than to us. The idea of coercing us, or subjugating us, is utterly preposterous. Whether the intention of evacuating Fort Sumter is to be received as an evidence of a desire for a peaceful solution of our difficulties with the United States, or the result of necessity, I will not undertake to say. I would fain hope the former. Rumors are afloat, however, that it is the result of necessity. All I can say to you, therefore, on that point is, keep your armor bright and your powder dry. [Enthusiastic cheering.]

The surest way to secure peace, is to show your ability to maintain your rights. The principles and position of the present administration of the United States—the Republican Party—present some puzzling questions. While it is a fixed principle with them never to allow the increase of a foot of slave territory, they seem to be equally determined not to part with an inch "of the accursed soil." Notwithstanding their clamor against the institution, they seemed to be equally opposed to getting more, or letting go what they have got. They were ready to fight on the accession of Texas, and are equally ready to fight now on their secession. Why is this? How can this strange paradox be accounted for? There seems to be but one rational solution—and that is, notwithstanding their professions of humanity, they are disinclined to give up the benefits they derive from slave labor. Their philanthropy yields to their interest. The idea of enforcing the laws, has but one object, and that is a collection of the taxes, raised by slave labor to swell the fund, necessary to meet their heavy appropriations. The spoils is what they are after—though they come from the labor of the slave. [Continued applause.]

[*Editorial note*: At this point in the speech, the Savannah reporter stopped transcribing Stephens's remarks and began summarizing the vice-president's speech.] Mr. Stephens reviewed at some length, the extravagance and profligacy of appropriations by the Congress of the United States for several years past, and in this connection took occasion to allude to another one of the great improvements in our new constitution, which is a clause prohibiting Congress form appropriating any money from the treasure, except by a two third vote, unless it be for some object which the executive may say is necessary to carry on the government.

When it is thus asked for, and estimated for, he continued, the majority may appropriate. This was a new feature. Our fathers had guarded the assessment of taxes by insisting that representation and taxation should go together. This was inherited from the mother country, England. It was one of the principles upon which the revolution had been fought. Our fathers also provided in the old constitution, that all appropriation bills should originate in the representative branch of Congress, but our new constitution went a step further, and guarded not only the pockets of the people, but also the public money, after it was taken from their pockets.

He alluded to the difficulties and embarrassments which seemed to surround the question of a peaceful solution of the controversy with the old government. How can it be done? Is perplexing many minds. The President seems to think that he cannot recognize our independence, nor can he, with and by the advice of the Senate, do so. The constitution makes no such provision. A general convention of all the States has been suggested by some.

Without proposing to solve the difficulty, he barely made the following suggestion:

"That as the admission of States by Congress under the constitution was an act of legislation, and in the nature of a contract or compact between the States admitted and the others admitting, why should not this contract or compact be regarded as of like character with all other civil contracts—liable to be rescinded by mutual agreement of both parties? The seceding States have rescinded it on their part, they have resumed their sovereignty. Why cannot the whole question be settled, if the north desire peace, simply by the

Congress, in both branches, with the concurrence of the President, giving their consent to the separation, and a recognition of our independence?" This he merely offered as a suggestion, as one of the ways in which it might be done with much less violence by constructions to the constitution than many other acts of that government. [Applause.] The difficulty has to be solved in some way or other—this may be regarded as a fixed fact.

Several other points were alluded to by Mr. Stephens, particularly as to the policy of the new government toward foreign nations, and our commercial relations with them. Free trade, as far as practicable, would be the policy of this government. No higher duties would be imposed on foreign importations than would be necessary to support the government upon the strictest economy.

In olden times the olive branch was considered the emblem of peace; we will send to the nations of the earth another and far more potential emblem of the same, the cotton plant. The present duties were levied with a view of meeting the present necessities and exigencies, in preparation for war, if need be; but if we have peace, and he hoped we might, and trade should resume its proper course, a duty of ten per cent upon foreign importations it was thought might be sufficient to meet the expenditures of the government. If some articles should be left on the free list, as they now are, such as breadstuffs, etc., then, of course, duties upon others would have to be higher—but in no event to an extent to embarrass trade and commerce. He concluded in an earnest appeal for union and harmony, on part of all the people in support of the common cause, in which we were all enlisted, and upon the issues of which such great consequences depend.

If, said he, we are true to ourselves, true to our cause, true to our destiny, true to our high mission, in presenting to the world the highest type of civilization ever exhibited by man—there will be found in our lexicon no such word as fail.

Mr. Stephens took his seat, amid a burst of enthusiasm and applause, such as the Athenaeum has never had displayed within its walls, within "the recollection of the oldest inhabitant."

Notes

Introduction

1. The Cornerstone Speech lacks an official title. The speech has been called the "Cornerstone Address" as well as the "Cornerstone Speech" throughout its history. While stylistically the titles of speeches are generally set off by quotation marks, the title appears so often in this text that I think including them would become a bit wearying for the reader; moreover, I hope to convince the reader that the speech, like the Gettysburg Address or the Declaration of Independence, has become so iconic and ubiquitous that it seems needless to add them. Stephens sometimes tried to diminish the speech by not giving it a title because his eternal connection to the speech often embarrassed him. He saw the speech as one of his worst moments. After the war, Stephens claimed that his emotions had bested him as he delivered it.

2. On March 22, 1861, the *Savannah Republican* published a brief report of Alexander H. Stephens's remarks. At that time, the speech was not referred to as the Cornerstone Speech. A full transcription of the speech first appeared in the *Savannah Republican* on March 23, 1861, under the title "Speech of Hon. A.H. Stephens." The speech had been recorded by Editor James R. Sneed. Stephens delivered the speech extemporaneously. No handwritten copy of the speech exists among extensive Stephens collections housed at the Library of Congress, Duke University, or the University of Georgia. On March 25, 1861, the *Southern Confederacy* of Atlanta became the first newspaper to reprint the *Savannah Republican* transcription. Within a few weeks, the speech had appeared in more than two hundred newspapers worldwide. During the war, the speech appeared in several published collections. After the war, Stephens claimed that he had been misquoted, but his later revisions never altered the original transcription's substance. Stephens never contested whether he said that slavery was the cornerstone of the Confederate States of America. He only argued that his message had been misunderstood. The first book to include a transcription of the speech was Garrett Davis, *Hon. Garrett Davis, of Kentucky. African slavery the cornerstone of the Southern confederacy. Speech by Hon. Alex. H. Stephens, of Georgia* (New York: E. D. Barker, 1862).

3. Annette Gordon-Reed, "America's Original Sin: Slavery and the Legacy of White Supremacy," *Foreign Affairs* 97 (1) (2018): 2–7; James W. Vander Zanden, "The Ideology of White Supremacy," *Journal of the History of Ideas* 20 (3) (1959): 385–402; Desmond King and Stephen Tuck, "De-Centering the South: America's Nationwide White Supremacist Order after Reconstruction," *Past & Present* 194 (2007): 213–53. Throughout this work, the term white supremacy is broadly defined as a belief that white people are superior and should therefore dominate society. In this context, whites believe they should have dominance over people of other backgrounds, especially where they co-exist. White supremacy exists in political, economic, and cultural systems in which whites overwhelmingly control power and material resources, and where conscious and unconscious expressions of white superiority and entitlement are widespread. White supremacy is a collective effort carried out by white people across class lines. The rhetoric used to reinforce white supremacy can bind together white people of varying social, economic, and cultural backgrounds into a singular white race. Like Rev. Dr. Martin

Luther King, Jr., this work argues that white supremacy was a structural pillar equal in weight to democracy itself in American society. However, the rhetoric and identity politics of white supremacy have evolved over time as expressions of white supremacy have become more overt, aggressive, and part of a call to action against expanding minority rights in America. The foundation of white-supremacist ideology was laid in the racist assumptions that bolstered defenses of American slavery. External threats to slavery's future existence and emancipation and debates over civil rights produced more aggressive expressions of white supremacy that sought to build a unified white racial identity that could undermine calls for black equality and civil liberties.

4. Historian James McPherson offers the following summary of Lost Cause interpretations of the American Civil War: "secession was not rebellion but rather a legal exercise of state sovereignty; the South fought not for slavery but for self-government; the Confederate soldiers fought courageously and won most of the battles but against long odds were finally worn down by overwhelming numbers and resources." James M. McPherson, "Long-Legged Yankee Lies: The Southern Textbook Crusade," in *The Memory of the Civil War in American Culture*, ed. Alice Fahs and Joan Waugh (Chapel Hill: Univ. of North Carolina Press, 2004), 64–78.

5. Although he was five foot, seven inches tall, not unusually short for a nineteenth-century American male, Stephens's relatively small stature and slight build earned him the nickname "Little Aleck." Many of his friends called him Aleck. I have refrained from referring to Alexander Stephens as "Little Aleck" because no one should be defined by their physical appearance.

6. Mark E. Neely, Jr., *Lincoln and the Democrats: The Politics of Opposition in the Civil War* (New York: Cambridge Univ. Press, 2017), chap. 3.

7. Ulrich B. Phillips, "The Central Theme of Southern History," *American Historical Review* 34 (1) (1928): 30–43; Samuel S. Hill Jr. et al., "South's Two Cultures," in *Religion and the Solid South* (Nashville: Abingdon Press, 1972), 54, 78.

8. George M. Fredrickson, *The Black Image in the White Mind: The Debate on Afro-American Character and Destiny, 1817–1914* (New York: Harper and Row, 1971), 63–64; Fredrickson, *The Arrogance of Race: Historical Perspectives on Slavery, Racism, and Social Inequality* (Middletown, CT: Wesleyan Univ. Press, 1988). The use of white-supremacist rhetoric to foster unity among white men is sometimes referred to as the "white men's democracy." Anthony Gene Carey, *Parties, Slavery, and the Union in Antebellum Georgia* (Athens: Univ. of Georgia Press, 1997); William Cooper, *The South and the Politics of Slavery, 1828–1856* (Baton Rouge: Louisiana State Univ. Press, 1978); John M. Sacher, *A Perfect War of Politics: Parties, Politicians, and Democracy in Louisiana, 1824–1861* (Baton Rouge: Louisiana State Univ. Press, 2003); Donald B. Cole, *A Jackson Man: Amos Kendall and the Rise of American Democracy* (Baton Rouge: Louisiana State Univ. Press, 2004); Sean Wilentz, *The Rise of American Democracy: Jefferson to Lincoln* (New York: W. W. Norton, 2005); Mark V. Wetherington, *Plain Folks' Fight: The Civil War and Reconstruction in Piney Woods Georgia* (Chapel Hill: Univ. of North Carolina Press, 2005); J. Mills Thornton, III, *Politics and Power in a Slave Society: Alabama, 1800–1860* (Baton Rouge: Louisiana State Univ. Press, 1978); Lacy K. Ford, *Deliver Us From Evil: The Slavery Question in the Old South* (New York: Oxford Univ. Press, 2009). While Ford does not specifically use the term white men's democracy, he describes a growing reliance among antebellum southern proslavery advocates of adopting the language of white supremacy to strengthen broad support for slavery among all white men. For an opposing view

of intraclass relations among white southerners, see Keri Merrit, *Masterless Men: Poor Whites and Slavery in the Antebellum South* (Cambridge: Cambridge Univ. Press, 2017).

9. Racism and white supremacy, of course, are not exclusive to the history of the American South. Both ideas have national and international origins, manifestations, and effects on race relations. My research embraces the interpretations of historian Laura Edwards, who argued that "many issues associated with the South in the historiography were actually national in scope." While the Lost Cause emerged as an effort made by white southern men to explain the Civil War's origins, results, and consequences, northern audiences also found many aspects of the Lost Cause attractive. Meanwhile, the postbellum emergence of more explicit brands of white-supremacist political ideologies was evident across the nation. Throughout my book, the fact that so many northern and southern audiences were interested in debating the Cornerstone Speech supports Edwards's contention that most aspects of southern history are in fact inseparable from the national past. Laura Edwards, "Southern History as U.S. History," *Journal of Southern History* 75 (3) (2009): 533–64.

10. W. J. Cash, *The Mind of the South* (New York: Knopf, 1941).

11. Edward A. Pollard, *The Lost Cause Regained* (New York: G. W. Carleton and Company, 1868), 115. According to Caroline Janney: "The Lost Cause is an interpretation of the American Civil War (1861–1865) that seeks to present the war, from the perspective of Confederates, in the best possible terms." Despite its rejection among most contemporary professional historians, the Lost Cause remains a powerful form of historical interpretation and memory among broad public audiences, especially in the South. Caroline Janney, "The Lost Cause," *Encyclopedia of Virginia*, accessed at https://www.encyclopediavirginia.org/lost_cause_the.

12. Gunner Myrdal, *An American Dilemma: The New in a White Nation*, second edition (New York: McGraw-Hill Book Company, 1962), vol. 1: 88. Myrdal argues that white supremacy became more important to white southerners after emancipation because it had to replace slavery as the primary means of justifying black inferiority.

13. Rollin G. Osterweis, *The Myth of the Lost Cause, 1865–1900* (Hamden, CT: Archon Books, 1973).

14. In 2018, select passages from the Cornerstone Speech appeared in more than two thousand national publications, such as the *New York Times*, *Wall Street Journal*, and *National Review*. Over the past decade, whenever a racial conflict happens in America, such as Charleston, Ferguson, and Charlottesville, journalists and opinion writers tend to reference the speech as either evidence of the South's longstanding support for white supremacy or proof that Confederate symbols contain racist origins.

15. Gary W. Gallagher and Alan T. Nolan, eds. *The Myth of the Lost Cause and Civil War History* (Bloomington: Indiana Univ. Press, 2000), introduction; Anne E. Marshall, *Creating a Confederate Kentucky: The Lost Cause and Civil War Memory in a Border State* (Chapel Hill: Univ. of North Carolina Press, 2010), 6. Historians lack consensus in explaining white supremacy's role in the Lost Cause. Charles Reagan Wilson's classic, *Baptized in Blood: The Religion of the Lost Cause, 1865–1920* (Univ. of Georgia Press, 1962) de-emphasizes the influence that constructions of race played among Lost Cause believers.

16. Maurice Halbwachs, *On Collective Memory* (Chicago: Univ. of Chicago Press, 1992); Michael Kammen, *Mystic Chords of Memory: The Transformation of Tradition in American Culture* (New York: Knopf, 1992).

17. Paul H. Buck, *The Road to Reunion: 1865–1900* (Boston: Little, Brown, 1937).

18. Thomas J. Pressly, *Americans Interpret Their Civil War* (Princeton: Princeton Univ. Press, 1954).

19. David Blight, *Race and Reunion: The Civil War in American Memory* (Cambridge: Harvard Univ. Press, 2001). The literature on Civil War memory is voluminous. Major studies that influenced my work include Nina Silber, *Romance of Reunion: Northerners and the South, 1865–1900* (Chapel Hill: Univ. of North Carolina Press, 1993); Alice Fahs, *The Imagined Civil War: Popular Literature of the North and South, 1861–1865* (Chapel Hill: Univ. of North Carolina Press, 2001); Kirk Savage, *Standing Soldiers, Kneeling Slaves: Race, War, and Monument in Nineteenth-Century America* (Princeton: Princeton Univ. Press, 1997); David Goldfield, *Still Fighting the Civil War: The American South and Southern History* (Baton Rouge: Louisiana State Univ. Press, 2002); Fred Hobson, *Tell About the South: The Southern Rage to Explain* (Baton Rouge: Louisiana State Univ. Press, 1983); Robert J. Cook, *Civil War Memories: Contesting the Past in the United States since 1865* (Baltimore: Johns Hopkins Univ. Press, 2017); and Cook, *Troubled Commemoration: The American Civil War Centennial, 1961–1965* (Baton Rouge: Louisiana State Univ. Press, 2007).

20. Caroline E. Janney, *Remembering the Civil War: Reunion and the Limits of Reconciliation* (Chapel Hill: Univ. of North Carolina Press, 2013).

21. M. Keith Harris, *Across the Bloody Chasm: The Culture of Commemoration among Civil War Veterans* (Baton Rouge: Louisiana State Univ. Press, 2014).

22. Adam H. Domby, *The False Cause: Fraud, Fabrication, and White Supremacy in Confederate Memory* (Charlottesville: Univ. of Virginia Press, 2020).

23. To be sure, distortions of slavery or omitting slavery from commemorations of the Civil War are common nationwide. David Blight's *Race and Reunion* undeniably demonstrates that Union and Confederate veterans and their communities were both eager to ignore African American contributions to the war and distort the harsh realities of antebellum slavery. While both North and South share much in common, the Lost Cause emerged as the most powerful expression of those distorted memories. The bulk of Lost Cause promoters were and still remain white southerners. Goldfield, *Still Fighting the Civil War*; Marc Howard Ross, *Slavery in the North: Forgetting History and Recovering Memory* (Philadelphia: Univ. of Pennsylvania Press, 2018); James Oliver Horton and Lois E. Horton, eds., *Slavery and Public History: The Tough Stuff of American Memory* (New York: W. W. Norton, 2006); Randolph Bergstrom, "Still Provoking: The Public History of Race and Slavery," *Public Historian* 36 (1) (2014): 7–8. Historians interested in the politics of Civil War memorials should consider the absence of northern monuments celebrating African American contributions to Union victory as an equally powerful statement of racial prejudice as the tens of thousands of Confederate monuments that can be found across the South. The politics of omission can have an equally powerful impact upon American memory compared to what Americans have chosen to commemorate by erecting memorials.

24. Raul Hilberg, *Perpetrators, Victims, Bystanders: The Jewish Catastrophe, 1933–1945* (New York: Aaron Asher Books, 1992).

25. David Gobel and Daves Rossell, *Commemoration in America: Essays on Monuments, Memorialization, and Memory* (Charlottesville: Univ. of Virginia Press, 2013); Polly Low, Graham Oliver, and P. J. Rhodes, *Cultures of Commemoration: War Memorials, Ancient and Modern* (Oxford: Oxford Univ. Press, 2012); Cook, *Troubled Commemora-*

tion; John Bodnar, *Remaking America: Public Memory, Commemoration, and Patriotism in the Twentieth Century* (Princeton: Princeton Univ. Press, 1992).

26. Thomas Lawrence Connelly, *The Marble Man: Robert E. Lee and His Image in American Society* (Baton Rouge: Louisiana State Univ. Press, 1978); James M. McPherson, *Embattled Rebel: Jefferson Davis as Commander in Chief* (New York: Penguin, 2014); Thomas Lawrence Connelly, *God and General Longstreet: The Lost Cause and the Southern Mind* (Baton Rouge: Louisiana State Univ. Press, 1995); Court Carney, "The Contested Image of Nathan Bedford Forrest," *Journal of Southern History* 67 (3) (2001): 601–30; Paul Ashdown, *The Myth of Nathan Bedford Forrest* (New York: Rowman & Littlefield, 2006); Wallace Hettle, *Inventing Stonewall Jackson: A Civil War Hero in History and Memory* (Baton Rouge: Louisiana State Univ. Press, 2011).

27. Another example of historians' de-emphasis of the Cornerstone Speech can be seen in Thomas A. Scott's *Cornerstones of Georgia History: Documents That Formed the State*. In that collection of primary sources, Scott decided to include the WPA slave narrative of Georgia Baker that largely praised Stephens as a benevolent enslaver. Scott included Stephens's Milledgeville Union Speech, delivered in protest of secession, but did not include or mention the Cornerstone Speech. Ironically, a book titled *Cornerstones of Georgia History* neglected to include the Cornerstone Speech. Thomas A. Scott, *Cornerstones of Georgia History: Documents That Formed the State* (Athens: Univ. of Georgia Press, 1995).

28. William C. Davis, *The Union that Shaped the Confederacy: Robert Toombs and Alexander H. Stephens* (Lawrence: Univ. Press of Kansas, 2001).

1. Laying the Cornerstone, 1830–1860

1. For a broad history of racism and white supremacy in America, see: Ibram X. Kendi, *Stamped from the Beginning: The Definitive History of Racist Ideas in America* (New York: Bold Type Books, 2017).

2. Miss Sallie Eola Reneau, Panola, Mississippi, to Alexander H. Stephens, Montgomery, Alabama, Mar. 23, 1861, General Correspondence, 1784–1886; 1861, Mar. 6–31, Alexander Hamilton Stephens Papers, Library of Congress; H. L. Byrd, Savannah, Georgia, to Alexander H. Stephens, Crawfordville, Georgia, Mar. 23, 1861, General Correspondence, 1784–1886; 1861, Mar. 6–31, Alexander Hamilton Stephens Papers, Library of Congress.

3. Catalog of literary books belonging to Alexander H. Stephens, Printed Materials, Box 7, Folder 10, Alexander H. Stephens Family Papers, MS3823, Hargrett Rare Book and Manuscript Library, University of Georgia. On March 22, 1861, the day after Stephens delivered the Cornerstone Speech, he received an invitation to join the Indiana State University's Athenian Society as an honorary member. Stephens received hundreds of similar invitations—many after Georgia seceded from the Union. He had developed a national reputation as an intellectual statesman. John Alexander, Bloomington, Indiana, to Alexander H. Stephens, Mar. 22,1861, Correspondence, 1861, Jan.–Dec., letter 1714, Alexander H. Stephens Papers, David M. Rubenstein Rare Book and Manuscript Library, Duke University.

4. Henry Louis Gates Jr., *Stony the Road: Reconstruction, White Supremacy, and the Rise of Jim Crow* (New York: Penguin, 2019), 14–15.

5. Neely, *Lincoln and the Democrats*, chap. 3.

6. Legal Papers, 1837–1882, letter 3901, Alexander H. Stephens Papers, David M. Rubenstein Rare Book and Manuscript Library, Duke University.

7. Narrative of Georgia Baker, *Federal Writers' Project: Slave Narrative Project, Volume 4, Georgia, Part 1, Adams-Furr* (Washington, DC: Federal Writer's Project, United States Work Projects Administration, 1936–1938), 37–54; Schott, *Alexander H. Stephens*, 66.

8. Susan M. Ryan, *The Grammar of Good Intentions: Race and the Antebellum Culture of Benevolence* (Ithaca: Cornell Univ. Press, 2005). Ryan argues that "benevolence . . . [was] a central paradigm in antebellum culture, one that provided Americans with ways of understanding, describing, and constructing their racial and national identities" (p. 5). Michael C. C. Adams, *Our Masters the Rebels* (Cambridge: Harvard Univ. Press, 1978), 3. The term "fictive kin" refers to familial relationships that are not based upon common bloodlines but rather through individual relationships built in response to their immediate environment or circumstance. Unlike many enslavers, Stephens did not father children among his enslaved laborers.

9. George McDuffie, "The Natural Slavery of the Negro," Laws of South Carolina, 1836, *Journal of the General Assembly of the State of South Carolina for the year 1835*.

10. Ford, *Deliver Us from Evil*, 511; Larry E. Tise, *Proslavery: A History of the Defense of Slavery in America, 1701–1840* (Athens: Univ. of Georgia Press, 2004), 80.

11. Historians have questioned whether southern elite male descriptions of white unity existed beyond their rhetoric. W. J. Cash argued that white supremacy bound together white men of differing levels of wealth. U. B. Phillips proclaimed that race was the central theme in southern history. Paul H. Buck agreed that poor white men held "a strong personal hatred for the negro and a firm conviction that slavery was essential." Likewise, Frank Owsley found that plain folk in the South supported their wealthier white neighbors because of the shared benefits of white supremacy. George Fredrickson also described race as central to white southern male identity. For decades this interpretation was shared among numerous southern historians, such as Eugene Genovese, Elizabeth Fox-Genovese, Barbara J. Fields, Fred Arthur Bailey, J. Wayne Flynt, Lacey K. Ford, Orville Vernon Burton, and J. William Harris. Recent scholars, such as Keri Merritt, David Williams, Jeff Forret, Betty Wood, David Brown, and Loren Schweninger, have questioned whether race and slavery unified white southerners. Those historians tend to emphasize the level of class consciousness and conflict that existed in antebellum society. They stress the extreme disparities in wealth and access to political power that separated property-owning white households from non-property-owning households. They have argued that the white man's democracy was largely a rhetorical tool employed by elite white men to court the political and social support of their poorer neighbors. My research argues that Alexander H. Stephens often employed the rhetoric of a common, classless white man's democracy to defend slavery from its critics. Whether such relations among all white men existed did not matter because Stephens, and to some degree pro-secession zealots, acted as if this imagined condition was real. Beyond a handful of critics of slavery, antebellum discussions of politics and race largely ignored poor whites (those who did not own property) and confined their audience to property holders. Most northern critiques of southern society lumped together white men as a single entity. Stephens likely misinterpreted important facets of southern society. He was so obsessed with interpreting the constitution and deciphering minute legal precedents that favored the South's sectional interests that he likely missed that significant portions of the white southern population did not share his belief that slavery had benefited all white men.

Among property owners, particularly slave owners, Stephens could confidently observe a shared commitment to slavery and white supremacy. Since he had experienced considerable upward social mobility—he had been born an orphan in difficult circumstances who rose to be become a major national political figure—Stephens had faith that other poor white men could transform themselves through education, thrift, and hard work. Stephens would have perceived the ownership of slaves as proof of an individual's social and economic worth. In his opinion, the shared goal of slave ownership and mastery over the black race was critical to securing the allegiance of poor white men. He, like so many, rarely thought about white men at the bottom of southern society.

12. Stephens's views on slavery were influenced by his reading of the works of George Fitzhugh. In *Cannibals all!*, Fitzhugh examined the ill effects that black emancipation had on various parts of the world, including France and its colonies. Fitzhugh also claimed that slavery "elevates those whites; for it makes them not the bottom of society, as at the North . . . but privileged citizens, like Greek and Roman citizens, with a numerous class far beneath them" George Fitzhugh, *Cannibals all! or, Slaves without masters* (Richmond: A. Morris, 1857), 320.

13. George W. Williams, "To the Citizens of Henry County," *Spirit of the South* (Eufaula, AL), May 20, 1861.

14. Thomas E. Schott, *Alexander H. Stephens of Georgia: A Biography* (Baton Rouge: Louisiana State Univ. Press, 1988), 177; Katharine Gerbner, *Christian Slavery: Conversion and Race in the Protestant Atlantic World* (Philadelphia: Univ. of Pennsylvania Press, 2019); James L. Gorman, Jeff W. Childers, and Mark W. Hamilton, eds., *Slavery's Long Shadow: Race and Reconciliation in American Christianity* (Grand Rapids, MI: Eerdmans, 2019); H. Shelton Smith, *In His Image . . . ; Racism in Southern Religion, 1780–1910* (Durham, NC: Duke Univ. Press, 1972).

15. For a discussion of biblical justifications of American slavery, see Stephen R. Haynes, *Noah's Curse: The Biblical Justification of American Slavery* (New York: Oxford Univ. Press, 2002). Historians disagree over whether race was the central factor that shaped southern evangelicalism. Alexander H. Stephens's religious views appeared to focus on race as a defining factor in determining one's relationship to God and to humanity. From this perspective, slavery was a divine institution set by nature. On the other hand, some scholars have emphasized that pro-slavery evangelicals focused less on race and more on the individual's role in salvation. John Patrick Daly, *When Slavery Was Called Freedom: Evangelicalism, Proslavery, and the Causes of the Civil War* (Lexington: Univ. Press of Kentucky, 2002).

16. Josiah Priest, *Slavery, As It Relates to the Negro, or African Race* (Albany, NY: C. Van Bethuysen and Co., 1843), 63.

17. Priest, *Slavery*, 92.

18. Ibid.

19. Alexander H. Stephens's views on the origins of the African race also shared much in common with Alexander McCaine, a South Carolina Methodist minister who vigorously defended slavery during the 1840s and 1850s. Alexander McCaine, *Slavery defended from Scripture, against the attacks of the abolitionists: in a speech delivered before the General Conference of the Methodist Protestant Church, in Baltimore, 1842* (Baltimore: W. Wooddy, 1842).

20. John Campbell, *Negro-mania: being an examination of the falsely assumed equality of the various races of men; demonstrated by the investigations of Champollion, Wilkinson [and*

others] *together with a concluding chapter, presenting a comparative statement of the condition of the Negroes in the West Indies before and since emancipation* (Philadelphia, PA: Campbell & Power, 1851).

21. For example, Elizabeth Hasser, Double Hills, Georgia, to Alexander H. Stephens, Mar. 1861, Correspondence, 1861, Jan.–Dec., letter 1718, Alexander H. Stephens Papers, David M. Rubenstein Rare Book and Manuscript Library, Duke University.

22. General Correspondence, 1784–1886, Alexander Hamilton Stephens Papers, Library of Congress. During March 1861, Stephens received more than one dozen requests from indigent students for funds to provide for their education. Some of those requests came from students located far from Stephens's local community. Few had ever met Stephens yet had been advised by others to contact him for assistance.

23. Milledgeville *Southern Recorder*, May 7, 1844; Carey, *Parties, Slavery, and the Union in Antebellum Georgia*, 74.

24. Carey, *Parties, Slavery, and the Union in Antebellum Georgia*, 75.

25. *Congressional Globe*, 28th Congress, 2nd Session, Appendix, 309–14; "The Hon. Alexander H. Stephens' Opinions on Slavery," *Georgia Telegraph* (Macon), Feb. 25, 1845; Schott, *Alexander H. Stephens*, 61–62.

26. Matthew Karp, *The Vast Southern Empire: Slaveholders at the Helm of American Foreign Policy* (Cambridge: Harvard Univ. Press, 2016). Stephens was among a group of nationalist southerners who promoted national expansion as long as the nation supported extending slavery across the globe.

27. "Mr. Alexander H. Stephens on Slavery," *Georgia Telegraph* (Macon), Mar. 4 1845; Carey, *Parties, Slavery, and the Union in Antebellum Georgia*, 74–75; "Speech of Mr. Stephens, Of Georgia, on the Joint Resolution for the Annexation of Texas," *Georgia Messenger* (Ft. Hawkins), March 6, 1845, 2; Schott, *Alexander H. Stephens*, 62.

28. Schott, *Alexander H. Stephens*, 130; Carey, *Parties, Slavery, and the Union in Antebellum Georgia*, chaps. 6 and 7; Davis, *The Union that Shaped the Confederacy*, chap. 2. Kenneth Coleman, ed., *A History of Georgia* (Athens: Univ. of Georgia Press, 1977), 137–38.

29. Schott, *Alexander H. Stephens*, 135.

30. Carey, *Parties, Slavery, and the Union in Antebellum Georgia*, 168.

31. Ibid., 186.

32. Ibid., 166–67.

33. Henry Cleveland, *Alexander H. Stephens in public and private. With letters and speeches before, during, and since the war* (Philadelphia: National Publishing Company, 1866).

34. Schott, *Alexander H. Stephens*, 168.

35. Ibid., 173.

36. Ibid., 116.

37. Daly, *When Slavery Was Called Freedom*, 136.

38. Schott, *Alexander H. Stephens*, 117.

39. *Congressional Globe Appendix*, 34th Congress, 1st Session, 1855–56, 728–29.

40. James Philemon Holcombe, *Is Slavery Consistent with Natural Law?* (Richmond: Virginia State Agricultural Society, 1858), 12.

41. Ibid., 15.

42. Cleveland, *Alexander H. Stephens*, 129.

43. Ibid.

44. W. E. B. Du Bois, *Suppression of the Slave Trade* (New York: Oxford Univ. Press, 1896),

chap. 11; Ronald T. Takaki, *A Pro-Slavery Crusade: The Agitation to Reopen the African Slave Trade* (New York: Free Press, 1971), 242.

45. "Hon. Alexander H. Stephens," *Upson Pilot* (Thomaston, GA), Apr. 14, 1859, 1; Schott, *Alexander H. Stephens*, 272–73.

46. Cleveland, *Alexander H. Stephens*, 129; "Mr. Stephens' Speech," *Daily Constitutionalist* (Augusta, GA), July 13, 1859, 1; *Citizen* (Washington, GA), July 9, 1859, 1; *Rutland Weekly Herald* (VT), July 14, 1859, 2; Schott, *Alexander H. Stephens*, 268–70.

47. "Mr. Stephens' Speech," *Daily Constitutionalist* (Augusta, GA), July 17, 1859, 3; "The Opposition Convention," *Daily Constitutionalist* (Augusta, GA), July 23, 1859, 3; "The Stephens' Dinner," *Southern Recorder* (Milledgeville, GA), July 5, 1859, 3; "Mr. Stephens' Speech," *Columbus Daily Times*, July 6, 1859, 2; Oration of J. H. Stephens at Augusta," *Daily Exchange* (Baltimore, MD), July 6, 1859, 1; "The Stephens' Oration," *National Era* (Washington, DC), July 7, 1859, 3; "Hon. A. H. Stephens," *Richmond Dispatch*, July 7, 1859, 1; "Prospects of Slavery," *Richmond Dispatch*, July 9, 1859, 2; "A. H. Stephens," *New Bern Daily Progress* (North Carolina), July 11, 1859, 2; "Upward and Onward," *Semi-Weekly Mississippian* (Jackson), July 12, 1859, 2; "Hon. Alexander H. Stephens," *Buffalo Weekly Express*, July 12, 1859, 2.

48. "Hon. A. H. Stephens of Georgia—His Inconsistency," *The National Era* (Washington, DC), July 28, 1859, 2.

49. *Upson Pilot* (Thomaston, Georgia), Aug. 27 1859, 1.

50. Carey, *Parties, Slavery, and the Union in Antebellum Georgia*, 223; "State Convention," *Daily Chronicle and Sentinel* (Augusta, GA), Apr. 12, 1860.

51. "Alexander H. Stephens of Ga.," *Columbus Daily Times*, June 1, 1860, 2.

52. Cleveland, *Alexander H. Stephens*, 674–94; Schott, *Alexander H. Stephens*, 300–301.

53. "The Home of Hon. Alex. H. Stephens," *New York Herald*, Sept. 29, 1860, 2; "Impending Danger to the Most Prosperous Nation in the World," *Daily Constitutionalist* (Augusta, GA), Oct. 7, 1860, 2.

54. Carey, *Parties, Slavery, and the Union in Antebellum Georgia*, 235–36; Michael Johnson, *Toward a Patriarchal Republic: The Secession of Georgia* (Baton Rouge: Louisiana State Univ. Press, 1977).

55. Alexander H. Stephens to Linton Stephens, Nov. 9, 1860, Stephens Papers, Manhattanville College of the Sacred Heart, Purchase, New York.

56. Carey, *Parties, Slavery, and the Union in Antebellum Georgia*, 235–36.

57. William W. Freehling and Craig M. Simpson, eds., *Secession Debated: Georgia's Showdown in 1860* (New York: Oxford Univ. Press, 1992), 31–50.

58. Schott, *Alexander H. Stephens*, 305.

59. Alexander H. Stephens, "The Assertions of a Secessionist. From the speech of A. H. Stephens, of Georgia, November 14, 1860" (New York: Loyal Publication Society, 1864), 6; Freehling and Simpson, Secession Debated, 51–79.

60. Stephens, "Assertions of a Secessionist," 8.

61. *Bradford Reporter* (Towanda, PA), Nov. 22 1860, 2.

62. "Alexander H. Stephens on the Crisis—Wisdom, Moderation and Justice," *Philadelphia Inquirer*, Nov. 23, 1860, 2, 4.

63. *Detroit Free Press*, Nov. 24, 1860, 2.

64. Schott, *Alexander H. Stephens*, 309.

65. Roy P. Basler, ed., *The Collected Works of Abraham Lincoln* (New Brunswick: Rutgers Univ. Press, 1953), vol. 4: 160; quoted in Schott, *Alexander H. Stephens*, 310.

66. Ibid., 160–61; Stephens "apples of gold" quotation was taken from Proverbs 25:11.
67. *Buffalo Daily Republic*, Nov. 17, 1860, 2.
68. *Milledgeville Federal Union*, Dec. 25, 1860.
69. Ralph Wooster, "The Georgia Secession Convention," *Georgia Historical Quarterly* 40 (1) (1956): 21–55.
70. *Journal of the Public and Secret Proceedings of the Convention of the People of Georgia. . . . 1861* (Milledgeville, GA, 1861), 112–13.
71. Ibid.
72. *Ordinances and Constitution of the State of Alabama: with the Constitution of the Provisional Government and of the Confederate States of America* (Montgomery: Montgomery Advertiser Book and Job Printing Office, 1861), 3.Ernest W. Winkler, ed., *Journal of the Secession Convention of Texas, 1861* (Austin, TX, 1912), 35–36.
73. Fulton Anderson, "Address of Fulton Anderson, of Mississippi," in *Rebellion Record, Supplement, First Volume*, ed. Frank Moore (G. P. Putnam & Henry Holt, 1864), 143–48.
74. Henry Benning, "Address of Henry L. Benning, of Georgia," in *Rebellion Record*, 148–56.
75. Schott, *Alexander H. Stephens*, 328.
76. Davis, *The Union That Shaped the Confederacy*, chap. 4.
77. "The Montgomery Convention," *Bradford Reporter* (Towanda, PA), Feb. 14, 1861.
78. Schott, *Alexander H. Stephens*, 328; Davis, *The Union That Shaped the Confederacy*, chap. 4; "Disunion Movement," *Grand Haven News* (Grand Haven, MI), Feb. 13, 1861, 2.
79. "Speech of A. H. Stephens, the First Vice President of the Southern Confederacy," *Jeffersonian Democrat* (Chardon, OH), Feb. 15, 1861, 2; *Baltimore Sun*, Feb. 12, 1861, 2.
80. *Delaware Gazette* (OH), Mar. 1, 1861.
81. "Important from Montgomery: Speech of Hon. Jefferson Davis. Declaration of the Policy of the Southern Confederacy," *New York Times*, Feb. 18, 1861, 8.
82. "Jefferson Davis' First Inaugural Address," *The Papers of Jefferson Davis*, Vol. 7 (Baton Rouge: Louisiana State Univ. Press, 1971), 45–51.
83. "Alexander H. Stephens, of Georgia, on the Constitution of the Confederate States," *Detroit Free Press*, Mar. 22, 1861, 1; *Southern Confederacy* (Atlanta), Mar. 14, 1861, 2; "Vice President Stephens in Atlanta," *Weekly Huntsville Advocate*, Mar. 27, 1861, 2.
84. "Speech of Vice President Stephens," *Southern Banner* (Atlanta), Mar. 20, 1861, 2.
85. "A Finality," *Chicago Tribune*, Mar. 21, 1861.
86. Leonidas W. Spratt, "The Philosophy of Secession; A Southern View, Presented in a Letter Addressed to the Hon. Mr. Perkins of Louisiana, in Criticism on the Provisional Constitution Adopted by the Southern Congress at Montgomery, Alabama" (Charleston, 1861).
87. "The Question," *The Liberator* (Boston), Mar. 15, 1861.
88. "A Finality," *Chicago Tribune*, Mar. 21, 1861.

2. The "Corner Stone Speech," 1861–1865

1. Michael E. Woods, "What Twenty-First Century Historians Have Said about the Causes of Disunion: A Civil War Sesquicentennial Review of the Recent Literature," *Journal of American History* 99 (2) (2012): 415–39; Desmond King and Stephen Tuck, "De-Centering the South: America's Nationwide White Supremacist Order after Reconstruction," *Past & Present* 194 (2007): 213–53.

2. John Stevens Cabot Abbott, *The History of the Civil War in America* (New York: Henry Bill, 1863), vol. 1: 34–35.

3. Cleveland, *Alexander H. Stephens*; "Mr. Stephens's Speech," *Savannah Republican*, Mar. 22, 1861, 2.

4. "Hon. Alexander H. Stephens, of Georgia, Vice-President," *Richmond Dispatch* (VA), Feb. 13, 1861, 1.

5. "Ugliness Looking Up—Beauty, Below Par," *Vicksburg Whig* (MS), Feb. 20, 1861.

6. Cleveland, *Alexander H. Stephens*. Cleveland's biography contains many examples of Stephens's orations. My analysis of Stephens oratorical traits was derived from reading those addresses as well as others found in the *Congressional Globe*.

7. "Mr. Stephens's Speech," *Savannah Republican*, Mar. 22, 1861, 2.

8. Ibid.

9. "Speech of Hon. A. H. Stephens," *Southern Banner* (Athens, GA), Apr. 3, 1861, 2.

10. Schott, *Alexander H. Stephens*, 51.

11. Stephens often described himself as a leader whose principles could not be swayed by public opinion. His actions and evolving rhetoric, however, often betrayed those sentiments. He often made statements only to recant them later if doing so benefited his current situation. "Speech of Hon. A. H. Stephens," *Southern Banner* (Athens, GA), Apr. 3, 1861, 2.

12. "Speech of Hon. A.H. Stephens," 2.

13. Ibid.

14. Stephens's commentary on the perceived shortcomings of the Founding Fathers was influenced by his reading of the writings of George Fitzhugh. George Fitzhugh, *Sociology for the South: or, The failure of free society* (Richmond: A. Morris, 1854).

15. "Speech of Hon. A. H. Stephens," *Southern Banner* (Athens, GA), Apr. 3, 1861, 2; Manisha Sinha, *The Counterrevolution of Slavery: Politics and Ideology in Antebellum South Carolina* (Chapel Hill: Univ. of North Carolina Press, 2003). Sinha's study of South Carolina argues that secession was a conservative, anti-democratic movement to protect and preserve racial slavery. Stephens's Cornerstone Speech reflected those same motivations. Stephens's believed that the CSA was revolutionary in its conservative foundations.

16. "Speech of Hon. A. H. Stephens," *Southern Banner* (Athens, GA), Apr. 3, 1861, 2. For additional information on the Confederacy's failed effort to gain foreign recognition, consult: Karp, *This Vast Southern Empire*; Don H. Doyle, *The Cause of All Nations: An International History of the American Civil War* (New York: Basic Books, 2014).

17. Constitution of the Confederate States of America, Article 9.1.

18. Spratt, "Philosophy of Secession."

19. "Disunion and the Slave Trade," *New York Times*, Jan. 5, 1861, 4.

20. "Speech of Hon. A. H. Stephens," 2.

21. Genesis 3:19.

22. "Speech of Hon. A. H. Stephens," 2.

23. Ibid., 2.

24. Ibid., 2.

25. Davis, "African Slavery, The Corner-stone of the Southern Confederacy," 78; "Speech of Hon. A. H. Stephens," *Weekly Advertiser* (Montgomery, AL), Apr. 3, 1861, 4; "Speech of Hon. A. H. Stephens," *Southern Advertiser* (Troy, AL), Apr. 9, 1861, 1.

26. "Mr. Stephens' Speech," *Savannah Daily Republican*, Mar. 22, 1861, 2.

27. *Daily Morning News* (Savannah, GA), Mar. 23, 1861, 1.
28. "Fancy Politicians," *Chicago Tribune*, Mar. 23, 1861, 2.
29. "New Mexico and Old Mexico," *Chicago Tribune*, Mar. 22, 1861, 2.
30. "A White Man's Government," *Southern Confederacy* (Atlanta, GA), Mar. 27, 1861, 1.
31. "Mr. Stephens' Speech," *Weekly Huntsville Advocate* (AL), Apr. 10, 1861, 3.
32. "Mr. Stephen's Speech in Savannah," *Southern Banner* (Athens, GA), Mar. 27, 1861, 2. This article included only a brief summary of the Cornerstone Speech. Most of the article focused on Stephens's earlier Atlanta address.
33. H. L. Byrd, Savannah, Georgia, Alexander H. Stephens, Crawfordville, Georgia, Mar. 23, 1861, General Correspondence, 1784–1886; 1861, Mar. 6–31, Alexander Hamilton Stephens Papers, Library of Congress; Harvey Leonidas Byrd, *Oglethorpe Medical and Surgical Journal* (Savannah, GA: Power Press of J. M. Cooper, 1861); Barry Sheehy, Cindy Wallace, and Vaughnette Goode-Walker, *Civil War Savannah: Savannah Immortal City* (Austin, TX: Emerald Book Company, 2011), 238.
34. Cornelius V. Grant, Savannah, Georgia, to Alexander H. Stephens, Montgomery, Alabama, Mar. 26, 1861, General Correspondence, 1784–1886; 1861, Mar. 6–31, Alexander Hamilton Stephens Papers, Library of Congress.
35. James A. Nisbet, Macon, Georgia, to Alexander H. Stephens, Mar. 28, 1861, General Correspondence, 1784–1886; 1861, Mar. 6–31, Alexander Hamilton Stephens Papers, Library of Congress.
36. "Mr. Stephens," *Augusta Chronicle and Sentinel* (GA), Mar. 28, 1861, 1; "Mr. Stephens," *Southern Messenger* (Greenville, AL), Apr. 3, 1861, 2.
37. *Alabama Beacon* (Greensboro, AL), April 5, 1861, 2; "Our Resources," *The Independent* (Gainesville, AL), Mar. 30, 1861, 2.
38. "Hon. A. H. Stephens at Savannah," *Wilmington Daily Herald* (NC), Mar. 28, 1861, 2; Kent McCoury, "Alfred Moore Waddell," *North Carolina History Project* https://northcarolinahistory.org/encyclopedia/alfred-moore-waddell-1834–1912/ accessed June 2, 2019. After the Civil War, Waddell played a central role in the 1898 Wilmington Race Riot as he led a coup d'état that toppled the city's elected government.
39. "The Republicans Throwing Off All Disguise," *New Bern Daily Progress* (NC), Apr. 17, 1861.
40. "Hon. John J. Crittenden," *Nashville Union and American* (TN), Apr. 2, 1861, 1.
41. William Christian, "The New Republic," *Civilian and Telegraph* (Cumberland, MD), Mar. 28, 1861.
42. *New York Express* article quoted in: "Resources and Prospects of the Southern Confederacy," *Richmond Enquirer*, Mar. 30, 1861, 2.
43. Unus, "Mr. Stephens on the Southern Constitution," *Lowell Patriot* (MA), Mar. 28, 1861, 2; Unus, "Mr. Stephens on the Southern Constitution," *Wayne County Herald* (Honesdale, PA), Apr. 4, 1861, 2.
44. "Another Great Principle," *Chicago Tribune*, Apr. 3, 1861, 2. Stephens's speeches alluded to Arthur Gobineau's *Essai sur des L'inégalité races humaines* (1853). Gobineau's work was translated in 1856 by Henry Hotze, who later represented Confederate interests in London. Doyle, *The Cause of all Nations*.
45. Henry M. Phillips, Deerfield, Massachusetts, to Alexander H. Stephens, Mar. 28, 1861, General Correspondence, 1784–1886; 1861, Mar. 6–31, Alexander Hamilton Stephens Papers, Library of Congress.
46. J. Bavaro Thomas, Independence, Iowa, to Alexander H. Stephens, Crawfordville,

Georgia, Mar. 26, 1861, General Correspondence, 1784–1886; 1861, Mar. 6–31, Alexander Hamilton Stephens Papers, Library of Congress.

47. William C. Wallace, Newark, New Jersey, to Alexander H. Stephens, Mar. 28, 1861, General Correspondence, 1784–1886; 1861, Mar. 6–31, Alexander Hamilton Stephens Papers, Library of Congress.

48. "'Popular Sovereignty' Exemplified," *The Guardian* (Buchanan County, IA), Apr. 16, 1861, 2.

49. "The Southern Confederacy," *New York Evening Post*, Mar. 27, 1861. Several Upper South newspapers reprinted the *New York Evening Post*'s account of the Cornerstone Speech. Newspapers that republished New York newspapers without additional editorials or criticism tended to support the Union. "The Southern Confederacy," *Delaware State Journal and Statesman* (Wilmington), Apr. 2, 1861, 1.

50. Allen Campbell, "The New Confederacy," *Massachusetts Spy* (Boston), Apr. 3, 1861.

51. Edward S. Bunker, Brooklyn, New York, to Alexander H. Stephens, Montgomery, Alabama, Mar. 28, 1861, General Correspondence, 1784–1886; 1861, Mar. 6–31, Alexander Hamilton Stephens Papers, Library of Congress.

52. Edward Williams, Boston, to Alexander H. Stephens, Mar. 28, 1861, General Correspondence, 1784–1886; 1861, Mar. 6–31, Alexander Hamilton Stephens Papers, Library of Congress.

53. "The Cornerstone of the Southern Confederacy," *Manhattan Express* (KS), Apr. 13, 1861, 2.

54. "Mr. Stephens's Speech," *New York Daily Tribune*, Mar. 27, 1861, 4.

55. Ibid.

56. Ibid.

57. "The Southern V.P.," *Portsmouth Journal of Literature and Politics*, Apr. 13, 1861, 2; "Mr. Stephens's Speech," *New York Daily Tribune*, Mar. 27, 1861, 4.

58. Allen Campbell, "The New Confederacy," *Massachusetts Spy* (Boston), Apr. 3, 1861.

59. "Mr. Stephens's Speech," New York Daily Tribune, Mar. 27, 1861, 4.

60. *The Times* (Bellow Falls, VT), Apr. 5, 1861, 2.

61. "The Principle of the Confederation," *Ebensburg Alleghanian* (PA), Apr. 11, 1861, 2.

62. Ibid.

63. I. M. Hatch, Rochester, New York, to Alexander H. Stephens, Montgomery, Alabama, Mar. 29, 1861, General Correspondence, 1784–1886; 1861, Mar. 6–31, Alexander Hamilton Stephens Papers, Library of Congress.

64. *Chicago Tribune*, Apr. 2, 1861, 2.

65. *Des Arc Semi-Weekly Citizen* (AR), June 18, 1861, 2; Doyle, *The Cause of All Nations*, 36.

66. "The Southern Confederacy," *Caledonian Mercury* (Edinburgh, Scotland), Apr. 13, 1861, 4.

67. Doyle, *The Cause of All Nations*, 36. In France, the word "cornerstone" became shorthand for opposition to the Confederate States of America.

68. "Mr. Forster, M.P., on the American War," *Leeds Mercury* (Leeds, West Yorkshire, England), Oct. 2, 1861, 3.

69. Ibid.

70. "The Just and Holy Cause of Slavery," *Leeds Mercury*, May 30, 1861, 4.

71. Hudson Strode, *Jefferson Davis, Confederate President* (New York: Harcourt. 1959), 24; Charles Dew, *Apostles of Disunion: Southern Secession Commissioners and the Causes of the Civil War* (Charlottesville: Univ. of Virginia Press, 2001), 24. Strode's biography

states that Jefferson Davis had been displeased with Stephens's Cornerstone Speech, but does not provide any primary sources to back up this claim.

72. James D. Richardson, *A Compilation of the Messages and Papers of the Confederacy* (Nashville: United States Publishing Company, 1906), vol. 1: 68.

73. "Movements of Vice President Stephens, of the Southern Confederacy," *Valley Spirit* (Chambersburg, PA), May 1, 1861, 1.

74. "Mr. Stephens's Speech," *New York Daily Tribune*, Mar. 27, 1861, 4.

75. Emory Thomas, *The Confederate Nation* (New York: Harper and Row, 1979); George Rable, *The Confederate Republic: A Revolution against Politics* (Chapel Hill: Univ. of North Carolina Press, 2000).

76. Gallagher and Nolan, eds., *The Myth of the Lost Cause*; W. Stuart Towns, *Enduring Legacy: Rhetoric and Ritual in the Lost Cause* (Tuscaloosa: Univ. of Alabama Press, 2012); William C. Davis, *The Cause Lost: Myths and Realities of the Confederacy* (Lawrence: Univ. Press of Kansas, 1996).

77. Doyle, *The Cause of All Nations*; Strode, *Jefferson Davis*. On Strode, see above, n. 71.

78. Pressly, *Americans Interpret Their Civil War*; David W. Blight, ed., *Beyond the Battlefield: Race, Memory, and the American Civil War* (Amherst: Univ. of Massachusetts Press, 2002); Cook, *Troubled Commemoration*; Richard E. Beringer, Herman Hattaway, Archer Jones, and William N. Still, Jr., *Why the South Lost the Civil War* (Athens: Univ. of Georgia Press, 1986).

79. James Conroy, *Our One Common Country: Abraham Lincoln and the Hampton Roads Peace Conference of 1865* (Guilford, CT: Lyons Press, 2014); William C. Harris, "The Hampton Roads Peace Conference: A Final Test of Lincoln's Presidential Leadership," *The Journal of the Abraham Lincoln Association* 21 (2000), 31–61.

80. Benjamin G. Cloyd, *Haunted by Atrocity: Civil War Prisons in American Memory* (Baton Rouge: Louisiana State Univ. Press, 2010).

81. Stephens left behind numerous writings and speeches that shed light on his views on Confederate defeat. Alexander H. Stephens, *A Constitutional View of the Late War Between the States Its Causes, Character, Conduct and Results* (Philadelphia, PA: National Publishing Company, 1868).

3. The Origins of a Dishonest Intellectual Tradition, 1865–1883

1. Myrta Lockett Avary, ed., *Recollections of Alexander H. Stephens* (Atlanta: Sunny South Publishing, 1910); Schott, *Alexander H. Stephens*, chaps. 21 and 22.

2. Schott, *Alexander H. Stephens*, 166; Janney, *Remembering the Civil War*, 87.

3. Avary, *Recollections of Alexander H. Stephens*.

4. Ibid.

5. Cook, *Civil War Memories*.

6. Avary, *Recollections of Alexander H. Stephens*, 235.

7. Ibid., 245.

8. Stephens, *Constitutional View*, vol. 1: 28.

9. Ibid., Introduction. Stephens's book filled nearly 900 pages. His introduction contains the most extensive commentary on the relationship between slavery and the causes of the Civil War. Cook, *Civil War Memories*, 42–43.

10. Gaines Foster, *Ghosts of the Confederacy: Defeat, the Lost Cause, and the Emergence of the New South* (New York: Oxford Univ. Press, 1987), 49.

11. Edward Pollard, *The Lost Cause: A New Southern History of the War of the Confederates* (New York: E. B. Treat & Company, 1866), 50. Two years later, Pollard published *The Lost Cause Regained* during the 1868 presidential election. In that document, a Democratic Party pamphlet, Pollard again neglected to mention the Cornerstone Speech but included Stephens's postbellum prediction of a looming race war in America. Stephens and Pollard agreed that white supremacy was more important in the postbellum era than ever before as conservative white men resisted black demands for civil equality. For an extended discussion of Edward Pollard's writings, see Jack P. Maddex, *The Reconstruction of Edward A. Pollard: A Rebel's Conversion to Postbellum Unionism* (Chapel Hill: Univ. of North Carolina Press, 1974).

12. Carey, *Parties, Slavery, and the Union in Antebellum Georgia*, 221.

13. Cleveland, *Alexander H. Stephens*; "Rev. Henry Whitney Cleveland," *Confederate Veteran* July 1907.

14. Cleveland, *Alexander H. Stephens*, 347.

15. Schott, *Alexander H. Stephens*, 488–89; *Tribune* (New York), June 10, 1871; *Enquirer* (Columbus, GA), Oct. 10, 1871; Mitchell Snay, *Horace Greeley and the Politics of Reform in Nineteenth-Century America* (New York: Rowman & Littlefield, 2011).

16. According to historian Numan V. Bartley, "The Georgia Bourbon Democrats supported a stable social order based on white supremacy, a closed political system resting on one-party politics, and a passive national stance that protected 'home rule.'" Numan V. Bartley, *The Creation of Modern Georgia*, second edition (Athens: Univ. of Georgia Press, 1990), 81.

17. Schott, *Alexander H. Stephens*, 488; Steven Hahn, *The Roots of Southern Populism: Yeoman Farmers and the Transformation of the Georgia Upcountry, 1850–1890* (New York: Oxford Univ. Press, 1983), 228–29; Coleman, ed., *A History of Georgia*, second edition (Athens: Univ. of Georgia Press, 1991), 217.

18. "It is as the Tribune says," *Christian Recorder*, May 4, 1872.

19. Bartley, *The Creation of Modern Georgia*, 126; Charles E. Wynes, "The Politics of Reconstruction, Redemption, and Bourbonism," in *A History of Georgia*, second edition, ed. Coleman, 207–24; "Mr. Stephens's Speech," *Atlanta Daily Sun*, Jan. 19, 1873, 2. When Stephens returned to Washington, DC, he joined thirty-seven other former Confederates serving in Congress.

20. "Rare Scene in Congress," *Junction City Weekly Union* (Junction City, KS), Jan. 17, 1874, 1. Stephens received letters of support for his remarks on the Civil Rights Bills from across the country. Peter McDermot, Jr. New York, New York, to Alexander H. Stephens, Washington, DC, Feb. 12, 1874, Correspondence, 1874 Jan–May, letter 2439, Alexander H. Stephens Papers, David M. Rubenstein Rare Book & Manuscript Library, Duke University.

21. "Rare Scene in Congress," *Junction City Weekly Union* (Junction City, KS), Jan. 17, 1874, 1.

22. Southern Democratic Congressmen were not alone in their criticism of Stephens's speech. The *Atlanta Daily Herald* accused Stephens of failing to "strike a blow at the mad and unnatural fanaticism of the hour." The newspaper questioned Stephens's commitment to the defense of white supremacy. "Mr. Stephens' Speech," *Atlanta Daily Herald*, Jan. 9, 1874, 1.

23. Ibid.

24. *Atlanta Daily Herald*, "A pamphlet containing the full history of the celebration of the

ninety-ninth anniversary of American independence in Atlanta, GA., July 4th, 1875" (Atlanta: Herald Stream Book and Job print, 1875), 38.

25. "Stephens's Address," *Atlanta Daily Herald*, July 5, 1875, 2.
26. Speech in *Congressional Record*, 43rd Congress, 1st Session, II, 378–82.
27. Ibid., 388.
28. Ibid.
29. "XLVTH Congress," *Hartford Courant*, Feb. 13, 1878, 3; *Raleigh News*, Jan. 23, 1878, 3; "The Lincoln-Cabinet Meeting," *The Inter Ocean* (Chicago), Feb. 12, 1878; *New York Times*, Feb. 13, 1878, 1; Schott, *Alexander H. Stephens*, 500.
30. "XLVTH Congress," *Hartford Courant*, Feb. 13, 1878, 3.
31. "XLVTH Congress," *Hartford Courant*, Feb. 13, 1878, 3.
32. Hahn, *Roots of Southern Populism*; Hébert, *Long Civil War in the North Georgia Mountains: Confederate Nationalism, Sectionalism, and White Supremacy in Bartow County, Georgia* (Knoxville: Univ. of Tennessee Press, 2017); Schott, *Alexander H. Stephens*, 507–8; "A. H. Stephens Speaks Truth," *Scranton Republican*, June 28, 1878, 2; "Alexander H. Stephens," *Savannah Morning News*, June 1, 1878, 1; "The Potter Committee at Work," *Savannah Morning News*, June 3, 1878, 1; "A Northern Democratic Opinion of Hon. A. H. Stephens," *Savannah Morning News*, Nov. 22, 1878; "Forty-Sixth Congress," *St. Mary's Democrat* (St. Mary: KS), Nov. 22, 1878. Technically, Stephens was not considered an Independent Democrat because the party kept him on the ballot during the 1878 election. Stephens campaigned and endorsed Independent candidates.
33. Schott, *Alexander H. Stephens*, 508–10.
34. Stephens did not endorse universal suffrage for black men. He believed that black males should attain a minimum level of education before casting a ballot. Stephens, who always held white supremacist beliefs, did not endorse similar barriers for white male voters. Schott, *Alexander H. Stephens*, 509.
35. Schott, *Alexander H. Stephens*, 519; *St. Landry Democrat* (Opelousas, LA), Mar. 10, 1883, 4; Minnie Harper to Alexander H. Stephens, Feb. 14, 1883, Correspondence, 1883, letter 3231, Alexander H. Stephens Papers, David M. Rubenstein Rare Book & Manuscript Library, Duke University.
36. *Dunn County News* (Menomonie, WI), Mar. 10, 1883, 4.
37. *Brooklyn Union* (Brooklyn, NY), Mar. 5, 1883, 2. The author of the *Brooklyn Union* article elaborated: "In his death the South has sustained a greater loss than it would in that of almost any other citizen, and the country is deprived of one whose services were not altogether nullified by his mistakes. Mr. Stephens was with those who rebelled against the Union, but was not of them until overwhelmed by the popular voice. . . . Though casting his fortune with the "lost cause" he did it reluctantly and with an innate belief that the Union arms would triumph. . . . His gifts compelled him to fight for a principle up to a certain point and then make as graceful a surrender as possible. . . . The greatest chance of his life to become a martyr for his convictions was when he so long and so ably obstructed the tide of secession; but he succumbed, as on lesser occasions, and, worse than that, did not maintain a dignified loyalty in retirement but accepted a second place in the Confederacy, doing what he would in his amiable way to strengthen it."
38. *Berkshire County Eagle* (Pittsfield, MA), Mar. 8, 1883; "Alexander Hamilton Stephens," *Prohibitionist and Journal of Reform* (Columbus, KS), Oct. 4, 1883; *Boston Journal*, Oct. 4, 1883.
39. *Rutland Daily Herald* (Rutland, VT), June 16, 1883.

40. *Jasper Weekly Courier* (IN), Mar. 9, 1883, 8.
41. "Mr. Alexander H. Stephens on Slavery," *Georgia Telegraph* (Macon), Mar. 4, 1845; Carey, *Parties, Slavery, and the Union in Antebellum Georgia*, 74–75; "Speech of Mr. Stephens, Of Georgia, on the Joint Resolution for the Annexation of Texas," *Georgia Messenger* (Ft. Hawkins, GA), Mar. 6, 1845, 2; Schott, *Alexander H. Stephens*, 62.
42. *Jasper Weekly Courier* (IN), Mar. 9, 1883, 8; *Public Press* (Northumberland, PA), Mar. 9, 1883, 2; "Death of Alex. Stephens," *Donaldsonville Chief* (LA), Mar. 10, 1883, 2. Gates, *Stony the Road*, Introduction; W.E.B. DuBois, *Black Reconstruction in America, 1860–1880* (New York: Free Press, 1998), 5; C. Vann Woodward, *Origins of the New South, 1877–1913* (Baton Rouge: Louisiana State Univ. Press, 1951), 351.
43. *New York Tribune* (New York), Mar. 9, 1883, 2; "Alexander H. Stephens," *St. Landry Democrat*, Mar. 24, 1883, 2. A few months prior to his death, Stephens drew strong criticism from many Georgia Democrats, including John B. Gordon, for commuting the sentences of dozens of African American prisoners who he deemed had been improperly convicted by local courts. At that time, some Democrats accused Stephens of harboring favorable sympathies toward African Americans. *St. Landry Democrat* (LA), Jan. 27, 1883, 4; *Louisiana Democrat* (Alexandria, LA), Jan. 24, 1883, 2.
44. Frank H. Norton, *The Life of Alexander H. Stephens* (New York: John B. Alden, 1883), 64; *Lake Charles Commercial* (Lake Charles, LA), May 19, 1883, 3.
45. *Telegraph-Bulletin* (Monroe, Louisiana), Mar. 14, 1883, 2.
46. *Ouachita Telegraph* (Monroe, LA), Mar. 10, 1883, 2; "Alexander H. Stephens," *Clarksdale Weekly Chronicle* (TN), Mar. 10, 1883, 2; *Milan Exchange* (TN), Mar. 10, 1883, 4; "Alexander H. Stephens," *Memphis Daily Appeal*, Mar. 6, 1883, 2; "Alexander H. Stephens Dead," *Pulaski Citizen* (TN), Mar. 8, 1883, 2; *Bolivar Bulletin* (TN), Mar. 8, 1883, 2; "Death of Gov. Stephens," *Shenandoah Herald* (Woodstock, VA), Mar. 7, 1883, 2.
47. "The Heritage of a Good Name," *Louisiana Democrat* (Monroe, LA), Apr. 4, 1883, 1.

4. Emancipationists Strike Back, 1865–1883

1. Blight, *Race and Reunion*.
2. John Stevens Cabot Abbott, *The History of the Civil War in America* (New York: Henry Bill, 1863), vol. 1: 34–35.
3. Horace Greeley, *The American Conflict: A History of the Great Rebellion in the.* . . . vol. 1: 416.
4. Stephens also received a large amount of mail from individuals expressing their regret for his imprisonment and support for his postbellum life. He also received letters from across the nation requesting his autograph. Moses Cooke, Flint, Michigan, to Alexander H. Stephens, Crawfordville, Georgia, Jan. 10, 1866, Correspondence, 1866 Jan–Aug, letter 1903, Alexander H. Stephens Papers, David M. Rubenstein Rare Book & Manuscript Library, Duke University. Stephens also received numerous requests for help from Confederate veterans or bureaucrats. See, for example, Unknown correspondent, Albany, Georgia, to Alexander H. Stephens, Crawfordville, Georgia, Correspondence, 1866 Jan–Aug, letter 1904.
5. *Cincinnati Enquirer*, Mar. 10, 1883. In 1883, at the time of Stephens's death, GATH published an extended analysis of his 1867 interview with him. For an extended discussion of Townsend's journalism, see: Mark Wahlgren Summers, *The Press Gang: Newspapers and Politics, 1865–1878* (Chapel Hill: Univ. of North Carolina Press, 2018).

6. *Cincinnati Enquirer*, Mar. 10, 1883.
7. In the Union Speech, Stephens warned that some slaveholders were supporting secession to advance their personal ambitions. The Emancipationists sometimes used this speech in combination with the Cornerstone Speech to demonstrate that, while Stephens's views on the viability of secession might have changed, his opinion that secession was driven by the interests of slaveholders remained constant. "Who Commenced the War?" *The Christian Recorder*, Aug. 4, 1866.
8. "Address by Gen. Stephen Thomas, as a mass meeting at Norwich, on Saturday, August 22d, 1868," *Vermont Journal* (Windsor) Aug. 29, 1868, 1.
9. "The Rights of Labor," *Chicago Tribune*, Feb. 22, 1868.
10. Constitutionalist, *A review of the first volume of Alexander H. Stephens's "War between the states"* (Philadelphia: J. B. Lippincott & Company, 1872), 17. In 1872, Stephens published a 273-page rebuttal in response to his critics. Alexander H. Stephens, *The reviewers reviewed: a supplement to the "War between the states," etc.*, with an appendix in review of "reconstruction," so called (New York: D. Appleton and Company, 1872).
11. "To the voters of the seventh congressional district of South Carolina," *Christian Recorder* (Philadelphia, PA), Nov. 9, 1882.
12. "Civil Rights in Congress," *Vermont Watchman and State Journal* (Montpelier, VT), Jan. 28, 1874.
13. Elliott's repudiation of Stephens's Cornerstone Speech was a source of pride for African Americans in South Carolina and across the nation. The act of a black man defying the former Confederate vice-president became a symbol of black resistance to white supremacy. "To the voters of the seventh congressional district of South Carolina," *Christian Recorder* (Philadelphia), Nov. 9, 1882; "Gen. R.B. Elliott, Statesman, Jurist and Orator. His Brilliant Career in South Carolina during the Reconstruction," *Christian Recorder* (Philadelphia), Oct. 2, 1884. Edward A. Johnson, *A School History of the Negro Race in America from 1619 to 1890* (Raleigh: Edwards and Broughton Printers, 1890), 168.
14. Henry Blumenthal, "Confederate Diplomacy: Popular Notions and International Realities," *Journal of Southern History* 32 (2) (1966): 151–71.
15. "Alexander H. Stephens' Vote," *Chicago Tribune*, Mar. 8, 1875, 4.
16. "Mr. Stoughton's Address. Delivered at Burlington, Vt., Thursday Evening, Aug. 10, 1876," *Enterprise and Vermonter* (Vergennes, VT), Aug. 18, 1876; Michael F. Holt, *By One Vote: The Disputed Presidential Election of 1876* (Lawrence: Univ. Press of Kansas, 2008).
17. "Carpenter's Picture," *Christian Recorder* (Philadelphia, PA), Feb. 21, 1878.

5. *Different Things to Different People, 1883–1911*

1. Avary, *Recollections of Alexander H. Stephens*, 172–74.
2. "Alexander H. Stephens's Prison Life," *Confederate Veteran* 1 (1893): 137–38; "Mr. Stephens's Prison Life," *Confederate Veteran*, Supplement to April Issue 2 (1894): 5. In 1923, Mildred Lewis Rutherford of Georgia, historian of the United Daughters of the Confederacy and Lost Cause promoter, published a history of the South that included a chapter entitled "Cruelties in Northern Prisons" that featured selections from Stephens's prison journal and personal correspondence. Rutherford falsely claimed that Stephens's experiences at Fort Warren "left him a cripple for life." Mildred Lewis

Rutherford, *Miss Rutherford's Scrap Book: Valuable Information about the South* (Charlottesville: Univ. of Virginia Press, 1923), vol. 1: 179.

3. "The Causes of the War," *Confederate Veteran*, Supplement to April Issue 2 (1894): 9–12.

4. "Texas UDC to the Sons of Veterans," *Confederate Veteran* 8 (1900): 406–7.

5. "Alexander H. Stephens, One of the Ablest Men and Most Unique Characters Prominent in the Confederacy," *Times-Democrat* (New Orleans, LA), Mar. 23, 1902, 18.

6. "Chat About Trees," *Richmond Dispatch*, Apr. 6, 1902, 10.

7. *Catholic Advance*, July 31, 1902, 3.

8. *Hartford Courant*, Sept. 5, 1902, 10.

9. *Evening Star*, Apr. 12, 1902, 30.

10. "Alexander H. Stephens," *The Inter Ocean* (Chicago, IL), Mar. 23, 1902.

11. "Dixon Pleased Large Audience," *Tampa Tribune* (Florida), Oct. 3, 1902, 1; Michelle K. Gillespie and Randal L. Hall, eds. *Thomas Dixon Jr. and the Birth of Modern America* (Baton Rouge: Louisiana State Univ. Press, 2009).

12. "Seeking Delay," *Boston Globe*, July 25, 1902, 11; *News and Observer* (Raleigh, NC), July 25, 1902, 4; "Massachusetts Will Not Give Up the Negro," *New York Times*, July 27, 1902, 2.

13. William H. Scott, *The history of the Rogers case: from July 22 to Sept. 4, with the speech of Rev. W.H. Scott before the governor of Massachusetts and the attorney-general, and Rev. W.H. Scott's address to the president of the U.S. on Feb. 26, 1902* (Massachusetts: N.p., 1902), 6–8.

14. Ibid.

15. "Monroe Rogers," *Greensboro Patriot* (NC), Dec. 10, 1902, 10; "Ten Years for Monroe Rogers," *Morning Post* (Raleigh, NC), Dec. 4, 1902, 7.

16. "Negrophilists Please Take Notice," *Robesonian* (Lumberton, NC), Dec. 9, 1902, 2.

17. "Work of the S.S. Convention," *Troy Messenger* (AL), Apr. 30, 1902, 3.

18. *Hartford Courant* (CT), Jan. 2, 1890, 7; *Democrat and Chronicle* (Rochester, NY), Jan. 5, 1890, 4.

19. Ren Davis and Helen Davis, *Atlanta's Oakland Cemetery: An Illustrated History and Guide* (Athens: Univ. of Georgia Press, 2012), xxv.

20. Mrs. L. W. Greene, "Ms. Horace Holden Gives Report on Preservation of Liberty Hall," *Atlanta Constitution*, Dec. 18, 1932, 29.

21. E. Ramsay Richardson, *Little Aleck: A Life of Alexander H. Stephens, Fighting Vice-President of the Confederacy* (Indianapolis, IN: Bobbs-Merrill, 1932), 20.

22. Micki McElya, *Clinging to Mammy: The Faithful Slave in Twentieth-Century America* (Cambridge: Harvard Univ. Press, 2007); Kevin M. Levin, *Searching for Black Confederates: The Civil War's Most Persistent Myth* (Chapel Hill: Univ. of North Carolina Press, 2019).

23. Edward J. Cashin, *A Confederate Legend: Sergeant Berry Benson in War and Peace* (Macon: Mercer Univ. Press, 2008), 184; Gracie Shepherd, "Family of researcher built local landmarks," *Augusta Chronicle*, Aug. 27, 2010.

24. Remsen Crawford, "Stephens," *Atlanta Constitution*, May 14, 1893, 14; Cleveland, *Alexander H. Stephens*, 101.

25. Remsen Crawford, "Stephens," *Atlanta Constitution*, May 14, 1893, 14.

26. "Harry Stephens," *Daily Constitution* (Atlanta), Feb. 2, 1881; Remsen Crawford, "Stephens," *Atlanta Constitution*, May 14, 1893, 14.

27. Remsen Crawford, "Stephens," *Atlanta Constitution*, May 14, 1893, 14.
28. "Crawfordsville's Big Day," *Knoxville Journal* (TN), May 25, 1893, 1; *Knoxville Tribune* (TN), May 25, 1893, 1; *Middleton Times-Press* (NY), May 25, 1893, 4.
29. *Huntsville Weekly Democrat* (AL), May 31, 1893, 2.
30. "Apotheosis of Jefferson Davis," *Omaha Daily Bee*, May 30, 1893, 4.
31. *Seattle Post-Intelligencer*, June 1, 1893, 4.
32. "Decoration Day," *Middlebury Register* (VT), June 2, 1893, 1; William A. Blair, *Cities of the Dead: Contesting the Memory of the Civil War in the South, 1865–1914* (Chapel Hill: Univ. of North Carolina Press, 2004).
33. "Decoration Day," *Great Bend Register* (KS), June 1, 1893, 3.
34. *Baltimore Sun*, May 25, 1893, 2; *Evening Star* (Washington, DC), May 24, 1893, 6; *Times-Democrat* (New Orleans, LA), May 24, 1893, 1; *The Sentinel* (Carlisle, PA), May 25, 1893, 2; *Muscatine News-Tribune* (IA), May 26, 1893, 8; *The Inter Ocean* (Chicago, IL), May 25, 1893, 4; *Evening Messenger* (Marshall, TX), May 4, 1893, 1; *Democratic Messenger* (Eureka, KS), May 12 ,1893, 4; *Los Angeles Times*, May 25, 1893, 2.
35. "Another Negro Outrage," *Staunton Spectator and General Advertiser* (VA), May 17, 1893, 2.
36. *Baltimore Sun*, May 15, 1893, 7; *Laurens Advertiser* (SC), May 30, 1893, 1; *Knoxville Journal* (TN), May 25, 1893, 1; *Atlanta Constitution*, May 25, 1893, 1; *Wilmington Morning Star*, May 17, 1893, 1; *Piedmont Inquirer* (AL), May 20, 1893, 4; *Montgomery Advertiser*, May 25, 1893, 1; *Evening Republican* (Meadville, PA), May 25, 1893, 1; *Buffalo Morning Express*, May 26, 1893, 1; *The Intelligencer* (Anderson, SC), May 17, 1893, 2; *St. Louis Dispatch*, May 26, 1893, 3; *Charlotte Observer*, May 25, 1893, 2; *Davenport Weekly Republican* (IA), May 27, 1893, 1; Grace Poon Ghaffari, "Myths America Lives By: White Supremacy and the Stories That Give Us Meaning," *Diverse: Issues in Higher Education* 36 (8) (2019): 24–25.
37. Philip H. Viles, *National Statuary Hall: Guidebook for a Walking Tour* (P. H. Viles: Washington, DC, 1997).
38. "Honoring the Great Commoner," *Atlanta Constitution*, Oct. 24, 1902, 6.
39. Ibid.
40. John E. Bruce, "The Negro's Rights Under the Law," *New York Times*, June 29, 1902, 7.
41. Quoted in Gillian Brockwell, "How Statues of Robert E. Lee and Other Confederates Got into the U.S. Capitol," *Washington Post*, Aug. 17, 2017.
42. *Montgomery Advertiser*, Feb. 13, 1920, 4; Grace Elizabeth Hale, "Granite Stopped Time: Stone Mountain Memorial and the Representation of White Southern Identity," in *Monuments to the Lost Cause: Women, Art, and the Landscapes of Southern Memory*, ed. Cynthia Mills and Pamela H. Simpson (Knoxville: Univ. of Tennessee Press, 2003), 219–33; Benjamin Forest and Juliet Johnson, "Confederate Monuments and the Problem of Forgetting," *Cultural Geographies* 26 (1) (2019): 127–31.
43. "Name County for Stephens," *Atlanta Constitution*, Apr. 29, 1905, 5.
44. "New Counties Will Bring About Warm Fight in the House Today," *Atlanta Constitution*, Aug. 11, 1905, 3; "Colonel Calvin Tells of Gen. W. A. Sanford," *Atlanta Constitution*, Aug. 20, 1905, 2; "Stephens County's Debut," *Atlanta Constitution*, Sept. 3, 1905, 4.
45. "Colonel Calvin Tells of Gen. W. A. Sanford," *Atlanta Constitution*, Aug. 20, 1905, 2; Steven Hoelscher, "Making Place, Making Race: Performances of Whiteness in the Jim Crow South," *Annals of the Association of American Geographers* 93 (3) (2003): 657–86.
46. "Effective Retort Made by Alexander Stephens of Georgia," *Logan Republican* (UT),

Jan. 28, 1905, 3; "Col. Mason's Reminiscences," *Ottawa Weekly Republic* (KS), Apr. 6, 1905, 2; "Wit on the Hustings," *Pemiscot Press* (Caruthersville, MO), Apr. 20, 1905, 3.

47. Savoyard, "Alexander H. Stephens," *Fayetteville Weekly Observer* (NC), 21; "Alexander H. Stevens," *Weekly Pioneer-Times* (Deadwood, SD), June 22, 1905, 4

48. Savoyard, "Alexander H. Stephens," *Fayetteville Weekly Observer* (NC), Sept. 21, 1905, 1; "Alexander H. Stevens," *Weekly Pioneer-Times* (Deadwood, SD), June 22, 1905, 4; *Mound City Republic* (KS), Mar. 2 1905, 1. During the semicentennial, newspaper editorials appeared across the northern United States that often hypothesized that Stephens would have been a superior president compared to Davis. See, for example, *Burlington Free Press* (VT), Mar. 11, 1911, 5.

49. Quoted in Myrdal, *An American Dilemma*, vol. 1: 354.

50. Clark Howell, "An Echo From The Past!" *Atlanta Constitution*, Apr. 2, 1905, 4.

51. Ibid.

52. Schott, *Alexander H. Stephens*, 506–17.

53. Joshua F. J. Inwood, "Geographies of Race in the American South: The Continuing Legacies of Jim Crow Segregation," *Southeastern Geographer* 51 (4) (2011): 564–77.

54. William H. Fleming, "Slavery and Race Problem in the South," *New York Age*, Oct. 25, 1906, 5.

55. Ibid.

56. Ibid.

57. Ibid.

58. Judge George Christian's speech can be located in: Frank B. Chilton, *Unveiling and Dedication of Monument to Hood's Texas Brigade on the Capitol Grounds at Austin, Texas, Thursday, October twenty-seven, nineteen hundred and ten, and minutes of the thirty-ninth annual reunion of Hood's Texas brigade association held in Senate chamber at Austin, Texas, October twenty-six and twenty-seven, nineteen hundred and ten, together with a short monument and brigade association history and Confederate scrap book* (Houston: F. B. Chilton, 1911), 166.

59. Ibid.

60. Charles Francis Adams, "The Modern Conception of History," *Wisconsin Alumni Magazine* 2 (1901): 53. Adams is quoted in Christian, *Report of the U.C.V. History Committee* (Richmond: U.C.V., 1909), 14.

61. Quoted in Blight, *Race and Reunion*, 359–60.

62. Christian, *Report of the U.C.V. History Committee*, 74, 78.

63. Ibid., 78–82.

64. Joseph Moreau, *Schoolbook Nation: Conflicts over American History Textbooks from the Civil War to the Present* (Ann Arbor: Univ. of Michigan Press, 2003), 56; James M. McPherson, "Long-Legged Yankee Lies: The Southern Textbook Crusade," *The Memory of the Civil War in American Culture*, ed. Alice Fahs and Joan Waugh (Chapel Hill: Univ. of North Carolina Press, 2004): 64–78.

65. Albert Bushnell Hart, "American History," *Baltimore Sun*, July 14, 1899, 6. Transcripts of the Cornerstone Speech also appeared in several published volumes of primary sources including Alexander Johnston's popular *Masterpieces of American Eloquence*. Alexander Johnston, ed. *Masterpieces of American Eloquence: Representative Orations Illustrating American Political History* (New York: G. P. Putnam, 1890), 164.

66. William P. Trent, *Southern Statesmen of the Old Regime: Washington, Jefferson, Randolph, Calhoun, Stephens, Toombs, and Jefferson Davis* (New York: T. Y. Crowell and Company, 1897), 288–90.

67. Edgar Sanderson, *Six Thousand Years of History* (New York: E. R. DuMont, 1899), 240.
68. Oliver Perry Temple, *East Tennessee and the Civil War* (Cincinnati, OH: R. Clarke Company, 1899), 135–36.
69. Benson John Lossing, *Harper's Popular Cyclopedia of United States History* (New York: Harper and Brothers, 1898–1899), vol. 2: 1347.
70. Francis J. Grimke, "Equality of rights for all citizens, black and white, alike. A discourse delivered in the Fifteenth street Presbyterian church, Washington, D.C., Sunday, March 7th, 1909, by the pastor, Rev. Francis J. Grimke" (Washington. DC: 1909).
71. John McElroy, "The Southern Confederacy," *National Tribune* (Washington, DC), Feb. 21, 1907, 2. For an extended discussion of how the Confederacy's pro-slavery stances impacted its relationship with Great Britain, see Ephraim Douglass Adams, *Great Britain and the American Civil War* (New York: Russell & Russell, 1958). Adams argues that the Cornerstone Speech did little to alter British attitudes toward the Confederacy. He found that the selection of William Lowndes Yancey as foreign ambassador deeply upset British leaders.

6. Civil War Semicentennial, 1911–1915

1. Rayford W. Logan, *The Negro in American Life and Thought, the Nadir 1877–1901* (New York: Dial Press, 1954).
2. David Blight, "Fifty Years of Freedom: The Memory of Emancipation at the Civil War Semicentennial, 1911–15," in *After Slavery: Emancipation and its Discontents*, ed. Howard Temperley (London: Frank Cass Publishers, 2000), 117–34; John Hope Franklin, "A Century of Civil War Observance," *Journal of Negro History* 47 (2) (1962): 97–107; Edmund Fong, "Reconstructing the 'Problem' of Race," *Political Research Quarterly* 61(4)(2008): 660–70.
3. Blight, *Race and Reunion*, 2, 13, 24, 31, 42, 53.
4. Du Bois, *Black Reconstruction*, 30.
5. Ibid.; Gates, *Stony the Road*; Kendi, *Stamped from the Beginning*; Robert Tracey McKenzie, *Lincolnites and Rebels: A Divided Town in the American Civil War* (Oxford: Oxford Univ. Press, 2009).
6. Louis Pendleton, *Alexander H. Stephens* (Philadelphia, PA: G. W. Jacobs and Company, 1908), 252–53; Doyle, *The Cause of All Nations*.
7. Pendleton, *Alexander H. Stephens*, 254. Several early-twentieth-century historians accused Stephens of ruining the Confederacy's chance to receive additional foreign aid and recognition. See, for example, Cecil Chesterton, *A History of the United States* (New York: George H. Doran Company, 1919), 234.
8. J. T. Graves, Clark Howell, and Walter Williams, eds., *Eloquent Sons of the South: A Handbook of Southern Oratory* (Boston: Chapple Publishing Company, 1909), vol. 2: 99–114.
9. "He Defends Lynch Law," *New York Times*, Aug. 12, 1903.
10. John Temple Graves, "Editorial by Hon. John Temple Graves, Editor of the New York American," *Atlanta Georgian*, June 14, 1914.
11. Berkeley Minor, "If Lee Could Have Stood at the Helm," *Times Dispatch* (Richmond, VA), Jan. 15, 1911, 3. Lost Cause promoters distorted Gen. Robert E. Lee's relationship with his black enslaved laborers as well as his supposed efforts to emancipate his human property. In fact, Lee was an abusive enslaver who never expressed any

support for emancipation and racial equality. For an excellent summary of Lee's record, see: Adam Serwer, "The Myth of the Kindly General Lee," *The Atlantic*, Jun. 4, 2017 (accessed Jun. 5, 2020), https://www.theatlantic.com/politics/archive/2017/06/the-myth-of-the-kindly-general-lee/529038/.

12. Ibid.

13. "The Cause of Secession," *The Citizen* (Honesdale, PA), Mar. 3, 1911, 1.

14. *Evening Capital News*, Oct. 30, 1912, 10.

15. *Boston Globe*, Mar. 11, 1911, 10.

16. Ibid.

17. "Honor is Shown Ottumwa's Dead," *Ottumwa Tri-Weekly Courier* (IA), June 1, 1911, 4.

18. Ibid.; Desmond King and Stephen Tuck, "De-Centering the South: America's Nationwide White Supremacist Order after Reconstruction," *Past & Present* 194 (2007): 213–53.

19. "The South Avenged," *Greenville Advocate* (AL), Nov. 25, 1914, 7; "Commencement at Fisk Uni.," *Nashville Globe*, June 16, 1911, 1; *Staunton Spectator and Vindicator* (VA), Aug. 11, 1911, 1; *Montgomery Advertiser*, Nov. 18, 1914, 4; *New York Age*, June 22, 1911, 1; *Brooklyn Daily Eagle*, Feb. 26, 1912, 10; "Tom's Cabin," *Farmer and Mechanic* (Raleigh, NC), Sept. 5, 1911, 12; *Oxford Banner* (NC), Sept. 9, 1911, 2.

20. "Address on South," *Morristown Gazette* (TN), July 12, 1911, 1.

21. Ibid.

22. *Bemidji Daily Pioneer* (MN), June 18, 1912, 4.

23. *Evening Journal*, June 8, 1912, 4.

24. Charles N. Lurie, "The State of the Union Half a Century Ago," *Evening Times*, Feb. 25, 1911, 7.

25. "Civil War Without a Cause," *Quad-City Times* (Davenport, IA), Sept. 8, 1912, 21.

26. Ibid.

27. *Norwich Bulletin*, June 22, 1911, 2.

28. "Apt Questions for Teachers," *Democratic Banner*, Apr. 4, 1911, 8; *News-Herald* (Hillsboro, OH), Apr. 6, 1911, 6.

29. E. J. Edwards, "Alexander H. Stephens' Remarkable Vitality in His Closing Years," *Pittsburgh Post-Gazette*, Feb. 22, 1911, 4.

30. "Maj. Harvey's Address," *Stafford County Republican* (KS), June 5, 1913, 1.

31. Ibid.

32. Ibid., 8.

33. "Blue and Gray Clasp Hands," *Indianapolis News*, May 30, 1914, 16.

34. "Speaker of Day," *Santa Ana Register* (CA), May 30, 1911, 4.

35. "A Virginia Woman's View of Slavery," *Times Dispatch* (Richmond, VA), June 24, 1911, 4.

36. "To Subjugate World Is Aim," *Shipping World* (London), May 31, 1915.

37. James Ford Rhodes, *History of the United States from the Compromise of 1850* (New York: Macmillan Company, 1904), vols. 6 and 7.

38. James Ford Rhodes, *Lectures on the American Civil War, delivered before the University of Oxford in Easter and Trinity terms 1912* (New York: Macmillan Company, 1913), 84–86; Blight, *Race and Reunion*, 357–58.

39. For an extended examination of the connections between romanticism and the Lost Cause, see Rollin G. Osterweis, *The Myth of the Lost Cause, 1865–1900* (Hamden, CT: Archon Books, 1973); Osterweis, *Romanticism and Nationalism in the Old South* (New

Haven: Yale Univ. Press, 1949). W. J. Cash also emphasized the role that romanticism had played in southern history. Cash, *The Mind of the South*.

40. James W. Mathews, "Dr. Gamaliel Bradford (1795–1839), Early Abolitionist," *Historical Journal of Massachusetts* 19 (1) (1991): 1–12.
41. Gamaliel Bradford, *Lee: The American* (Mineola: Dover Publications, 2004); "Gamaliel Bradford Honored," *Atlanta Constitution*, Dec. 12, 1926, 47; "Gamaliel Bradford's Journal," *Galveston Daily News* (TX), Nov. 19, 1933, 3; "The South Owes Appreciation to Gamaliel Bradford," *Montgomery Advertiser*, Apr. 24, 1926, 4.
42. Gamaliel Bradford, *Confederate Portraits* (Boston: Houghton Mifflin, 1914), 5, 153–54.
43. Ibid., 155.
44. Ibid., 153–54.
45. Ibid., 153–54; Thomas L. Connelly, *The Marble Man: Robert E. Lee and His Image in American Society* (Baton Rouge: Louisiana State Univ. Press, 1977).
46. Cloyd, *Haunted by Atrocity*, chap. 4.
47. "A Sorrowful Story," *Godwin's Weekly: A Thinking Paper for Thinking People* (Salt Lake City, UT), Mar. 11, 1911, 2.
48. "Recollections of Alexander H. Stephens," *Montgomery Advertiser*, Aug. 27, 1911, 11. *Times Dispatch* (Richmond, VA) and several other southern newspapers printed excerpts of Stephens's Fort Warren journal. "Diary of A. H. Stephens, While in Fort Warren," *Times Dispatch* (Richmond, VA), Jan. 15, 1911, 3. Stephens's prison journal appeared in newspapers nationwide. "A Sorrowful Story," *Godwin's Weekly: A Thinking Paper for Thinking People* (Salt Lake City, UT), Mar. 11, 1911, 2. Interest in Alexander H. Stephens's historical writings increased during the Civil War Semicentennial. Across the South, funds were donated to libraries to purchase Confederate histories. Stephens's *Constitutional History* was considered one of a handful of standard histories of the Civil War. *Lafayette Advertiser*, Jan. 19, 1912, 4; "New Books Received as C&H Public Library," *Calumet News*, Aug. 29, 1911, 5.
49. "A Sorrowful Story," Godwin's Weekly, , Mar. 11, 1911, 2; *San Francisco Call*, Oct. 10, 1912, 10; *Washington Herald* (Washington, DC), May 15, 1914, 2; *Bridgeport Evening Farmer* (CT), Aug. 27, 1913, 5; *The Sun* (New York), Nov. 15, 1911, 6; *Wheeling Intelligencer* (WV), Jan. 2, 1915, 11.
50. "Brantley to Speak to Honor Stephens," *Montgomery Monitor* (Mt. Vernon, Montgomery County, GA), 14, 1912. On July 4, 1912, the United Daughters of the Confederacy, Crawfordville Chapter, held a barbecue and celebration to honor Alexander H. Stephens's one-hundredth birthday. The event was held at Stephens's home, Liberty Hall. Proceeds from the event were used to maintain the historic property, which had been set aside as a public park. "Anniversary of Stephens to be Celebrated," *McDuffie Progress* (Thomson, GA), June 28, 1912, 1; "Stephens: Centennial of Birth of Alexander Stephens," *Athens Banner*, June 18, 1912, 5; *Milledgeville News* (GA), June 28, 1912, 1.
51. "Nation Misled by False Dogmas," *Times Dispatch* (Richmond, VA), May 23, 1912, 14; *Richmond Palladium and Sun-Telegram* (IN), Feb. 12, 1912, 6; "Will Celebrate Centenary of Stephens," *Las Vegas Optic*, Feb. 12, 1912, 2; "Centenary of Noted Southerner Will Be Observed Tomorrow," *Calumet News* (MI), Feb. 10, 1912, 1. The National News Association circulated a biographical sketch of Stephens that accompanied a story detailing plans to honor the deceased Confederate leader. Using a conciliatory tone that held up Stephens as an exemplar of statesmanship, industry, and intellect,

the paper praised efforts to honor him. The biography made no mention of the Cornerstone Speech or Stephens's postbellum opposition to Reconstruction.

52. "Secession Movement in Georgia," *Athens Banner* (GA), Apr. 26, 1912, 6; "The Famous Provisional Congress," *Athens Banner*, Apr. 26, 1912, 7.

53. "Alexander H. Stephens, Daisy St. Germain, 8th Grade A," *The Herald* (New Orleans, LA), Feb. 5, 1914, 4.

54. "Gen. Lee and Slavery," *Troy Messenger* (AL), Mar. 12, 1913, 6.

55. Melvyn Stokes, *D. W. Griffith's the Birth of a Nation: A History of the Most Controversial Motion Picture of All Time* (Oxford: Oxford Univ. Press, 2008).

7. Old Times There Are Not Forgotten, 1915–1965

1. "Speech at Columbus, Ohio, 16 September 1859," Basler, ed., *The Collected Works of Abraham Lincoln*, vol. 3: 423.

2. "The New Lincoln Letter," *Montgomery Advertiser*, Nov. 7, 1917, 4.

3. *Atlanta Constitution*, Oct. 19, 1926; *Atlanta Constitution*, July 20, 1927.

4. "Mrs. High Tells of Movement to Erect Stephens Statue," *Atlanta Constitution*, Mar. 13, 1927, 47.

5. *Atlanta Constitution*, July 20, 1927; *Atlanta Constitution*, Jan. 17, 1928, 6.

6. Cameron McWhirter, *Red Summer: The Summer of 1919 and the Awakening of Black America* (New York: Henry Holt, 2011).

7. "Neval Thomas Fights Statue for Stephens," *Pittsburgh Courier*, Apr. 10, 1926, 2.

8. Ibid.

9. "Georgians Make Visit to Coolidge," *Anniston Star* (AL), Dec. 8, 1927, 3.

10. *Atlanta Constitution*, Jan. 17, 1928, 6.

11. Ibid., 6.

12. *Atlanta Constitution*, Feb. 12, 1928, 41; *Atlanta Constitution*, Feb. 19, 1928, 47.

13. "Uncle Sam Has on Hand A New 'Housing Problem,'" *Piute County* (Junction, UT), Jan. 20, 1928, 1.

14. Alexander H. Stephens, "Remarks in regard to the Know-Nothing organization," *Congressional Globe*, vol. 24, Feb. 28, 1855; "Stephens on Tolerance," *Atlanta Constitution*, Aug. 20, 1928, 4.

15. "Stephens on Tolerance," *Atlanta Constitution*, Aug. 20, 1928, 4.

16. Jesse O. Thomas, "Below the Mason-Dixon Line," *Pittsburgh Courier*, Sept. 28, 1935, 18.

17. Ibid.

18. Ibid.

19. Abraham Lincoln to A. H. Stephens, Jan. 19, 1860, in *Some Lincoln Correspondence with Southern Leaders Before the Outbreak of the Civil War: From the Collection of Judd Stewart* (New York: Publisher Unknown, 1909), 6–8; "Four Spurious Lincoln Letters," *Bulletin of the Abraham Lincoln Association* 21 (1) (1930): 8.

20. "Stephens Memorial Park Emerges as Lovely Shrine at Crawfordville," *Atlanta Constitution*, Apr. 15, 1934, 21; "Crawfordville Historic District," Taliaferro County, Georgia, *National Register of Historic Places Registration Form* (Washington, DC: National Park Service, 2006).

21. "History of the Georgia Forestry Commission," Georgia Forestry Commission, http://www.gfc.state.ga.us/about-us/history/index.cfm; Elizabele Vadconcelos, "Georgia State

Parks," *New Georgia Encyclopedia*, https://www.georgiaencyclopedia.org/articles /geography-environment/georgia-state-parks.

22. Mrs. L. W. Greene, "Ms. Horace Holden Gives Report on Preservation of Liberty Hall," *Atlanta Constitution*, Dec. 18, 1932, 29.

23. *Advertiser Journal* (Haleyville, AL), Aug. 24, 1933, 6; *Sumter County Journal* (York, AL), July 6, 1933, 1; *Atlanta Constitution*, May 10, 1934, 21.

24. Ibid.

25. Frank Drake, "Stephens Memorial Park Emerges as Lovely Shrine at Crawfordville," *Atlanta Constitution*, Apr. 15, 1934, 21.

26. Ibid.

27. "Program Is Completed for Bench Dedication," *Atlanta Constitution*, July 17, 1935, 3.

28. Randolph Fort, Associated Press, "Stephens Is Honored at Park Dedication," *Atlanta Constitution*, July 19, 1935, 10.

29. Georgia Baker Interview, Federal Writers' Project, *Slave Narratives: Volume IV Georgia Narratives, Part 1* (Washington, DC: Library of Congress, 1941), 37–57.

30. Horton and Horton, eds., *Slavery and Public History*; Stephanie J. Shaw, "Using the WPA Ex-Slave Narratives to Study the Impact of the Great Depression," *Journal of Southern History* 69 (3 (2003): 623–58; Library of Congress, "The Limitations of the Slave Narrative Collection," https://www.loc.gov/collections/slave-narratives-from-the -federal-writers-project-1936-to-1938/articles-and-essays/introduction-to-the-wpa -slave-narratives/limitations-of-the-slave-narrative-collection/.

31. Quoted in Kathryn Allamong Jacob, *Testament to Union: Civil War Monuments in Washington, D.C.* (Baltimore, MD: Johns Hopkins Univ. Press, 1998), 5.

32. Norman P. Hesseltine, "Was Lee a Traitor?" *Berkshire Eagle* (Pittsfield, MA), May 24, 1935, 14.

33. Ibid.

34. Milton A. Miller, "Pioneers of Oregon Will Meet Feb. 14," *Capital Journal* (Salem, OR), Feb. 8, 1936; Henry H. Simms, "The Controversy Over the Admission of the State of Oregon," *Mississippi Valley Historical Review* 32 (3) (1945): 368; Rudolph Von Abele, *Alexander H. Stephens, a Biography* (New York: Knopf, 1946), 111.

35. Milton A. Miller, "Pioneers of Oregon Will Meet Feb. 14," *Capital Journal* (Salem, OR), Feb. 8, 1936.

36. "Dr. Stone Aids Opposition to History Book," *Kokomo Tribune* (IN), Nov. 3, 1938, 1–2; Fremont Wirth, *The Development of America* (New York: American Book Company, 1937).

37. Ralph McGill, "What is 'The Last Ditch'?" *Atlanta Constitution*, Mar. 24, 1948, 10.

38. Hudson Strode, *Jefferson Davis: Confederate President* (New York: Harcourt Brace, 1955), vol. 2: 24–25.

39. Davis quoted in: Dew, *Apostles of Disunion*, 14–15; James Richardson, ed., *Messages and Papers of the Confederacy* (Nashville: United States Publishing Company, 1905), vol. 1: 67–68.

40. Jefferson Davis, *The Rise and Fall of the Confederate Government* (New York: D. Appleton and Company, 1881), vol. 1: 78.

41. Thomas Rountree, "Hudson Strode: The Legend and the Legacy," *Alabama English* 2 (1990): 17–24; "Alabama's Man of Letters: Remembering Hudson Strode," *AL.com*.

Dec. 25, 2011, https://www.al.com/entertainment/2011/12/alabamas_man_of_letters _rememb.html; "Prof. Hudson Strode Dead at 83," *New York Times*, Sept. 23, 1976.

42. Evidence of Strode's popularity among contemporary Lost Cause believers can be found in the interpretation of Jefferson Davis at the First White House of the Confederacy house museum in Montgomery, Alabama. Strode's works are prominently displayed and have been incorporated into the museum's primary tour and exhibits. Both Strode and the museum present an overly sympathetic view of Jefferson Davis that ignores his central role in the Confederacy's demise. First White House of the Confederacy (website) http://www.firstwhitehouse.org/jefferson-davis-as-seen-by-author-hudson-strode/.

43. D. W. Brogan, "Not Fort Sumter," *Montgomery Advertiser*, May 11, 1960, 4.

44. Ibid.

45. Jones Osborn, "The Editor's Notebook," *Yuma Daily Sun* (AZ), Apr. 3, 1961, 1.

46. Ruth Hard Bonner, "Books in Town," *Brattleboro Reformer* (VT), Jan. 17, 1962, 4.

47. Ibid.

48. David Blight, "*Patriotic Gore* is Not Really Much Like Any Other Book by Anyone," *Slate*, Mar. 22, 2012, https://slate.com/human-interest/2012/03/edmund-wilsons -patriotic-gore-one-of-the-most-important-and-confounding-books-ever-written -about-the-civil-war.html.

49. Edmund Wilson, *Patriotic Gore: Studies in the Literature of the American Civil War* (Oxford: Oxford Univ. Press, 1962); W. Emerson Wilson, "Civil War Myths Exploded," *Morning News* (Wilmington, DE), Apr. 30, 1962, 15.

50. Earle Bowden, "Dixie Pauses Today to Remember an Independent Nation That Almost Was," *Pensacola News*, Apr. 26, 1962, 5.

51. Library of Congress, *The American Civil War: A Centennial Exhibition* (Washington, DC: Library of Congress, 1961). This book was produced as a companion piece to a Library of Congress exhibition.

52. "100 YEARS AGO," *Roanoke Leader* (AL), Mar. 23, 1961, 1.

53. Ibid.

54. Sergeant Dalzell, "Civil War Album: 100 Years Ago Today," *Courier-Journal* (Louisville, KY), Mar. 21, 1961, 7; *Pittsburgh Post Gazette*, Mar. 21, 1961, 27.

55. Norman Shavin, Mike Edwards, Willard Wright, "A Non-Partisan Account of Events of This Week 100 Years Ago," *Atlanta Constitution*, Mar. 26, 1961, 14.

56. "Jules Loh," Obituary, https://obits.lohud.com/obituaries/lohud/obituary.aspx?n=jules -loh&pid=150057810; Paul Rubin, "Jules Loh, One of the Great Reporters Who Ever Lived, Dies at 79," *Phoenix New Times*, Sept. 22, 2010, https://www.phoenixnewtimes .com/news/jules-loh-one-of-the-great-reporters-who-ever-lived-dies-at-79-6650293.

57. Jules Loh, "Nation's Negro Crisis Has Roots Reaching 344 Years into History," *The Post-Crescent* (Appleton, WI), Aug. 4, 1963, 7.

58. "Editor's Note," *Greenville News* (SC), Aug. 4, 1963, 30.

59. Vanessa Siddle Walker, *The Lost Education of Horace Tate* (New York: New Press, 2018), 238–44. Walker's book includes the history of Crawfordville, Georgia's African American community.

60. Associated Press, "Beating of Rights Worker Investigated," *Longview Daily News* (Longview, WA), May 27, 1965, 1.

61. United Press International, "Attempt to Integrate Set in Crawfordville," *Statesville Record and Landmark* (NC), May 28, 1965, 2; United Press International, "Negroes

Plan Protests in State Park," *Santa Maria Times* (CA), May 29, 1965, 2; United Press International, "New Georgia Protests Planned Against Firing of Negro Educators," *The Record* (Hackensack, NJ), May 29, 1965, 2.

62. United Press International, "Crawfordville Jails 12 at Coin Laundry," *Atlanta Constitution*, May 29, 1965, 3.

63. United Press International, "County's Only White School Closed," *Palm Beach Post* (West Palm Beach, FL), Sept. 2, 1965, 30.

64. Donald Lee Grant, *The Way It Was In The South: The Black Experience in Georgia* (Athens: Univ. of Georgia Press, 2001), 524; Associated Press, "42 Georgia Negro Pupils Are Shifted," *Courier-Journal* (Louisville, KY), Nov. 18, 1965, 10; United Press International, "Negroes Taken from Bus Path," *Corvallis Gazette-Times* (OR), Oct. 1, 1965, 2.

8. Heritage and Hate, 1990–2019

1. Blight, *Race and Reunion*, 24, 27.

2. Neo-Confederates are a broad group of contemporary right-of-center actors who have grafted the Lost Cause's dishonest intellectual legacy onto contemporary political movements associated with America's culture wars against liberalism, gay rights, civil equality, gun rights, secularism, and federal tyranny. Many Neo-Confederate groups began decades ago, such as the Sons of Confederate Veterans and United Daughters of the Confederacy. Others, such as the League of the South and Abbeville Institute, began in reaction to America's contemporary culture wars. Although many Neo-Confederates groups have been classified by the Southern Poverty Law Center and American Defamation League as hate groups, some Neo-Confederate organizations lack that designation, but continue to espouse beliefs that give credence to racist ideologies. No Neo-Confederate would consider themselves to be a modern-day "liberal." The overwhelming majority of Neo-Confederates align themselves politically with Republican and Libertarian parties, most notably the recent Tea Party movement, which fused these ideologies into a more coherent lobbying platform. Peter Applebome's *Dixie Rising* warns that "neo-Confederate groups are not a monolith. They range from hard-right and overtly racist politics to a relatively benign mix of monument polishing, history, nostalgia, and agrarian conservativism suspicious of both big government and big business." Peter Applebome, *Dixie Rising: How the South is Shaping American Values, Politics, and Culture* (New York: First Harvest, 1996), 2. Even the "benign" segments of Neo-Confederates that Applebome references are staunchly determined to prevent the removal from public view of monuments that celebrate a shared white heritage that they perceive to be under attack from the left.

3. Ken Burns, Ric Burns, Geoffrey C. Ward, and David G. McCullough, *The Civil War* (videorecording, PBS Home Video), 1997. https://search.ebscohost.com/login.aspx?direct=true&db=cat07161a&AN=aul.1871164&site=eds-live&scope=site.

4. Ken Burns, *The Civil War*; "Civil War Audience 'Discovers' Storyteller-Writer Shelby Foote," *Milwaukee Sentinel*, Sept. 25, 1990.

5. Lars-Erik Nelson, "Hurricane Carol Flagged Insensitivity," *Daily News* (NY), July 26, 1993, 27; John M. Coski, *The Confederate Battle Flag: America's Most Embattled Emblem* (Cambridge, MA: Harvard Univ. Press, 2005), 196–97; "Raw Racism Gets a Black Eyes in the Senate," *National Catholic Register* 29 (36) (1993): 28; Celeste M. Walls,

"You Ain't Just Whistling Dixie: How Carol Moseley-Braun Used Rhetorical Status to Change Jesse Helms' Tune," *Western Journal of Communication* 68 (3) (2004): 343–64.

6. Nelson, "Hurricane Carol flagged insensitivity," *Daily News* (NY), July 26, 1993, 27; Bill Theobald, "Capitol Controversy," *Victoria Advocate* (TX), Sept. 25, 2018.

7. Nelson, "Hurricane Carol flagged insensitivity," *Daily News* (NY), July 26, 1993, 27

8. Library of Congress, "NAACP's Campaign for the Removal of the Confederate Flag," https://www.loc.gov/exhibits/naacp/towards-a-new-century.html; NAACP, "When Heritage Means Hate," https://www.naacp.org/field-resources/confederate-symbols/.

9. Coski, *The Confederate Battle Flag*, chap. 12; Gregory P. Kane, "A Flag That Symbolized the Opposite of the American Ideal," *Baltimore Sun*, July 11, 1994, 43.

10. Robert May, "Why the South Treasured States' Rights," *Journal and Courier* (Lafayette, IN), Sept. 11, 1994, 10. See also James L. Roark, "Slavery Issue at the Heart of Secession," *Atlanta Constitution*, Nov. 15, 1999, 9.

11. Derrick Z. Jackson, "The Confederacy's Favorite Cabinet Nominee," *Chicago Tribune*, Jan. 16, 2001, 15; W. Scott Poole, *Never Surrender: Confederate Memory and Conservatism in the South Carolina Upcountry* (Athens: Univ. of Georgia Press, 2004). Liberals are broadly defined as individuals who support civil equality achieved through the positive use of government power. Many Neo-Confederates believe that liberals and Marxists are indistinguishable because of their shared belief in the prospects for enlightened governance at the federal level. Most American liberals, however, would reject claims that their support for increased government regulation of banking, industry, and the environment, as well as enforceable equal rights legislation, among other issues, would label them as Marxists. American liberals continue to espouse a belief in American free market capitalism, even when they support a more equitable distribution of its benefits.

12. "Sen. Moseley-Braun Needs to Practice Tolerance," *St. Louis Post-Dispatch*, July 31, 1993, 15.

13. Frederic Emile, Baron d'Erlanger, was a German-born Parisian banker who married the daughter of a John Slidell, a wealthy Louisiana merchant, lawyer, and politician. This analysis correctly points out that Erlanger issued bonds in 1863 to support the Confederate government. The accusations that Erlanger's actions were motivated by his Jewish religious beliefs remains unproven and unlikely. Erlanger's father has converted from Judaism to Christianity before his birth. Erlanger's mother was a Christian.

14. Nation of Islam Research Group, "WITH LIBERTY & JUSTICE FOR WHITE: AMERICA'S FLASE FLAG CONTROVERSY," June 25, 2015, https://noirg.org /articles/with-liberty-justice-for-white-americas-false-flag-controversy/; Nation of Islam Research Group, "WHITE JEWS PLAY 'THE RACE CARD' AGAINST BLACK JEWS," July 16, 2018, https://noirg.org/articles/white-jews-play-the-race-card-against -black-jews/; Nation of Islam Research Group, "Lincoln's Tricky Deal: The Emancipation Proclamation," Nov. 22, 2012, https://noirg.org/articles/lincolns-tricky-deal-the -emancipation-proclamation/; Nation of Islam Research Group, "A LOOK AT SLAVERY THEN AND NOW HALF-TRUTHS AND HISTORY: THE DEBATE OVER JEWS AND SLAVERY," Feb. 22, 2012, https://noirg.org/articles/a-look-at-slavery -then-and-now-half-truths-and-history-the-debate-over-jews-and-slavery-2/.

15. Darren Dochuk, *From Bible Belt to Sun Belt: Plain Folk Religion, Grassroots Politics, and the Rise of Evangelical Conservatism* (New York: Norton, 2011).

16. Michael Hill and Thomas Fleming, "The New Dixie Manifesto: States' Rights Shall Rise Again," *Washington Post*, Oct. 29, 1995.

17. Tony Horwitz, *Confederates in the Attic: Dispatches from the Unfinished Civil War* (New York: Vintage, 1998).

18. Southern Poverty Law Center, "League of the South," https://www.splcenter.org /fighting-hate/extremist-files/group/league-south.

19. Michael Hill, "If the South was Right then why are there Rainbow Confederates?" League of the South, https://leagueofthesouth.com/if-the-south-was-right-then-why -are-there-rainbow-confederates/.

20. Ibid.; Michael Hill, "Queer empire," League of the South, June 27, 2015, https:// leagueofthesouth.com/queer-empire/. The LOS also has a problem with the SCV efforts to incorporate Confederate veterans into memorials and commemorations of Union veterans and American veterans in general. The LOS argues that Confederate veterans fought for very different reasons than other soldiers in American history. The LOS views SCV efforts as another example of the corrupting influence that multiculturalism has on Confederate memory.

21. John A. Simpson, *Edith D. Pope and Her Nashville Friends: Guardians of the Lost Cause in the* Confederate Veteran (Knoxville: Univ. of Tennessee Press, 2003); Reda C. Goff, "The *Confederate Veteran Magazine*," *Tennessee Historical Quarterly* 31 (1) (1972): 45–60; Josephine King Evans, "Nostalgia for a Nickel: The '*Confederate Veteran*,'" *Tennessee Historical Quarterly* 48 (4) (1989): 238–44.

22. Heidi Beirich, "The Struggle for the Sons of Confederate Veterans: A Return to White Supremacy in the Early Twenty-First Century?" in *Neo-Confederacy: A Critical Introduction*, ed. Euan Hague, Heidi Beirich, and Edward H. Sebesta (Austin: Univ. of Texas Press, 2008).

23. Ibid.

24. Southern Poverty Law Center, "SCV Once Again Elects Radical National Leaders," *Intelligence Report*, Oct. 19, 2005, https://www.splcenter.org/fighting-hate/intelligence -report/2005/scv-once-again-elects-radical-national-leaders.

25. Southern Poverty Law Center, "Racial Divisions Along the Neo-Confederate Spectrum," Mar. 2, 2017, https://www.splcenter.org/hatewatch/2017/03/02/racial -division-along-neo-confederate-spectrum.

26. Heidi Beirich and Mark Potok, "Sons of Confederate Veterans Back in Extremist Hands, Many Leave Group," Southern Poverty Law Center, July 27, 2005, https://www .splcenter.org/fighting-hate/intelligence-report/2005/sons-confederate-veterans-back -extremist-hands-many-leave-group; Beirich, "The Struggle for the Sons of Confederate Veterans."

27. Tara McPherson, "I'll Take My Stand in Dixie-Net: White Guys, the South, and Cyperspace," in *Race in Cyberspace*, ed. Beth E. Kolko, Lisa Nakamura, and Gilbert B. Rodman (New York: Routledge, 2000). McPherson argues that Neo-Confederates have used the internet to create a renewed sense of place to celebrate their identity. Many media scholars worried that the internet would decrease users' sense of place, but the World Wide Web seems to have aided the expansion of Neo-Confederate identity beyond the geographic confines of the American South.

28. Sons of Confederate Veterans, "Education Committee Papers," https://scv.org /education-committee-papers/.

29. Sons of Confederate Veterans, "Black History Month Black Confederate Heritage," https://scv.org/wp-content/uploads/2019/08/blackhistory-1.pdf; Levin, *Searching for Black Confederates*.

30. Make Dixie Great Again, https://www.makedixiegreatagain.com/.
31. W.F. Jenkins Sons of Confederate Veterans Camp #690, Facebook, https://www.facebook .com/W.F.Jenkins.SCV.Camp690/, Sept. 15, 2019.
32. Ibid.
33. David Goldfield, *Still Fighting the Civil War: The American South and Southern History* (Baton Rouge: Louisiana State Univ. Press, 2013), 5; Applebome, *Dixie Rising*.
34. Diane R. Stepp, "Man, This Dude Sure Covers Dixie," *Atlanta Journal-Constitution*, Mar. 1, 2003, G1.
35. Dixie Outfitters, "Revisiting The 'Cornerstone Speech,'" https://dixieoutfitters.com /2018/08/29/revisiting-the-cornerstone-speech/.
36. "Black Neo-Confederate H. K. Edgerton Discusses Beliefs," *Intelligence Report: Southern Poverty Law Center*, Sept. 15, 2000, accessed June 15, 2019, https://www.splcenter.org /fighting-hate/intelligence-report/2000/black-neo-confederate-hk-edgerton-discusses -beliefs.
37. Dixie Outfitters, "Revisiting The 'Cornerstone Speech,'" https://dixieoutfitters. com/2018/08/29/revisiting-the-cornerstone-speech/.
38. Geoff Fox, "Southern Shopping," *Tampa Tribune*, June 30, 2008, 1–2; Dixie Outfitters, "Our Mission," accessed Sept. 16, 2019, https://dixieoutfitters.com/our-mission/; Applebome, *Dixie Rising*; "Confederate T-shirts Spark Fashion Fight," *Sioux City Journal* (IA), Apr. 7, 2001, 20.
39. Dixie Outfitters, "Revisiting The 'Cornerstone Speech,'" https://dixieoutfitters.com /2018/08/29/revisiting-the-cornerstone-speech/.
40. WallBuilders, "About Us," accessed Sept. 14, 2019, https://wallbuilders.com/.
41. WallBuilders, "Confronting Civil War Revisionism: Why the South Went to War," accessed Sept.14, 2019, https://wallbuilders.com/confronting-civil-war-revisionism-south -went-war/. Although WallBuilders generally supports President Donald J. Trump's policies, the group's name is unrelated to his efforts to build a wall along the Mexico–US Border. According to WallBuilders, its name derives from the Old Testament Book of Nehemiah and the Israelites' efforts to rebuild Jerusalem's walls.
42. RenewAmerica, "About RenewAmerica," http://www.renewamerica.com/about.htm.
43. Jake Jacobs, "Thomas Woods' 1861 "Secessionist-Libertarianism": a defense of a slave-civilization gone with the wind!," http://www.renewamerica.com/columns/jacobs /141205.
44. Young Americans for Liberty, https://yaliberty.org/.
45. CSA II: The New Confederate States of America, "Our Platform," http://www.new csa.com/ourplatform.
46. CSA II: The New Confederate States of America, accessed Sept. 11, 2019, http:// www.newcsa.com/.
47. For a representative example of how journalists have used the Cornerstone Speech in recent times, see DeWayne Wickham, "Debunking Myths of Black History," *USA Today*, Feb. 14, 2005. *USA Today* opinion writer Wickham used the Cornerstone Speech to debunk the widely held notion that the Civil War was fought over states' rights and not slavery. Wickham points out that Stephens "was no loose cannon. He helped draft the Confederate constitution . . . which forbade the Confederate congress from enacting any law 'denying or impairing' the right of whites to own slaves." While Confederates cared about states' rights, the most important of those rights was the right to enslave African Americans forever.

48. Ibram X. Kendi, *Stamped from the Beginning: The Definitive History of Racist Ideas in America* (New York: Nation Books, 2016).

Conclusion

1. LeeAnna Keith, *The Colfax Massacre: The Untold Story of Black Power, White Terror, and the Death of Reconstruction* (New York: Oxford Univ. Press, 2008); "The Colfax Massacre," Christian Recorder, May 1 ,1873.
2. Eric Foner, *Reconstruction: America's Unfinished Revolution, 1863–1877* (New York: Harper & Row, 1988).
3. "Colfax Riot," *The Historical Marker Database*, https://www.hmdb.org/m.asp?m=34602, accessed Jan. 20, 2020.

Bibliography

PRIMARY SOURCES

Archival Collections

Congressional Globe
Congressional Record
Duke University, David M. Rubenstein Rare Book and Manuscript Library
    Alexander H. Stephens Papers
Library of Congress
    Alexander Hamilton Stephens Papers
Manhattan College of the Sacred Heart
    Stephens Papers
University of Georgia, Hargrett Rare Book and Manuscript Library
    Alexander H. Stephens Family Papers

Newspapers and Periodicals

Advertiser Journal (Haleyville, AL)
Alabama Beacon (Greensboro, AL)
Anniston Star (Anniston, AL)
Athens Banner (Athens, GA)
Atlanta Constitution
Atlanta Daily Herald
Atlanta Daily Sun
Atlanta Georgian
Atlanta Journal
Atlanta Journal-Constitution
Baltimore Sun
Bemidji Daily Pioneer (MN)
Berkshire County Eagle (Pittsfield, MS)
Bolivar Bulletin (TN)
Boston Globe
Bradford Reporter (Towanda, PA)
Brattleboro Reformer (Brattleboro, VT)
Bridgeport Evening Farmer (Bridgeport, CT)
Brooklyn Daily Eagle (NY)
Buffalo Daily Republic (NY)
Buffalo Morning Express and Illustrated Buffalo Express
Burlington Free Press (Burlington, VT)
Caledonian Mercury (Edinburgh, Scotland)
Calumet News (MI)

Capital Journal (Salem, OR)
The Catholic Advance (Wichita, KS)
Charlotte Observer
Chicago Tribune
Christian Recorder (Philadelphia, PA)
Cincinnati Enquirer
Citizen (Honesdale, PA)
Citizen (Washington, GA)
Civilian and Telegraph (Cumberland, MD)
Clarksdale Weekly Chronicle (TN)
Columbus Daily Times (Columbus, GA)
Corvallis Gazette-Times (Corvallis, OR)
Courier Journal (Louisville, KY)
Daily Constitutionalist (Augusta, GA)
Daily Morning News (Savannah, GA)
Daily News (NY)
Davenport Weekly Republican (IA)
Delaware Gazette (OH)
Delaware State Journal and Statesman (Wilmington, DE)
Democrat and Chronicle (Rochester, NY)
Democratic Messenger (Eureka, KS)
Des Arc Semi-Weekly Citizen (IA)
Detroit Free Press
Donaldson Chief (Donaldson, LA)
Dunn County News (Menomonie, WI)
Ebensburg Alleghanian (Ebensburgh, PA)
Enquirer (Columbus, GA)
Enterprise and Vermonter (Vergennes, VT)
Evening Capital News
Evening Journal
Evening Messenger (Marshall, TX)
Evening Republican (Meadville, PA)
Farmer and Mechanic (Raleigh, NC)
Fayetteville Weekly Observer (Fayetteville, NC)
Galveston Daily News (TX)
Georgia Messenger (Ft. Hawkins, GA)
Georgia Telegraph (Macon, GA)
Godwin's Weekly: A Thinking Paper for Thinking People (Salt Lake City, UT)
Grand Haven News (MI)
Great Bend Register (KS)
Greensboro Patriot (NC)
Greenville Advocate (AL)
The Guardian (Buchanan County, IA)
Hartford Courant (CT)
The Herald (New Orleans, LA)
Huntsville Weekly Democrat (AL)
The Independent (Gainesville, AL)

Indianapolis News
Intelligence Report (Montgomery, AL)
The Intelligencer (Anderson, SC)
The Inter Ocean (Chicago, IL)
Jasper Weekly Courier (Jasper, IN)
Junction City Weekly Union (Junction City, KS)
Knoxville Journal (TN)
Knoxville Tribune (TN)
Kokomo Tribune (IN)
Lafayette Advertiser (LA)
Lake Charles Commercial (LA)
Las Vegas Optic
Leeds Mercury (Leeds, England)
The Liberator (Boston, MA)
Longview Daily News (WA)
Los Angeles Times
Louisiana Democrat (Alexandria, LA)
Manhattan Express (KS)
Marion Times-Standard (Marion, AL)
Massachusetts Spy (Boston, MA)
McDuffie Progress (Thomson, GA)
Memphis Daily Appeal
Miami News
Middlebury Register (Middlebury, VT)
Middleton Times-Press (NY)
Milan Exchange (TN)
Milledgeville News (GA)
Milledgeville Southern Recorder (GA)
Milwaukee Sentinel
Montgomery Advertiser
Montgomery Monitor (Mt. Vernon, GA)
Morning Post (Raleigh, NC)
Morristown Gazette (TN)
Mound City Republic (KS)
Nashville Globe
Nashville Union and American
National Catholic Register (Denver, CO)
National Era (Washington, DC)
New Bern Daily Progress (New Bern, NC)
New York Age
New York Evening Post
New York Times
News-Herald (Hillsboro, OH)
News-Press (Fort Myers, FL)
Noblesville Ledger (IN)
Norwich Bulletin (CT)
Ottawa Weekly Republic (KS)

Ottumwa Tri-Weekly Courier (IA)
Ouachita Telegraph (LA)
Oxford Banner (NC)
Palm Beach Post (West Palm Beach, FL)
Pemiscot Press (Caruthersville, MO)
Pensacola News
Philadelphia Inquirer
Phoenix New Times
Piedmont Inquirer (AL)
Pittsburgh Courier
Pittsburgh Post Gazette
Piute County (Junction, UT)
Post-Crescent (Appleton, WI)
Prohibitionist and Journal of Reform (Columbus, KS)
Public Press (Northumberland, PA)
Quad-City Times (Davenport, IA)
The Record (Hackensack, NJ)
Richmond Dispatch
Richmond Palladium and Sun-Telegram (IN)
Roanoke Leader (AL)
The Robesonian (Lumberton, NC)
San Francisco Call
Santa Ana Register (CA)
Santa Maria Times (CA)
Savannah Morning News
Savannah Republican
Scranton Republican (PA)
Semi-Weekly Mississippian (Jackson, MS)
Sentinel (Carlisle, PA)
Shenandoah Herald (Woodstock, VA)
Southern Banner (Athens, GA)
Southern Confederacy (Atlanta, GA)
Southern Recorder (Milledgeville, GA)
Spirit of the South (Eufaula, AL)
Stafford County Republican (KS)
St. Landry Democrat (Opelousas, LA)
St. Louis Dispatch
St. Mary's Democrat (St. Mary's: KS)
Statesville Record and Landmark (Statesville, NC)
Staunton Spectator and Vindicator (Staunton, VA)
Sumter County Journal (York, AL)
Telegraph-Bulletin (Monroe, LA)
The Times (London, England)
Times Dispatch (Richmond, VA)
Times-Democrat (New Orleans, LA)
Tribune (NY)
Troy Messenger (AL)

Upson Pilot (Thomaston, GA)
USA Today
Valley Spirit (Chambersburg, PA)
Vermont Journal (Windsor, VT)
Vermont Watchman and State Journal (Montpelier, VT)
Vicksburg Whig
Victoria Advocate (TX)
Washington Herald (DC)
Wayne County Herald (Honesdale, PA)
Weekly Pioneer-Times (Deadwood, SD)
The Wheeling Intelligencer (WV)
Wilmington Daily Herald (NC)
Wilmington Morning Start (NC)

Published Primary Sources

Atlanta Daily Herald. *A pamphlet containing the full history of the celebration of the ninety-ninth anniversary of American independence in Atlanta, GA., July 4th, 1875.* Atlanta: The Herald Stream Book and Job print, 1875.

Avery, I. W. *In Memory: The Last Sickness, Death, and Funeral Obsequies, of Alexander H. Stephens, Governor of Georgia.* Atlanta: U.P. Sisson, 1883.

Chilton, Frank B. *Unveiling and Dedication of Monument to Hood's Texas Brigade on the Capitol Grounds at Austin, Texas, Thursday, October twenty-seven, nineteen hundred and ten, and minutes of the thirty-ninth annual reunion of Hood's Texas brigade association held in Senate chamber at Austin, Texas, October twenty-six and twenty-seven, nineteen hundred and ten, together with a short monument and brigade association history and Confederate scrap book.* Houston: F.B. Chilton, 1911.

Confederate Veteran Magazine

Davis, Garrett. *Hon. Garrett Davis, of Kentucky. African slavery the cornerstone of the Southern confederacy. Speech by Hon. Alex. H. Stephens, of Georgia.* New York: E. D. Barker, 1862.

Grimke, Francis J. *Equality of rights for all citizens, black and white, alike. A discourse delivered in the Fifteenth street Presbyterian church, Washington, D.C., Sunday, March 7th, 1909, by the pastor, Rev. Francis J. Grimke.* Washington, DC: 1909. McCaine, Alexander. *Slavery defended from Scripture, against the attacks of the abolitionists: in a speech delivered before the General Conference of the Methodist Protestant Church, in Baltimore, 1842.* Baltimore: W. Wooddy, 1842.

McDuffie, George. "The Natural Slavery of the Negro." *Laws of South Carolina, 1836, Journal of the General Assembly of the State of South Carolina for the year 1835.*

Moore, Frank, ed. *Rebellion Record, Supplement, First Volume.* New York: G.P. Putnam & Henry Holt, 1864.

Richardson, James D. ed., *Messages and Papers of the Confederacy,* Volume 1. Nashville: United States Publishing Company, 1905.

Scott, William H. *The history of the Rogers case: from July 22 to Sept. 4, with the speech of Rev. W.H. Scott before the governor of Massachusetts and the attorney-general, and Rev. W.H. Scott's address to the president of the U.S. on Feb. 26, 1902.* Massachusetts: Publisher Not Identified, 1902.

Spratt, Leonidas W. *The Philosophy of Secession; A Southern View, Presented in a Letter*

Addressed to the Hon. Mr. Perkins of Louisiana, in Criticism on the Provisional Constitution Adopted by the Southern Congress at Montgomery, Alabama. Charleston: 1861.

Stephens, Alexander H. *The Assertions of a Secessionist. From the speech of A.H. Stephens, of Georgia, November 14, 1860.* New York: Loyal Publication Society, 1864.

Websites and Social Media

AL.com
CSA II: The New Confederate States of America.com
DixieOutfitters.com
Facebook.com
Instagram.com
League of the South.com
Ludwig von Mises Institute.com
Make Dixie Great Again.com
Nation of Islam Research Group.com
Reddit.com
Renew America.com
Sons of Confederate Veterans.com
Southern Poverty Law Center.com
Thomas Woods Radio.com
Wallbuilders.com

Contemporary Commentaries and Histories

Abbott, John Stevens Cabot. *The History of the Civil War in America*, vol. 1. New York: Henry Bill, 1863.

Avary, Myrta Lockett. *Recollections of Alexander H. Stephens.* Atlanta: Sunny South Publishing Company, 1910.

Beck, Nemias Bramlette. *Alexander H. Stephens: Orator.* 1937.

Bradford, Gamaliel. *Confederate Portraits.* Boston: Houghton Mifflin Company, 1914.

Bradford, Gamaliel. *Lee: The American.* Rev. ed., 1927. Reprint, Mineola: Dover Publications, 2004.

Byrd, Harvey Leonidas. *Oglethorpe Medical and Surgical Journal.* Savannah: Power Press of J. M. Cooper, 1861.

Campbell, John. *Negro-mania: being an examination of the falsely assumed equality of the various races of men; demonstrated by the investigations of Champollion, Wilkinson [and others] together with a concluding chapter, presenting a comparative statement of the condition of the Negroes in the West Indies before and since emancipation.* Philadelphia: Campbell & Power, 1851.

Chesterton, Cecil. *A History of the United States.* New York: George H. Doran Company, 1919.

Cleveland, Henry. *Alexander H. Stephens in Public and Private.* Philadelphia: National Publishing Company, 1866.

Constitutionalist. *A review of the first volume of Alexander H. Stephens's "War between the states."* Philadelphia: J. B. Lippincott & Company, 1872.

Davis, Jefferson. *The Rise and Fall of the Confederate Government*, vol. 1. New York: D. Appleton and Company, 1881.

Du Bois, W. E. B. *Black Reconstruction in America, 1860-1880.* New York: Free Press, 1998.

———. *Suppression of the Slave Trade.* New York: Oxford Univ. Press, 1896.

Fitzhugh, George. *Cannibals all! Or, Slaves without masters.* Richmond: A. Morris, 1857.

———. *Sociology of the South: or, The failure of free society.* Richmond: A. Morris, 1854.

Gobineau, Arthur. *Essai sur L'inégalité races humaines.* Paris: Firmin Didot Freres, 1853.

Graves, J. T., Clark Howell, and Walter Williams, eds. *Eloquent Sons of the South: A Handbook of Southern Oratory.* Vol. 2. Boston: Chapple Publishing Company, 1909.

Greeley, Horace. *The American Conflict: A History of the Great Rebellion in the United States of America, 1860–65.* Hartford: O.D. Case & Co., 1864.

Holcombe, James Philemon. *Is Slavery Consistent with Natural Law?* Richmond: Virginia State Agricultural Society, 1858.

Johnson, Edward A. *A School History of the Negro Race in America from 1619 to 1890.* Raleigh, VA: Edwards and Broughton Printers, 1890.

Johnston, Alexander, ed. *Masterpieces of American Eloquence: Representative Orations Illustrating American Political History.* New York: G. P. Putnam, 1890.

Johnston, Richard Malcom, and William Hand Browne. *Life of Alexander H. Stephens.* Philadelphia: J. B. Lippincott & Company, 1878.

Lossing, Benson John. *Harper's Popular Cyclopedia of United States History*, vol. 2. New York: Harper and Brothers, 1898–1899.

Norton, Frank H. *The Life of Alexander H. Stephens.* New York: John B. Alden, 1883.

Pendleton, Louis. *Alexander H. Stephens.* Philadelphia: G. W. Jacobs and Company, 1908.

Pollard, E. A. *Southern History of the War.* New York: C. B. Richardson, 1866.

———. *The Lost Cause: A New Southern History of the War of the Confederates.* New York: E. B. Treat & Company, 1866.

Priest, Josiah. *Slavery, As It Relates to the Negro, or African Race.* Albany: C. Van Bethuysen & Co., 1843.

Rhodes, James Ford. *History of the United States from the Compromise of 1850.* New York: Macmillan & Co., 1928.

———. *Lectures on the American Civil War, delivered before the University of Oxford in Easter and Trinity terms 1912.* New York: Macmillan Company, 1913.

Sanderson, Edgar, et al. *Six Thousand Years of History.* New York: E. R. DuMont, 1899.

Stephens, Alexander H. *The Assertions of a Secessionist.* New York: Royal Publication Society, 1864.

———. *A Constitutional View of the Late War between the States.* 2 vols. Philadelphia: National Publishing Company, 1868.

———. *Recollections of Alexander H. Stephens: His Diary Kept When a Prisoner at Fort Warren, Boston Harbour, 1865.* Reprint, New York: Da Capo Press, 1971.

———. *The reviewers reviewed: a supplement to the "War between the states," etc., with an appendix in review of "reconstruction," so called.* New York: D. Appleton and Company, 1872.

Temple, Oliver Perry. *East Tennessee and the Civil War.* Cincinnati: The R. Clarke Company, 1899.

Toombs, Robert Augustus. *The Correspondence of Robert Toombs, Alexander Stephens, and Howell Cobb.* Washington, DC: American Historical Association, 1913.

Trent, William P. *Southern Statesmen of the Old Regime; Washington, Jefferson, Randolph, Calhoun, Stephens, Toombs, and Jefferson Davis*. New York: T. Y. Crowell and Company, 1897.

SECONDARY SOURCES
Articles
Adams, Charles Francis. "The Modern Conception of History." *Wisconsin Alumni Magazine* 2 (1901).

Appleby, Joyce. "Reconciliation and the Northern Novelist, 1865–80." *Civil War History* 10 (1964): 117–29.

Associated Press. "42 Georgia Negro Pupils Are Shifted." *Courier-Journal* (Louisville, KY), Nov. 18, 1965.

———. "Beating of Rights Worker Investigated." *Longview Daily News* (Longview, WA), May 27, 1965.

Blight, David. "*Patriotic Gore* is Not Really Much Like Any Other Book by Anyone." *Slate*, Mar. 22, 2012, https://slate.com/human-interest/2012/03/edmund-wilsons-patriotic -gore-one-of-the-most-important-and-confounding-books-ever-written-about-the-civil -war.html.

Blumenthal, Henry. "Confederate Diplomacy: Popular Notions and International Realities." *Journal of Southern History* 32 (2) (1996): 151–71.

Bonner, Ruth Hard. "Books in Town." *Brattleboro Reformer* (VT), Jan. 17, 1962.

Bowden, Earle. "Dixie Pauses Today to Remember an Independent Nation That Almost Was." *Pensacola News*, Apr. 26 1962.

Brockwell, Gillian. "How Statues of Robert E. Lee and Other Confederates Got into the U.S. Capitol." *Washington Post*, Aug. 17 2017.

Brogan, D. W. "Not Fort Sumter." *Montgomery Advertiser*, May 11, 1960.

Brown, David. "Attacking Slavery from Within: The Making of the Impending Crisis of the South." *Journal of Southern History* 70 (3) (2004): 541-76.

Bruce, John E. "The Negro's Rights Under the Law." *New York Times*, June 29, 1902, 7.

Campbell, Allen. "The New Confederacy." *Massachusetts Spy* (Boston), Apr. 3 1861.

Carney, Court. "The Contested Image of Nathan Bedford Forrest." *Journal of Southern History* 67 (3) (2001): 601–30.

Centner, Christopher M. "Neo-Confederates at the Gate: The Rehabilitation of the Confederate Cause and the Distortion of History." *Skeptic* 9 (3) (2002): 60–66.

Dalzell, Sergeant. "Civil War Album: 100 Years Ago Today." *Courier-Journal* (Louisville, KY), Mar. 21, 1961.

Davis, David Brion. "The Enduring Legacy of the South's Civil War Victory." *New York Times* Aug. 26, 2001.

Drake, Frank. "Stephens Memorial Park Emerges as Lovely Shrine at Crawfordville." *Atlanta Constitution*, Apr. 15, 1934.

Edwards, E. J. "Alexander H. Stephens in Closing Years of His Life." *Post-Crescent* (Appleton, WI), June 24, 1911.

———. "Alexander H. Stephens in His Closing Years." *Anaconda Standard* (Anaconda, MT), Feb. 22, 1911.

———. "Alexander H. Stephens' Remarkable Vitality in His Closing Years." *Pittsburgh Post-Gazette*, Feb. 22, 1911.

Edwards, Laura. "Southern History as U.S. History." *Journal of Southern History* 75 (3) (2009): 533–64.

Essex, Jamey S. "'The Real South Starts Here'—Whiteness, the Confederacy, and Commodification at Stone Mountain." *Southeastern Geographer* 42 (2) (2002): 211–27.

Evans, Josephine King. "Nostalgia for a Nickel: The "Confederate Veteran."" *Tennessee Historical Quarterly* 48 (4) (1989): 238–44.

Fleming, William H. "Slavery and Race Problem in the South." *New York Age*, Oct. 25, 1906, 5.

Fong, Edmund. "Reconstructing the 'Problem' of Race." *Political Research Quarterly* 61 (4) (2008): 660–70.

Forest, Benjamin, and Juliet Johnson. "Confederate Monuments and the Problem of Forgetting." *Cultural Geographies* 26 (1) (2019): 127–31.

Fort, Randolph. "Stephens Is Honored at Park Dedication." *Atlanta Constitution*, July 19, 1935.

Forts, Franklin. "Living with Confederate Symbols." *Southern Cultures* 8 (2002): 60–75.

Fox, Geoff. "Southern Shopping." *Tampa Tribune*, June 30, 2008.

Franklin, John Hope. "A Century of Civil War Observance." *Journal of Negro History* 47 (2) (1962): 97–107.

Ghaffari, Grace Poon. "Myths America Lives By: White Supremacy and the Stories That Give Us Meaning." *Diverse: Issues in Higher Education* 36 (8) (2019): 24–25.

Goff, Reda C. "The *Confederate Veteran Magazine*." *Tennessee Historical Quarterly* 31 (1) (1972): 45–60.

Gordon-Reed, Annette. "America's Original Sin: Slavery and the Legacy of White Supremacy." *Foreign Affairs* 97 (1) (2018): 2–7.

Graves, John Temple. "Editorial by Hon. John Temple Graves, Editor of the New York American." *Atlanta Georgian*, June 14, 1914.

Greene, Mrs. L. W. "Ms. Horace Holden Gives Report on Preservation of Liberty Hall." *Atlanta Constitution*, Dec. 18, 1932.

Gulley, H. E. "Women and the Lost Cause: Preserving a Confederate Identity in the American Deep South." *Journal of Historical Geography* 19 (2) (1993): 125–41.

Harris, William C. "The Hampton Roads Peace Conference: A Final Test of Lincoln's Presidential Leadership." *Journal of the Abraham Lincoln Association* 21 (2000): 31-61.

Hesseltine, Norman P. "Was Lee a Traitor?" *Berkshire Eagle* (Pittsfield, MA), May 24, 1935.

Hill, Michael. "If the South was Right Then Why Are there Rainbow Confederates?" *League of the South*, Aug. 13, 2014. Accessed at https://leagueofthesouth.com/if-the-south-was -right-then-why-are-there-rainbow-confederates/

———. "Name Changes: Principles Remain the Same." *Southern Patriot*, 4 (4) (1997): 25–26.

———. "The Battlecry of Rainbow Confederates." *League of the South*, July 4, 2015. Accessed at https://leagueofthesouth.com/the-battlecry-of-rainbow-confederates/

Hill, Michael, and Thomas Fleming. "New Dixie Manifesto: States' Rights Will Rise Again." *Washington Post*, Oct. 29 1995, C03.

Hoelscher, Steven. "Making Place, Making Race: Performances of Whiteness in the Jim Crow South." *Annals of the Association of American Geographers* 93 (3) (2003): 657–86.

Howell, Clark. "An Echo from the Past!" *Atlanta Constitution*, Apr. 2 1905, 4.

Inwood, Joshua F. J. "Geographies of Race in the American South: The Continuing Legacies of Jim Crow Segregation." *Southeastern Geographer* 51 (4) (2011): 564–77.

Jackson, Derrick Z. "The Confederacy's Favorite Cabinet Nominee." *Chicago Tribune*, Jan. 16, 2001.

Jones, Robert R. "James L. Kemper and the Virginia Redeemers Face the Race Question: A Reconsideration." *Journal of Southern History* 38 (3) (1972): 393–414.

Kane, Gregory P. "A Flag That Symbolized the Opposite of the American Ideal." *Baltimore Sun*, July 11, 1994, 43.

King, Desmond, and Stephen Tuck. "De-Centering the South: America's Nationwide White Supremacist Order after Reconstruction." *Past & Present* 194 (2007), 213–53.

Ledbetter, Billy D. "White Texans' Attitudes toward the Political Equality of Negroes, 1865–1870." *Phylon* 40 (3) (1979): 253–63.

Loh, Jules. "Nation's Negro Crisis Has Roots Reaching 344 Years into History." *Post-Crescent* (Appleton, WI), Aug. 4 1963.

Lurie, Charles N. "The State of the Union Half a Century Ago." *Evening Times*, Feb. 25, 1911.

Mathews, James W. "Dr. Gamaliel Bradford (1795–1839), Early Abolitionist." *Historical Journal of Massachusetts* 19 (1) (1991): 1–12.

McElroy, John. "The Southern Confederacy." *National Tribune* (Washington, DC), Feb. 21, 1907, 2.

McGill, Ralph. "What is 'The Last Ditch'?" *Atlanta Constitution*, Mar. 24, 1948.

Miller, Milton A. "Pioneers of Oregon Will Meet Feb. 14." *Capital Journal* (Salem, OR), Feb. 8, 1936.

Nelson, Lars-Erik. "Hurricane Carol Flagged Insensitivity." *Daily News* (NY), July 26, 1993.

New York Times. "Important from Montgomery: Speech of Hon. Jefferson Davis. Declaration of the Policy of the Southern Confederacy," *New York Times*, Feb. 18, 1861, 8.

Osborn, Jones. "The Editor's Notebook." *Yuma Daily Sun* (AZ), Apr. 3, 1961.

Phillips, Ulrich B. "The Central Theme of Southern History." *American Historical Review* 34 (1) (1928), 30–43.

Radford, J. P. "Identity and Tradition in the Post-Civil War South." *Journal of Historical Geography* 18 (1) (1992): 91–103.

Roark, James L. "Slavery Issue at the Heart of Secession." *Atlanta Constitution*, Nov. 15, 1999.

Rountree, Thomas. "Hudson Strode: The Legend and the Legacy." *Alabama English* 2 (1990): 17–24.

Rubin, Paul. "Jules Loh, One of the Great Reporters Who Ever Lived, Dies at 79." *Phoenix New Times*, Sept. 22, 2010.

Savoyard. "Alexander H. Stephens." *Fayetteville Weekly Observer* (NC), Sept. 21, 1905, 1.

Serwer, Adam. "The Myth of the Kindly General Lee." *The Atlantic*, Jun. 4, 2017 (accessed Jun. 5, 2020), https://www.theatlantic.com/politics/archive/2017/06/the-myth-of-the-kindly-general-lee/529038/.

Shavin, Norman, Mike Edwards, Willard Wright. "A Non-Partisan Account of Events of This Week 100 Years Ago." *Miami News*, Mar. 26, 1961.

Shaw, Stephanie J. "Using the WPA Ex-Slave Narratives to Study the Impact of the Great Depression." *Journal of Southern History* 69 (3) (2003): 623–58.

Simms, Henry H. "The Controversy Over the Admission of the State of Oregon." *Mississippi Valley Historical Review* 32 (3) (1945): 355–74.

Theobald, Bill. "Capitol Controversy." *Victoria Advocate* (TX), Sept. 25 2018.

Thomas, Jesse O. "Below the Mason-Dixon Line." *Pittsburgh Courier*, Sept. 28, 1935.

Trent, William P. "Tendencies of Higher Life in the South." *Atlantic Monthly* 79 (June 1897): 766–78.

United Press International. "Attempt to Integrate Set in Crawfordville," *Statesville Record and Landmark* (Statesville, NC), May 28, 1965.

———. "County's Only White School Closed." *Palm Beach Post* (West Palm Beach, FL), Sept. 2, 1965.

———. "Crawfordville Jails 12 at Coin Laundry." *Atlanta Constitution*, May 29, 1965.

———. "Negroes Plan Protests in State Park." *Santa Maria Times* (Santa Maria, CA), May 29, 1965.

———. "Negroes Taken from Bus Path." *Corvallis Gazette-Times* (Corvallis, OR), Oct. 1, 1965.

———. "New Georgia Protests Planned against Firing of Negro Educators." *The Record* (Hackensack, NJ), May 29, 1965.

Walls, Celeste M. "You Ain't Just Whistling Dixie: How Carol Moseley-Braun Used Rhetorical Status to Change Jesse Helms' Tune." *Western Journal of Communication* 68 (3) (2004): 343–64.

Webster, Gerald R., and Jonathan I. Leib. "Whose South Is It Anyway? Race and the Confederate Battle Flag in South Carolina." *Political Geography* 20 (3) (2001): 271–99.

Wickham, DeWayne. "Debunking myths of black history." *USA Today*, Feb. 14, 2005.

Will, George F. "Save Your Confederate Money, Boys." *Washington Post*, Dec. 28, 1995, 23.

Wilson, W. Emerson. "Civil War Myths Exploded." *Morning News* (Wilmington, DE), Apr. 30, 1962, 15.

Winberry, John J. "'Lest We Forget': The Confederate Monument and the Southern Townscape." *Southeastern Geographer* 23 (2) (1983): 107–21.

Woods, Michael E. "What Twenty-First Century Historians Have Said about the Causes of Disunion: A Civil War Sesquicentennial Review of the Recent Literature." *Journal of American History* 99 (2) (2012): 415–39.

Zanden, James W. Vander. "The Ideology of White Supremacy." *Journal of the History of Ideas* 20 (3) (1959): 385–402.

Books

Adams, Ephraim Douglass. *Great Britain and the American Civil War*. New York: Russell & Russell, 1958.

Adams, Michael C. C. *Our Masters the Rebels*. Cambridge: Harvard Univ. Press, 1978.

Applebome, Peter. *Dixie Rising: How the South Is Shaping American Values, Politics, and Culture*. New York: Times Books, 1996.

Ashdown, Paul. *The Myth of Nathan Bedford Forrest*. New York: Rowman & Littlefield, 2006.

Ayers, Edward L. *What Caused the Civil War? Reflections on the South and Southern History*. New York: Norton, 2005.

Bailey, Fred Arthur. *Class and Tennessee's Confederate Generation*. Chapel Hill: Univ. of North Carolina Press, 1987.

Bartley, Numan V. *The Creation of Modern Georgia*, second edition. Athens: Univ. of Georgia Press, 1990.

Basler, Roy P., ed. *The Collected Works of Abraham Lincoln*, Volume IV. New Brunswick: Rutgers Univ. Press, 1953.

Beringer, Richard E., Herman Hattaway, Archer Jones, and William N. Still, Jr. *Why the South Lost the Civil War.* Athens: Univ. of Georgia Press, 1986.

Blair, William A. *Cities of the Dead: Contesting the Memory of the Civil War in the South, 1865–1914.* Chapel Hill: Univ. of North Carolina Press, 2004.

Blight, David W. *Beyond the Battlefield: Race, Memory, and the American Civil War.* Amherst: Univ. of Massachusetts Press, 2002.

———. *Race and Reunion: The Civil War in American Memory.* Cambridge: Harvard Univ. Press, 2001.

Bodnar, John. *Remaking America: Public Memory, Commemoration, and Patriotism in the Twentieth Century.* Princeton: Princeton Univ. Press, 1992.

Bonner, Robert E. *Mastering America: Southern Slaveholders and the Crisis of American Nationhood.* New York: Cambridge Univ. Press, 2009.

Braden, Waldo W., ed. *Oratory in the New South.* Baton Rouge: Louisiana State Univ. Press, 1979.

Brundage, W. Fitzhugh. *The Southern Past: A Clash of Race and Memory.* Cambridge, MA: Harvard Univ. Press, 2005.

Buck, Paul H. *The Road to Disunion: 1865–1900.* Boston: Little, Brown, 1937.

Burton, Orville Vernon. *In My Father's House Are Many Mansions: Family and Community in Edgefield, South Carolina.* Chapel Hill: Univ. of North Carolina Press, 1985.

Carey, Anthony. *Parties, Slavery, and the Union in Antebellum Georgia.* Athens: Univ. of Georgia Press, 1997.

Cash, W. J. *The Mind of the South.* New York: Knopf, 1941.

Cashin, Edward J. *A Confederate Legend: Sergeant Berry Benson in War and Peace.* Macon, GA: Mercer Univ. Press, 2008.

Chadwick, Bruce. *The Reel Civil War.* New York: Knopf, 2001.

Clark, Thomas D. *The Rural Press and the New South.* Baton Rouge: Louisiana State Univ. Press, 1948.

———. *The Southern Country Editor.* Indianapolis: Bobbs-Merrill, 1948.

Clayton, Bruce. *The Savage Ideal: Intolerance and Intellectual Leadership in the South, 1890–1914.* Baltimore, MD: Johns Hopkins Univ. Press, 1972.

Cloyd, Benjamin G. *Haunted by Atrocity: Civil War Prisons in American Memory.* Baton Rouge: Louisiana State Univ. Press, 2010.

Cobb, James C. *Away Down South: A History of Southern Identity.* Oxford: Oxford Univ. Press, 2005.

———. *Redefining Southern Culture: Mind and Identity in the Modern South.* Athens: Univ. of Georgia Press, 1999.

Cole, Donald B. *A Jackson Man: Amos Kendall and the Rise of American Democracy.* Baton Rouge: Louisiana State Univ. Press, 2004.

Coleman, Kenneth, ed. *A History of Georgia.* Athens: Univ. of Georgia Press, 1991.

Commager, Henry Steele. *Fifty Basic Civil War Documents.* Malabar: R.E. Krieger Publishing Company, 1982.

Connelly, Thomas L. *God and General Longstreet: The Lost Cause and the Southern Mind.* Baton Rouge: Louisiana State Univ. Press, 1995.

———. *The Marble Man: Robert E. Lee and His Image in American Society.* New York: Knopf, 1977.

Conroy, James. *Our One Common Country: Abraham Lincoln and the Hampton Roads Peace Conference of 1865.* Guilford, CT: Lyons Press, 2014.

Cook, Robert J. *Civil War Memories: Contesting the Past in the United States since 1865*. Baltimore, MD: Johns Hopkins Univ. Press, 2017.

———. *Troubled Commemoration: The American Civil War Centennial, 1961–1965*. Baton Rouge: Louisiana State Univ. Press, 2007.

Cooper, William J. *Jefferson Davis and the Civil War Era*. Baton Rouge: Louisiana State Univ. Press, 2008.

———. *The South and the Politics of Slavery, 1828–1856*. Baton Rouge: Louisiana State Univ. Press, 2003.

Coski, John M. *The Confederate Battle Flag: America's Most Embattled Emblem*. Cambridge: Harvard Univ. Press, 2005.

Cox, Karen L. *Dixie's Daughters: The United Daughters of the Confederacy and the Preservation of Confederate Culture*. Gainesville: Univ. Press of Florida, 2003.

Cullen, Jim. *The Civil War in Popular Culture*. Washington, DC: Smithsonian Institution Press, 1995.

Daly, John Patrick. *When Slavery Was Called Freedom: Evangelicalism, Proslavery, and the Causes of the Civil War*. Lexington: Univ. Press of Kentucky, 2002.

Davis, Ren, and Helen Davis. *Atlanta's Oakland Cemetery: An Illustrated History and Guide*. Athens: Univ. of Georgia Press, 2012.

Davis, William C. *The Cause Lost: Myths and Realities of the Confederacy*. Lawrence: Univ. Press of Kansas, 1996.

———. *The Union that Shaped the Confederacy: Robert Toombs and Alexander H. Stephens*. Lawrence: Univ. Press of Kansas, 2001.

Dew, Charles. *Apostles of Disunion: Southern Secession Commissioners and the Causes of the Civil War*. Charlottesville: Univ. Press of Virginia, 2001.

Dochuk, Darren. *From Bible Belt to Sun Belt: Plain Folk Religion, Grassroots Politics, and the Rise of Evangelical Conservatism*. New York: Norton, 2011.

Domby, Adam H. *The False Cause: Fraud, Fabrication, and White Supremacy in Confederate Memory*. Charlottesville: Univ. of Virginia Press, 2020.

Doyle, Don H. *The Cause of All Nations: An International History of the American Civil War*. New York: Basic Books, 2015.

Durden, Robert F. *The Gray and the Black*. Baton Rouge: Louisiana State Univ. Press, 1972.

Egerton, John. *The Americanization of Dixie: The Suburbanization of America*. New York: Harper's Magazine Press, 1974.

Fahs, Alice. *The Imagined Civil War: Popular Literature of the North and South, 1861–1865*. Chapel Hill: Univ. of North Carolina Press, 2001.

Fahs, Alice, and Joan Waugh, eds. *The Memory of the Civil War in American Culture*. Chapel Hill: Univ. of North Carolina Press, 2004.

Federal Writers' Project. *Slave Narratives: Volume IV Georgia Narratives, Part 1*. Washington, D.C.: Library of Congress, 1941.

Fields, Barbara. *Slavery and Freedom on the Middle Ground: Maryland during the Nineteenth Century*. New Haven: Yale Univ. Press, 1985.

Flint, Colin, ed. *Spaces of Hate: Geographies of Discrimination and Intolerance in the U.S.A.* New York: Routledge, 2004.

Flynt, J. Wayne. *Poor but Proud: Alabama's Poor Whites*. Tuscaloosa: Univ. of Alabama Press, 1989.

Foner, Eric. *Reconstruction: America's Unfinished Revolution, 1863–1877*. New York: Harper and Row, 1988.

———. *The Story of American Freedom*. New York: Norton, 1998.

Ford, Lacy K. *Deliver Us from Evil: The Slavery Question in the Old South*. Oxford: Oxford Univ. Press, 2009.

Forret, Jeff. *Race Relations at the Margins: Slaves and Poor Whites in the Antebellum Country-side*. (Baton Rouge: Louisiana State Univ. Press, 2006.

Foster, Gaines. *Ghosts of the Confederacy: Defeat, the Lost Cause, and the Emergence of the New South*. New York: Oxford Univ. Press, 1987.

Fox-Genovese, Elizabeth and Eugene Genovese. *Slavery in White and Black: Class and Race in the Southern Slaveholders' New World Order*. Cambridge: Cambridge Univ. press, 2008.

Franklin, John Hope. *The Militant South, 1800–1861*. Champaign: Univ. of Illinois Press, 2002.

Fredrickson, George M. *The Arrogance of Race: Historical Perspectives on Slavery, Racism, and Social Inequality*. Middletown, CT: Wesleyan Univ. Press, 1988.

———. *The Black Image in the White Mind: The Debate on Afro-American Character and Destiny, 1817–1914*. New York: Harper & Row, 1971.

Freehling, William W. and Craig M. Simpson, eds. *Secession Debated: Georgia's Showdown in 1860*. New York: Oxford Univ. Press, 1992.

Freeman, Douglas Southall. *The South to Posterity: An Introduction to the Writing of Confederate History*. New York: Charles Scribner's Sons, 1939.

Gallagher, Gary W., and Alan T. Nolan, eds. *The Myth of the Lost Cause and Civil War History*. Bloomington: Indiana Univ. Press, 2000.

Gates, Henry Louis, Jr. *Stony the Road: Reconstruction, White Supremacy, and the Rise of Jim Crow*. New York: Penguin, 2019.

Gerbner, Katharine. *Christian Slavery: Conversion and Race in the Protestant Atlantic World*. Philadelphia: Univ. of Pennsylvania Press, 2019.

Gillespie, Michelle K., and Randal L. Hall. *Thomas Dixon Jr. and the Birth of Modern America*. Baton Rouge: Louisiana State Univ. Press, 2009.

Gobel, David, and Daves Rossell. *Commemoration in America: Essays on Monuments, Memorialization, and Memory*. Charlottesville: Univ. of Virginia Press, 2013.

Goldfield, David D. *Still Fighting the Civil War*. Baton Rouge: Louisiana State Univ. Press, 2002.

Gorman, James L., Jeff W. Childers, and Mark W. Hamilton, eds. *Slavery's Long Shadow: Race and Reconciliation in American Christianity*. Grand Rapids, MI: Eerdmans Publishing Company, 2019.

Grant, Donald L. *The Way It Was in the South: The Black Experience in Georgia*. Athens: Univ. of Georgia Press, 2001.

Hague, Euan, Heidi Berich, and Edward H. Sebesta. *Neo-Confederacy: A Critical Introduction*. Austin: Univ. of Texas Press, 2008.

Hahn, Steven. *The Roots of Southern Populism: Yeoman Farmers and the Transformation of the Georgia Upcountry, 1850–1890*. New York: Oxford Univ. Press, 1983.

Halbwachs, Maurice. *On Collective Memory*. Chicago: Univ. of Chicago Press, 1992.

Harris, J. William. *Society and Culture in the Slave South*. London: Routledge, 1992.

Harris, M. Keith. *Across the Bloody Chasm: The Culture of Commemoration among Civil War Veterans*. Baton Rouge: Louisiana State Univ. Press, 2014.

Haynes, Stephen R. *Noah's Curse: The Biblical Justification of American Slavery*. New York: Oxford Univ. Press, 2002.

Hébert, Keith S. *The Long Civil War in the North Georgia Mountains: Confederate Nationalism, Sectionalism, and White Supremacy in Bartow County, Georgia*. Knoxville: Univ. of Tennessee Press, 2017.

Hettle, Wallace. *Inventing Stonewall Jackson: A Civil War Hero in History and Memory*. Baton Rouge: Louisiana State Univ. Press, 2011.

Hilberg, Raul. *Perpetrators, Victims, Bystanders: The Jewish Catastrophe, 1933–1945*. New York: Aaron Asher Books, 1992.

Hill, Samuel S., Jr., et al. *Religion and the Solid South*. Nashville, TN: Abingdon Press, 1972.

Hobson, Fred. *Tell About the South: The Southern Rage to Explain*. Baton Rouge: Louisiana State Univ. Press, 1983.

Holman, C. Hugh. *The Immoderate Past: The Southern Writer and History*. Athens: Univ. of Georgia Press, 1977.

Holt, Michael F. *By One Vote: The Disputed Presidential Election of 1876*. Lawrence: Univ. Press of Kansas, 2008.

Horton, James Oliver, and Lois E. Horton, eds. *Slavery and Public History: The Tough Stuff of American History*. New York: New Press, 2006.

Horwitz, Tony. *Confederates in the Attic: Dispatches from the Unfinished Civil War*. New York: Vintage, 1998.

Jacob, Kathryn Allamong. *Testament to Union: Civil War Monuments in Washington, D.C.* Baltimore, MD: Johns Hopkins Univ. Press, 1998.

Janney, Caroline E. *Remembering the Civil War: Reunion and the Limits of Reconciliation*. Chapel Hill: Univ. of North Carolina Press, 2013.

Johnson, Michael. *Toward a Patriarchal Republic: The Secession of Georgia*. Baton Rouge: Louisiana State Univ. Press, 1977.

Kammen, Michael. *Mystic Chords of Memory: The Transformation of Tradition in American Culture*. New York: Knopf, 1992.

Karp, Matthew. *This Vast Empire: Slaveholders at the Helm of American Foreign Policy*. Cambridge: Harvard Univ. Press, 2016.

Kendi, Ibram X. *Stamped from the Beginning: The Definitive History of Racist Ideas in America*. New York: Nation Books, 2016.

Kolko, Beth E., Lisa Nakamura, and Gilbert B. Rodman. *Race in Cyberspace*. New York: Routledge, 2000.

League of the South. *The Grey Book: Blueprint for Southern Independence*. College Station, TX: Traveller Press, 2004.

Levin, Kevin M. *Searching for Black Confederates: The Civil War's Most Persistent Myth*. Chapel Hill: Univ. of North Carolina Press, 2019.

Loewen, James W. *Lies Across America: What Our Historic Sites Get Wrong*. New York: Touchstone, 2000.

Logan, Rayford W. *The Negro in American Life and Thought, The Nadir 1877–1901*. New York: Dial Press Incorporated, 1954.

Low, Polly, Graham Oliver, and P. J. Rhodes, *Cultures of Commemoration: War Memorials, Ancient and Modern*. Oxford: Oxford Univ. Press, 2012.

Maddex, Jack P. *The Reconstruction of Edward A. Pollard: A Rebel's Conversion to Postbellum Unionism*. Chapel Hill: Univ. of North Carolina Press, 1974.

Marshall, Anne E. *Creating a Confederate Kentucky: The Lost Cause and Civil War Memory in a Border State*. Chapel Hill: Univ. of North Carolina Press, 2010.

McElya, Micki. *Clinging to Mammy: The Faithful Slave in Twentieth-Century America*. Cambridge: Harvard Univ. Press, 2007.

McKenzie, Robert Tracey. *Lincolnites and Rebels: A Divided Town in the American Civil War*. Oxford: Oxford Univ. Press, 2009.

McPherson, James M. *Embattled Rebel: Jefferson Davis as Commander in Chief*. New York: Penguin, 2014.

McWhirter, Cameron. *Red Summer: The Summer of 1919 and the Awakening of Black America*. New York: Henry Holt, 2011.

Merrit, Keri. *Masterless Men: Poor Whites and Slavery in the Antebellum South*. Cambridge: Cambridge Univ. Press, 2017.

Mills, Cynthia, and Pamela H. Simpson, eds. *Monuments to the Lost Cause: Women, Art, and the Landscapes of Southern Memory*. Knoxville: Univ. of Tennessee Press, 2003.

Mitchell, Don. *Cultural Geography: A Critical Introduction*. Oxford: Blackwell, 2000.

Moreau, Joseph. *Schoolbook Nation: Conflicts over American History Textbooks from the Civil War to the Present*. Ann Arbor: Univ. of Michigan Press, 2003.

Myrdal, Gunner. *An American Dilemma: The New in a White Nation*, vol. 1. Second edition. New York: McGraw-Hill Book Company, 1962.

Neely, Mark, Jr. *Lincoln and the Democrats: The Politics of Opposition in the Civil War*. New York: Cambridge Univ. Press, 2017.

Neff, John R. *Honoring the Civil War Dead: Commemoration and the Problem of Reconciliation*. Lawrence: Univ. Press of Kansas, 2005.

Nolen, Claude H. *The Negro's Image in the South: The Anatomy of White Supremacy*. Lexington: Univ. Press of Kentucky, 1967.

O'Brien, Michael. *The Idea of the American South: 1920–1941*. Baltimore, MD: Johns Hopkins Univ. Press, 1979.

Osterweis, Rollin G. *Romanticism and Nationalism in the Old South*. New Haven: Yale Univ. Press, 1949.

———. *The Myth of the Lost Cause, 1865–1900*. Hamden, CT: Archon Books, 1973.

Piston, William Garrett. *Lee's Tarnished Lieutenant: James Longstreet and His Place in Southern History*. Athens: Univ. of Georgia Press, 1987.

Poole, W. Scott. *Never Surrender: Confederate Memory and Conservativism in the South Carolina Upcountry*. Athens: Univ. of Georgia Press, 2004.

Pressly, Thomas J. *Americans Interpret Their Civil War*. Princeton: Princeton Univ. Press, 1954.

Richardson, E. Ramsay. *Little Aleck: A Life of Alexander H. Stephens, Fighting Vice-President of the Confederacy*. Indianapolis: Bobbs-Merrill, 1932.

Rutherford, Mildred Lewis. *Miss Rutherford's Scrap Book: Valuable Information about the South*, vol. 1. Charlottesville: Univ, of Virginia Press, 1923.

Ryan, Susan M. *The Grammar of Good Intentions: Race and the Antebellum Culture of Benevolence*. Ithaca: Cornell Univ. Press, 2005.

Sacher, John M. *A Perfect War of Politics: Parties, Politicians, and Democracy in Louisiana, 1824–1861*. Baton Rouge: Louisiana State Univ. Press, 2003.

Savage, Kirk. *Standing Soldiers, Kneeling Slaves: Race, War, and Monument in Nineteenth-Century America*. Princeton, NJ: Princeton Univ. Press, 1999.

Schott, Thomas E. *Alexander H. Stephens of Georgia: A Biography*. Baton Rouge: Louisiana State Univ. Press, 1988.

Schweninger, Loren. *Families in Crisis in the Old South: Divorce, Slavery, and the Law*. Chapel Hill: Univ. of North Carolina Press, 2012.

Scott, Thomas A. *Cornerstones of Georgia History: Documents That Formed the State*. Athens: Univ. of Georgia Press, 1995.

Shackel, Paul A. *Memory in Black and White: Race, Commemoration, and the Post-Bellum Landscape*. Walnut Creek, CA: AltaMira Press, 2003.

Silber, Nina. *Romance of Reunion: Northerners and the South, 1865–1900*. Chapel Hill: Univ. of North Carolina, 1993.

Simpson, John A. *Edith D. Pope and Her Nashville Friends: Guardians of the Lost Cause in the Confederate Veteran*. Knoxville: Univ. of Tennessee Press, 2003.

Sinha, Manisha. *The Counterrevolution of Slavery: Politics and Ideology in Antebellum South Carolina*. Chapel Hill: Univ. of North Carolina Press, 2003.

Smith, H. Shelton. *In His Image: Racism in Southern Religion, 1780–1910*. Durham: Duke Univ. Press, 1972.

Smith, John David, and J. Vincent Lowery, eds. *The Dunning School: Historians, Race, and the Meaning of Reconstruction*. Lexington: Univ. Press of Kentucky, 2013.

Snay, Mitchell. *Horace Greeley and the Politics of Reform in Nineteenth-Century America*. New York: Rowman & Littlefield, 2011.

Stampp, Kenneth M. *The Imperiled Union*. New York: Oxford Univ. Press, 1980.

Stephenson, Wendell H. *The South Lives in History: Southern Historians and Their Legacy*. Baton Rouge: Louisiana State Univ. Press, 1955.

———. *Southern History in the Making: Pioneer Historians of the South*. Baton Rouge: Louisiana State Univ. Press, 1964.

Stokes, Melvyn. *D. W. Griffith's the Birth of a Nation: A History of the Most Controversial Motion Picture of All Time*. Oxford: Oxford Univ. Press, 2008.

Strode, Hudson. *Jefferson Davis: American Patriot, 1808–1861*. New York: Harcourt, Brace, 1955.

———. *Jefferson Davis: Confederate President*. New York: Harcourt, Brace and Company, 1959.

———. *Jefferson Davis: Tragic Hero; The Last Twenty-five Years, 1865–1889*. New York: Harcourt, Brace & World, 1964.

———, ed. *Jefferson Davis: Private Letters, 1823–1889*. New York: Harcourt, Brace, & World, 1966.

Summers, Mark Wahlgren. *The Press Gang: Newspapers and Politics, 1865–1878*. Chapel Hill: Univ. of North Carolina Press, 2018.

Takaki, Ronald T. *A Pro-Slavery Crusade: The Agitation to Reopen the African Slave Trade*. New York: Free Press, 1971.

Temperley, Howard, ed. *After Slavery: Emancipation and its Discontents*. London: Frank Cass Publishers, 2000.

Thelen, David, ed. *Memory and American History*. Bloomington: Indiana Univ. Press, 1990.

Thornton III, J. Mills. *Politics and Power in a Slave Society: Alabama, 1800–1860*. Baton Rouge: Louisiana State Univ. Press, 1978.

Tise, Larry E. *Proslavery: A History of the Defense of Slavery in America, 1701–1840*. Athens: Univ. of Georgia Press, 2004.

Towns, W. Stuart Towns. *Enduring Legacy: Rhetoric and Ritual in the Lost Cause*. Tuscaloosa: Univ. of Alabama Press, 2012.

Viles, Philip H. *National Statuary Hall: Guidebook for a Walking Tour*. Washington, DC: P. H. Viles, 1997.

Von Abele, Rudolph. *Alexander H. Stephens, a Biography*. New York: Knopf, 1946.

Walker, Vanessa Siddle. *The Lost Education of Horace Tate*. New York: New Press, 2018.

Warren, Robert Penn. *The Legacy of the Civil War: Meditations on the Centennial*. New York: Random House, 1961.

Weaver, Richard M. *The Southern Tradition at Bay: A History of Postbellum Thought*. Edited by George Core and M. E. Bradford. New Rochelle, N.Y.: Arlington House, 1968.

Wesley, Charles H. *The Collapse of the Confederacy*. Washington, D.C.: Associated Publishers, Inc., 1937.

Wetherington, Mark V. *Plain Folk's Fight: The Civil War and Reconstruction in Piney Woods Georgia*. Chapel Hill: Univ. of North Carolina Press, 2005.

Wilentz, Sean. *The Rise of American Democracy: Jefferson to Lincoln*. New York: Norton, 2005.

Williams, David. *Rich Man's War: Class, Caste, and Confederate Defeat in the Lower Chattahoochee Valley*. Athens: Univ. of Georgia Press, 1998.

Wilson, Charles R. *Baptized in Blood: The Religion of the Lost Cause, 1865–1920*. Athens: Univ. of Georgia Press, 1962.

Wilson, Chris, and Paul Groth, eds. *Everyday America: Cultural Landscape Studies after J. B. Jackson*. Berkeley: Univ. of California Press, 2003.

Wilson, Clyde. *Why the South Will Survive*. Athens: Univ. of Georgia Press, 1981.

Wilson, Edmund. *Patriotic Gore: Studies in the Literature of the American Civil War*. Oxford: Oxford Univ. Press, 1962.

Wirth, Fremont. *The Development of America*. New York: American Book Company, 1937.

Wood, Betty. *The Origins of American Slavery: Freedom and Bondage in the English Colonies*. New York: Hill and Wang, 1997.

Index